FINAN
MANA

Knowledge Sk

Financial Times Management is a new business created to deliver the knowledge, skills and understanding that will enable students, managers and organisations to achieve their ambitions, whatever their needs, wherever they are.

Financial Times Pitman Publishing, part of Financial Times Management, is the leading publisher of books for practitioners and students in business and finance, bringing cutting-edge thinking and best practice to a global market.

To find out more about Financial Times Management and Financial Times Pitman Publishing, visit our website at:

www.ftmanagement.com

F R A M E W O R K S

Each book in the Frameworks series is a
comprehensive and concise introduction to
the subject. The books are well structured
and provide a step-by-step guide to essential
principles. They develop a basic framework
of understanding to underpin further study of
core business, financial and legal subjects in
the higher education curriculum.

F R A M E W O R K S

Company Law

Twelfth Edition

M C Oliver
and
Enid A Marshall

MA, LLB, PhD, Associate RICS, ACIArb, FRSA, Solicitor
Reader in Business Law at the University of Stirling

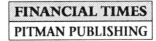

FINANCIAL TIMES
PITMAN PUBLISHING

LONDON · HONG KONG · JOHANNESBURG
MELBOURNE · SINGAPORE · WASHINGTON DC

FINANCIAL TIMES MANAGEMENT
128 Long Acre, London WC2E 9AN
Tel: +44 (0)171 447 2000
Fax: +44 (0)171 240 5771
Website: www.ftmanagement.com

A Division of Financial Times Professional Limited

Twelfth edition published in 1994

© Pearson Professional Limited 1994

ISBN 0 273 63423 2

British Library Cataloguing in Publication Data
A CIP catalogue record for this book can be obtained from the British Library.

10 9 8 7 6 5 4 3

Printed and bound in Singapore

The Publishers' policy is to use paper manufactured from sustainable forests.

Contents

Preface to the twelfth edition

The aim of this book remains, as was the case in its first edition, 'to be as simple as possible, in the hope that readers will pursue the subject in more advanced books'.

Company law continues to be a rapidly-changing subject, and there is no promise of any respite. New statutory material on single member private limited companies and on insider dealing has made this an appropriate time for a new edition.

The opportunity has been taken to introduce some new features. First, where Scots law is distinctive, attention is now drawn to it by its incorporation in square brackets in the text immediately after the English material. This should increase the usefulness of the book to students in Scotland. Secondly, as a book of these dimensions can give only the briefest account of decided cases, cross-references to pages of Josephine R. Bisacre's *Casebook on Company Law* (Pitman Publishing) have been added to the text (indicated by '[B]' after the date). Students will thus have easy access to further information on many of the cases. Thirdly, there is now fuller treatment of EC law.

Finally, while the full Table of Statutes has been retained, there has been added a new Table of arrangement of major Statutes. It is hoped that this new Table will aid access to the provisions sought, now that the neat consolidation of 1985 is receding further into the distance with every amending Act.

The law is intended to be stated as at the end of July 1993.

I wish to record my thanks to Linda Macpherson for her meticulous work in the preparation of the Tables of Cases and Statutes and the Index.

Enid A. Marshall
September 1993

Table of cases

Table of statutes

Table of arrangement of major statutes

Companies Act 1985

PART XIII ARRANGEMENTS AND RECONSTRUCTIONS
ss. 425–427A

PART XIIIA TAKEOVER OFFERS
ss. 428–430F

PART XIV INVESTIGATION OF COMPANIES AND THEIR AFFAIRS; REQUISITION OF DOCUMENTS
ss. 431–453

PART XV ORDERS IMPOSING RESTRICTIONS ON SHARES (SECTIONS 210, 216, 445)
ss. 454–457

PART XVI FRAUDULENT TRADING BY A COMPANY
s. 458

PART XVII PROTECTION OF COMPANY'S MEMBERS AGAINST UNFAIR PREJUDICE
ss. 459–461

PART XVIII FLOATING CHARGES AND RECEIVERS (SCOTLAND)

CHAPTER I FLOATING CHARGES

ss. 462–466

CHAPTER II RECEIVERS

ss. 467–485 (Repealed by Insolvency Act 1986, s. 438)

CHAPTER III GENERAL

ss. 486–487

PART XIX RECEIVERS AND MANAGERS (ENGLAND AND WALES)
ss. 488–500 (Repealed by Insolvency Act 1986, s. 438)

PART XX WINDING UP OF COMPANIES REGISTERED UNDER THIS ACT OR THE FORMER COMPANIES ACTS
ss. 501–650 (Repealed by Insolvency Act 1986, s. 438)

CHAPTER VI MATTERS ARISING SUBSEQUENT TO WINDING UP

ss. 651–658

Insolvency Act 1986

Financial Services Act 1986

(Parts I to III omitted as irrelevant to contents of this book.)

PART VI TAKEOVER OFFERS
s. 172

PART VII INSIDER DEALING
ss. 173–178
(ss. 173–176 repealed by Criminal Justice Act 1993, s. 79)
(Parts VIII to X omitted as irrelevant to contents of this book.)

Companies Act 1989

PART I COMPANY ACCOUNTS
ss. 1–23

PART II ELIGIBILITY FOR APPOINTMENT AS COMPANY AUDITOR
ss. 24–54

PART III INVESTIGATIONS AND POWERS TO OBTAIN INFORMATION
ss. 55–91

PART IV REGISTRATION OF COMPANY CHARGES
ss. 92–107

PART V OTHER AMENDMENTS OF COMPANY LAW
ss. 108–145

PART VI MERGERS AND RELATED MATTERS
ss. 146–153

PART VII FINANCIAL MARKETS AND INSOLVENCY
ss. 154–191

PART VIII AMENDMENTS OF THE FINANCIAL SERVICES ACT 1986
ss. 192–206

PART IX TRANSFER OF SECURITIES
s. 207

PART X MISCELLANEOUS AND GENERAL PROVISIONS
ss. 208–216

Criminal Justice Act 1993
(Parts I to IV omitted as not relevant to the contents of this book)

PART V INSIDER DEALING
ss. 52–64
(Part VI omitted as not relevant to the contents of this book)

1

The basic principles of company law

1. The subject-matter of this book

The aim of this book is to give an elementary account of the law which applies to registered companies, i.e. to companies registered under the Companies Act 1985, in England and Wales and in Scotland.

To a large extent the company law applicable to England and Wales does not differ from that applicable to Scotland. For the advantage of Scottish students, such differences as exist are indicated in square brackets in the text.

Students may approach their study of company law with the notion that it consists of a dull mass of complex rules and restrictions, coupled with even more complex exceptions, all to be searched for in a bulky volume of legislation of which the Companies Act 1985 is the principal part. There is only a vestige of truth in that notion. Company law is much more interesting than that.

It is true to say that there are very many detailed statutory provisions applicable to registered companies, and that their bulk is constantly on the increase. Against this, however, one must balance the following factors:

(a) the basis of common law and equity on which the legislation has been superimposed;

(b) the fact that the subject is a modern one;

(c) the circumstance that the latest consolidation is as recent as 1985–86; *and*

(d) the recognition that the more complex the statutory provisions are, the greater is the likelihood that they will not feature in ordinary examination questions at an elementary level.

A little more must be said about each of these encouraging factors.

2. The basis of common law and equity

There has never been a codification of company law in this country. There have been several *consolidating* Acts, each in its turn gathering into a single Act all the pre-existing statutory provisions with the result that the earlier provisions are repealed and re-enacted in a more convenient and compact form in a new Act.

The rules of common law and of equity continue as the base on which all the statutory provisions are superimposed, and where no statutory provision exists to cover the situation, the rules of common law and equity are applicable.

Despite the great mass of legislation, therefore, company law is still partly to be found in, and enlivened by, decided cases.

Further information on many of the cases mentioned in this book can be found in Josephine R. Bisacre's *Casebook on Company Law* (Pitman Publishing), and references in the text [B] after the date of a case are references to that casebook, followed by the page number in that book.

3. A modern subject

By legal standards company law is a modern subject. The system of registration of companies had its origins in an Act of 1844. The principle of limited liability, which was introduced in 1855, was then combined with the registration system in the Joint Stock Companies Act 1856.

Neither the 1844 Act nor the 1855 Act applied to Scotland. Both the system of registration and the principle of limited liability were introduced to Scotland by the Act of 1856.

Six years later, there was passed the first of a series of consolidating Acts—the Companies Act 1862.

Since that date the pattern has been for amendments to company law to be made by separate new Acts passed as the need for them became evident, and then, when the consolidating Act plus its often numerous amendments became too cumbersome, to have a new consolidating Act passed so as to accommodate all the existing legislation once more in a single Act.

Such consolidating Acts were passed in 1908, 1929 and 1948. The current consolidation is that of 1985–86.

4. The consolidation of 1985–86

By 1985 a new consolidating Companies Act had been long overdue, to replace the 1948 Act which had been heavily amended by Acts of 1967, 1972, 1976, 1980 and 1981 in particular. As a result of all these amending Acts, it had become increasingly difficult to find what the present statutory provisions were.

However, the consolidation which was at last accomplished in 1985 did not precisely follow the pattern of earlier consolidating Acts (*see* 3). It consisted, for the first time, not of a single Act but of four Acts:

(a) the Companies Act 1985;

(b) the Company Securities (Insider Dealing) Act 1985;

(c) the Business Names Act 1985; *and*

(d) the Companies Consolidation (Consequential Provisions) Act 1985.

The last is of a transitional nature, and need not be further mentioned. The first is the principal Act and throughout this book references to sections are references to sections of that Act unless the context indicates otherwise. The provisions of the second and third Acts, each of which has a restricted subject-matter, will be dealt with at appropriate points in later chapters.

However, these four Acts of 1985 are not the end of the story of our present consolidation. In the very same year Parliament was already passing an Act—the Insolvency Act 1985—substantially amending the law relating to disqualification of company directors and the law relating to insolvency generally, including insolvent companies. The position reached called for a further consolidation of the *affected parts* of the 1985 consolidation, and this took the form of two Acts of 1986:

(a) the Company Directors Disqualification Act 1986; *and*

(b) the Insolvency Act 1986.

The first of these latest consolidating Acts is dealt with principally in the chapter on directors (Chapter 16). The second is a much longer Act and must be looked at in several chapters, particularly those concerned with the winding up of companies (Chapters 28–31).

Two further major amending Acts have since been passed:

(a) the Financial Services Act 1986; *and*

(b) the Companies Act 1989.

The first of these two Acts made substantial alterations to the provisions of the consolidating Acts dealing with prospectuses, insider dealing and take-over offers, while the second implemented the Seventh and Eighth European Company Law Directives on consolidated accounts and on the regulation of auditors respectively. It also made many other alterations, including extension of investigation powers, amendment of the Financial Services Act 1986 and the abolition of the *ultra vires* doctrine.

Finally, Part V of the Criminal Justice Act 1993 amended and restated the provisions relating to insider dealing, wholly repealing the consolidating Act of 1985 on this subject.

The Companies Act 1985 remains the principal Act, but it must be remembered that not a few sections of it have now been amended or repealed by later provisions which are to be found *either* in later consolidating Acts (namely the Company Directors Disqualification Act 1986 and the Insolvency Act 1986) *or* in later amending Acts (principally the Financial Services Act 1986 and the Companies Act 1989).

In all, therefore, the student now approaching his study of company law is faced with six consolidating Acts of 1985–86 and their subsequent amendments. He does, however, enjoy a considerable advantage over his counterpart of a few years ago. A student of 1983, for instance, had to look to no fewer than eleven Acts, i.e. to the then principal Act (the Companies Act 1948) and ten later Acts which amended it.

It must, however, be remembered that, in addition to the Acts themselves, there is a great mass of subordinate legislation consisting of rules and regulations. Most of these add details to the provisions in the Acts, e.g. the Companies (Tables A–F) Regulations 1985 and the Insolvency Rules 1986 [for Scotland, the Insolvency (Scotland) Rules 1986], but some actually amend the Acts themselves, e.g. the Companies (Single Member Private Limited Companies) Regulations 1992.

It can confidently be expected that in the next one or two years a further consolidation will take place, removing the present need to consult amendments superimposed on the existing consolidated provisions. On the other hand, it must be admitted that company law is a fast-moving subject and further amendments are never far away.

5. Complex statutory provisions and examination questions

Many of the readers of this book will be studying for examinations on company law, usually at a comparatively elementary level (though it may not seem elementary to them).

Be comforted! No self-respecting examiner would set questions calling for a knowledge of complex statutory provisions. The rote learning required for success in such questions is out-moded and frowned upon. Even experts in company law would shy from giving an answer without close scrutiny of the actual wording and context of the statutory provision, and the only examination question which could justifiably be set on complex provisions would be an open-book examination taken by advanced students of company law, for whom this book is not intended.

Complicated provisions have been enacted mainly because *in practice* they were found to be necessary or desirable. The student of this book should first grasp the *principles* and the *general objects* of company law.

As regards principles, two are fundamental:

(a) the concept of *legal personality; and*
(b) the theory of *limited liability.*

As regards the general objects, much of the detail will fall into place once the student appreciates the fact that most of the statutory rules are intended for one of two purposes:

(a) the *protection of creditors* (e.g. the rules preventing reduction of capital without proper safeguards); *and*

(b) the *protection of investors* (e.g. the rules concerning offers of shares to the public and concerning the accounts).

6. EC legislation
Much of the reform of company law in recent years has resulted from this country's membership of the European Community.

Legislation emanating from EC institutions may take the form of:

(a) regulations, which are directly enforceable in member states; *or*
(b) Directives, which require the member state to alter its law so as to comply with the Directive, although it has a discretion as to the means by which it achieves that end; *or*
(c) decisions.

The binding force of EC law in the United Kingdom was established by the European Communities Act 1972.

A series of Directives has the general aim of harmonisation of the company laws of the member states. There are, however, often options allowed in the Directives, with the result that harmonisation is by no means complete since one member state may choose a different option from other member states.

Some of the Directives have been already enacted by the EC Council of Ministers, while others are still in draft form.

The following have already been enacted:

(a) First Directive (March 1968) on the capacity of a company and its directors and questions of publicity and nullity of a company. Section 9 of the European Communities Act 1972 made changes in this country's company law in compliance with this Directive, especially noteworthy being the modification of the *ultra vires* doctrine.
(b) Second Directive (December 1976) on the formation of public limited companies and the maintenance and alteration of their capital. This was implemented in this country by the Companies Acts 1980 and 1981.
(c) Third Directive (October 1978) on mergers of public limited companies within the same state. This was implemented in this country, along with the Sixth Directive, by the Companies (Mergers and Divisions) Regulations 1987 (SI 1987, No. 1991). The Regulations amended the Companies Act 1985 and added Schedule 15A to it. (This Schedule was renumbered 15B by s. 114 Companies Act 1989.)
(d) Fourth Directive (July 1978) on the annual accounts of certain types of companies. This was implemented in this country by the Companies Act 1981.
(e) Sixth Directive (December 1982) on the division of public limited companies within the same state.

(f) Seventh Directive (June 1983) on consolidated accounts. This was implemented in this country by the Companies Act 1989.

(g) Eighth Directive (April 1984) on auditors. This was implemented in this country by the Companies Act 1989.

(h) Eleventh Directive (December 1989) on disclosure requirements for branches opened in another member state. This was implemented in this country by the Companies Act 1985 (Disclosure of Branches and Bank Accounts) Regulations 1992 (SI 1992, No. 3178).

(i) Twelfth Directive (December 1989) on single-member private limited companies. This was implemented in this country by the Companies (Single Member Private Limited Companies) Regulations 1992 (SI 1992, No. 1699).

There are the following draft Directives:

(a) Fifth Directive on the structure of public limited companies and the powers and obligations of their organs.

(b) Ninth Directive on the conduct of groups.

(c) Tenth Directive on cross-border mergers of public limited companies.

(d) Thirteenth Directive on take-over bids.

In addition to the programme of harmonising the company law of the member states by the use of directives, there are two other EC movements aimed at establishing by EC regulations supranational bodies to co-exist with, but be separate from, the national law of the member states. These are:

(a) the European Economic Interest Grouping ('EEIG'); *and*

(b) the proposed European Company Statute ('ECS').

An EEIG (provided for by a regulation of July 1985 which became applicable in July 1989) is an entity set up by persons in two or more member states with a view to fostering co-operation in activities ancillary to their main business (e.g. development and research). An EEIG is subject in some respects to the national law of the states in which it is registered (e.g. as to the use of its name and to certain winding-up rules), but it is not a profit-making body, its members have unlimited liability for its debts, public investment in it is not permitted and the number of its employees is limited to 500.

The proposed ECS would make available a European company form, subject to new EC legislation, though to some extent governed by the national law of the state of its registration. Divergent views, especially as to the aspect of worker-participation, require to be reconciled before this proposal becomes an actuality.

7. The starting-point

Every subject should have a starting-point which a beginner with no previous knowledge can understand. Here it is suggested that the easiest way of beginning to study company law is to imagine that you yourself are about to 'go into business', i.e. that you have a little money saved or lent to you and are about to start a small business.

The first legal question which arises is: in which legal form shall the business operate? In order to decide this question it is necessary to examine the legal forms of a business and understand the differences between them. There are three:

(a) You may be a *sole trader.*
(b) You may form a *partnership* with one or more other persons.
(c) You may form a *limited company* by registration under the Companies Act.

Each of these must now be considered in turn.

8. A sole trader

A sole trader is so called because *he alone* bears the responsibility for running the business, and *he alone* takes the profits.

He may of course be helped by his wife and family, or he may employ other people to work for him, but this does not alter the fact that the management is entirely in his hands. A person in this position has not formed any kind of 'association' in law.

9. A partnership

In a partnership the members 'associate', i.e. they form collectively an association in which they all participate, as a rule, in management and in sharing the profits. The basic rules governing such an association are to be found in the Partnership Act 1890.

(a) *Number of partners.* Obviously there must be at least two members in a partnership, but there may be more. There is, however, in most cases a maximum number. Section 716 Companies Act 1985, as amended by s. 145 and Schedule 19 Companies Act 1989, states that this maximum is 20, but exempts from this provision partnerships of solicitors, accountants, members of a recognised stock exchange and other partnerships prescribed by regulations made by the Secretary of State for Trade and Industry. If a partnership not covered by any of the exemptions has a membership of more than 20, the members must *incorporate* themselves by registering as a company under the Companies Act.

(b) *Liability of partners.* In a partnership the legal position of the members is not very different from that of a sole trader. If the firm gets into financial difficulties, all the partners may find that their creditors are seeking to make them bankrupt, and since all the partners are liable for the debts of the firm, they are not protected against the possibility of total bankruptcy. At the same time, just because they are liable for the firm's debts, they may find that tradesmen are willing to give them credit on the grounds, for example, that one of the partners is known to be a very wealthy person.

(c) *Legal position of partners.* The members of a partnership may sue and be sued collectively by using the name of the firm, but this is a matter of legal procedure only, and does not alter the fact that the action is being brought by or against the *partners*. [In Scotland, a partnership is a legal person distinct from the individuals of whom it is composed and the action is brought by or against the partnership.] All the partners are *agents* for each other, i.e. each one can bind the others when he makes contracts on behalf of the firm. It follows that each partner is a *principal*. They are therefore all in a *fiduciary relation* with each other, i.e. they must not only tell each other the truth in conducting the business, but they must disclose the whole truth. For instance, no partner may make a secret profit. The word 'fiduciary' comes from the Latin *fides*, meaning trust or confidence.

(d) *Rights of partners.* Usually the rights of the partners are regulated by a contract drawn up between them and put in writing, called the 'articles' of partnership or the 'partnership deed' [in Scotland, the deed of co-partnery]. The partners may make what arrangements they like in this contract, but when they have not made any provision at all the position is regulated by the Partnership Act 1890. A partnership need not be created formally, however, and may arise through an oral agreement or even by conduct.

10. A limited partnership

There is a special type of partnership which is very rare but should be mentioned. It is called a *limited partnership* and is regulated by the Limited Partnerships Act 1907. Here it is possible for all the partners except one to be 'limited partners'. A limited partner puts into the firm a certain amount of money, e.g. £500, and then he is not responsible for the debts of the firm above that figure. This means that he can lose his £500, but cannot be made bankrupt or made to pay more than this sum. The £500 is the 'limit' of his liability. He cannot, however, take part in the management of the firm.

There must always be at least one partner whose liability for the firm's debts is not limited in this way, and he is called a 'general partner'. He manages the business, bears the risk, but normally gets the bulk of the profits. Limited partnerships are very rare because in the same year in which they were introduced the Companies Act 1907 made it possible to form a *private company*, which is a much more convenient way of running a small business. The ordinary type of partnership described in **9** above, however, is very common and will be referred to later when a comparison will be drawn between it and the limited company (*see* 4: **7**)

11. The meaning of the word 'company'

Partnerships often describe themselves as 'Smith, Brown and Co.', but this is misleading because they are not companies in the strict sense of the word. The difficulty is caused by the fact that the word 'company' has a variable meaning and can be used in many ways. The meaning depends on the context. When a partnership describes itself in this way the partners may simply be indicating that there are other persons in their association besides Smith and Brown. They are *not* indicating that their business is a company registered under the Companies Act.

12. A limited company formed by registration under the Companies Act

If you choose this form for your business you are *incorporating* it, i.e. you are forming a corporation. You are also going to acquire *limited liability*. The actual process of incorporation by registration forms the subject-matter of Chapters 2–4 and there is much detail to be learnt about it, but before this process is described it is essential to clarify the two legal concepts which have already been mentioned as being the basis of company law, i.e. legal personality and limited liability (*see* **13–16** below).

13. The concept of legal personality

A *human* person is a man, woman or child and usually recognisable as such, but a *legal* person is not quite the same thing. In the first place, a legal person is not always human. In the second place, in some societies (though not in ours today) a human person is not necessarily a legal person.

A legal person can be described as any person, human or otherwise, who has rights and duties at law, i.e. who can seek the aid of the court and against whom the aid of the court can be sought by others. It is clear that in a modern civilised community all human persons fall into this category, but slaves when slavery was lawful, did not: they were regarded as property, not persons, and they could be owned and dealt with as property. Today it is almost universally true that no one may own another person. In a modern state all human persons, whatever their sex or age, can enforce their rights in the court and can be made liable for breach of their legal duties by the court.

A human person is, therefore, a legal person all his life, i.e. from birth to death. But it is important to remember that for some purposes he has pre-natal rights and the courts protect him even before he is born, while for other purposes his rights remain enforceable after death for specified periods. Students learn more about this when they study criminal law and the law of tort [in Scots law, delict], but is outside the proper scope of this book.

Although all human persons are legal persons, not all legal persons are human. Non-human legal persons are called *corporations*, a word derived from the Latin *'corpus'* (body). A corporation is a legal person created by a process other than natural birth. It is therefore sometimes called an *artificial* legal person, but it should not be called 'fictitious', because it really exists. For instance, if you have a carnation in your button-hole it may be a real one or an artificial one, but it can hardly be said to be fictitious if it is there.

14. Types of corporation

There are many types of corporations and they can be classified in various ways, e.g.:

(a) *sole* (where one human being constitutes the corporation and has a dual personality, one corporate and the other human or natural, e.g. the Crown);
(b) *aggregate* (where the corporation consists of two or more persons).

Another classification is into:

(a) *lay* (e.g. Imperial Chemical Industries or the Institute of Chartered Secretaries and Administrators);
(b) *ecclesiastical* (e.g. the Archbishop of Canterbury).

A third classification is into:

(a) *trading* (e.g. Imperial Chemical Industries);
(b) *non-trading* (e.g. the Institute of Chartered Secretaries and Administrators).

Thus the particular type of corporation which we are about to study is a lay trading corporation aggregate.

For our purposes, however, by far the most useful classification is based on the method of formation. Corporations may exist as a result of:

(a) *common law*, e.g. the Crown or a bishop;
(b) *prescription*, i.e. the corporation has existed so long that the law presumes that it had a charter which was lost;
(c) *royal charter*;
(d) *statute*;
(e) *registration under the Companies Act*.

The corporation we are studying is formed in this last way.

NOTE: Students are often confused by being told that a corporation can be statutory, i.e. formed by statute, and that this is a different method of formation from registration under the Act. They feel that both these types of corporation are 'statutory'. The difference, however, is that a statutory corporation is directly created by a particular Act of Parliament which is passed for that specific purpose. The Companies Act, on the other hand, does not itself create any corporations at all. It merely lays down a *process* by which any two or more persons who so desire can themselves create a corporation by complying with the rules for registration which the Act prescribes.

15. The nature of the corporate person

The corporate legal person is very different from the natural or human legal person. It has neither body, mind nor soul. In the *Case of Sutton's Hospital* (1612), it was said that it 'is invisible, immortal, and rests only in intendment and consideration of the law'. Corporations 'cannot commit treason, nor be outlawed, nor excommunicated, for they have no souls'. A corporation is not subject to 'death of the natural body'.

All corporations, then, however they came into existence, have *perpetual succession*, i.e. they were not born and so cannot die. They have been created by a process of law and can only be destroyed by a process of law and until so destroyed will continue to exist. They will exist even if all their human members are dead, for every corporation is a *separate* legal person from those legal persons who compose it.

In the latter part of this book the methods of destruction or dissolution are dealt with.

16. Limited liability

Students sometimes confuse the idea of limited liability with the principle outlined above concerning the independent legal personality of a corporation. It is true that in a large number of corporations the members have limited liability, but this is not necessarily so. Later we shall see that the Act itself provides for the creation of an unlimited company, i.e. a company where the members have unlimited liability.

The meaning of liability must be understood: it means the *extent to which a person can be made to account at law*. He is either fully liable, i.e. he can be made to pay the full amount of the debts owed, or he is liable only to a limited extent, i.e. he can be made to pay towards those debts only up to a certain limit, but not beyond it. In our company we shall see that the member's liability for the debts of the company is normally limited to the amount unpaid on his shares. Thus, if he buys 100 £1 shares 'at par', i.e. at £1 per share, and pays up 50p on each share, he has paid up £50 and can be made to pay another £50, but he cannot be made to pay more than £100 in all. This is so even if the debts of the company amount to many thousands of pounds.

Notice that it is only the *members'* liability for the *company's* debts which is limited. The company itself, the artificial legal person, is always fully liable and so has unlimited liability. It follows that so long as there are assets available to pay the debts, it must pay them. It will be seen later (*see* **18**) that these debts must be paid in a strict order laid down by the law and certain classes of creditor receive preferential treatment.

Of course a company, like a human person, may not have enough assets to pay its debts. It will then be dissolved by liquidation, while a human person in such a case would be made bankrupt. This condition of insolvency is in no way related to limited liability. Insolvency is a simple matter of *fact*: a person cannot pay his debts because he has not enough money. Liability is a matter of *law*: a person is liable to pay his debts to a limited or unlimited extent regardless of whether he has enough money. Thus, *ability* to pay one's debts must never be confused with *liability* to pay them.

17. Implications of the creation of a registered company

Now that we have considered the concepts of legal personality and limited liability, we must turn to the implications of the creation of this artificial legal person in the form of a registered company. This involves the study of the most famous of all company law cases: *Salomon v. Salomon & Co. Ltd* (1897) [B5]. The case, however, can only be thoroughly understood if a student already knows the order of distribution of a company's assets when it goes into liquidation. This is therefore given below and should be carefully studied and thoroughly learnt.

18. The order of distribution of a company's assets in liquidation

On liquidation the usual important distinction between capital and revenue ceases and these merge to become, collectively, the company's *assets* which the liquidator must assemble and distribute in the following order:

(a) Secured creditors with *fixed* charges usually take payment out of their security. If their security is inadequate, they rank as unsecured creditors for the balance of their debts.

(b) The costs of liquidation (including the liquidator's remuneration).

(c) Preferential creditors. (Schedule 6 Insolvency Act 1986 lists them, and will be studied later: *see* 31:**2**.)

(d) Secured creditors with *floating* charges.

(e) Unsecured creditors.

(f) Debts due to members *as members*, e.g. dividends declared but not yet paid, and interest on calls paid in advance: s. 74 Insolvency Act 1986.

(g) Repayment of capital to members *pari passu* (i.e. proportionately in relation to their shareholdings) unless the articles or terms of issue provide otherwise. (Often they give priority to the preference shareholders, but this is a modification by contract of the basic rule.)

(h) Surplus assets divisible among the members *pari passu*, unless the articles or terms of issue provide otherwise.

From this order it is apparent that the law protects the creditors of the company at the expense of the members. Even a debt due to a member in his capacity of member is deferred below the claims of the unsecured creditors by s. 74 Insolvency Act 1986.

Moreover, the normal rule by which secured creditors rank before unsecured ones is reversed by s. 175 Insolvency Act 1986, which provides that preferential debts (which are unsecured) rank *before* secured creditors with floating charges. Floating charges are often over the whole of the company's assets generally, so if s. 175 did not make this provision there would be a much greater risk to the preferential creditors who include, of course, the Revenue.

A secured creditor part of whose debt is preferential and who realises his security for less than the amount owing to him may appropriate the proceeds of sale to that part of his debt which is non-preferential, thus leaving his preferential claim outstanding: *Re William Hall (Contractors)* (1967).

Debenture-holders, being simply creditors, fall into **(a) (d)** or **(e)** according to whether they have a fixed charge, a floating charge, or are 'naked', i.e. unsecured and have no charge at all.

Finally, under s. 107 Insolvency Act 1986, the assets of a company must be applied to its liabilities *pari passu*, subject to the claims of its preferential creditors. Thus unsecured creditors all rank equally and if the assets are insufficient to discharge their debts in full, they will each receive a proportionate amount. Even a *judgment* creditor has no priority although he has brought a successful action for his debt. If, therefore, a contract is made which would result in a distribution of the company's property in a manner contrary to s. 107, the court will refuse to give effect to it, even though it was made for good business reasons and without any thought for the effect of insolvency on the arrangement agreed under it: *British Eagle International Air Lines* v. *Compagnie Nationale Air France* (1975).

NOTE: Students often ask whether a floating charge which has *crystallised* (21:7) and so become fixed is promoted, as it were, from **(d)** to **(a)** on crystallisation. This is not the case. One of the events which causes crystallisation is liquidation, and if the holders of floating charges which had crystallised were in the same position as the holders of fixed charges, there would be no need to put the holders of floating charges into a separate category as shown above.

19. *Salomon v. Salomon & Co. Ltd* (1897) [B5]

The facts of this leading case were as follows:

> Salomon ran a boot business which he decided to incorporate. He formed a registered company by the process of registration, and then sold his business to the company. The only members of the company were Salomon, his wife, and his children, who by luck or judgment were just sufficient in number to form a registered company. (The minimum number of subscribers required to form a public company was seven until the Companies Act 1980 reduced it to two, and it was not possible to form a private company with the smaller minimum number of members until 1907.) All the members knew of and approved the entire arrangement.
>
> Salomon's wife and children each held one share in this company, and the remainder were held by Salomon himself. In payment for the business these shares were allotted to Salomon fully paid up, but part of the purchase-price was left outstanding as a debt due to Salomon from the company. He was careful to see that it was secured by a floating charge over the company's assets.
>
> When at length the company went into liquidation, these assets were insufficient to pay all the debts. The unsecured trade creditors claimed that they were entitled to such assets as existed, on the grounds that the whole transaction was a sham, and that the secured debentures originally issued to Salomon were therefore invalid. They regarded the company as in essence the same person as Salomon himself, since he controlled it.

The House of Lords either had to agree that this was so, thereby rejecting the whole principle of incorporation and the theory of the corporate legal personality, or had to hold that once a corporation had been formed, it was an entirely different legal person from the members who composed and controlled it. They chose the latter course, and accordingly the company was treated as a different legal person from Salomon. It followed that since the debentures originally issued to him were secured by a floating charge, the holder had priority over the unsecured trade creditors, who in consequence received nothing.

This famous case established beyond all doubt the existence of the 'veil of incorporation', i.e. the legal personality of the corporation through which the identity of the members cannot be perceived.

20. Application of *Salomon* v. *Salomon & Co. Ltd*

It is a consequence of the principle of *Salomon* v. *Salomon & Co. Ltd* that the property of the company belongs to the company and not to the individual members of the company.

Thus in *Macaura* v. *Northern Assurance Co. Ltd* (1925) [B9] Macaura, having sold timber to a company in which he and his nominees were the sole shareholders, insured the timber against fire by policies taken out in his own name. Macaura was also a creditor of the company. Most of the timber was destroyed by fire. HELD: Neither as a shareholder nor as a creditor did Macaura have any insurable interest in the timber, since it was an asset owned by the company. Lord Wrenbury said:'The corporator even if he holds all the shares is not the corporation.'

Similarly, in a Privy Council case *Lee* v. *Lee's Air Farming Ltd* (1961) [B10] Lee was, apart from a solicitor who held one share, the sole shareholder and the governing director of a company. He was employed at a salary as chief pilot and was killed in an aircrash while piloting the company's aircraft. The question in the case was whether he was a 'worker' for the purposes of a Workers' Compensation Act. HELD: Since the company was a person distinct from its shareholders, Lee was a servant of the company and so a 'worker', even though he was the controlling shareholder and sole director.

The best known recent Scottish application is the House of Lords case *Woolfson* v. *Strathclyde Regional Council* (1978) [B23].

C Ltd was the occupier of a retail shop. Its issued share capital was 1,000 shares, of which 999 were held by W and one by W's wife. W was the sole director of C Ltd and managed the business. The premises were owned partly by W and partly by S Ltd, the shares in which were held as to two-thirds by W and as to the remaining one-third by W's wife. The local highway authority made a compulsory purchase order in respect of the shop, and W claimed compensation for disturbance under the Land Compensation (Scotland) Act 1963 on the basis that he, C Ltd and S Ltd should all be treated as a single entity embodied in W himself. HELD: W, C Ltd and S Ltd were separate legal persons; W was neither the occupier nor the owner occupier of the premises and was therefore not entitled to compensation.

Several other instances of the application of *Salomon* v. *Salomon & Co. Ltd* will be discovered in later chapters.

21. Lifting the veil of incorporation
The principle of the separate legal personality of the company is not, however, without its exceptions. Both at common law and under the

provisions of the Act there are instances of the veil being 'lifted', or 'pierced', so that the identity of the members can be seen, not through a glass darkly, but face to face. A few of the instances are given in the next two paragraphs. Others will be seen at appropriate points in later chapters.

22. Cases illustrating lifting of the veil
The following are a few instances of cases where the court has decided that in the interests of justice and equity the veil of incorporation should be lifted.

> In *Gilford Motor Co. Ltd* v. *Horne* (1933) [B28] a managing director's contract of employment included a covenant in restraint of trade by which he undertook that, on the termination of his employment, he would not solicit the company's customers. However, on the termination of his employment, he formed a new company consisting virtually of himself and sent out circulars to his former employer's customers. HELD: The new company was a mere channel, a mere cloak or sham for the purpose of enabling the former managing director to commit a breach of the covenant. An injunction was therefore granted against him and the new company to restrain any further breach of the covenant.

> In *Jones* v. *Lipman* (1962) there had been a written agreement for the sale of land by Lipman to Jones. Lipman asked to be released from the contract, and on Jones' refusal transferred the land to a company in which he himself and his solicitor's clerk were the sole shareholders and sole directors. HELD: Jones was entitled to specific performance. Russell J. said: 'The defendant company is the creature of the first defendant, a device and a sham, a mask which he holds before his face in an attempt to avoid recognition by the eye of equity'.

There are several cases where the court has lifted the veil to identify the relationship within a group of companies. Thus, in *Smith, Stone & Knight Ltd* v. *Birmingham Corporation* (1939) a subsidiary company was held to be an agent of its holding company, while conversely in *Wm Cory & Son Ltd* v. *Dorman Long & Co. Ltd* (1936) a parent company was held to be the agent of its subsidiary. In *D.H.N. Food Distributors Ltd* v. *Tower Hamlets London Borough Council* (1976) [B20], where two subsidiary companies were wholly owned by the holding company and had no separate business operations, the court held it just to treat the group as a single entity. The authority of this last case, however, has been doubted: Lord Keith in the House of Lords in the *Woolfson* case considered that the *D.H.N.* case was clearly distinguishable on its facts from the *Woolfson* case and that it was appropriate to pierce the corporate veil only where special circumstances existed indicating that it was a mere façade concealing the true facts; in the later case of *National Dock Labour Board* v. *Pinn & Wheeler Ltd* (1989) [B25] the Court of Appeal applied the *Woolfson* approach in deciding that where a group of companies had been set up for good commercial reasons the veil of incorporation should not be lifted.

A particularly striking instance of lifting the veil is *Re Bugle Press Ltd* (1961) which arose out of a 'take-over bid' (*see* 32:**6**). Two out of the three shareholders in a company formed themselves into a new company which made a take-over bid for all the shares of the first company. These two shareholders accepted the bid, but the third rejected it. As, however, he held only one-tenth of the shares, the new company became entitled to acquire his shares compulsorily under s. 209 Companies Act 1948 (now s. 428 Companies Act 1985). HELD: The compulsory acquisition would not be allowed because the section was being abused for the purpose of enabling the majority shareholders in the first company to evict the minority shareholder. The court was thus lifting the veil so as to reveal that the new company was in reality the same in identity as the majority shareholders of the first company. Harman L.J. said that the new company was 'nothing but a little hut built round' the two majority shareholders and that the whole scheme was a 'hollow sham'.

23. Provisions of the Act illustrating lifting of the veil

Some of the sections of the Act which have the effect of lifting the veil of incorporation are as follows:

(a) Section 24, as amended by the Companies (Single Member Private Limited Companies) Regulations 1992 (SI 1992, No. 1699), (*see* 2:**33**). Under this section as amended the members of a *public* company, if they fall below two in number, can lose the protective shield of the company as regards its debts.

(b) Section 349 (*see* 2:**10**). Under this section an officer of the company or any person on its behalf who omits to place the company's name on a negotiable instrument which he signs on behalf of the company may be personally liable to the holder for the specified amount.

(c) Section 433 (*see* 22:**4**). This concerns the power of an inspector appointed by the Department of Trade and Industry to investigate the affairs of any company within the same group as the company primarily under investigation.

(d) Section 442 (*see* 22:**8**). This concerns the power of the Department of Trade and Industry to investigate membership.

(e) Section 283 (*see* 16:**3**). The device of the corporation cannot be used to evade the provision that a sole director must not also be secretary of the company.

(f) Section 324 and Schedule 13 (*see* 16:**16**). Here a person is deemed interested in shares or debentures if he has a certain degree of control over the company which holds them.

(g) Section 227, inserted by the Companies Act 1989 (*see* 18:**12**). This section requires the directors of a parent company to prepare group accounts, disregarding the separate corporate personalities of the companies in the group and emphasising their economic unity.

(h) Section 346 and Schedule 13 (*see* 16:**30**). Under this provision a director is identified with a body corporate controlled by him.

(i) Section 203 (*see* 12:**15**). Here again a person is deemed interested in shares if he has a certain degree of control over the company which holds them.

An instance from the Insolvency Act 1986 is:

(j) Section 214 Insolvency Act 1986 (*see* 2:**33**). By this provision a director guilty of wrongful trading may be declared by the court to be liable to make such contribution to the company's assets as the court thinks proper.

If these examples are examined closely, it will be seen that the expression 'lifting the veil' is used in more than one way. In its strict sense, it is applied to cases where the personality of the corporation is penetrated to reveal the *members* of the company as individuals, e.g. in *Re Bugle Press Ltd* or under s. 24. In these cases it is as though one were looking at the bricks rather than the building. The emphasis is on the composition, not the structure. In a wider sense, however, the expression covers in a loose and academically unsatisfactory way cases where the personality of the corporation is swept aside in order to reach the *officers* of the company, e.g. under s. 349. Here it is not a matter of the law substituting composition for structure, since the officers do not compose the corporation, but rather enabling an injured outsider to pursue his remedy against the persons responsible for his injury, whether they are members or not. If there is any rationale behind these cases, it may be that the *corporation* ought not to be made liable for wrongful acts done by *individuals* purporting to act on its behalf or in its name.

24. The arrangement of this book
It is appropriate to conclude this first chapter by taking a bird's eye view of the individual topics which are dealt with in the succeeding chapters and noting in passing some of the essential terminology of our subject.

25. Registration

As is already known, a registered company comes into existence through a process of registration. This involves the filing with the registrar of companies of certain documents, of which, at the beginning of the company's life, the most important are the company's memorandum of association and articles of association. The certificate of incorporation, issued by the registrar in response to compliance with the registration procedure laid down in the Act, is the company's birth certificate.

This material — the memorandum of association, the articles of association and registration — comprises Chapters 2–4.

Throughout company law, there are many further requirements for registration with the registrar, including the filing of resolutions, accounts and reports.

The object of all the registration requirements is to secure publicity for important matters concerning the company. The information filed with the registrar may be consulted by any member of the public who is interested in any way in the company — it may be as a prospective creditor or prospective investor.

26. Setting the company going

Although, with the issue of the company's certificate of incorporation, the company is formally in existence as a legal person, there are normally many arrangements to be made before the company can be said to be a 'going concern'.

The company may require to obtain a further certificate in order to be entitled to trade and enter into contracts. Chapter 5 deals with this.

The persons who take steps to set the company going are called 'promoters'. They are in a fiduciary relationship to the company and must make full disclosure of any profit which they obtain from their position. Although the persons who sign the memorandum of association (and so become the company's first members) are not normally promoters, the Act has provisions aimed at ensuring that these persons also do not obtain for themselves an undisclosed profit. Chapter 6 deals with these matters.

27. Raising capital

The company, if it is to trade on a large scale, will normally wish to raise capital, directly or indirectly, from the public. Offers of listed and unlisted shares to the public are the subject-matter of Chapter 7.

Those who offer shares to the public will want the offer to be successful. They will, however, realise that it is possible that not all the shares offered will in fact be taken up, and to safeguard themselves against such a failure they will arrange for the shares to be 'underwritten', i.e. to be taken up by a financial house, in return for a commission, in so far as the public does not take up the offer. The provisions of the Act which regulate the paying of underwriting commission are given in Chapter 8.

Where a person applies to the company for shares and receives from the company the shares applied for, the company is said to 'allot' the shares. The 'allottee' is then the first holder of these shares. He may later choose to sell his shares to another person, who will be a 'transferee' (not an allottee, because the term 'allottee' is used only of a person who obtains his shares *from the company*). The price paid for shares allotted is paid to the company. The provisions of the Act on allotment and payment for shares are in Chapters 9 and 10.

Finally in this group of chapters is Chapter 11 on capital itself. It deals with what the company may do with its capital, once obtained, e.g. the procedure by which it may alter its amount or structure.

28. Shareholders and members

Capital is divided into shares and the persons who hold the shares are, obviously enough, referred to as 'shareholders'. In the ordinary type of company the word 'shareholders' is synonymous with 'members'. There are, however, some companies (in particular companies limited by guarantee) where the company has no share capital, and so has no shareholders, but does have members.

In the normal trading company with which we are concerned in this book, Chapters 12–14 are on closely related topics. Chapter 12 deals with shares (how they may be transferred, used as security for a loan, etc.), Chapter 13 with membership (how one becomes a member, who may be members, etc.) and Chapter 14 with the register of members, which must be kept by the company — another instance of the emphasis placed on publicity as a protection for prospective investors and creditors.

29. Operation of the company

It has been seen how the company is formed by registration, and, by the raising of capital divisible into shares held by the members, is in a position to operate as a legal person.

As the company is an *artificial* legal person, however, its operations must be initiated by resolutions passed at meetings of the members or by the board of directors. The Act requires the company to hold certain meetings of its members (*see* Chapter 15), but these are, on all but rare occasions, sparsely attended, and in practice the day-to-day management of the company is in the hands of the directors or other persons to whom the directors have delegated their own power. Chapters 16 and 17 are concerned with the directors, the secretary, and meetings of the board of directors.

30. Accounts and related matters

The Act requires the company to have annual accounts and to give to such accounts a degree of publicity which varies according to the size of the company. The provisions are described in Chapter 18.

There are also requirements for the accounts to be audited (*see* Chapter 19), and some restrictions placed by the common law and by the Act on the distribution of dividends to the shareholders (*see* Chapter 20).

31. Debentures

A debenture is a document by which a company acknowledges that a loan has been made to it. The company may or may not give to the lender security over some or the whole of its property, so that the creditor may have recourse to that property in the event of the company's failing to make due repayment of the loan.

Although, from the point of view of investors, shares and debentures are similar in that they both provide a home for a sum of money, with the prospect of increased capital value and the payment of an annual return on the money invested, they are in law radically different from one another. Shareholders are the members who comprise the company itself, whereas debenture-holders are creditors of the company, i.e. are outsiders. Also, the return received by shareholders in the form of a dividend is due only where there are available profits, whereas the interest paid on debentures is, like the loan itself, a debt due by the company, even when the company is making a loss.

Chapter 21 is devoted to debentures and the related matters of charges (including floating charges) and receivers.

32. Investigations and inspections

The Department of Trade and Industry has certain powers of investigation and inspection over registered companies. These are dealt with in Chapter 22.

33. Majority rule and minority protection

A principle, known as 'the rule in *Foss* v. *Harbottle*' [B239], is to the effect that an individual shareholder is not permitted to bring an action against any person who has injured the company if the majority of the shareholders are opposed to that step, i.e. the company as a separate legal person can act only through its majority shareholders.

There are, however, exceptions to the rule in *Foss* v. *Harbottle*, because the common law and the Act both recognise that there are certain circumstances where the minority shareholders require to have protection from the majority.

The rule in *Foss* v. *Harbottle* and the exceptions to it are explained in Chapter 23.

34. Insider dealing

The Company Securities (Insider Dealing) Act 1985 is part of the criminal law. It is aimed at preventing a person who has some inside information about a company from abusing his position by dealing in the company's shares or debentures in such a way as to make a private gain. The Act was amended by the Financial Services Act 1986 and repealed by the Criminal Justice Act 1993. Chapter 24 outlines this somewhat complex topic.

35. Private companies

Throughout the text there are many references to exemptions and privileges available to private companies. It may be found convenient to have the principal distinguishing provisions gathered together in a separate chapter, and this is done in Chapter 25.

36. Administration orders

Where a company is likely to be unable to pay its debts but has not yet gone into liquidation, the court may make an administration order directing that the company's affairs be managed by an 'administrator' appointed by the court. The procedure is aimed at rescuing the company from liquidation, or at least ensuring a more advantageous sale of the company's assets than would otherwise be possible in a liquidation. The provisions, which are in the Insolvency Act 1986, are outlined in Chapter 27.

37. Dissolution and winding up

A company's life is brought to an end by dissolution. There are several modes of dissolution, as explained in Chapter 26, but of these the one on which there are copious statutory provisions, now in the Insolvency Act 1986, is winding up or liquidation.

Some of the more important aspects of winding up are outlined in Chapters 28–31, entitled 'Contributories', 'Voluntary winding up', 'Winding up by the court' and 'Provisions of general application in winding up', respectively.

38. Arrangements and reconstructions

Finally Chapter 32 gives a brief account of schemes of arrangement and reconstruction of which a company may avail itself.

2

The memorandum of association

1. Who may form a registered company?

Section 1 tells us who may form a company under the Companies Act and by what process. It starts with the basic rule that any two or more persons may form a company. An exception is made to that basic rule by the Companies (Single Member Private Limited Companies) Regulations 1992 (SI 1992, No. 1699) which permit a private company to be formed by one person only. The purpose must always be a lawful purpose. No company may have an illegal object. The persons must subscribe their names to, i.e. sign, a document called a *memorandum of association*. They must also comply with the requirements of the Companies Act 1985 in respect of registration.

If they fulfil these conditions they can form an incorporated company, i.e. a corporation registered under the Act with or without limited liability. This means that the members' liability for the company's debts may be limited or unlimited (*see* **3**).

2. Public and private companies

A company may be a public company or a private company. The Act gives a statutory definition of a public company and defines a private company as any company which is not a public company. Of the total of over 900,000 companies now registered, over 99 per cent are private companies but the comparatively small number of public companies includes many large companies well known to the ordinary person.

Section 1 defines a public company as a company which is *either*:

(a) limited by shares: *or*
(b) limited by guarantee with a share capital (*see* **29**);

provided that in either case:

(a) its memorandum states that it is to be a public company; *and*
(b) the statutory provisions governing the registration of a public company have been complied with.

A public company, accordingly, is always a limited company. It follows that an unlimited company is necessarily a private company.

It should also be noted that s. 1 prohibits a company limited by guarantee from having a share capital unless it did so before 22 December 1980 (i.e. the date when the Companies Act 1980 came into force). Companies limited by guarantee *with* a share capital are therefore of diminishing importance and will cease to exist in time.

3. Limited and unlimited companies

Section 1 enlarges on the subject of liability. A company may be:

(a) *limited by shares* (i.e. the liability of the members is limited by the memorandum to the amount unpaid on their shares); *or*

(b) *limited by guarantee* (i.e. the liability of the members is limited by the memorandum to the amount which the members have undertaken or guaranteed to contribute to the assets of the company on winding up); *or*

(c) *unlimited* (i.e. there is no limit to the liability of the members. Here, although the association is a corporation and not a partnership, the extent of the members' liability is the same as that of partners. Unlike partners, however, they are not directly liable to the creditors, but are only directly liable to the company).

4. The contents of the memorandum

The contents of the memorandum are prescribed in the main by s. 2. The document must contain:

(a) The name of the company (*see* **7–13**).

If the company is a public company, s. 25 requires its name to end with the words 'public limited company' and by s. 1 the memorandum must state that the company is to be a public company (*see* **2**).

If the company is a private company, the last word of its name must be 'limited': s. 25.

(b) The domicile of the company, i.e. whether the registered office is to be in England and Wales, Scotland or Wales (*see* **14–15**).

(c) The objects of the company (*see* **17–27**).

(d) The limitation of the liability of the members, if the company is limited by shares or guarantee (*see* **28–33**)

(e) Unless the company is an unlimited company, the amount of share capital, divided into shares of a fixed amount (*see* **34**).

These five (in a public company six) clauses are usually referred to as the *compulsory clauses* and each of them is considered separately later in this chapter. Other clauses, however, are often included.

Where the memorandum states that the registered office is to be in Wales, s. 25 permits it to state a private company's name with 'cyfyngedig' as the last word, instead of 'limited'. Similarly, under the same section, the name of a Welsh public company may end with the words 'cwmni cyfyngedig cyhoeddus', instead of 'public limited company'.

Furthermore, none of these expressions is required to be given in full. Section 27 permits abbreviations to be used in all cases, as follows:

for 'limited', 'ltd';
for 'public limited company', 'plc';
for 'cyfyngedig', 'cyf',
for 'cwmni cyfyngedig cyhoeddus', 'ccc'.

5. The form of the memorandum
By s. 2 the memorandum must be signed by each subscriber in the presence of at least one witness. Anyone may be a witness so long as he is old enough to understand what he is doing.

The same section requires each subscriber to take at least one share and for there to be shown against his name the number of shares he takes.

Model forms of memorandum for the different types of companies are to be found in the Companies (Tables A-F) Regulations 1985. The model form for a public company limited by shares is in Table F of the Schedule to these Regulations, while Table B gives the model for a private company limited by shares. The models must be followed as closely as circumstances admit: s. 3. In both forms, after the compulsory clauses, appears what is known as the *association clause* by which the subscribers bind themselves together to form a company, but no mention of this clause is made in the Act itself.

6. Alteration of the memorandum
Section 2 of the Act also deals with the legal rules relating to alteration of the memorandum. This is an important provision governing the *whole document* and states that a company may not alter the clauses in its memorandum except in the cases, in the mode and to the extent for which the Act expressly provides.

The result of this provision is that each clause of the memorandum must be separately studied, for the rules regarding alteration of the clauses are not all the same.

Section 18 provides that where a company is required to send to the registrar any document relating to an alteration in its memorandum, it must also send to him a printed copy of the memorandum as altered. Alterations of objects under s. 4 are exempted from this provision since s. 6 already contains a requirement for a printed copy of the memorandum as altered to be sent to the registrar (*see* **27**).

Section 711 requires the registrar to publish his receipt of any such document in the *Gazette* and gives the term 'official notification' to publication in this manner. If an alteration of the memorandum has not been officially notified by the registrar at the material time and if the company cannot show that it was known at that time to the person concerned, the company cannot rely on the alteration against that person: s. 42.

7. The choice of a name for the company

Regarding the choice of a name, s. 26, which prohibits the registration of certain names, must be complied with. There is also some important case-law on this topic.

Section 26 prohibits a company from being registered by a name:

(a) which includes the words 'limited', 'unlimited' or 'public limited company', or their abbreviations, anywhere except at the end of the name;
(b) which is the same as any name appearing in the index of names kept by the registrar under s. 714; *or*
(c) the use of which would in the opinion of the Secretary of State constitute a criminal offence or be offensive.

As indicated in **(b)**, s. 714 requires the registrar to keep an index of company names. However, in determining whether any name is the same as another appearing in the index, s. 26 lists certain words or printing characteristics which are to be disregarded. These are as follows:

(a) the word 'the' when it is the first word of the name;
(b) the words 'company', 'and company', 'company limited', 'and company limited', 'limited', 'unlimited', and 'public limited company' when they are the last word or words of the name;
(c) abbreviations of any of the words in **(b)** above when they appear at the end of the name; and
(d) type and case of letters, spaces between letters, accents and punctuation marks.

Finally there is the provision, in a phrase which has already become immortal: 'and "and" and "&" are to be taken as the same'. Presumably this means that one cannot rely on an ampersand to constitute a difference.

If, despite these rules, a company is registered by a name so similar to that of another that the public are likely to be deceived, the court will grant an injunction [in Scots law an interdict] restraining it from using that name.

> Thus in *Ewing* v. *Buttercup Margarine Co. Ltd* (1917) [B55] the plaintiff, who carried on business under the name of the Buttercup Dairy Co., obtained an injunction against the defendant on the grounds that the public might think that the two businesses were connected.

[A comparable Scottish case is *Chill Foods (Scotland) Ltd* v. *Cool Foods Ltd* (1977) [B53] in which an established company was granted an interdict to restrain a new company with a name likely to cause confusion from trading in the same line of business in the same area.]

The same considerations will apply where a company chooses an invented word, rather than a real one, as part of its name.

In *Exxon Corporation* v. *Exxon Insurance Consultants International Ltd* (1981) [B57], the plaintiffs, after a long period of research to find a suitable name, invented the word 'Exxon' as part of it. The defendant company later used the same word as part of its name although it had no connection with the plaintiffs' business. The plaintiffs sought an injunction to restrain the defendant from using the word 'Exxon' on the grounds that its use was an infringement of their copyright, the word being an 'original literary work' within s. 2 Copyright Act 1956. They also sought an injunction to restrain the defendant from passing off its goods as the plaintiffs' goods by using a similar name. HELD: The plaintiffs were entitled to an injunction restraining the defendant from passing off its goods as the plaintiffs' goods by the use of the word 'Exxon'. However, they were not entitled to an injunction restraining infringement of copyright since the word 'Exxon' was not an 'original literary work'. A 'literary work', said Stephenson L.J., is 'something . . . intended to afford either information and instruction or pleasure in the form of literary enjoyment', and the word 'Exxon' did not do either of these things.

The courts view much more favourably the use of a purely descriptive word with a definite meaning and in common use. If the names of two companies contain such a word, a very trifling distinction between them will suffice to make them acceptable.

Thus in *Aerators Ltd* v. *Tollitt* (1902) the plaintiff was refused an injunction restraining the defendant from using the name of *Automatic Aerators Patents Ltd* and Farwell J. said: 'If the name is simply a word in ordinary use representing a machine or an article of commerce, the probability of deception is out of all proportion less than it would be in the case of an invented or fancy word'.

8. Names requiring the approval of the Secretary of State

Section 26 requires the company to obtain the approval of the Secretary of State before it is registered by any name which:

(a) in his opinion would be likely to give the impression that the company is connected with the Government or any local authority; *or*

(b) includes any word specified in regulations made under s. 29.

Where a company carries on business under a name which is not its corporate name, s. 2 Business Names Act 1985 provides that these rules apply to its business name as well.

The regulations mentioned in **(b)** are to be found in SI 1981, No. 1685, entitled 'The Company and Business Names Regulations 1981'. The statutory instrument was made under authority of the Companies Act 1981, but now has effect as if made under s. 29 Companies Act 1985 and ss. 3, 6 Business Names Act 1985. It contains in its Schedule a long list of words for the use or registration of which the approval of the Secretary of State is required, together with the names of the 'relevant bodies' whose objections in each case must first be sought.

Where a company proposes to adopt a corporate name which contains any of the listed words, the appropriate person must first, under s. 29 Companies Act 1985, make a written request to the relevant body to indicate whether it has any objections to the proposal and, if so, why. He must then submit to the registrar a statement that the request has been made and a copy of any response received from the relevant body, together with:

(a) in the case of a company seeking to register under the 1985 Act, the statutory declaration required by s. 12 (*see* 4:**1**);
(b) in the case of an existing company, a copy of the special resolution changing the company's name (*see* **12**).

The expression 'the appropriate person' means, in the case of **(a)**, the person making the declaration and, in the case of **(b)**, a director or secretary of the company: s. 29.

Where a company proposes to use a business name which contains any of the listed words, it is required by s. 3 Business Names Act 1985 to make a similar request to the relevant body and submit a similar statement to the Secretary of State along with a copy of the relevant body's response.

9. Disclosure of corporate name by company using business name

Section 4 Business Names Act 1985 requires any company using a business name to state:

(a) its corporate name; *and*
(b) an address in Great Britain at which service of any document relating to its business will be effective;

in legible characters on all business letters, orders for goods or services to be supplied to the business, invoices and receipts issued in the course of the business and written demands for payment of business debts.

Such a company is also required, in any premises where it carries on business and to which customers or suppliers have access, to display a notice containing the same information in a prominent position. Further, the company must immediately give the same information in writing to any person with whom business is conducted and who asks for it.

Section 5 Business Names Act 1985 gives a civil remedy to the other party to any business transaction in which a company has infringed the provisions in s. 4. It states that where the defaulting company brings legal proceedings to enforce a right arising out of a contract made in the course of the business, the action will be dismissed if the defendant shows that owing to the company's breach of s. 4:

(a) he has been unable to pursue a claim against the company arising out of that contract; *or*
(b) he has suffered some financial loss in connection with that contract:

unless the court thinks it just and equitable to permit the proceedings to continue.

The section makes it clear, however, that if it is the other party who sues the defaulting company, the company will be able to enforce any rights which it may have against the plaintiff, despite the fact that it has infringed s. 4.

10. Publication of the company's name

Once a company has chosen its name, it must comply with ss. 348–350 Companies Act 1985 regarding publication.

(a) *Publication of name.* Sections 348–350 make it compulsory to have the name painted or affixed on the outside of *business premises*, engraved on the *seal* if it has a seal, and mentioned on all *business documents and negotiable instruments*.

We have already seen in **4** that the word 'limited' or 'cyfyngedig' must appear in the name of a limited company so as to indicate the true legal position of the members regarding the company's debts. Where the name of a public company contains the words 'cwmni cyfyngedig cyhoeddus', s. 351 requires the fact that it is a public limited company to be stated in English also on all business documents and in a notice in the business premises.

Conversely, however, under s. 34, any person who carries on business under a name of which 'limited' or 'cyfyngedig' is the last word, without being incorporated with limited liability, commits an offence. Section 33 contains a similar provision, stating that any person who is not a public company and who carries on business under a name which includes, as its last part, the words 'public limited company', or their equivalent in Welsh, commits an offence.

Finally, s. 33 also makes it an offence for a public company to use a name which may reasonably be expected to give the impression that it is a private company in circumstances where the fact that it is a public company is likely to be material.

(b) *Fines for non-compliance.* Other provisions in ss. 348–350 impose fines on the company and the officers for non-compliance with the sections. The fines need not be learned in detail, but a distinction should be noted between 'officer' and 'officer in default' in these provisions. In the case of failure to comply with the provision as to having the name painted or affixed on the business premises, the fine is on the company and every officer who is in default, whereas in the case of failure to comply with the other provisions as to publication the fine is on the company and any officer using the seal or issuing or signing the business document or negotiable instrument.

Section 730 states that the expression 'officer in default' means an officer who *knowingly and wilfully* authorises or permits the default, while s. 744, the main definition section, alphabetically arranged, defines 'officer' as including *director, manager or secretary.*

(c) *Personal liability.* Section 349 has an important provision. It not only imposes a fine on the officer for signing a negotiable instrument without the company's name on it, but it states that he will be personally liable to the holder of such a negotiable instrument for the amount thereof unless it is duly paid by the company. This could be a serious matter for an officer of a company, as a negotiable instrument may be for any amount and could involve him in personal liability which far exceeds the amount of the fine. The omission of any part of the name is sufficient to render him personally liable in this way.

Thus in *Hendon* v. *Adelman* (1973), where an ampersand was omitted, and in *Penrose* v. *Martyr* (1858), *British Airways Board* v. *Parish* (1979) and *Lindholst & Co. A/S* v. *Fowler* (1988) where the word 'limited' was not on the instrument, the officers were in every case held personally liable. The court does not rectify the error so as to enable the officer to escape liability: *Blum* v. *O.C.P. Repartition S.A.* (1988).

In *Stacey & Co. Ltd* v. *Wallis* (1912), however, it was held not only that the abbreviation 'Ltd' was permissible — a rule now enshrined in s. 27 (*see* **4**) — but also that it did not matter whereabouts on the instrument the company's name appeared, so long as it was correctly stated. Similarly, in *Banque de l'Indochine et de Suez S.A.* v. *Euroseas Group Finance Co. Ltd* (1981) it was held that 'Co.' was an acceptable abbreviation for 'Company'. Further, if the error in the name is caused by the holder of the instrument, it may be that he will not be able to enforce the resulting liability against the officer who signed it: *Durham Fancy Goods Ltd* v.

Jackson (Michael) (1968) but the authority of this case has been doubted in the later cases of *Lindholst* and *Blum*.

Confusion can arise where a company uses a business name. In *Maxform S.p.A.* v. *Mariani and Goodville Ltd* (1981), however, it was held that the word 'name' in what is now s. 349 means the registered corporate name and the fact that the company uses a business name does not prevent the application of the section.

11. Power to dispense with the word 'limited'

There are certain cases where, even in a limited company, the last word of the name need not be 'limited'.

Section 30 provides that where a *private company limited by guarantee* has for its objects the promotion of commerce, art, science, education, religion, charity or any profession and its memorandum or articles comply with certain requirements, it is exempt from the provisions of the Act relating to the use of the word 'limited' as part of its name, the publishing of its name and the sending of lists of members to the registrar of companies.

The requirements are that the company's memorandum or articles:

(a) require its profits or other income to be applied in promoting its objects;
(b) prohibit the payment of dividends to its members; *and*
(c) require all the assets which would otherwise be available to its members to be transferred, on its winding up, either to another body with *similar* objects or to one which has for its objects the *promotion of charity*.

Where a company is seeking registration a statutory declaration that it is one to which s. 30 applies may be made by a solicitor engaged in its formation or by a person named as a director or secretary in the statement delivered under s. 10 (*see* 4:1). This declaration may be delivered to the registrar who may accept it as sufficient evidence of that fact and who may refuse to register a company by a name which does not include 'limited' unless he has received such a declaration. Where a company is already in existence but is seeking to change its name and dispense with the word 'limited', the declaration may be made by a director or the secretary.

A company to which s. 30 applies and which does not have the word 'limited' in its name is prohibited by s. 31 from altering its memorandum or articles so that the section ceases to apply to it. If, however, it appears to the Secretary of State that such a company has carried on any business other than the promotion of the listed objects, or has infringed the provisions of its memorandum or articles stated in (a) or (b) above, he may direct the company to change its name by a resolution of the directors so that its name ends with 'limited'. This resolution must be filed with the registrar under s. 380 (*see* 15:**34**).

12. Voluntary change of name

Section 28 tells us how we can change the company's name. It provides that a company may change its name by special resolution. This is a general permission to any company to change its name at any time and as often as it wishes, but of course the new name must not contravene the statutory rules described above.

Where a company changes its name, s. 28 requires the registrar to enter its new name on the register in place of its former name and to issue an altered certificate of incorporation. The change of name takes effect from the date on which the altered certificate is issued, but it does not affect the company's legal position. Thus legal proceedings by or against it may be continued under the new name.

13. Compulsory change of name

Under the above rules a company may change its name voluntarily. There are, however, three cases where it can be *directed* to change its name and must comply with the direction:

(a) If a company is registered by a name which is either *the same* as one appearing in the index (*see* **7**) at the time of its registration or, in the opinion of the Secretary of State, *too similar* to such a name, the Secretary of State may, within 12 months, give a *written direction* to the company to change its name within a specified period.

The same rule applies if a company is registered by a name which is the same as, or too similar to, one which should have appeared in the index at the time of its registration, even though it did not: s. 28.

(b) If it appears to the Secretary of State that a company has provided *misleading information* for the purpose of its registration by a particular name, or has given undertakings or assurances which have not been fulfilled, he may, within five years, give a *written direction* to the company to change its name within a specified period: s. 28.

(c) Section 32 empowers the Department of Trade and Industry to *direct* a company to change its name if, in their opinion, its registered name gives *so misleading an indication of the nature of its activities* as to be likely to cause harm to the public.

Section 32 requires the company to comply with such a direction within six weeks unless it applies to the court within three weeks to set the direction aside. The court may set the direction aside or confirm it, in which latter case it must specify the period within which the company must comply.

14. The distinction between domicile and residence

In the case of a public company the second clause of the memorandum will be, as explained in **4**, a statement that the company is to be a public company. The alteration of the memorandum with regard to this clause is best considered in Chapter 25 on private companies.

We come now, therefore, to the second or, in the case of a public company, the third compulsory clause of the memorandum. This states the country in which the registered office of the company is situated, thus giving the company's domicile. Section 351 requires both the domicile and the registered number of the company to be mentioned in all business letters and order forms. The registered number of a company is given on its certificate of incorporation (*see* 4:**2**).

Domicile must be distinguished from *residence*. The domicile of a company is the place where it was incorporated or registered, and this domicile adheres to the company throughout its existence. A company can have only one domicile, which cannot be changed.

The test of residence, on the other hand, is not registration but the place where the company does its business, i.e. the place of its management and control. This will usually be the place where the board of directors meets. The main importance of residence is with regard to taxation, for which purpose a company may have more than one residence.

15. The importance of the registered office

Although the domicile of the company cannot be changed, the address of the registered office within that domicile can be changed freely at any time to suit the company's convenience. Section 351 requires that address to be mentioned in all business letters and order forms.

Section 287, as substituted by s. 136 Companies Act 1989, makes it compulsory for a company to have a registered office at all times. Its intended situation must, under s. 10, be specified in the statement delivered to the registrar prior to incorporation (*see* 4:**1**). The company may change the situation of its registered office by giving notice in the prescribed form to the registrar. The change takes effect upon the notice being registered by the registrar, but for the next 14 days documents may still be validly served on the company at its previous registered office.

Section 711 requires the registrar to publish in the *Gazette* the receipt by him of notice of any change in the situation of a company's registered office. If the change had not been officially notified by the registrar at the material time and if the company cannot show that it was known at that time to the person concerned, the company cannot rely on it against that person as regards service of any document on the company: s. 42.

The importance of the registered office is that it is the address where writs may be served on the company and where communications may be sent. It is also the address at which the following registers and documents must normally be kept:

(a) the register of members: s. 353,

(b) the register of debenture holders: s. 190;

(c) the register of directors and secretaries: s. 288;

(d) the register of directors' interests in shares and debentures: s. 325 and Schedule 13, Part IV;

(e) the register of charges: s. 411, inserted by s. 101 Companies Act 1989;

(f) copies of instruments creating the charges: s. 411, inserted by s. 101 Companies Act 1989;

(g) minute books of general meetings: s. 383;

(h) the register of interests in shares: s. 211.

This list must be carefully learnt. The order in which the eight items are memorised is not important, but they have been arranged above as far as possible so that they fall into couples in order to facilitate learning them.

There are some exceptions to the requirement that all these items must be kept at the registered office — in particular, the register of members may be kept at the office where the work of making it up is done if that office is not the company's registered office: s. 353.

NOTE: All these documents are open to members free; **(e)** and **(f)** are also open to creditors free, while **(b)** is open to debenture-holders free; **(a)** to **(f)** are open to the public on payment of the prescribed fee, while **(h)** is open to the public free.

By s. 723A, inserted in the 1985 Act by s. 143 Companies Act 1989, the Secretary of State is empowered to make provision by regulations as to the time, duration and manner of inspection and as to the provision of copies.

The section also provides that where there is power to charge a fee, the regulations may make provision as to the amount of the fee and the basis of its calculation. The sections in the Act which provide for a fee to be charged, therefore, do not now specify any particular fee, but state that the fee charged will be 'such fee as may be prescribed'.

A company is free to allow more extensive facilities for inspection than the statutory facilities, and may also, if it chooses, charge a lesser fee than that prescribed or no fee at all.

16. The statutory books

Often the student is required to state what are the statutory books. This is a list of the registers and documents which every company is required by law to keep. There are eight items here:

(a) the register of members: s. 352;

(b) the register of directors and secretaries: s. 288;
(c) the register of directors' interests in shares and debentures: s. 325;
(d) directors' service contracts: s. 318;
(e) the register of charges: s. 411, inserted by s. 101 Companies Act 1989;
(f) the minute books of general and directors' meetings: s. 382;
(g) the register of interests in shares: s. 211;
(h) the accounting records, which are:

  (*i*) receipts and expenditure;
  (*ii*) assets and liabilities;
  (*iii*) statements of stock held and sales and purchases of goods: s. 221, as substituted by s. 2 Companies Act 1989.

NOTE: The two lists are very similar. Most of the statutory books must normally be kept at the registered office since they appear in both lists. But the minute books of directors' meetings and the accounting records may be kept at any convenient place; they do not appear in the first list and therefore there is no obligation to keep them at the registered office. Directors' service contracts must be kept at an appropriate place, defined as the registered office or the place where the register of members is kept (if other than the registered office), or the principal place of business.

On the other hand, while there is no obligation to keep a register of debenture-holders at all, most companies do so in practice, in which case the register must be kept either at the registered office or at the office where the work of making it up is done.

Directors' service contracts are open to members free. The accounting records are open to the officers of the company at all times, though not to members: s. 222, as substituted by s. 2 Companies Act 1989.

17. The objects of the company

The third, or, in the case of a public company, the fourth compulsory clause in the memorandum sets out the objects of the company. It is with this clause that the famous doctrine of *ultra vires* has been associated.

We must first look briefly at the meaning and effects of this doctrine before dealing with the new provisions made as to the objects by the Companies Act 1989.

18. The *ultra vires* doctrine

The doctrine of *ultra vires* means that a company may only carry out acts which are expressly or by necessary implication sanctioned by its objects. Any other acts are void and cannot later be ratified, even by the unanimous consent of members.

This doctrine has never applied to chartered companies. A chartered corporation will have objectives set out in its charter, but nevertheless it has full legal capacity, so that even if it acts outside those objects the transaction is valid. However, if it persistently violates its charter, the charter may be forfeited.

Statutory corporations and registered companies, on the other hand, are in a different position. A statutory corporation has its objects set out in the Act of Parliament creating it, while a registered company, created by a procedure authorised by Act of Parliament, has its objects stated in its memorandum. By the *ultra vires* doctrine, both statutory corporations and registered companies have their capacity limited to their stated objects, and anything purported to be done beyond these objects is void and cannot be ratified even by the unanimous consent of members.

Theoretically, the *ultra vires* doctrine was a protection for members and creditors of a registered company. By consulting the company's memorandum they could discover whether the particular transaction being proposed was beyond the company's objects and therefore void.

In practice, however, no such consultation would be made and so there was no protection acquired. Companies could find themselves hindered from new developments, and unwary creditors might be left without any valid claim in respect of business transactions which appeared to be ordinary but which were in fact not within the company's objects.

Persons forming a company considered it prudent to avoid the operation of the *ultra vires* doctrine by drafting their objects clause so widely that the company could effectively do anything. The result has been that most companies now have very lengthy objects clauses, ranging from A to Z, and often from AA to ZZ, covering every conceivable object and ending with general terms authorising the company to do anything else which happened to have been omitted.

The effects of the doctrine, as shown in the considerable case law which had accumulated, were generally regarded as unfortunate and ripe for at least revision, if not abolition, by the time of the UK's entry into the European Communities in 1972. The legislation in s. 9 European Communities Act 1972 modified the doctrine, but still left some difficulties.

On consolidation of company legislation in 1985, the provisions of s. 9 of that 1972 Act modifying the doctrine became s. 35 Companies Act 1985.

In 1985 the Department of Trade and Industry appointed Dr Dan Prentice of Oxford University to carry out a study of the legal and commercial implications of abolishing the doctrine. His report was published in 1986, and, after a period of consultation with interested bodies including the Law Societies new provisions on this whole area of company law were adopted by s. 108 Companies Act 1989. That section substitutes for s. 35 Companies Act 1985 three new sections — ss. 35, 35A and 35B.

The general effect of the new provisions is to abolish the *ultra vires* doctrine as it operated 'externally', i.e. as regards outsiders, thus removing the disadvantages which they could previously suffer, but to retain the doctrine as it operated 'internally', i.e. as regards members, thus affording members protection against the actions of directors.

19. Company's capacity not limited by its memorandum

The leading provision in s. 35 is that the validity of an act done by a company shall not be called into question on the ground of lack of capacity by reason of anything in the company's memorandum. The purpose of this provision is to give security to commercial transactions entered into between the company and outsiders. The provision, in effect, abolishes the 'external' operation of the *ultra vires* doctrine.

The next provision in s. 35 is aimed at preserving an individual shareholder's right to go to court to seek an injunction [in Scots law an interdict] to restrain a proposed *ultra vires* act: the 'internal' operation of the *ultra vires* doctrine has been considered a valuable safeguard for shareholders *vis-à-vis* the directors. The provision is that a member of a company may bring proceedings to restrain the doing of an act which would, but for the leading provision in s. 35 mentioned above, be beyond the company's capacity.

This personal right of an individual shareholder is limited by a further provision that he cannot bring such proceedings if the act in question is to be done in fulfilment of a legal obligation arising from a previous act of the company. The purpose of this provision is that honest third parties who have entered into a legal contract with a company should not suffer because of limits, of which they were unaware, on the directors' authority.

Section 35 then provides that it remains the duty of the directors to observe any limitations on their powers flowing from the company's memorandum, and action by the directors which, but for the leading provision in s. 35, would be beyond the company's capacity may only be ratified by the company by special resolution.

A further provision in s. 35 is that a resolution ratifying such action does not affect any liability incurred by the directors or any other person; relief from any such liability must be agreed to separately by special resolution. The purpose of this specific provision is the preservation of the right of the company to obtain damages from the directors for their breach of duty in failing to observe the limitations on their powers flowing from the memorandum. There is some authority for the proposition that ratification of an unauthorised act of an agent authorises the agent retrospectively. Application of this proposition to the directors could have had the effect of wiping out their breach of duty and so their liability. Hence the specific provision.

20. Powers of directors to bind the company

Section 35A provides that in favour of a person dealing with a company in good faith, the power of the board of directors to bind the company, or authorise others to do so, is to be deemed to be free of any limitation under the company's constitution.

This provision covers the situation where the memorandum and articles of a company place limitations on the powers of the directors. It can happen that the directors exceed their powers, but still are within the *company's* powers. This is a contrast with the situation referred to in s. 35 above, where the question was as to the capacity of the *company itself*. Under s. 35 a special resolution was required to ratify the transaction, but under s. 35A there is no such requirement, because the section provides that the directors' power is to be *deemed to be free of limitation*.

The outsider must be 'acting in good faith' in order to take the benefit of s. 35A, but further provisions of the section assist him in this respect. It is provided that a person is to be presumed to have acted in good faith unless the contrary is proved, and it is also provided that a person is not to be regarded as acting in bad faith *merely because* he knows that an act is beyond the powers of the directors under the company's constitution. The third party is therefore in a very strong position.

Section 35A refers to the limitations as being 'under the company's constitution'. A company's constitution is usually regarded as being contained in its memorandum and articles, and limitations on directors' powers would normally be found in these documents. However, it is possible that the company might, perhaps temporarily, place limitations on directors' powers by passing a resolution in a general or class meeting or by an agreement between its members or between members of any class. The section provides that the expression 'company's constitution' extends to such resolutions and agreements.

The reference in s. 35A to the possibility that the board of directors would authorise others to bind the company would apply to the situation where the board of directors had authorised persons (e.g. a managing director) to act on its behalf.

As with s. 35, the right of a member to bring proceedings to restrain the directors from exceeding their powers is preserved, but no such proceedings can be brought if the act in question is to be done in fulfilment of a legal obligation arising from a previous act of the company.

Section 35A also specifically provides that any liability incurred by directors or any other person for exceeding their powers is not affected by its provisions.

21. No duty to inquire as to capacity of company or authority of directors

Section 35B provides that a party to a transaction with a company is not bound to inquire as to whether it is permitted by the company's memorandum or as to any limitation on the powers of the board of directors to bind the company or authorise others to do so.

22. Invalidity of certain transactions involving directors

As we have seen, s. 35A protects honest third parties from limits on the authority of directors. An exception is made to this protection by s. 322A — a new section inserted in Part X of the Companies Act 1985 (which is on enforcement of fair dealing by directors) by s. 109 Companies Act 1989. The aim is to prevent s. 35A being used by directors as a vehicle for fraud and to assist the company in recovering property or money lost through transactions with its directors.

Section 322A applies where a company enters into a transaction to which the parties include:

(a) a director of the company or of its holding company, *or*
(b) a person connected with such a director or a company with whom such a director is associated,

and the board of directors exceed any limitation on their powers under the company's constitution.

The provision of the section is that the transaction is voidable at the instance of the company.

Whether or not the company takes advantage of that provision by setting the transaction aside, any of the parties mentioned in **(a)** or **(b)** above, and any director of the company who authorised the transaction, is liable:

(a) to account to the company for any gain which he has made directly or indirectly by the transaction; *and*
(b) to indemnify the company from any loss or damage resulting from the transaction.

A person *other than a director* is not liable in these respects if he shows that at the time when the transaction was entered into he did not know that the directors were exceeding their powers.

The section provides that the transaction ceases to be voidable if:

(a) restitution of any money or other asset which was the subject-matter of the transaction is no longer possible; *or*
(b) the company is indemnified for any loss or damage resulting from the transaction: *or*
(c) rights acquired *bona fide* for value by a person who was not a party to the transaction would be affected by the avoidance; *or*
(d) the transaction is ratified by the company in general meeting, by ordinary or special resolution or otherwise.

Section 322A does not affect the operation of s. 35A in relation to any party other than a director or connected person etc. The result may be that a transaction may be voidable under s. 322A, and valid under s. 35A in favour of a party other than a director or connected person etc. It could be a complex matter for the court to sever the void aspects of the transaction from the valid ones. It has therefore been considered preferable to give the court power to *affirm* the transaction as well as to sever it or set it aside. The application to court in this connection may be made by the company or by the party other than the director or connected person etc., and the court order affirming, severing or setting aside the transaction may be on such terms as appear to the court to be just.

By s. 322B, inserted by the Companies (Single Member Private Limited Companies) Regulations 1992 (SI 1992, No. 1699), where a private limited company with only one member enters into a contract with the sole member of the company and that sole member is also a director of the company, the company must, unless the contract is in writing, ensure that the terms of the contract are either set out in a written memorandum or are recorded in the minutes of the next board meeting. The provision does not apply to contracts in the ordinary course of the company's business, and failure to comply with the provision does not affect the validity of the contract.

23. Statement of company's objects

As was explained in **18** above, it had become the practice, in order to avoid the *ultra vires* doctrine, to list in the objects clause every conceivable object. In addition, *powers*—which a company would by implication have—to carry out the stated objects had also come to be specified in the objects clause, and the distinction between objects and powers was often blurred.

The 1989 Act seeks to discourage these elaborations by making them superfluous. To do this, it inserts s. 3A in the 1985 Act: s. 110 Companies Act 1989.

Section 3A provides that where a company's memorandum states that the object of the company is to carry on business as a general commercial company, then:

(a) the object of the company is to carry on any trade or business whatsoever; *and*

(b) the company has power to do all such things as are incidental or conducive to the carrying on of any trade or business by it.

24. Charitable companies

The *ultra vires* doctrine was considered by Parliament, when passing the 1989 Act, to be of particular importance and value to charitable companies, since the control of these companies by the Charities Commission and the Attorney-General through the courts was based on the limitations on their capacity and powers set out in their objects clauses. Parliament therefore wished to disturb the existing system as little as possible, but at the same time to protect honest third parties who had given full consideration and did not know that a transaction was beyond the objects of the company or beyond the powers of the directors.

The justification for the distinct treatment of charitable companies is that people who donate money to a charity expect it to be used for the charity's expressed purposes and not misapplied or put to some other purpose, whether charitable or not.

Section 111 Companies Act 1989 substitutes for s. 30 Charities Act 1960 new provisions consisting of ss. 30, 30A, 30B and 30C, the general effect of which is to preserve some elements of the *ultra vires* doctrine in charitable companies, while conferring on third parties a lesser degree of protection than they now have under ss. 35 and 35A Companies Act 1985 in relation to commercial companies.

Section 30B Charities Act 1960 accordingly provides that ss. 35 and 35A Companies Act 1985 do not apply to the acts of a company which is a charity *except in favour of a person who*:

(a) gives full consideration in money or money's worth in relation to the act in question, *and*
(b) does not know that the act is not permitted by the company's memorandum or, as the case may be, is beyond the powers of the directors,

or who does not know at the time the act is done that the company is a charity.

Ratification under s. 35 or under s. 322A (*see* **22**) of the 1985 Act is ineffective in the case of a company which is a charity without the prior written consent of the Charity Commissioners.

In order that the third party may be made aware that he is dealing with a company which is a charity, s. 30C Charities Act 1960 provides that if the word 'charity' or the word 'charitable' is not included in the company's name, the fact that the company is a charity must be stated in all the company's business letters, notices and other official publications and in all bills of exchange, promissory notes, and orders for money or goods purporting to be signed by or on behalf of the company.

[In Scotland different legislation applies to charitable companies. The Charities Act 1960 does not apply to Scotland nor is there any body corresponding to the Charity Commissioners.

The legislation which first provided for the supervision of charities in Scotland was Part I (ss. 1-15) of the Law Reform (Miscellaneous Provisions) (Scotland) Act 1990. The Act conferred supervisory powers on the Lord Advocate and the Court of Session.

However, as regards the *ultra vires* doctrine, there are provisions in

s. 112 Companies Act 1989 relating to charitable companies in Scotland which have the same general effect as the provisions in s. 111 applicable to charitable companies in England.]

25. Gratuitous payments by companies

One further matter connected with a company's objects must be considered: namely, how far a company may make gratuitous payments out of its assets for various purposes.

Charitable donations seem never to have been challenged in the courts, being regarded as permissible on the grounds that they preserve goodwill. As regards *educational* donations, the court may hold that these are incidental or conducive to the attainment of the company's objects as in *Evans* v. *Brunner, Mond and Co. Ltd* (1921), where a donation for scientific research by chemical manufacturers was held *intra vires*.

In *Parke* v. *Daily News* (1962), however, where a gratuitous payment had been made to the employees of a company who had become redundant on an amalgamation, the court decided that *ex gratia* payments out of the assets were only valid if they were:

(a) bona fide;

(b) reasonably incidental to the carrying on of the company's business; *and*

(c) made for the benefit and prosperity of the company.

> Thus in *Re W. and M. Roith* (1967), the controlling director of a company, after many years' service without any contract, was given a service agreement providing for payment of a pension to his executors on trust for his wife. He died in office two months later and the pension was paid for several years. Then the company went into liquidation. The executors claimed the capitalised value of the pension, but the liquidator rejected their claim. HELD: The payment of the pension was not reasonably incidental to the carrying on of the company's business, nor undertaken bona fide for the benefit and prosperity of the company, and the claim was therefore rightly rejected.

However, some doubt was thrown on these rules by later cases including the decision of the Court of Appeal in *Re Horsley & Weight Ltd* (1982) [B69]. There it was held that provided an act is expressly authorised by the memorandum, the question whether it will benefit or promote the prosperity of the company is irrelevant. A company's objects did not need to be commercial. They could be charitable or philanthropic. All that was required was that they should be legal.

In any event, s. 719 resolved the difficulty to a limited extent by providing that the powers of a company include power to provide for its past and present employees and those of any of its subsidiaries on the *cessation or transfer* of the whole or any part of its undertaking or that of the subsidiary in question. Moreover, under the section the company may exercise the power even when it is not in its best interests to do so. Any such provision, if made before the commencement of winding up may by s. 719 be made out of distributable profits (*see* 20:**3-5**), while if made after the commencement of winding up, it may, by s. 187 Insolvency Act 1986, be made out of the assets available to shareholders.

Section 719 Companies Act 1985 imposes certain conditions on the exercise of the power. It must be sanctioned:

(a) in a case not falling under **(b)** or **(c)** below, by an *ordinary resolution; or*

(b) if so authorised by the memorandum or articles, a *directors' resolution; or*

(c) if the memorandum or articles require the sanction of a resolution for which a higher majority is necessary, a *resolution of that kind.*

Furthermore, any other requirement of the memorandum or articles must also be observed.

If, before winding up has commenced, the company has decided to make a payment in accordance with these conditions, the fact that it later goes into liquidation will not affect the position. Section 187 Insolvency Act 1986 expressly authorises the liquidator to make the payment in these circumstances, although if the company is being wound up by the court his power to do so is subject to the control of the court.

If winding up has already commenced, s. 187 Insolvency Act 1986 authorises the liquidator, after providing for the costs of winding up and discharging the company's liabilities, to exercise the company's power to make a payment. The conditions stated in s. 719 of the 1985 Act above, however, again apply with the exception of **(b)** which can have no application to a company in liquidation since on winding up the powers of directors cease (*see* 29:**3(d)** and 30:**9(f)**).

It should be noted that if there should be any conflict between the rules governing the power to make a payment to employees under s. 187 Insolvency Act 1986 and the normal rules relating to distribution of assets in liquidation (*see* 1:**18**), the former prevail.

26. Alteration of objects

Section 4, as substituted by s. 110 Companies Act 1989, enables the company to alter its objects at any time by *special resolution.*

Since the 1989 Act there has no longer been any restriction on the purposes for which an alteration of objects may be made. It is, however, still possible for an application to be made to court against an alteration of objects, and s. 4, as substituted by s. 110 Companies Act 1989, provides that *if* an application is made to court under s. 5, an alteration does not have effect except in so far as it is confirmed by the court.

In the case of a company which is a charity, any alteration of the objects clause requires the prior written consent of the Charity Commissioners: s. 30A Charities Act 1960 as substituted by s. 111 Companies Act 1989. [This provision does not apply to Scotland.]

27. Objections to alterations

Once the special resolution is passed, the company must wait for a period of 21 days to see whether or not any application to the court is made to cancel the alteration: s. 5. If the 21 days elapse without such an application having been made, s. 6 requires the company, within a further period of 15 days, to deliver to the registrar a printed copy of the memorandum as altered.

It may be, however, that during the permitted period of 21 days specified in s. 5 an application to the court for cancellation of the alteration is made. Such an application can be made only by:

(a) the holders of at least 15 per cent of the issued share capital, or any class thereof, or, if the company is not limited by shares, 15 per cent of the members; *or*

(b) the holders of at least 15 per cent of any debentures secured by a floating charge and issued before 1 December 1947.

NOTE: One person may hold the requisite 15 per cent and so be able to apply to the court on his own.

The court may make such order as it thinks fit, or may adjourn the proceedings in order that an arrangement may be made for the purchase of the shareholdings or other interests of the dissentient persons. The court order may provide for the purchase by the company of the shares of any members and for the resulting reduction of capital (*see* 13:**20**). It can also make any alterations to the memorandum or articles which are thereby rendered necessary and prohibit the company from making subsequent alterations to these documents. The company may then make such alterations only with the leave of the court.

As soon as an application is made, s. 6 requires the company to notify the registrar. Then when the court order is made, the company must deliver to the registrar within 15 days an office copy of the order and, if it confirms the alteration, a printed copy of the altered memorandum.

28. The liability clause

The fourth or, in the case of a public company, the fifth compulsory clause of the memorandum states that the liability of the members is limited if in fact this is the case.

In the normal trading company, as we have seen, the members' liability will be limited to the amount, if any, unpaid on their shares. But in a company limited by guarantee, it will be limited to the amount which the members have agreed to contribute to the assets in the event of liquidation. This amount will be the sum specified in the fifth or, in the case of a public company, the sixth clause of the memorandum of such a company.

29. Companies limited by guarantee

Some details concerning companies limited by guarantee may be considered here. Such companies have normally been formed for educational or charitable purposes, and may or may not have a share capital. If there is a share capital, then a member has a double liability, for he is liable not only up to the amount unpaid on his *shares*, but also up to the amount of the *guarantee* whatever it may be.

Model forms of memorandum for companies limited by guarantee with a share capital are found in Table D of the Schedule to the Companies (Tables A-F) Regulations 1985, but it should be borne in mind that no more companies of this type can be created (*see* 2).

If there is no share capital, the member is liable only up to the amount of the guarantee which is, as stated above, not payable until liquidation (*see* Table C in the Schedule). Companies limited by guarantee with no share capital normally obtain their funds through subscriptions or endowments.

30. Alteration of liability

Sections 49-52 provide re-registration procedures enabling a limited company to become unlimited and an unlimited company to become limited.

A company cannot, however, use *both* procedures. Thus once a limited company has re-registered as unlimited under s. 49 it cannot re-convert itself into a limited company under s. 51 or vice versa.

31. Re-registration of limited company as unlimited

Section 49 states that a *limited* company may be re-registered as *unlimited* by application to the registrar. The application must be framed in the prescribed form, signed by a director or the secretary, and lodged with the registrar together with certain other documents.

The application must set out such alterations in the memorandum and, if articles have been registered, in the articles as are necessary to conform with the requirements of the Act as regards unlimited companies with share capital or, if the company is not to have a share capital, as are necessary in the circumstances. If articles have not been registered, appropriate printed articles must be annexed and their registration requested.

The application must be accompanied by:

(a) the *form of assent* to the company's being registered as unlimited, subscribed by *all the members;*

(b) a *statutory declaration* by the directors that the persons subscribing the form of assent constitute the whole membership of the company; *and*

(c) a printed copy of the *memorandum* and, if articles have been registered, of the *articles* incorporating the alterations set out in the application.

Section 50 requires the registrar to retain the application and other documents, to register the articles if annexed, and to issue to the company an appropriate certificate of incorporation. On the issue of this certificate the status of the company is changed from limited to unlimited, and the alterations in the memorandum and, if articles were previously registered, in the articles take effect as if made by resolution of the company.

The section provides that the certificate of incorporation is conclusive evidence of compliance with the requirements of s. 49 as to re-registration.

It must be remembered, however, that owing to the definition of a public company in s. 1 (*see* 2), the procedure laid down in s. 49 is confined to private companies: s. 49.

32. Re-registration of unlimited company as limited

Section 51 states that an *unlimited* company may be registered as *limited* if a *special resolution* is passed to that effect and an application made to the registrar. The application must be framed in the prescribed form, signed by a director or the secretary, and lodged with the registrar, together with certain other documents on or after the day on which a copy of the resolution is received by him (*see* 15:**34**).

The resolution must state whether the company is to be limited by shares or by guarantee and, if limited by shares, what the share capital is to be. It must also provide for such alterations to the memorandum and articles as are necessary to conform with the statutory requirements.

The application must be accompanied by a printed copy of the memorandum and articles as altered.

Section 52 requires the registrar to retain the application and other documents, and to issue to the company an appropriate certificate of incorporation. On the issue of this certificate the status of the company is changed from unlimited to limited, and the alterations in the memorandum and articles specified in the resolution take effect.

The section provides that the certificate of incorporation is conclusive evidence of compliance with the requirements of s. 51 as to re-registration.

It must again be stressed that this procedure is confined to *private* companies: s. 51.

33. Other statutory provisions regarding liability

There are a number of other statutory provisions regarding liability, some of which are of importance while others are rarely used. They are as follows:

(a) Section 16 provides that the liability of a member cannot be increased without his written consent.

(b) Section 24, as amended by the Companies (Single Member Private Limited Companies) Regulations 1992 (SI 1992, No. 1699), provides that where a public company carries on business for more than six months without having at least two members, any person who, for the whole or any part of the period that it carries on business after those six months:

(*i*) is a member of the company; *and*

(*ii* knows that it is carrying on business with only one member, is liable, jointly and severally with the company, for the payment of the company's debts contracted during that period or the relevant part of it. Such a person thus *loses the protection of limited liability*.

The horrifying effect of this section can be avoided by a member quite easily, since under s. 122 Insolvency Act 1986 a reduction of members below the statutory minimum is a ground for winding up by the court, and under s. 124 of that Act this is one of the occasions on which a member can present a winding-up petition and so protect himself.

(c) By s. 306 the memorandum may provide that the *directors* in a limited company shall have *unlimited liability*, but they must be notified of this, before accepting office, by the promoters, existing directors, manager or secretary.

If they are not notified, then, though their liability will still be unlimited, the person responsible for the failure to notify them is liable for any damage which they may sustain.

(d) Section 307 provides that a limited company with authority in its articles may by special resolution alter its memorandum so as to make the liability of a director or manager unlimited.

Section 306 and s. 307 are rarely used in practice.

(e) Section 213 Insolvency Act 1986 deals with *fraudulent trading*. The section provides that where, in the course of liquidation, it appears that the company's business has been carried on with intent to defraud creditors or for any fraudulent purpose, the liquidator may apply to the court, which may declare that any persons knowingly parties to the carrying on of the business in that way are to be liable to make such contributions to the company's assets as the court thinks proper.

The provision is in the nature of a punitive provision and therefore the declared sum may be, or contain, a punitive element as well as a compensatory element: *Re a Company No. 001418 of 1988* [B285].

To be a 'party' within this section, a person must take some *positive steps* in the carrying on of the company's business in a fraudulent manner: *Re Maidstone Buildings Provisions Ltd* (1971).

However, a creditor who accepts money knowing that it has been procured by carrying on the business with intent to defraud other creditors for the very purpose of paying him is a 'party' within the section: *Re Gerald Cooper Chemicals Ltd* (1978) [B284]. 'A man who warms himself with the fire of fraud cannot complain if he is singed,' said Templeman J. of the creditor in question. He further held that even an isolated transaction can be within the section provided that it amounts to a fraud on a creditor perpetrated in the course of carrying on business.

Lastly, in *Re Sarflax Ltd* (1979) [B283] it was held that the expression 'carrying on business' had a wider meaning than carrying on trade. It included the collection of assets acquired in the course of business and their distribution in discharge of business liabilities provided there was a 'continuous course of active conduct'. The court further held that the mere preference of one creditor over another did not amount to an 'intention to defraud' within the section.

(f) Section 214 Insolvency Act 1986 deals with *wrongful trading by a director.* The provisions were introduced by the Insolvency Act 1985. The provisions apply where:

(*i*) the company has gone into insolvent liquidation, i.e. its assets are insufficient for the payment of its debts and other liabilities and the expenses of the winding up; *and*

(*ii*) the director concerned, at some time before the commencement of the winding up, knew or ought to have concluded that there was no reasonable prospect that the company would avoid going into insolvent liquidation.

In these circumstances the liquidator may apply to the court, which may declare that the director concerned is to be liable to make such contribution to the company's assets as the court thinks proper.

No order is made if the director succeeds in satisfying the court that, on becoming aware of (*ii*) above, he took every step which he ought to have taken with a view to minimising the potential loss to the company's creditors. The standard applied is that of a reasonably diligent director.

For applications of s. 214 see *Re Produce Marketing Consortium Ltd* (1989) [B288] and *Re Purpoint Ltd* (1991) [B291].

(g) Sections 216 and 217 Insolvency Act 1986 deal with the *use of prohibited company names.* They too were introduced by the Insolvency Act 1985.

The provisions apply to a person who has been a director of a company which has gone into *insolvent liquidation* within 12 months of his holding that office. Section 216 prohibits such a person, within the next five years after the commencement of the liquidation, from being a director of, or otherwise taking part in the promotion or management of, a company which has the same name as the first company or a name so similar as to suggest an association with that company. The prohibition may be lifted by leave of the court or in prescribed circumstances. For an instance of the use of a similar name being allowed by the court subject to conditions see *Re Bonus Breaks Ltd* (1991) [B293].

By s. 217 a person who in contravention of s. 216 becomes a director or otherwise becomes involved in the management of a company is personally liable for that company's debts incurred during his period of office.

The object of these provisions is to remedy the situation in which directors of a company which had failed might mislead the public by immediately becoming directors of another company with a closely similar name.

34. The capital clause

Consideration of this topic will be postponed, since it requires a chapter to itself. Two points, however, should be noted at this stage:

(a) The figure given in the capital clause of the memorandum is the *nominal* or *authorised* capital of the company. The Act does not state any *minimum figure* for share capital in the case of a private company. This can, in theory, be of any amount, provided the subscribers to the memorandum take at least one share each. Thus one private company was incorporated with a capital of ½d divided into two shares of ¼d each. Presumably today the minimum capital for a private company would be 1p.

In the case of a public company, however, s. 11 requires the capital clause of the memorandum to state a figure which is *not less than the authorised minimum*. Section 118 defines the authorised minimum as £50,000 or such other sum as the Secretary of State may specify by order made by statutory instrument. Presumably the definition is designed to allow the Secretary of State sufficient latitude to take account of inflation.

(b) The shares must have a *fixed value* which can also be of any amount. This fixed value is called the *par* or *nominal* value of the share.

Once the share is allotted, the holder will be able to sell it at its current *market* value, which is a fluctuating figure and may be either above or below the par value according to the prosperity and prospects of the company. When the market value is *above* the par value, the share is said to be standing *at a premium*. When the market value is *below* the par value, the share is said to be standing *at a discount*.

Similarly, when shares are first issued by the company, they may be issued at par or at a premium, although not at a discount.

35. Other clauses in the memorandum

The compulsory clauses of the memorandum have now been separately considered in this chapter, but of course the memorandum may have other clauses containing matters which might equally well have been put in the articles instead.

The alteration of any such non-compulsory clauses is governed by s. 17 which states that they may be altered by special resolution, with the same provision for dissentients to apply to the court to cancel the alteration as was made by s. 5 regarding alterations of the objects clause, except that debenture-holders have no right of application.

There are, however, three cases where s. 17 does not apply:

(a) If the memorandum expressly, or by reference to the articles, lays down a method of alteration of the particular clause, then that method must be used.

(b) If the memorandum prohibits alteration, then the clause can only be altered with the leave of the court under s. 425.

(c) Section 17 does not apply to class rights. The nature of class rights and the method of alteration required will be considered later.

3

The articles of association

1. The nature of the articles of association

The articles of a company are the regulations for its internal management, corresponding to the partnership deed in a partnership. The management of every company is governed by articles, though not every company need *register* articles with the registrar, as will be seen later.

2. The Companies (Tables A-F) Regulations 1985

Section 3 and 8 of the Companies Act 1985 authorise the Secretary of State to make, by statutory instrument, regulations specifying forms of memorandum and forms of articles for the different categories of registered companies. The regulations made under these sections of the Act are the Companies (Tables A-F) Regulations 1985 (SI 1985, No. 805), and the forms of memorandum and articles are to be found in the Schedule to these regulations.

Section 3, which deals with the forms of memorandum, provides that the forms specified in the Schedule must be adhered to as nearly as circumstances admit.

The forms specified are:

(a) Table B for a private company limited by shares;

(b) Table C for a company limited by guarantee and not having a share capital;

(c) Table D, Part I, for a public company limited by guarantee and having a share capital;

(d) Table D, Part II, for a private company limited by guarantee and having a share capital;

(e) Table E for an unlimited company having a share capital; *and*

(f) Table F for a public company limited by shares.

The forms in both Parts of Table D are of diminishing importance because, by s. 1, it has not been permissible since 22 December 1980 to form any new company limited by guarantee with a share capital.

The forms in Tables C and E are necessarily for private companies since a public company, by its definition in s. 1, must have a share capital and must be a limited company.

Section 8 deals with forms of articles. The forms of articles specified in the Schedule are:

(a) Table A for a company (public or private) limited by shares;

(b) Table C for a company limited by guarantee and not having a share capital;

(c) Table D, Part III, for a company (public or private) limited by guarantee and having a share capital; *and*

(d) Table E for an unlimited company having a share capital.

Again because of the definition of a public company, the forms of articles in Tables C and E are necessarily for private companies only.

As regards Tables C, D and E, s. 8 provides that these forms must be adhered to as closely as circumstances admit. There is no corresponding provision regarding Table A. The articles of a company limited by shares, therefore, do not need to be in any specified form.

By s. 8A, inserted in the 1985 Act by s. 128 Companies Act 1989, the Secretary of State may by regulations prescribe a Table G containing articles appropriate for a 'partnership company', i.e. a company limited by shares whose shares are intended to be held to a substantial extent by or on behalf of its employees.

The provisions of the Act relating to Table A require further consideration, and constant reference will be made throughout the book to the contents of Table A.

3. The nature of Table A

Table A consists of the regulations for the management of the commonest category of registered company, i.e. a public or private company limited by shares. Many of the clauses in it must eventually be learnt, but at this stage it is best simply to glance at the headings in order to see the type of material normally found in the articles of companies limited by shares. The headings may be grouped as follows:

(a) shares (share capital, share certificates, lien on shares, calls on shares and forfeiture, transfer of shares, transmission of shares, alteration of share capital, purchase by company of its own shares);

(b) meetings (general meetings, notice of general meetings, proceedings at general meetings, votes of members);

(c) directors (number of directors, alternate directors, powers of directors, delegation of directors' powers, appointment and retirement of directors, disqualification and removal of directors, remuneration and expenses of directors, directors' appointments and interests, directors' gratuities and pensions, proceedings of directors (including board meetings));

(d) company secretary;

(e) minutes;

(f) company's seal;

(g) financial matters (dividends, accounts, capitalisation of profits);

(h) notices;

(i) winding up; *and*

(j) indemnity.

4. The obligation to register articles

Section 7 provides that a company limited by shares *may* register articles, i.e. may do so if it wishes, while a company limited by guarantee or an unlimited company *shall* (i.e. *must*) do so.

The articles must be signed by the subscribers to the memorandum, i.e. the same persons sign both documents.

5. The application of Table A

It is clear from s. 7 that a company limited by shares need not register articles, though other types of companies are required to do so. The section does not, however, tell us what happens if a company limited by shares does not register articles.

Section 8 deals with this situation. First the section gives a general permission for the articles of any company to adopt the Table A provisions, but there then follows a provision of great importance. It deals exclusively with companies limited by shares, and states that Table A applies to such companies *automatically, unless excluded or modified.*

It is essential to grasp the fact of the automatic application of Table A. The result of it is that if a company limited by shares does not register any articles, Table A automatically applies. Moreover, even if the company *does* register articles of its own, Table A will still apply automatically unless it has been excluded or modified.

The company can easily exclude Table A by express words to that effect in its articles. Modification can be either *express*, as where the company's articles state that some clauses of Table A will apply with certain alterations, or *implied*, as where the company's articles are inconsistent with Table A, in which case they will prevail.

6. Companies formed prior to 1985

A question which arises in connection with Table A is whether a company is always governed by the Table A prescribed under authority of s. 8 of the 1985 Act or, if it was formed prior to 1985, by the Table A of the particular Companies Act under which it was registered. Each Act had a Table A of its own, and each differed to some extent from the others, so this can be an important point.

The rule here is that a company is always governed by the Table A of the Act *under which it was registered* with *one exception*: under s. 370 the *method of service of notice of company meetings* is regulated in every case by the Table A prescribed by the 1985 Act, no matter when the company was formed, unless the company's own articles stipulate some other method.

7. Statutory requirements regarding articles
By s. 7 articles must be:

(a) printed;
(b) in numbered paragraphs;
(c) signed by the subscribers to the memorandum in the presence of at least one witness.

8. The duties of the subscribers to the memorandum
The duties of the subscribers must at some stage be noted, and since we have already come across three of them, they can now conveniently be listed in full:

(a) They must sign the memorandum (*see* 2:5).
(b) They must sign the articles.
(c) They must take at least one share each (*see* 2:5).
(d) They normally appoint the first directors (*see* 16:4).
(e) They must sign the statement required by s. 10 on the registration of the company (*see* 4:1).

9. Alteration of the articles
Section 9 provides that a company may alter its articles by special resolution. This may be done at any general meeting and as often as required. It should be noted, however, that s. 9 merely lays down a procedure whereby *some only* of the shareholders can validly alter the articles. There is nothing in it to override the basic principle of company law that all the shareholders, acting together, can do anything which is within the capacity of the company. Hence the articles can also be altered by their unanimous agreement: *Cane* v. *Jones* (1980) [B215]. Section 380, which requires all special resolutions to be filed with the registrar, also requires such unanimous agreements to be filed with him (*see* 15:34).

There are certain important rules regarding alteration:

(a) Under s. 9, the alteration is subject to the provisions of the memorandum, and if the two documents conflict, the memorandum will prevail.
(b) The alteration must be lawful. It must not conflict with the provisions of the Act, nor with the general law.
(c) If, in response to an application by the prescribed minority for the cancellation of an alteration of the company's objects clause, the court has

made an order under s. 5 prohibiting any alteration to the articles, the company may not alter them without the leave of the court (*see* 2:**27**).

(d) If, in response to an application by the prescribed minority for the cancellation of a resolution by a public company to be re-registered as a private company, the court has made an order under s. 54 prohibiting any alteration to the articles, the company may not alter them without the leave of the court (*see* 25:**5**).

(e) If, in response to a petition on the ground that the company's affairs are being conducted in a manner unfairly prejudicial to the members or some part of the members, the court has made an order under s. 461 prohibiting any alteration to the articles, the company may not alter them without the leave of the court (*see* 23:**9**).

(f) Under s. 16, the alteration may not increase the liability of any member without his written consent (*see* 2:**33**).

(g) If the alteration concerns class rights, s. 127 protects dissentients, i.e. persons who disagree. (Section 127 and class rights are discussed in 11:**14**).

(h) The alteration must be *bona fide* for the benefit of the company as a whole. Provided this condition is satisfied, individual hardship is irrelevant: *Allen* v. *Gold Reefs of West Africa* (1900) [B79]; *Shuttleworth* v. *Cox Bros & Co. Ltd* (1927); *Sidebottom* v. *Kershaw, Leese & Co. Ltd* (1920).

(i) If the alteration involves a breach of contract, it will still be valid, but the injured party will have all the normal remedies against the company for the breach: *Southern Foundries (1926) Ltd* v. *Shirlaw* (1940) [B136].

NOTE: The first seven of these rules have a restrictive effect on the company's statutory power to alter its articles freely by special resolution under s. 9, while the last two rather emphasise its power to alter its articles as it wishes.

Section 18 provides that where a company is required to send to the registrar any document relating to an alteration in its articles, it must also send him a printed copy of the articles as altered. Section 711 requires him to publish his receipt of any such document in the *Gazette*. If an alteration has not been officially notified by the registrar at the material time and if the company cannot show that it was known at that time to the person concerned, the company cannot rely on it against that person: s. 42.

10. The legal effect of the articles

Section 14 states that the memorandum and articles bind the company and the members as though signed and sealed by each member, and as though they contained covenants by each member to observe their provisions.

The section also provides that money payable by the member to the company under the memorandum or articles is a *specialty debt*, i.e. the period of limitation is 12 years and not the normal six. [This provision does not apply to Scotland, *'specialty debt'* not being a term of Scots law. By the Prescription and Limitation (Scotland) Act 1973 the prescriptive period would be 20 years.] It appears, however, that this is not the case as regards debts owed by the company to the members, e.g. declared dividends (*see* 20:**10**).

The effect of the articles is therefore as follows:

(a) The company is bound to the members *in their capacity of members.*
(b) The members *in their capacity of members* are bound to the company.
(c) The members are contractually bound *to each other.*
(d) The company is *not bound to any person*, except to members in their capacity of members.

Each of these will be considered in turn. It should, however, be noted as a preliminary that the precise effect of the statutory provisions has been the subject of considerable controversy and there have been many apparently conflicting decisions by the courts.

11. Company bound to members in their capacity of members

Section 14 does *not* state that the memorandum and articles bind the company and the members as though signed and sealed *by the company* and as though they contained covenants *by the company* to observe their provisions. However, case law indicates that the company is bound.

In *Wood* v. *Odessa Waterworks Co.* (1889), a case decided by Stirling J., a company which had applied its profits to the construction of works instead of paying a dividend to the shareholders passed a resolution proposing to give to the shareholders debenture bonds carrying interest. The company's articles empowered the directors with the sanction of the company to declare a dividend 'to be paid' to shareholders. HELD: What was proposed by the resolution was not in accordance with the articles and therefore the directors were restrained by injunction from acting on the resolution.

A Court of Appeal case to a similar effect was *Salmon* v. *Quin & Axtens Ltd* (1909): By the company's articles the powers of general management were vested in the directors except that no resolution of the directors for acquiring or letting premises was to be valid if Salmon, a managing director, dissented. The directors passed a resolution for acquiring and letting premises, despite Salmon's dissent, and at an extraordinary meeting of shareholders resolutions were passed by a simple majority affirming the directors' action. HELD: Since the company's resolutions were inconsistent with the articles, the company could be restrained from acting upon them.

Wood's case was approved as accurate subject to the observation that it might well be that the court would not enforce the covenant as between individual shareholders in most cases (*see* **13**).

However, in *Re Compania de Electricidad de la Provincia de Buenos Aires Ltd* (1980) it was held that the limitation period in actions by members against the company for unpaid dividends was six years, since such actions were not actions upon a specialty for the purposes of the Limitation Act 1939 (now the Limitation Act 1980). Under that Act the limitation period would have been 12 years if the contract had been regarded as sealed *by the company*.

12. Members as members bound to company

The memorandum and articles constitute a contract between the company and its members *in respect of their ordinary rights as members*. This was stated by Astbury J. in *Hickman* v. *Kent or Romney Marsh Sheep-Breeders' Association* (1915). The judgment in the case contains a comprehensive review of decided cases.

A clause in the articles of the association provided for disputes between the association and any of its members to be referred to arbitration. Hickman, who was a member as a flock owner, issued a writ against the association and its secretary claiming an injunction to restrain the association from employing that secretary and for other purposes. The defendants asked for the proceedings to be stayed and the matters in dispute to be referred to arbitration. HELD: Hickman's action was a breach of the arbitration clause in the articles and the matters had to be referred to arbitration.

This case was approved by the Court of Appeal in *Beattie* v. *E. & F. Beattie Ltd* (1938), also relating to an arbitration clause in the articles. The essential difference, however, was that here it was a director who was arguing that a member's action against the company and himself should be stayed on the ground that the articles were a contract giving him the right to demand arbitration. HELD: There was no contractual force in the articles as between the company and its directors as such. Sir Wilfred Greene M.R., who gave the leading judgment, said: 'The contractual force given to the articles of association by the section is limited to such provisions of the articles as apply to the relationship of the members in their capacity as members'.

13. Members contractually bound to each other

The memorandum and articles constitute a contract between individual members but the rule in *Foss* v. *Harbottle* (1843) (*see* **1:33**) normally prevents an individual member from enforcing that contract against another individual member except through the company, or, if it is in liquidation, through the liquidator.

> The dissenting speech of Lord Herschell in the House of Lords in *Welton* v. *Saffery* (1897) is often quoted from in this connection. The decision in the case was that, as it was *ultra vires* to issue shares at a discount, the holders of such shares were not relieved from liability to calls in the winding up.

> Lord Herschell said: 'The articles constitute a contract between each member and the company, and . . . there is no contract in terms between the individual members of the company; but the articles do not any the less, in my opinion, regulate their rights *inter se*. Such rights can only be enforced by or against a member through the company, or through the liquidator representing the company; but I think that no member has, as between himself and another member, any right beyond that which the contract with the company gives'.

It is different, however, where the right given to a member by the articles is a personal right. The contract can then be directly enforced by one member against another member without the aid of the company.

> In *Rayfield* v. *Hands* (1960) [B86], Clause 11 of the articles of a private company provided: 'Every member who intends to transfer shares *shall* inform the directors, who *will* take the said shares equally between them at a fair value'. The plaintiff, a member, informed the defendants, the directors, of his wish to transfer his shares. The directors denied liability to take and pay for them. HELD: *(a)* 'Will' indicated an *obligation* to take the shares. *(b)* The article created a *contractual relationship* between the *plaintiff as a member* and the *defendants as members*.

It is submitted that *(a)* above is correct in that it probably gives effect to the intention behind the clause, although one may well wonder why, if obligation was intended, the word 'shall' was not used again. But *(b)* is more difficult to understand. The defendants in the case were in fact members, but the clause imposed the obligation to buy the shares on the *directors*. If one of them had not been a member, would he too have been bound? Can an article which refers to a person as a director, or employee, or coal-supplier, bind him *as a member* if he also happens to be one? And how far does such an article give a *direct right of action* between one member and another?

The case is difficult to reconcile with other cases on the topic of the legal effect of the articles, but it should be noted that it does not stand entirely alone. Much the same reasoning appears to have been adopted by

Plowman J. in *Re Richmond Gate Property Co. Ltd* (1965), a case which concerned a managing director's claim for remuneration, and where in his judgment Plowman J. said: 'The effect of Article 9, coupled with Article 108 of Table A, *coupled with the fact that the applicant was a member of the company*, in my judgement is that a *contract exists between himself and the company*'.

14. Company not bound to members in any other capacity than that of members

This rule is seen clearly in the leading case of *Eley* v. *Positive Government Security Life Assurance Co. Ltd* (1876) [B81], from which it follows that a person cannot rely on the articles as a contract of employment or supply since they only bind the company to members in respect of their membership rights, and not contractual rights of other kinds. This is so whether he is a member or not.

> In *Eley* v. *Positive Government Security Life Assurance Co. Ltd* (1876), the articles provided that E should be the company's solicitor *for life*. He was employed by the company and took shares in it, but later the company dismissed him from his employment with it. He sued for breach of contract. HELD: His action failed, for the articles on which he relied were not a contract between the company and any other person, except in respect of their *membership* rights.

However, the terms of a separate contract, e.g. with a director, may by implication be incorporated into the company's contract with him from the terms of the articles.

> An example is *Re New British Iron Co. Ltd, ex parte Beckwith* (1898). The articles provided that the remuneration of the directors should be £1000 per annum. The directors, who were also members, accepted office, but were not paid. HELD: The directors were entitled to recover the arrears of remuneration on the basis of the separate contract between the company and themselves, of which the articles were evidence.

Further, where a person performs services for the company at its request without any contract, he may sue in *quasi-contract* for a reasonable sum (*quantum meruit*) for the work done. A clause in the articles then may be *evidence* of what the parties thought reasonable, and though unable of itself to create contractual rights of this type, may be of evidential value in a quasi-contractual claim such as was made in *Craven-Ellis* v. *Canons Ltd* (1936).

> In *Craven-Ellis* v. *Canons Ltd* (1936), C was appointed the company's managing director by a contract in writing and under the company's

seal, by a resolution of the board of directors. The articles imposed a share qualification on the directors, none of whom ever obtained it. C sued for his salary under the contract and, alternatively, for reasonable remuneration (*quantum meruit*) for work done, in quasi-contract. HELD: His claim on the *contract* failed, for under the articles his appointment could not be valid owing to his failure to take up his qualification shares. His claim in *quasi-contract*, however, succeeded, for he had performed services for the company at its request.

Although *Eley* v. *Positive Government Security Life Assurance Co. Ltd* has been described above as the leading case, some doubt as to its authority has been created by cases such as *Rayfield* v. *Hands* (*see* **13** above), and the only safe conclusion to draw is that this is an uncertain and controversial area of the subject.

4

Registration

1. Documents to be delivered to the registrar on registration

We have now dealt with the memorandum and articles of association and it remains to consider the next step after preparation of these documents, i.e. registration with the registrar of companies in Cardiff if the company's registered office is to be in England or Wales, or with the registrar of companies in Edinburgh if the company's registered office is to be in Scotland.

By ss. 10 and 12 the memorandum and articles, if any, must be delivered to the registrar, who retains and registers them. But this is not enough, and the complete list of documents which must be delivered to him is as follows:

(a) the memorandum: s. 10;

(b) the articles, if any: s. 10;

(c) a statement signed by the subscribers of the memorandum:

> (*i*) containing the names and particulars of the directors and secretary and a consent signed by each of them to act in the relevant capacity; *and*
>
> (*ii*) specifying the intended situation of the company's registered office: s. 10 and Schedule 1;

(d) a statutory declaration of compliance signed by a solicitor engaged in the formation of the company, or a person named as director or secretary in the statement delivered under s. 10: s. 12.

The statement of capital formerly required under s. 47 Finance Act 1973 to comply with an EC Directive in force when the UK joined the EC was removed from the list by s. 141 Finance Act 1988 following a change in the Directive which allowed capital duty to be abolished.

2. The certificate of incorporation

Once the required documents have been delivered the registrar, under s. 12, must satisfy himself that all the requirements of the Act in respect of registration have been complied with. He then, in accordance with s. 13, issues a certificate of incorporation (the company's 'birth' certificate) and, under s. 705, allocates to the company its registered number.

Section 13 provides that from the date of incorporation mentioned in the certificate the subscribers of the memorandum become a body corporate by the name contained in the memorandum. This occurs even if the date mentioned in the certificate is *not* in fact the date when it was signed by the registrar: *Jubilee Cotton Mills* v. *Lewis* (1924) [B35]. If the company's memorandum states that it is to be a public company, the certificate of incorporation must also contain a statement to that effect.

The certificate, once issued, is conclusive evidence that the company has been duly registered and, if it contains a statement to that effect, that the company is a public company. Section 711 requires the registrar to publish notice of its issue in the *Gazette*.

The company is now formed, i.e. it is now a 'registered' corporation.

The certificate is not, however, conclusive evidence that the company is lawful: A company registered with objects which are illegal or immoral can be struck off the register by the court: *Bowman* v. *Secular Society Ltd* (1917), followed in *R.* v. *Registrar of Companies, ex parte Attorney General* (1991) [B34].

3. Summary of the statutory provisions studied so far

It is at this stage helpful to look at the first two chapters of Part I of the Act and to see that some comprehension of them should now have been achieved. Chapter I (ss. 1–24) is headed 'Company Formation' and Chapter II (ss. 25–34) 'Company Names'. The groups of provisions may be listed:

Sections 1–3 deal with formation and the memorandum in general.
Sections 4–6 deal with alterations of the company's objects.
Sections 7–9 deal with the articles.
Sections 10–21 deal with the procedure for, and the effect of, registration.
Sections 22–24 deal with the company's membership.
Sections 25–34 deal with the company's name.

4. The expenses of formation

A registration fee of £50 is payable under the Companies (Fees) Regulations 1988 (SI 1988, No. 887).

In addition, the cost of professional services and preparing the requisite documents must be defrayed.

The capital duty of £1 per cent formerly payable under s. 47 Finance Act 1973 was abolished by s. 141 Finance Act 1988.

5. Form of documents delivered to the registrar

Throughout the statutory provisions there are many requirements for documents to be delivered to the registrar.

If a document is in legible form, it must under s. 706, as substituted in the 1985 Act by s. 125 Companies Act 1989:

(a) state in a prominent position the company's registered number;
(b) satisfy any requirements prescribed by regulations; *and*
(c) conform to such requirements as the registrar may specify for the purposes of enabling him to copy the document.

By s. 707, as substituted in the 1985 Act by s. 125 Companies Act 1989, a requirement to deliver a document to the registrar is satisfied if the information is given in any non-legible form prescribed by regulations or approved by the registrar. This provision is intended to facilitate the use of information technology in the registrar's office.

6. Abolition of doctrine of deemed notice

Because of the right of the public to inspect the documents registered with the registrar, the courts developed the doctrine of constructive notice, according to which any person was deemed to have notice of, i.e. know of, the matters included in the company's file kept by the registrar. The same doctrine applied to the documents made available by the company for inspection at its registered office.

Section 711A, inserted in the 1985 Act by s. 142 Companies Act 1989, abolishes the doctrine of constructive or deemed notice, by providing that a person is not to be taken to have notice of any matter merely because of its being disclosed in any document kept by the registrar (and so available for inspection) or made available by the company for inspection.

However, this provision does not affect the question whether a person is affected by notice of any matter where he has failed to make such inquiries as ought reasonably to be made.

7. Differences between a company limited by shares and a partnership

It is sometimes convenient at this stage to set out the differences between a company limited by shares and a partnership. The process of incorporation has been completed and its implications discussed, so that comparisons can now be drawn. There are a large number of differences, but the most important are as follows:

(a) A limited company is an *artificial legal person*.

A partnership is not. It is an association of two or more legal persons, in the same way as a company, but the *association itself* has no legal personality and outsiders deal directly with the members. [In Scotland a partnership has a legal personality distinct from the individual partners.]
(b) In a limited company the *liability* of the members is *limited* to the amount unpaid on their shares.

In a partnership, the *liability* of the partners is *unlimited* except in the case of a limited partnership, and even then there must be at least one general partner with unlimited liability.

(c) A limited company must be *formed by the process of registration* described above.

A partnership may be formed quite *informally*, e.g. orally, or even by conduct, though it is wise to have a written agreement or articles, often called the deed of partnership [or, in Scotland, the contract of co-partnery].

(d) In a *public* limited company the *shares* are usually *freely* transferable.

In a partnership no partner may transfer his share without the *consent* of the others.

(e) In a limited company the members are *not ipso facto agents* of the company.

In a partnership each partner is an *agent* of the others, and each therefore is also a principal. A partnership is thus a collection of principals and agents.

(f) In a limited company the *death or bankruptcy* of a member (or even of all the members) has *no effect* on the existence of the company.

In a partnership death or bankruptcy of a partner causes *dissolution* unless the articles provide otherwise.

(g) A limited company is subject to many *special rules of law*, both statutory and otherwise.

In a partnership the partners are *free* to make any arrangement they like which would be lawful between private persons.

5

Commencement of business and contracts

1. Commencement of business

A *private* company can commence business on incorporation. Once it has received its certificate of incorporation, nothing further is required.

A company registered as a *public* company on its *original incorporation*, however, must obtain a *second* certificate, often called a *trading certificate*, before it can commence business or exercise its borrowing powers. In order to obtain its trading certificate, the company must comply with s. 117.

2. Procedure for obtaining trading certificate

In order to obtain its trading certificate the company must apply to the registrar. The application must be made in the prescribed form and be accompanied by a statutory declaration signed by a director or the secretary of the company.

The statutory declaration must state:

(a) that the nominal value of the company's allotted share capital is not less than the authorised minimum (*see* 2:**34**);
(b) the amount paid up on the company's allotted share capital;
(c) the amount of the company's preliminary expenses and the persons who paid them; *and*
(d) any amount paid or benefit given to any promoter and his consideration for it.

Any shares allotted under a share scheme for employees must be disregarded for the purposes of **(a)** above unless they are paid up at least as to one quarter of their nominal value and the whole of any premium.

Finally, s. 711 requires the registrar to publish in the *Gazette* the receipt by him of such a declaration.

3. Issue of trading certificate

If the registrar is satisfied as to **(a)** above and has received the statutory declaration, s. 117 requires him to issue a trading certificate.

This certificate is conclusive evidence that the company is entitled to do business and exercise its borrowing powers.

If the company is not issued with a trading certificate within a year from incorporation, it may be wound up by the court under s. 122 Insolvency Act 1986 (*see* 30:1).

4. Contracts
In studying the contracts of a company, it is important first to grasp the situations which may arise.

In the case of a *private* company, there are only two:

(a) contracts made on behalf of the company before incorporation;
(b) contracts made after incorporation.

Owing to s. 117, however, in the case of a *public* company, there are three:

(a) contracts made on behalf of the company before incorporation;
(b) contracts made after incorporation but before obtaining the trading certificate;
(c) contracts made after obtaining the trading certificate.

These situations must be dealt with separately.

5. Pre-incorporation contracts
The rules here are the same for both public and private companies. Clearly no legal person, natural or artificial, can contract before he or it exists. Therefore a contract made by a promoter on behalf of the company before incorporation never binds the company, because the company is not yet formed. It has no legal existence. Even if the parties act on the contract, it will not bind the company: *Re Northumberland Avenue Hotel Co.* (1886). Similarly, in the Scottish case *Tinnevelly Sugar Refining Co. Ltd* v. *Mirrlees, Watson & Yaryan Co. Ltd* (1894) [B45] the new company was held to have no title to sue for damages where machinery supplied to it on the order of two promoters proved defective.

Problems formerly arose, however, with regard to the promoter. It must be remembered that he was not automatically bound simply because the company was not yet in existence. He was bound only if he had shown an intention to be bound, and this intention was deduced from his conduct and the surrounding circumstances. Similarly, he could not enforce the contract unless he had shown such an intention, since the right to enforce a contract normally accompanies liability to perform it.

Although the principle was clear enough, the question of whether the promoter had shown an intention to be bound often rested on subtle differences in the words used. Thus in *Kelner* v. *Baxter* (1866), the directors were held personally liable on a pre-incorporation contract where they had signed it 'A, B and C, on behalf of the X Company'. But in *Newborne* v. *Sensolid Ltd* (1954), Newborne was held unable to enforce the contract (and therefore presumably not bound by it) because he had signed it 'Leopold Newborne and Co. Ltd', even though underneath he had added his own name, 'Leopold Newborne'.

The position is now governed by s. 36C, inserted in the 1985 Act by s. 130 Companies Act 1989. It had its origin in the European Communities Act 1972 and provides that, unless otherwise agreed, a pre-incorporation contract has effect as a contract entered into by *the person purporting to act as agent for the company* and he is personally liable on it.

> In *Phonogram Ltd* v. *Lane* (1982) [B41] a company to be called Fragile Management Ltd was about to be formed to manage a group of 'pop' artists who intended to perform under the name 'Cheap Mean and Nasty'. The group's manager, Mr Brian Lane, entered into an arrangement with Phonogram under which, in anticipation of a subsequent contract between Fragile Management and Phonogram, the latter were to finance the group by providing £12,000, payable in two instalments of £6000 each. Phonogram duly paid the first instalment by a cheque made out to Jelly Music Ltd, a company of which Mr Lane was a director, for purely administrative reasons. The cheque was accompanied by a letter addressed to Mr Lane and stating that if the contract was not completed within a certain period, 'you will undertake to repay us the £6000'. A copy of the letter was enclosed which Mr Lane was asked to sign and return to Phonogram. He did so, signing 'for and on behalf of Fragile Management Ltd'.
>
> The contract was never completed and Phonogram accordingly issued a writ against Mr Lane claiming repayment of the money. Mr Lane asserted that he was not personally liable to repay it since he had throughout been acting on behalf of Fragile Management Ltd, even though it had not yet been incorporated. HELD: The fine distinctions adopted by the common law were no longer relevant. 'Unless there is a clear exclusion of personal liability, s. [36C] should be given its full effect. It means that in all cases such as the present, where a person purports to contract on behalf of a company not yet formed, then however he expresses his signature he himself is personally liable on the contract' (*per* Lord Denning M.R.).

6. Contracts made after incorporation but before issue of trading certificate

This situation can arise, as we have seen, only in the case of a *public* company.

Section 117 provides that failure to obtain its trading certificate will not affect the validity of any transaction entered into by a company.

If, however, a company contravenes the section by entering into a transaction before its trading certificate has been issued, and then fails to comply with its resulting obligations within 21 days from being called upon to do so, the directors become jointly and severally liable to indemnify the other party to the transaction in respect of any loss which he has suffered through such failure.

7. Contracts made after issue of the trading certificate in the case of a public company and after incorporation in the case of a private company

These are, of course, valid subject to the provisions of ss. 35 and 35A on the capacity of the company and the authority of the directors (*see* 2:**19,20**).

There are, however, some statutory provisions relating to form and other matters which must be studied.

8. Form of contracts made by companies

Section 36, as substituted by s. 130 Companies Act 1989, provides that under the law of England and Wales a contract may be made:

(a) by a company, by writing under its common seal; *or*
(b) on behalf of a company, by any person acting under its authority, express or implied.

Any formalities required by law in the case of a contract made by an individual also apply, unless a contrary intention appears, to a contract made by or on behalf of a company.

Section 36A, inserted in the 1985 Act by s. 130 Companies Act 1989, relates to the execution of documents by a company. It provides that under the law of England and Wales.:

(a) A document may be executed by a company by the affixing of its common seal.
(b) A company need not have a common seal, and provisions **(c), (d)** and **(e)** below apply whether the company does or does not have a common seal.
(c) A document signed by a director and the secretary, or by two directors, and expressed (in whatever form of words) to be executed by the company has the same effect as if executed under the common seal of the company.
(d) A document executed by a company which makes it clear on its face that it is intended by the person or persons making it to be a deed has effect, upon delivery, as a deed; and it is presumed, unless a contrary intention is proved, to be delivered upon its being executed.
(e) In favour of a purchaser a document is deemed to have been duly executed by a company if it purports to be signed by a director and the secretary, or by two directors, and, where it makes it clear on its face, that

it is intended by the person or persons making it to be a deed, to have been delivered upon its being executed; a 'purchaser' means a purchaser in good faith for valuable consideration and includes a lessee, mortgagee or other person who for valuable consideration acquires an interest in property.

[Section 36B, inserted in the 1985 Act by s. 72 Law Reform (Miscellaneous Provisions) (Scotland) Act 1990, relates to the execution of documents in Scotland:

(a) As in England and Wales, a company need not have a common seal.
(b) Where any Act provides for a document to be executed by a company by affixing its common seal, then the signing of the document on behalf of the company by a director and the secretary, or by two directors, or by two persons authorised to sign the document on behalf of the company has the same effect as if the document were executed under the common seal of the company.
(c) The same rule applies to documents which require to be *authenticated* under the law of Scotland, i.e. two signatures are required; there need be no witnesses, and the document is regarded as probative (i.e. it does not require to be proved genuine).
(d) Documents which do not require to be authenticated are validly executed if signed on behalf of the company by one person, who may be a director or the secretary or a person authorised to sign the document on behalf of the company.]

Section 37 provides that a bill of exchange or promissory note will be in order if made, accepted or endorsed in the name of the company by a person acting under its authority.

Schedule 17 to the 1989 Act contains further minor amendments to company contracts: s. 130 Companies Act 1989.

Section 41 of the 1985 Act, as amended by Schedule 17 to the 1989 Act, provides that a document is sufficiently authenticated by the signature of a director, secretary or other authorised officer of the company. [This does not apply to Scotland.]

9. The official seal
Section 39, as amended by s. 130 and Schedule 17 Companies Act 1989, provides that a company which has a common seal and whose objects comprise the transaction of business in foreign countries may, if authorised by its articles, have for use in any place outside the United Kingdom an official seal. This is a facsimile (copy) of the common seal, with the addition on its face of the name of the place where it is to be used.

6

Promoters and subscribers to the memorandum

1. The legal position of a promoter

There is no general statutory definition of a promoter, though he was indirectly described in s. 56 as a person 'engaged or interested in the formation of the company', and s. 67 gave a definition for the purpose of ss. 67–69 only, which dealt with compensation for mis-statements in a prospectus. That definition was:

> ' "promoter" means a promoter who was party to the preparation of the prospectus, . . . but does not include any person by reason of his acting in a professional capacity for persons engaged in procuring the formation of the company'.

These provisions were repealed by the Financial Services Act 1986, which uses the term 'promoter' without any definition. It is clear that in the normal way persons assisting the promoters by 'acting in a professional capacity' do not thereby become promoters themselves. Thus the solicitor or counsel who drafts the articles, or the accountant who values the assets of a business to be purchased, are merely giving professional assistance to the promoters. They will be paid for their services, but they will not be implicated further. Perhaps the true test of whether a person is a promoter is whether he has a *desire* that the company shall be formed, and is prepared to take some steps, which may or may not involve other persons, to implement it.

While the accurate description of a promoter may be difficult, his legal position is quite clear. He is said to be in a *fiduciary* position towards the company, analogous to the relation of an agent with his principal, and, like an agent, he may not make a secret profit. The fiduciary relation requires *full disclosure* of the relevant facts, including any profit made. Students of the law of contract will recall many examples of this relation.

NOTE: It is important to understand that it is not the profit made by the promoter which the law forbids, but the non-disclosure of it. Provided full disclosure is made, as was done in *Salomon* v. *Salomon & Co. Ltd*, the profit is permissible. It must be disclosed to an independent board of directors, if there is one, but if as is often the case in a private company, the promoter is himself the only director, it must be disclosed to the shareholders. Frequently they will be the promoter's own family, and he will in practice be free to make what arrangements he likes, since their fortunes rise and fall with his.

2. Remedies of the company against a promoter

As regards public companies, s. 103 imposes strict rules on the valuation of non-cash consideration for an allotment of shares (*see* 9:**18–20**). These statutory rules greatly diminish the importance of the remedies evolved by the courts against a promoter for non-disclosure of profit in a public company. In private companies, however, these remedies remain the only sanction and continue to be of significance. In theory, the remedies apply with respect to all companies, public or private.

If any profit made is not disclosed, the company has a remedy against the promoter which varies according to the circumstances. These can be divided into two possible situations:

(a) *Where the promoter was not in a fiduciary position when he acquired the property which he is selling to the company, but only when he sold it to the company*:

Here the promoter, as in Salomon's case, has had the property for a considerable period of time. He can hardly be said to be in a fiduciary position towards the company if he bought a business 10 years before its formation, and though the moment at which his fiduciary relation arises may be difficult to determine, it can at least be said that it does not arise until he contemplates, i.e. considers the possibility of, forming a company to take over his business.

The remedy for non-disclosure in such a case is that the company may rescind the contract with the promoter, which of course means that it restores the property to him and recovers its money.

(b) *Where the promoter was in a fiduciary position both when he acquired the property, and when he sold it to the company*:

Here the promoter bought the property with a view to selling it to the company, and the company will then have a choice of remedy. It may:

(*i*) rescind the contract as in **(a)** above: *Erlanger* v. *New Sombrero Phosphate Co.* (1878) [B36]; *or*

(*ii*) retain the property, paying no more for it than the promoter, thereby depriving him of his profit: *Gluckstein* v. *Barnes* (1900) [B39]; *or*

(*iii*) where the above remedies would be inappropriate, such as when the property has been altered so as to render rescission impossible, and the promoter has already received his inflated price, the company may sue the promoter for breach of the duty to disclose.

The measure of damages will be the amount of the profit made by the promoter: *Re Leeds and Hanley Theatres of Varieties Ltd* (1902).

3. Renumeration of promoters

It is clear that a promoter, if he makes proper disclosure, may expect to be rewarded for his efforts. In practice he is recompensed in *one* of the following ways:

(a) He may sell his own property to the company for *cash* at an over-valuation of which proper disclosure has been made.

(b) He may sell his own property to the company for *fully paid shares*, again having fully disclosed any over-valuation.

(c) He may be given an *option* to take up further shares in the company *at par* (i.e. at their *nominal* value) after their true value has risen and is reflected in their market price.

(d) The articles may provide for a fixed sum to be paid to him. Such a provision has no contractual effect and he cannot sue to enforce it (3:**10, 14**), but if it is acted on—and the promoter can in practice probably make sure that it is—the company cannot recover its money.

It must again be borne in mind that in a public company s. 103 will normally operate to prevent any over-valuation.

4. Disqualification of promoters

Section 1 Company Directors Disqualification Act 1986 empowers the court to make a disqualification order against a promoter which can prohibit him from taking part in the promotion of a company for a period of up to 15 years.

This Act is of very wide application and is fully considered in 16:**20**.

5. Valuation of non-cash assets acquired from subscriber

The subscribers to the memorandum are not normally the promoters of the company. Nevertheless, s. 104 provides that where, in a public company, a subscriber sells non-cash assets to the company, those assets must be valued by an independent person in the same way as is prescribed by s. 103 in relation to payment for shares: ss. 108–111 (*see* 9:**18–20** and 10:1).

Section 104 prohibits a public company from entering into an agreement with a subscriber for the transfer by him, within two years from the date of issue of its trading certificate, of a non-cash asset to the company for a consideration equal to *one-tenth or more of the nominal value of its issued share capital* unless four conditions are satisfied. These are:

(a) The consideration to be received by the company and any consideration other than cash to be given by it must have been *valued*.

(b) A report on the consideration so received and given must have been made to the company during the six months immediately preceding the agreement.

(c) The terms of the agreement must have been approved by an *ordinary resolution* of the company.

(d) Not later than the giving of notice of the meeting at which the resolution is proposed, copies of the resolution and the report must have been *circulated to the members* and, if the subscriber in question is not then a member, to him.

Section 111 requires a copy of the resolution, together with the report, to be delivered to the registrar within 15 days of the passing of the resolution, while s. 711 requires the registrar to publish in the *Gazette* the receipt by him of the report.

6. Report on non-cash assets acquired from subscriber

Section 109 provides that s. 108 applies to the valuation and report, requiring the valuation to be made by an independent person qualified to be an auditor of the company (the 'valuer'), or some other qualified person chosen by him (*see* 9:**18** and **19**).

Further, s. 110 entitles the person making the valuation or report to require from the company's officers any necessary information and explanation.

Under s. 109 the report must:

(a) state the consideration to be received by the company, describing the asset in question (specifying the amount to be received in cash) and the consideration to be given by the company (specifying the amount to be given in cash);

(b) state the method and date of valuation;

(c) be accompanied by a note by the valuer:

(*i*) that it appeared reasonable to him to arrange for the valuation to be made by another person if in fact it was so made;

(*ii*) that the method of valuation was reasonable;

(*iii*) that it appears to him that there has been no material change in the value of the consideration in question since the valuation; *and*

(*iv*) that on the basis of the valuation the value of the consideration, together with any cash to be paid for the shares, is not less than the amount treated as paid up on the shares allotted; *and*

(d) contain a note that on the basis of the valuation the value of the consideration to be received by the company is not less than the value of the consideration to be given by it.

7. Effect of contravention of s. 104

Section 105 provides that where a public company enters into any

agreement with a subscriber to its memorandum which contravenes
s. 104 and *either*:

(a) the subscriber has not received a report, *or*
(b) there has been some other contravention of ss. 104, 108 or 109 which
he knew or ought to have known amounted to a contravention,

the company is entitled to recover from him any consideration which it
gave under the agreement or a sum equivalent in value, and the agreement itself is *void*.

Special rules apply, however, where the agreement involves an *allotment of shares* in the company. In such a case, and regardless of whether
there has also been a contravention of s. 103, the agreement remains
enforceable in so far as it is for the allotment of shares, and the allottee is
liable to pay the company the nominal value of the shares plus any
premium. In a proper case, however, the court may grant relief from
liability under s. 113. Further, s. 115 expressly preserves the enforceability
of any undertaking given by the subscriber to do work or provide services
or do anything else in respect of the allotment.

7
Offers of shares to the public

1. The raising of capital

A company raises its share capital in the first instance by issuing shares to optimistic persons who hope to benefit by investing their money in a rapidly developing enterprise. It repeats this process as many times as is required in the course of its existence, so that the first issue of shares may well be followed by other later issues as the company's business expands and new capital is needed.

In the raising of capital, there is an important distinction between a public company and a private company. A public company will normally wish to attract applications for its shares, i.e. to raise capital, from the public. This has given rise to many statutory provisions designed to protect the investing public. These provisions are now in Parts IV and V of the Financial Services Act 1986. That Act wholly repealed Part III of the Companies Act 1985 which consolidated the then applicable law relating to prospectuses.

References in this chapter are to sections of the Financial Services Act 1986 unless the contrary is indicated.

As regards private companies there are only two statutory provisions to note:

(a) A private company must not apply for its shares to be listed on the Stock Exchange: s. 143.

(b) A private company must not issue any advertisement offering its shares, unless the circumstances in which the advertisement is issued are covered by an order made by the Secretary of State for Trade and Industry exempting the company from this provision.

> For the detailed list of categories of circumstances in which such an order may be made *see* s. 160A (discussed in **15** below). The general effect is that the advertisement must be of a private character or be addressed to a person sufficiently expert to appreciate the risks involved, but the Secretary of State has a wide discretion: s. 170, as substituted by s. 199 Companies Act 1989.

This chapter is therefore, apart from the exception in **(b)** above, confined to public companies.

There are three main methods by which a company may raise capital from the public:

(a) *By making a direct invitation to the public.*

(b) *By an offer for sale.* Here the company sells all the shares to an *issuing house*, i.e. a company or firm whose business is finance, and which may be involved in many types of financial enterprise, including the handling of new issues.

The issuing house sells the shares to the public at a higher price than it paid for them by publishing a document called an 'offer for sale' with an application form attached.

This method is more common than **(a)** above, as it relieves the company from the administrative work of a new issue, and at the same time ensures that the whole issue is sold, i.e. the issue here is *underwritten firm* (*see* 8:4).

(c) *By placing.* Here an issuing house may *either* subscribe for the issue itself and then invite other persons—normally its clients— to purchase from it at a higher price, *or* it may, without itself subscribing, find persons who wish to buy the shares. In the latter situation the issuing house is a mere agent, and will be paid a commission called 'brokerage' for its services.

2. Listed and unlisted securities

Part IV (i.e. ss. 142–57) of the Financial Services Act 1986 deals with the *official listing of securities.* Its leading provision is that no investment shall be admitted to the Official List of the Stock Exchange except in accordance with Part IV of the Act: s. 142.

The investments (referred to in the Act as 'securities') to which Part IV applies are specified in detail in Schedule 1 to the Act, taken along with s. 142. They include shares, stock, debentures and certain other investments. At this stage in the study of company law it will be convenient to refer only to shares.

A company which wishes its shares to be freely marketable will want to have them admitted to the Official List of the Stock Exchange. It will, therefore, require to comply with Part IV of the Act.

The provisions in Part IV had their origin in three EC Directives:

(a) the Admissions Directive (dealing with the conditions for admission to listing);

(b) the Listing Particulars Directive (relating to the drawing up, scrutiny and distribution of listing particulars); *and*

(c) the Interim Reports Directive (relating to the regular publication of information by listed companies).

Before the 1986 Act these Directives had been given effect to in the UK by the Stock Exchange (Listing) Regulations 1984. These Regulations were repealed by the 1986 Act, and the provisions of Part IV of the Act take their place.

Part V (i.e. ss. 158–71) deals with *offers of unlisted securities*. These provisions, by s. 158, relate to investments (or 'securities') which are not listed. Again, for what are investments for the purposes of Part V reference must be made to Schedule 1, from which, taken along with s. 158, it will be found that shares, stock, debentures and certain other investments are again included.

3. Applications for listing

An application for listing must, by s. 143, be made to 'the competent authority' in the way required by the 'listing rules'. These terms are explained in s. 142.

'The competent authority' means the Council of the Stock Exchange, except that, by s. 157, the Secretary of State for Trade and Industry may by order transfer the Council's functions in that connection to another body either at the request of the Council or if it appears to him:

(a) that the Council is exercising those functions in a way which is unnecessary for the protection of investors and fails to take into account the proper interests of issuers and proposed issuers of shares; *or*
(b) that it is necessary to do so for the protection of investors.

'Listing rules', referred to in s. 143 above, are rules made by the competent authority for the purposes of Part IV of the Act.

By s. 142 any functions of the competent authority under the provisions may be exercised by any committee, sub-committee, officer or servant of the authority except that listing rules must be made by the authority itself or if made by a committee or sub-committee be confirmed by the authority within 28 days.

Section 143 provides that no application for the listing of shares can be made except by or with the consent of the issuer of the shares.

By s. 144 the competent authority may impose other requirements on an applicant in addition to compliance with the listing rules.

Also by s. 144 the competent authority may refuse an application for listing:

(a) if it considers that, because of any matter relating to the issuer, the admission would be detrimental to the interests of investors; *or*
(b) in the case of shares already officially listed in another EC state, if the issuer has failed to comply with his obligations in connection with that listing.

The competent authority must notify the applicant of its decision within six months, but if there is no notification, the application must be taken to have been refused.

4. The content of listing rules

Several provisions of the Act specify particular matters which may be included in listing rules. The competent authority has, however, a general power as regards the making of listing rules for admission, not restricted by the specific matters mentioned: s. 144.

Listing rules may require as a condition of admission to the Official List:

(a) the submission to, and approval by, the authority of a document (called 'listing particulars') in such form and containing such information as may be specified in the rules; *and*
(b) the publication of that document.

The rules may alternatively provide that in specified cases a document other than listing particulars be published as a condition of admission.

By s. 153 listing rules may make provision as to the action which may be taken by the competent authority where there is non-compliance with listing rules. Provision may be included:

(a) authorising the competent authority to publish the fact that an issuer has contravened any provision of the rules; *and*
(b) if the rules require an issuer to publish any information, authorising the authority itself to publish it if the issuer fails to do so.

By s. 155 listing rules may require the payment of fees to the competent authority for applications for listing and for retaining shares in the Official List.

Finally, s. 156 sets out a number of general provisions on listing rules, including the following:

(a) Listing rules may make different provision for different cases.
(b) Listing rules may authorise the competent authority to dispense with or modify the application of the rules in particular cases.
(c) Listing rules must be made in writing, be printed and made available to the public with or without payment. A person must not be taken to have contravened any listing rule if he shows that it had not been made available in this way.

5. Listing particulars

The details of the information required to be stated in listing particulars are as specified in listing rules. The competent authority may also, under s. 144, require further information to be stated as a condition of admission to the Official List. In addition, there is imposed, by s. 146 of the Act, a *general duty of disclosure* in listing particulars.

The general duty of disclosure covers all such information as investors and their professional advisers would reasonably require, and reasonably expect to find in listing particulars, for the purpose of making an informed assessment of:

(a) the assets and liabilities, financial position, profits and losses, and prospects of the issuer of the shares; *and*
(b) the rights attaching to the shares.

This provision relates only to information which is within the knowledge of any person responsible for the listing particulars or which it would be reasonable for him to obtain by making inquiries.

Further, in deciding what information comes under the general duty of disclosure, regard must be had:

(a) to the nature of the shares and of the issuer of them;
(b) to the nature of the persons likely to consider acquiring them;
(c) to the fact that certain matters may reasonably be expected to be within the knowledge of such professional advisers as the persons mentioned in **(b)** may reasonably be expected to consult; *and*
(d) to any information available to investors or their professional advisers under this or any other Act.

6. Supplementary listing particulars

Section 147 provides that if at any time after the preparation of listing particulars for submission to the competent authority under s. 144 and before the commencement of dealings in the shares there is a *significant change* affecting any matter in the required particulars or a *significant new matter* arises which would have had to be included if it had arisen when the particulars were prepared, the issuer must submit to the competent authority for its approval, and (if approved) publish, 'supplementary listing particulars' of the change or of the new matter as the case may be.

Where the issuer is not aware of the change or new matter in question, he is not under any duty to submit or publish supplementary listing particulars unless he is notified of the change or new matter by a person responsible for the listing particulars, but it is the duty of any person responsible for the listing particulars who is aware of the matter to give notice of it to the issuer.

7. Exemptions from disclosure in listing particulars

By s. 148 the competent authority may authorise the omission from listing particulars or supplementary listing particulars of any required information if its disclosure would be:

(a) contrary to the public interest; *or*
(b) seriously detrimental to the issuer.

As regards **(a)**, the Secretary of State or the Treasury may issue a certificate stating that the disclosure of any information would be contrary to the public interest.

As regards **(b)**, no authority can be granted if the non-disclosure would be likely to mislead a person considering the acquisition of the shares as to any facts which it is essential for him to know in order to make an informed assessment.

8. Registration of listing particulars

Section 149 provides that on or before the date on which listing particulars or supplementary listing particulars are published a copy of the particulars must be delivered to the registrar of companies for registration, and a statement that a copy has been delivered to him must be included in the particulars.

If particulars are published without a copy of them having been delivered to the registrar, the issuer and any person who is knowingly a party to the publication is guilty of an offence and liable to a fine.

9. Compensation for false or misleading particulars

Section 150 provides that, with the exemptions stated in s. 151, the *person responsible for* any listing particulars or supplementary listing particulars is liable to pay compensation to any person who has acquired any of the shares in question and suffered loss as a result of any untrue or misleading statement in the particulars or the omission of any of the required particulars or failure to comply with s. 147 as to supplementary listing particulars.

10. Exemption from liability to pay compensation

Section 151 provides for certain exemptions from the liability to pay compensation under s. 150.

A person is exempt from liability if he satisfies the court that at the time when the particulars were submitted to the competent authority he *reasonably believed*, after having made reasonable inquiries, that the statement was true and not misleading or that the omission was proper *and*:

(a) that he continued in that belief until the shares were acquired; *or*

(b) that they were acquired before it was reasonably practicable to bring a correction to the attention of persons likely to acquire the shares; *or*

(c) that before the shares were acquired he had taken all reasonable steps to secure that a correction was brought to the attention of those persons; *or*

(d) that he continued in that belief until after the commencement of dealings in the shares and that the shares were acquired after such a lapse of time that he ought in the circumstances to be reasonably excused.

Section 151 also deals with *statements made by experts* and included in the particulars.

The term 'expert' in this section includes any engineer, valuer, accountant or other person whose profession, qualifications or experience give authority to a statement made by him.

A person is exempt from liability for a loss caused by a statement purporting to be made by another person as an expert and included in the particulars with the expert's consent if he satisfies the court that at the time when the particulars were submitted to the competent authority he believed on reasonable grounds that the expert was competent to make the statement and had consented to its inclusion in the form and context in which it appeared *and*:

(a) that he continued in that belief until the time when the shares were acquired; *or*

(b) that the shares were acquired before it was reasonably practicable to bring the fact that the expert was not competent or had not consented to the attention of persons likely to acquire the shares; *or*

(c) that before the shares were acquired he had taken all reasonable steps to secure that that fact was brought to the attention of those persons; *or*

(d) that he continued in that belief until after the commencement of dealings in the shares and that the shares were acquired after such a lapse of time that he ought in the circumstances to be reasonably excused.

Section 151 further provides that a person is exempt from liability if he satisfies the court:

(a) that before the shares were acquired a *correction* (or, in the case of an expert's statement, the fact that the expert was not competent or had not consented) had been published in a way calculated to bring it to the attention of persons likely to acquire the shares; *or*

(b) that he took all reasonable steps to secure such publication and reasonably believed that it had taken place before the shares were acquired.

Section 151 also deals with statements made by an *official person* or contained in a *public official document* and included in the particulars. A person is exempt from liability for any loss resulting from such a statement if he satisfies the court that the statement is accurately and fairly reproduced.

Further, a person is exempt from liability if he satisfies the court that the person suffering the loss acquired the shares *with knowledge* that the statement was false or misleading, or of the omitted matter or of the change or new matter, as the case may be.

A further exemption from liability arises in relation to failure to submit *supplementary listing particulars*: a person is exempt from liability if he satisfies the court that he reasonably believed that the change or new matter in question was not such as to call for supplementary listing particulars.

11. Persons responsible for listing particulars

The liability to pay compensation under s. 150 is imposed on *persons responsible for listing particulars or supplementary listing particulars*. Section 152 provides that these persons are:

(a) the issuer of the shares;
(b) where the issuer is a body corporate, the directors of that body;
(c) where the issuer is a body corporate, persons named in the particulars as having agreed to become directors;
(d) persons stated in the particulars as having accepted responsibility for any part of the particulars;
(e) any other persons who have authorised the contents of any part of the particulars.

As regards **(b)**, a person is not responsible for any particulars if they are published without his knowledge or consent and on becoming aware of their publication he immediately gives reasonable public notice that they were published without his knowledge or consent.

A person who under **(d)** or **(e)** has accepted responsibility for, or authorised, only *part* of the particulars is responsible only for that part and only if it is included in the form and context to which he has agreed.

A further limitation is that neither **(b)** nor **(c)** applies to any director certified by the competent authority as a person to whom the provision should not apply because of his having an interest, or because of other circumstances, making it inappropriate for him to be responsible.

Finally, where the issuer pays or is liable to pay compensation under s. 150, no account is taken of that payment or liability in any question as to the amount paid on subscription for the shares or as to the amount paid up on them.

12. Advertisements in connection with listing applications

Section 154 provides that where listing particulars are published in connection with an application for the listing of any shares no advertisement or other information of a kind specified by listing rules can be issued unless the contents of the advertisement or other information have been submitted to the competent authority and that authority has either:

(a) approved those contents; *or*
(b) authorised the issue of the advertisement or information without such approval.

13. Discontinuance and suspension of listing

Section 145 provides that the competent authority may, in accordance with the listing rules, discontinue the listing of any shares if satisfied that there are special circumstances which prevent normal regular dealings in the shares. The competent authority may also, in accordance with the listing rules, suspend the listing of any shares.

14. Definitions for Part V

It is now time to turn to the provisions of Part V of the Act, which is concerned with offers of *unlisted* securities. As with the provisions in Part IV, attention will be confined to shares, though the provisions also relate to other securities (as defined in Schedule 1) as well as to shares.

As a preliminary to the study of Part V, the definitions of three expressions which are used throughout Part V should be noted:

(a) *Advertisement offering shares.* For the purposes of Part V an advertisement is said to offer shares if:

(*i*) it invites a person to enter into an agreement for subscribing for or otherwise acquiring or underwriting any shares; *or*

(*ii*) it contains information calculated to lead directly or indirectly to a person entering into such an agreement: s. 158.

(b) *Approved exchange.* The term approved exchange, when used of dealings in any shares, means a recognised investment exchange approved by the Secretary of State for the purposes of Part V. The Secretary of State must give notice of the exchanges which are, for the time being, approved exchanges: s. 158.

(c) *Prospectus.* By s. 159 a prospectus is a document containing information about shares which are being admitted to dealings on an approved exchange.

15. Offers of shares on admission to approved exchange

The two leading provisions in Part V are in ss. 159 and 160. Section 159 relates to advertisements offering shares which are being admitted to dealings on an approved exchange, and s. 160 relates to other advertisements offering shares.

Section 159 provides that, with some exceptions, no person must issue an advertisement offering any shares on the occasion of their admission to dealings on an approved exchange unless:

(a) a prospectus containing information about the shares has been submitted to and approved by the exchange and delivered for registration to the registrar of companies; *or*

(b) the advertisement is such that no agreement can be entered into in pursuance of it until a prospectus has been submitted, approved and delivered as in **(a)** above.

The provision does not apply if a prospectus relating to the shares has been delivered for registration in the previous 12 months *and* the approved exchange certifies that it is satisfied that persons likely to consider acquiring the shares will have sufficient information to enable them to decide whether to do so from that prospectus and any information published in connection with the admission of the shares.

By s. 161 there are further exceptions to the requirements of s. 159:

(a) It does not apply to any advertisement offering shares if the offer is conditional on their *admission to listing* under Part IV or if the shares have been listed under Part IV within the previous 12 months and the approved exchange certifies that persons likely to consider acquiring them will have sufficient information to enable them to decide whether to do so.

(b) It does not apply if other shares issued by the same person (not necessarily shares of the same class as those in the present offer) are *already dealt in* on an approved exchange and the exchange certifies to the same effect as in **(a)** above.

(c) It does not apply if, in the case of shares dealt in on an exchange in a *country outside the UK*, the Secretary of State considers that the law of the other country provides investors in the UK with protection at least equivalent to that of Part IV or Part V and makes an order specifying circumstances in which the requirement is not to apply.

In addition, by s. 160A, inserted by s. 198 Companies Act 1989, the Secretary of State may by order exempt from s. 159 any of the following advertisements *when issued in such circumstances as may be specified in the order*:

(a) advertisements appearing to him to have a private character, whether because of a connection between the issuer and the addressee or otherwise;

(b) advertisements appearing to him to deal with investments only incidentally;

(c) advertisements issued to persons appearing to him to be sufficiently expert to understand any risks involved; *and*

(d) such other classes of advertisements as he thinks fit.

By the same section the Secretary of State may exempt an advertisement *issued in any circumstances whatsoever* if:

(e) it relates to securities appearing to him to be of a kind which can be expected normally to be bought or dealt in only by persons sufficiently expert to understand any risks involved.

However, an order under s. 160A, if it falls into categories **(a)**, **(b)** **(c)** or **(e)** above, may be annulled by a resolution of either House of Parliament, and an order in category **(d)** cannot be made unless a draft of it has been laid before, and approved by a resolution of, each House of Parliament.

16. Other advertisements offering shares

Other advertisements offering shares, i.e. advertisements where there is no admission of the shares to dealings on an approved exchange, are divided, by s. 160, into 'primary' offers and 'secondary' offers.

A primary offer is an advertisement (not issued in connection with admission to dealings on an approved exchange) inviting persons to enter into an agreement for *subscribing for or underwriting* the shares to which it relates or containing information calculated to lead directly or indirectly to their doing so.

A secondary offer is an advertisement (not issued in connection with admission to dealings on an approved exchange) inviting persons to enter into an agreement for *acquiring* the shares to which it relates or containing information calculated to lead directly or indirectly to their doing so. The advertisement must in the case of a secondary offer be issued:

(a) by a person who has acquired the shares from the issuer directly or indirectly *with a view to issuing the advertisement; or*
(b) by a person who is a *controller* of the issuer and who is acting with the consent or participation of the issuer in issuing the advertisement.

The main provision in s. 160 is that (with exceptions) no person must issue an advertisement offering shares which is a primary or secondary offer unless:

(a) he has delivered a prospectus to the registrar for registration; *or*
(b) the advertisement is such that no agreement can be entered into in pursuance of it until a prospectus has been delivered to the registrar for registration.

This provision, however, does not apply to a secondary offer if a prospectus has already been delivered to the registrar in respect of an offer of the same shares made in the previous six months.

The further exceptions under s. 161 and the possible exemptions under s. 160A apply in relation to s. 160 as they do in relation to s. 159 (*see* **15**).

17. Contents of prospectus

By s. 162 a prospectus must contain such information and comply with such other requirements as may be prescribed by rules made by the Secretary of State.

Compliance with requirements imposed by the law of a country outside the UK may be treated as compliance with the rules, if the rules so provide.

If it appears to the Secretary of State that an approved exchange has rules on prospectuses which provide investors with protection at least equivalent to that provided by rules made by himself, he may direct that any prospectus must comply with the rules of the exchange instead of his own rules.

In addition to information required to be included in a prospectus by s. 162, there is under s. 163 a *general duty of disclosure*. The provisions of s. 163 match those relating to the general duty of disclosure in listing particulars in s. 146 (*see* 5).

18. Supplementary prospectus

Section 164 requires a supplementary prospectus to be delivered for registration by the person who delivered the prospectus if a *significant change* occurs or a *significant new matter* arises after registration of the prospectus and while an agreement can still be entered into in pursuance of the offer. The provisions correspond to those in s. 147 relating to supplementary listing particulars (*see* 6), with the substitution of 'the person who delivered the prospectus for registration' for 'the issuer', and of 'person responsible for the prospectus' for 'person responsible for the listing particulars'.

19. Exemptions from disclosure in prospectus

By s. 165, if in the case of any approved exchange the Secretary of State so directs, the exchange has power to authorise the omission from a prospectus or supplementary prospectus of any required information. The provisions are otherwise the same as those relating to exemptions from disclosure in listing particulars (*see* 7).

20. Compensation for false or misleading prospectus

Section 166 provides that, with the exemptions stated in s. 167, the *person responsible for* a prospectus or supplementary prospectus is liable to pay compensation to any person who has acquired the shares to which the prospectus relates and has suffered loss as a result of any untrue or misleading statement in the prospectus or the omission of any of the required particulars or failure to comply with s. 164 (supplementary prospectus). These provisions correspond to those of s. 150 relating to listing particulars.

21. Exemption from liability to pay compensation

The provisions of s. 167 are to the same general effect as those of s. 151 (*see* 10).

References in s. 151 to 'the time when the particulars were submitted to the competent authority' become in s. 167 'the time when the prospectus was delivered for registration', and there is in s. 167 no reference to the commencement of dealings in the shares.

22. Persons responsible for prospectus

Section 168 lists the same persons as being responsible for a prospectus as are listed in s. 152 as being responsible for listing particulars (*see* **11**).

Instead of the reference in s. 152 to publication without the person's knowledge or consent there is substituted in s. 168 a reference to delivery for registration without the person's knowledge or consent, and instead of certification by the competent authority in s. 152 there is substituted in s. 168 a reference to certification by an approved exchange.

23. Rules made by the Secretary of State

Section 169 provides that the Secretary of State may make rules:

(a) regulating the terms on which a person may offer shares by an advertisement under Part V; *and*

(b) otherwise regulating his conduct with a view to ensuring that the persons to whom the offer is addressed are treated equally and fairly.

24. Non-statutory remedies for mis-statements in listing particulars or prospectus

We have now considered the main statutory provisions on listing particulars and prospectus, but there are two other remedies for mis-statements which are available to an injured party under the general law. The injured party must be a person intended to be influenced by the listing particulars or the prospectus and not a person who bought shares on the stock market or unlisted securities market; see *Al-Nakib Investments (Jersey) Ltd* v. *Longcroft* (1990) [B101], where a shareholder subscribed for shares in a rights issue and also made further purchases on the stock market.

The remedies are:

(a) damages for fraud; *and*

(b) rescission of the contract of allotment.

25. Damages for the tort of deceit or fraud

This remedy exists at *common law* for the plaintiff who can prove that he suffered damage by acting on a deceitful statement addressed to him. Thus, as a rule, only allottees taking their shares directly from the company may sue for deceit, though exceptionally a transferee may be able to prove that he was intended to be affected by the statement.

[The Scottish terms corresponding to 'tort' and 'deceit' are 'delict' and 'fraud' respectively.]

Deceit was defined in *Derry* v. *Peek* (1889), as 'a false statement made *knowingly*, without belief in its truth, or *recklessly*, careless whether it be true or false'. Thus in law something less immoral than a deliberate lie amounts to deceit: the defendant may merely have been reckless, i.e. he did not care whether the statement was true or not. But not caring involves considering the possibility that the statement might be false, and making it just the same, regardless of the consequences to the plaintiff. Thus the defendant is equally liable whether he made the false statement *knowing* that it was untrue, or *thinking that it might be,* for in both cases the possibility of deception was in his mind.

It is clear from this that to succeed in a claim for fraud, the plaintiff has to prove a certain state of mind in the defendant. This may well be 'as much a fact as the state of his digestion', but it is even harder to prove. Consequently the statutory remedy of compensation under s. 150 or s. 166 Financial Services Act 1986 is a much more reliable remedy; to recover compensation under those sections fraud need not be proved, and the mere untruth of the statement is enough. It is then for the defendant to show, if he can, that he reasonably believed that the statement was true, and so escape liability.

The action for damages for fraud may be brought either against the company or against the directors.

Before the Companies Act 1989, if the plaintiff sued the *company*, he had to rescind his contract to take the shares. He was not permitted to sue the company for fraud and at the same time remain a member. However, s. 111A Companies Act 1985, inserted by s. 131 Companies Act 1989, now provides that a person is not debarred from obtaining damages from a company merely because he holds shares in the company.

If he sues the *directors*, he need not rescind, though he may of course do so if he wishes.

26. Rescission

This remedy exists in *equity* for the plaintiff who can prove a mis-statement, either innocent or fraudulent.

The rules here are the ordinary rules of misrepresentation familiar to students of contract, so that the plaintiff must prove a mis-statement of fact which had an effect on his mind and induced him to buy the shares. He may then rescind and return the shares, receiving his money back with interest. But it is important to remember that this is an equitable remedy which is basically discretionary and may be lost in certain circumstances.

Thus the plaintiff will not be allowed to rescind if:

(a) he displays laches, i.e. delays in taking proceedings; delay defeats equity;

(b) he does some act showing a clear manifestation of ownership, e.g. attends meeting or tries to sell the shares;
(c) the company goes into liquidation; here the rights of creditors are involved, and the law always favours creditors at the expense of members.

By s. 2 Misrepresentation Act 1967 damages in lieu of rescission may be recovered if the misrepresentation has not been fraudulent or has been negligent.

[In Scotland s.10 Law Reform (Miscellaneous Provisions) (Scotland) Act 1985 provides that damages may be recovered for negligent misrepresentation.]

8

Underwriting commission and brokerage

1. The meaning and purpose of underwriting

For all companies the raising of capital is a matter of practical importance, since without capital a newly formed company can neither start nor purchase a business. For public companies it is also a legal necessity for, as was seen in 5:**2** and 5:**3**, no trading certificate will be granted unless the company's allotted share capital reaches the authorised minimum. The success of any issue to the public, however, depends on many factors and will always be doubtful to some extent, and therefore to ensure that the shares will be taken up even if the issue is a failure as far as the public are concerned, a company normally arranges for it to be underwritten.

This involves entering into an agreement with an *underwriter,* i.e. a financial house which undertakes to buy as many of the shares as are not taken up by the public. If the issue is a large one, several underwriting agreements may be made with different underwriters, since one alone may not be prepared to bear the risk. Alternatively, the principal underwriters may pass on the risk by entering into a *sub-underwriting agreement,* i.e. arranging for one or more other underwriters to underwrite them, while they underwrite the whole of the company's issue. If the issue is being handled by an issuing house by means of an offer for sale, the issuing house will make the same sort of arrangement.

2. Underwriting commission

The underwriters make their profit by charging a commission on the number of shares underwritten. This commission is still payable even if the issue is a complete success so that all the shares are bought by the public and the underwriters are not compelled to take up any of them. Where the underwriters have entered into a sub-underwriting agreement, the underwriting commission is passed on to the sub-underwriter and is known as *sub-underwriting commission,* while the principal underwriters retain some part of it, called *overriding commission,* for their services. Thus overriding commission is the difference between underwriting and sub-underwriting commission.

3. Statutory control of underwriting commission

A company which has been in existence for some years and is making, for instance, its third issue of shares to raise capital for expansion may have revenue reserves out of which it can pay the underwriting commission, or funds in its share premium account which, under s. 130, may lawfully be used for this purpose although a capital reserve. But a new company making its first issue will have no reserves of any kind. Any commission paid, therefore, will have to be provided out of the capital obtained from the issue, and this clearly reduces the amount of capital which the company will ultimately derive from that issue. Since the preservation of capital is one of the most important aims of the Act, ss. 97–98 permit the payment of underwriting commission only on certain conditions.

4. Power of company to pay underwriting commission

Section 97, as amended by the Financial Services Act 1986, provides that it is lawful to pay underwriting commission if:

(a) it is authorised by the articles; *and*

(b) it does not exceed 10 per cent of the price at which the shares are issued, or the rate specified in the articles, whichever is the less; *and*

(c) it complies with any rules made by the Secretary of State under s. 169 Financial Services Act 1986 (*see* 7:**23**).

Table A, Article 4, authorises the payment of commission.

It will be noted that s. 97 does not mention the word 'underwriter' and that it is very loosely phrased so that it might appear to cover the payment of a commission to anyone who undertakes to buy shares in a company. This was not, of course, what it was intended to do, but misuse of the section has sometimes occurred.

It will also be seen that the section uses the words: 'subscribe (absolutely or conditionally)'. To subscribe *conditionally* is to enter into the kind of agreement described above in **1**, i.e. to undertake to buy as many shares as are not taken up by the public. The underwriter here is agreeing to take up the shares only on a condition, namely, that the public do not do so. To subscribe *absolutely* is to agree to take up the shares, i.e. underwrite them *firm*, and then re-sell them at a higher price to the public. Thus an issuing house making an offer for sale, as described in 7:**1**, is in effect underwriting firm. Either way the company can be sure that the entire issue will be taken up, and that the risk of its failure lies with the underwriters.

NOTES: (1) Section 98 states that a company may not pay underwriting commission out of capital 'except as permitted by s. 97', i.e. unless it complies with the conditions laid down in s. 97. It does not, however, refer to the payment of commission out of revenue, i.e. profits, and this therefore seems to be unrestricted by the section.

(2) Section 98 refers not only to *commission*, but also to *discount* or *allowance*. This is because it is possible to pay a commission by allowing a discount: thus it makes no difference whether £1 shares are issued at £1 and the underwriters then receive 5p for each share underwritten, or whether they are issued to the underwriters at 95p. Either way the company is left with 95p for each £1 share issued. Thus s. 98 is the only *statutory* exception to the rule that shares may not be issued at a discount.

(3) Section 98 refers only to shares and does not mention debentures, since they are not capital and can therefore be issued at a discount freely.

5. Brokerage
Brokerage is the sum paid to a person by the company for *placing* shares. Sections 97–98 do not restrict it in any way, and s. 98 expressly states that ss. 97–98 in no way affect the payment of 'lawful brokerage'.

Lawful brokerage is reasonable brokerage, but it must be paid to a person carrying on the business of broker, and not to a private person: *Andreae* v. *Zinc Mines of Great Britain* (1918).

9

Allotment

1. The meaning of allotment

Although allotment is only one of several methods by which a person can become a member of a company, it is one of considerable importance and complexity owing to the large number of statutory provisions which apply to it. When this method of acquiring membership is employed, shares are taken to be allotted when a person acquires the unconditional right to be included in the company's register of members in respect of them: s. 738.

2. Basic feature of allotment

In this chapter the rules governing allotment are considered. It will be seen that its basic feature is that the investor acquires the shares from the *company* and not from a previous holder.

3. The contract to take shares

Listing particulars or a prospectus issued by a company or an offer for sale made by an issuing house is not an offer in the contractual sense, but merely an invitation to treat. It is the applicant for the shares who makes the offer, and it is the company which accepts or rejects it. The transaction is governed by the normal rules of contract and no special form is required. In practice, the applicant makes his application in writing on the application form issued to him, but in theory it could be oral.

NOTE: Where the contract is made by post, as it usually is, the ordinary rules of contract again apply to the position.

These rules are fully dealt with in textbooks on the law of contract, and they are outside the scope of this book.

There are, however, two points of importance where special rules apply regarding:

(a) the persons to whom the shares are offered; *and*
(b) variation of the offer to buy shares.

These will now be discussed in turn.

4. The persons to whom the shares are offered

Sections 89–96 deal with *pre-emption rights* for existing shareholders. Under these sections existing shareholders normally have a statutory right to be offered shares in proportion to their present holdings whenever a new issue is made (*see* **10–13**).

Pre-emption rights were introduced by the Companies Act 1980. Before that Act such rights were given only by the company's articles or, in the case of listed companies, by the rules of the stock exchange.

5. Variation of the offer to buy shares

The law of contract requires the acceptance of an offer to be entire. If the acceptance introduces a new term, or varies the offer to the slightest degree, it will amount in law to a counter-offer and itself require acceptance by the original offeror.

This rule could obviously lead to difficulty where the issue of shares is *over-subscribed*, i.e. where the public have applied for more shares than the company is issuing. This is a common occurrence, and the company usually deals with it by 'scaling down' the numbers of shares applied for, or by holding a ballot, or some other method intended to be a fair solution. The law of contract would allow the company either to accept an applicant's offer, or to reject it, but it would not allow any variation of the offer by allotting the applicant a lesser number of shares than the number for which he applied.

In consequence the application form is worded: 'I agree to accept—shares, or such lesser number as may be allotted to me', and the company is then able to accept the offer by allotting the applicant any number of shares not in excess of the number for which he applied. This may, of course, involve sending the applicant back a cheque for the difference between the price of the shares applied for and those ultimately allotted.

6. Conditional applications

An application for shares, like any other offer, may be conditional, i.e. subject to a *condition precedent*. Then if the condition is not fulfilled, no contract for the shares can result.

> Thus in *Simpson's Case* (1869), the applicant for the shares made his offer conditional on his being given a building contract by the company. He was allotted the shares, but was never given the building contract, so that the condition on which he had made his application was never fulfilled. HELD: He was not bound to pay up the amount unpaid on the shares.

This is exactly the result to be expected, of course, from the ordinary law of contract.

7. Applications subject to a condition subsequent

With regard to a *condition subsequent*, however, the ordinary law of contract does *not* apply to applications for shares. In most types of contract the parties may agree that their contractual relationship shall be terminated on the happening of an event: this is one form of discharge by agreement. Such arrangements are often made when a contract is to endure for a considerable period of time, and either or both of the parties fear a change in circumstances which might render it no longer beneficial to them. But in shareholding, as in marriage, it would hardly be in the public interest if the parties to the agreement decided that on the happening of a certain event their contract should be terminated, for the company's creditors could never be certain how many of the present members might suddenly become entitled to have their capital returned to them.

The law, of course, permits an allotment to be set aside for fraud or error, just as it permits a marriage to be destroyed by certain events or conduct, but it will not allow the parties themselves to agree to discharge their contract on the happening of an event which they, but not the law, find sufficient to make termination of their of their relationship desirable. Their contractual freedom is restricted: they may make, but not break, their agreement.

It follows, therefore, that an applicant who is allotted shares in the company may not set the allotment aside merely because he and the company have agreed that it should become invalid on the happening of an event. Once the applicant becomes a member, he is liable to pay for the shares. Similarly, where he has applied for shares and at the same time made a *collateral agreement* with the company, i.e. another contract *side by side* with his contract to take the shares, he cannot set the allotment aside merely because the company has broken the collateral agreement.

> Thus in *Elkington's Case* (1867), the applicants for £10 shares relied on an agreement which they had made with the company that they should pay 30s. per share in *cash*, and the balance should be set off against goods with which they were to supply the company. The company never ordered the goods. HELD: The applicants were liable to pay the balance due on the shares in cash, since the arrangement concerning the goods merely amounted to a collateral agreement, and not to a condition precedent.

A collateral agreement of this type will of course, if a valid contract in itself, give rise to all the normal remedies for breach if either party should break it. But it in no way affects the validity of the allotment.

Here is yet another example of the law's preference of creditors to members.

8. The statutory provisions on allotment

The statutory provisions on allotment are in ss. 80–116, as amended by the Financial Services Act 1986 and the Companies Act 1989. Of these sections, ss. 97–98, on underwriting commissions, have already been considered (*see* Chapter 8); other sections are dealt with in this chapter. Important changes in this part of company law were made by the Companies Act 1980. It is essential to notice, in each case, to which companies the particular section applies.

9. Authority of company required for allotment

Section 80 is the most comprehensive of all the sections on allotment. It applies to *all companies, public and private* and provides that the directors may not allot *'relevant securities'* of the company unless they are *authorised* to do so by either:

(a) a general meeting; *or*
(b) the articles.

It should be noted that Table A contains no such authority.

'Relevant securities' are defined as shares in the company *excluding those*:

(a) shown in the memorandum as having been taken by the subscribers to it; *or*
(b) allotted under a share scheme for employees.

The expression includes, however, a *right to subscribe for*, or *convert any security into*, shares in the company other than those comprised in (b) above. Thus it would include a convertible debenture (*see* 21:1).

The company's authority to the directors may be general or particular, conditional or unconditional, but in all cases must state:

(a) the maximum amount of relevant securities which may be allotted under it; *and*
(b) the date on which it will expire.

The date of expiration must not be more than five years from whichever of the following dates applies:

(a) where on the company's original incorporation the authority was contained in the articles, the *date of incorporation*;
(b) where this is not the case, the *date of the resolution* giving the authority.

Whether given by the articles or by a resolution, the authority may always be revoked or varied by the company in general meeting.

The authority may be renewed by a resolution of the general meeting as many times as is desired, but never for a period exceeding five years.

The resolution must always state the amount of relevant securities to be allotted, or which still remains to be allotted, as well as the date on which the renewed authority will expire.

Any resolution mentioned in the section, regardless of whether it gives, varies, revokes or renews the authority, may be an *ordinary* resolution, even if it alters the articles of the company (*see* 3:**9**). It must, however, by s. 380, be filed with the registrar (*see* 15: **34**) who, under s. 711, is required, in the case of a *public* company, to publish his receipt of it in the *Gazette*.

Although it can be seen that the rules imposed by s. 80 are stringent, the validity of an allotment is not affected if they are broken. A director who knowingly and wilfully contravenes the section is, however, liable to a fine: s. 80.

A concession is given to private companies by s. 115 Companies Act 1989, which inserts a new section (s. 80A) in the 1985 Act at this point. By s. 80A in a private company the authority may be given for an indefinite period or for a fixed period of more than five years. The procedure is for the company to elect by 'elective resolution' under s. 379A (*see* 15:**37**) that the provisions of s. 80A should apply to the giving of authority instead of those of s. 80.

10. Pre-emption rights

Section 89 prohibits any company, public or private, from allotting to any person *equity securities* which are to be paid up wholly in cash unless it has first offered to each holder of *relevant shares* or *relevant employee shares*, on terms at least as favourable, a proportion of them equal in nominal value to that already held by him of the total relevant shares or relevant employee shares already issued.

Under s. 94 'holder' includes any person who holds shares on any day within the 28 days immediately preceding the date of the offer.

Further, it is not enough for the company merely to make such an offer: the prohibition on allotment endures until either the period for the acceptance of the offer has expired (*see* **11**) or the company has, in every case, been notified of its acceptance or refusal: s. 89.

It is important to note the three technical expressions used in s. 89 and printed in italics above. They are defined in s. 94, and it will be seen that the most crucial of the definitions is that of *relevant shares*.

(a) *Relevant shares* means shares in the company *excluding*:
    (*i*) shares having a limit on their right to participate in distributions of both dividend and capital; *and*
    (*ii*) shares which are held or are to be allotted in pursuance of a share scheme for employees.
(b) *Relevant employee shares* means shares which would be relevant shares

within **(a)** above if they were not held in pursuance of a share scheme for employees.

(c) *Equity security* means a relevant share in the company *excluding those*:
  (*i*) shown in the memorandum as having been taken by the subscribers to the memorandum; *or*
  (*ii*) issued as bonus shares.

A reference to allotment of equity securities includes, however, a *right to subscribe for*, or *convert any security into*, relevant shares(*see* **9**).

It often happens that the company's memorandum or articles contain a clause giving a pre-emption right to holders of a *particular class* of shares in the event of any further issue of shares of that class. Where such a clause exists, the provisions of s. 89 apply *only to the balance of the securities which remains unallotted*. Thus such shareholders have 'double' pre-emption rights—the first as holders of a particular class of shares, and the second as members of the company.

11. Procedure for making pre-emption offer

Section 90 deals with the procedure for communicating pre-emption offers to shareholders. Whether made under s. 89 or under a clause in the memorandum or articles, s. 90 requires the company's offer of the new shares to be in writing and made to the holder either personally or by posting it to his registered address in the UK. If this is impossible because he has no registered address in the UK or is the holder of a share warrant (*see* 12:**26**), it may be published in the *Gazette*.

The offer must state a period of at least 21 days during which it may be accepted. It cannot be revoked before the end of that period.

12. Contravention of rules governing pre-emption rights

Where there is any contravention of s. 89 or of a class pre-emption clause in a company's memorandum or articles or of communication provisions in s. 90, then s. 92 provides that the company, and every officer who knowingly authorised or permitted the contravention, are jointly and severally liable to compensate any person entitled to receive an offer for any damage suffered or expenses incurred owing to the contravention.

Such a person must, however, commence proceedings within two years.

13. Exclusion, withdrawal or modification of pre-emption rights

In the case of a *private* company s. 91 permits the above rules to be entirely excluded by the company's memorandum or articles. Even in the case of a *public* company, however, s. 95 permits the company to dispense with or modify the statutory pre-emption rights given by s. 89 if it so desires.

Where the directors have been given a *general* authority to exercise the company's power of allotment under s. 14 (*see* 9), s. 95 permits the articles or a special resolution of the company to empower them to allot equity securities either entirely free from any pre-emption rights, or with those rights modified in whatever manner they decide.

Section 95 also includes a provision, of much narrower application, that the company may by special resolution withdraw or modify the pre-emption rights as regards any specified allotment. In this case it is immaterial whether the directors' authority to allot the equity securities in question is general or particular.

Whenever the directors' authority to allot is revoked or expires, their power or the special resolution to dispense with or modify the pre-emption rights terminates with it. In consequence, on the renewal of their authority a special resolution will be required to renew that power or special resolution if the company desires to do so.

A special resolution passed under s. 95 must, like all special resolutions, be filed with the registrar under s. 380. In the case of a *public* company the registrar is then required, under s. 711, to publish his receipt of it in the *Gazette*.

14. Further rules regarding specified allotments

Further rules apply where the special resolution to withdraw or modify the pre-emption rights relates to a particular specified allotment and therefore falls under s. 95.

Section 95 provides that no such special resolution, or special resolution for its renewal, can be proposed unless:

(a) it is recommended by the directors; *and*

(b) a written statement by the directors has been circulated with the notice of the relevant meeting giving:

  (*i*) their reasons for recommending it;

  (*ii*) the amount to be paid to the company in respect of the allotment; *and*

  (*iii*) the directors' justification of that amount.

There are penalties for false or misleading matter in the statement.

15. Minimum amount to be paid before allotment

The three sections considered above (i.e. s. 80 as to authority required for allotment, s. 89 as to pre-emption rights and s. 95 as to disapplication of such rights) all apply to both public and private companies. The sections now to be considered apply to *public companies only*.

Section 101 provides that a public company may not allot a share unless it is paid up at least as to *one-quarter of its nominal value and the whole of any premium on it*.

If the company makes an allotment which contravenes this rule, s. 101 requires the shares in question to be treated *as if the minimum amount had been received*, but renders the allottee liable to pay that amount, less the value of any consideration applied in payment for the allotment, with interest at the appropriate rate. *Bonus shares* are not affected by these two provisions unless the allottee knew or ought to have known of the contravention.

None of the above provisions applies to shares allotted under a *share scheme for employees*.

Section 112 extends the liability of the allottee under s. 101 to *subsequent holders* unless the subsequent holder is exempted from such liability. Where a person becomes liable through a contravention of s. 101 to pay an amount in respect of the shares, any subsequent holder also becomes liable, jointly and severally with him, unless *either*:

(a) he is a purchaser for value without actual notice of the contravention at the time of the purchase; *or*

(b) he derived title to the shares from a person who acquired them after the contravention and was not himself so liable.

There is thus a chain of liability which can be broken only by an innocent purchaser (the *bona fide purchaser for value*).

Finally, if a company contravenes s. 101, the company and any officer of it who is in default is liable to a fine: s. 114.

16. Allotment for non-cash consideration

The Companies Act 1980 introduced special rules to apply in public companies where the consideration to be furnished by the allottee for the allotment is not in cash but in some other form. It is entirely proper for an allottee to furnish consideration for the allotment in a form other than money, but the detailed rules on this topic will be found in Chapter 10.

Section 102 prohibits any public company from allotting shares as fully or partly paid up otherwise than in cash if the consideration consists of or includes an undertaking which is to be or may be performed *more than five years after the date of the allotment*.

Where the company makes an allotment which contravenes that provision, the allottee becomes liable to pay to the company an amount equal to the nominal value of the shares, together with any premium—i.e. he becomes liable to pay for his shares in *cash*, with interest at the appropriate rate.

The same rule applies where the terms of the contract for allotment, without any fault on the part of the company, have not been complied with by the allottee within the prescribed period.

In both these cases—i.e. whenever the allottee becomes liable to pay for his shares in cash—any subsequent holder also becomes liable, jointly and severally with the allottee, to pay for the shares in cash unless *either*:

(a) he is a purchaser for value without actual notice of the contravention at the time of the purchase; *or*
(b) he derived title to the shares from a person who acquired them after the contravention and was not himself so liable: s. 112.

Once again, therefore, as with the extension of s. 101 to subsequent holders (*see* 15), liability in a subsequent holder does not arise if the chain is broken.

Finally, if a company contravenes s. 102, the company and any officer of it who is in default is liable to a fine: s. 114.

17. Exemption from liability under s. 102

Section 113 provides that where a person is liable to a company under s. 102 regarding payment for his shares, he may apply to the court for relief from that liability.

The court may then exempt him from liability if it appears just and equitable to do so.

The overriding principle to which the court must have regard in considering whether to grant an exemption order is that a company which allots shares should receive money or money's worth at least equal in value to the aggregate of the nominal value of the shares and any premium: *Re Ossory Estates* (1988) (exemption order granted).

18. Valuation of non-cash consideration

Section 103 gives detailed rules for the valuation of non-cash consideration in public companies. The section prohibits any public company from allotting shares as fully or partly paid up otherwise than in cash unless:

(a) the consideration has been valued in accordance with s. 108;
(b) a report on its value has been made to the company by a person appointed by the company during the six months immediately preceding the allotment; *and*
(c) a copy of the report has been sent to the proposed allottee.

If a company contravenes s. 103, the company and any officer of it who is in default is liable to a fine: s. 114.

Section 108 requires the valuation and report to be made by an *independent person*, i.e. a person qualified to act as the company's auditor. Thus the company's auditor is not precluded from acting in this capacity, if the company desires him to do so. The term 'valuer' is applied to the independent person.

If the valuer thinks it reasonable to do so, he may arrange for the valuation to be made by some other person provided such person appears to him to have the requisite knowledge and experience and is *neither* an officer or servant of the company or of any company in the same group *nor* a partner or employee of any such officer or servant. Such other person must then make a report to the valuer which will enable him to make his own report as required by s. 103.

Whoever carries out the valuation or makes the report under s. 103 is entitled, under s. 110, to require any information and explanation which he thinks necessary from the company's officers. Any person who responds by knowingly or recklessly making a statement to him which is misleading, false or deceptive in a material particular is guilty of an offence and liable to penalties.

Lastly, s. 111 requires the company receiving the report to deliver a copy of it to the registrar for registration at the same time that it files its return of allotments for the shares in question (*see* **24**). The registrar must then, under s. 711, publish his receipt of it in the *Gazette*.

19. Contents of valuer's report

Section 108 requires the valuer's report to state:

(a) the nominal value of the shares to be wholly or partly paid for by the consideration in question;

(b) the amount of any premium payable on them;

(c) the description of the consideration and the method and date of valuation;

(d) the extent to which the nominal value of the shares and any premium are to be treated as paid up:

    (*i*) by the consideration;

    (*ii*) in cash.

Where a valuation is made by some person other than the valuer the latter's report, under s. 108, must also state:

(e) the fact that the valuation was made by some other person;

(f) that other person's name and relevant knowledge and experience; *and*

(g) the description of the consideration valued by him and the method and date of valuation.

Finally, s. 108 requires the valuer's report either to contain or to be accompanied by a *note* by him:

(a) that it appeared reasonable to him to arrange for the valuation to be made by another person if in fact it was so made;

(b) that the method of valuation was reasonable;

(c) that it appears to him that there has been no material change in the value of the consideration in question since the valuation; *and*

(d) that on the basis of the valuation the value of the consideration, together with any cash to be paid for the shares, is not less than the amount treated as paid up on the shares allotted.

20. Effect of contravention of ss. 103 and 108

Where a public company allots shares in contravention of s. 103 and *either*:

(a) the allottee has not received a report; *or*
(b) there has been some other contravention of s. 103 or s. 108 which the allottee knew or ought to have known amounted to a contravention;

the allottee becomes liable to pay to the company an amount equal to the nominal value of the shares together with any premium, or such proportion of that amount as is treated as paid up by the consideration, with interest at the appropriate rate.

Section 112 applies the now familiar provision previously encountered in relation to s. 101 and s. 102 (*see* **15** and **16**) to the effect that whenever the allottee becomes liable through a contravention of the section to pay an amount under it in respect of the shares, any subsequent holder also becomes liable, jointly and severally with the allottee, to pay the amount in question unless *either*:

(a) he is a purchaser for value without actual notice of the contravention at the time of the purchase; *or*
(b) he derived title to the shares from a person who acquired them after the contravention and was not himself so liable.

Thus once again a subsequent holder or purchaser is not liable if a previous holder or purchaser was not liable. Further, s. 113 again applies to any person liable under s. 103 (*see* **17**).

21. Cases where valuation of non-cash consideration is not required

Section 103 gives two cases where no valuation is required even though a public company is allotting shares for non-cash consideration. These are:

(a) Where the company makes an *arrangement* for an allotment of its shares on terms that all or part of the consideration for them is to be provided by the transfer to it, or the cancellation, of shares in another company (whether or not shares in that other company are *issued* to it).

For this exception to apply, however, the arrangement must be open to *all* the holders of the shares of the other company in question.
(b) Where the company is making an allotment of its shares in connection with a *merger* between itself and another company.

Both these operations are considered in more detail in Chapter 32.

22. Disclosure in prospectus where issue not fully subscribed

It is necessary also to deal with s. 84 which relates to allotment where an issue has not been fully subscribed.

Section 84 prohibits any allotment of shares in a public company, whether *for cash or otherwise,* unless *either*:

(a) the shares are fully subscribed; *or*
(b) the offer states that, even if the shares are not fully subscribed, those subscribed for will be allotted in any event.

If shares are prohibited from being allotted by that section and 40 days have elapsed after the first issue of the prospectus, all money received from applicants for shares must be repaid to them at once. If it is not repaid within 48 days after the issue of the prospectus, the directors become jointly and severally liable to repay it with interest at 5 per cent from the end of the 48th day, unless they can prove that the default in repayment was not due to their misconduct or negligence.

23. Effect of allotment which is irregular under s. 84

Section 85 deals with the effect of any allotment which is irregular under s. 84.

It provides that such an allotment is *voidable* by the applicant within one month after the date of the allotment even if the company is in liquidation.

It also makes a director who knowingly contravenes s. 84 liable to compensate the company and the allottee for the resulting loss or damage, but stipulates that the action to recover this compensation must be brought within *two years* — an unusual period of limitation, found also, however, in s. 92 in connection with contravention of the rules as to pre-emption rights (*see* **12**).

24. The return of allotments

The final section on allotment to be considered is s. 88, dealing with the return of allotments. This important document must be delivered to the registrar within one month of the allotment whenever any limited company, public or private, allots shares. In the case of a public company, s. 711 then requires the registrar to publish his receipt of the return in the *Gazette.*

Section 88 provides that the company must deliver:

(a) a return of allotments, stating:
    (*i*) the number and nominal amount of the shares allotted;
    (*ii*) the names, addresses and descriptions of the allottees;
    (*iii*) the amount paid and payable on each share; *and*
(b) where shares are allotted as fully or partly paid up *otherwise than in cash*:

(*i*) a written contract constituting the title of the allottee to the shares,

(*ii*) the contract of sale or for services or other consideration for which the allotment was made, *and*

(*iii*) a return stating the number and nominal amount of the shares so allotted, the extent to which they are paid up, and the consideration for which they were allotted.

Where there is no written contract available the company must deliver particulars of it.

Section 88 must be studied and learnt very carefully. It is not difficult to understand, but it is not easy to learn. It will help if it is seen that in *every case* the company will have to deliver the return under **(a)** above, but will only have to deliver the contracts and return under **(b)** where the shares have been paid for *otherwise than in cash*, i.e. with property, goods or services.

Where the company makes a *capitalisation issue* (20:**13**) and issues bonus shares paid up out of undistributed profits or reserves, it is nevertheless necessary not only **(a)** to make a return of allotments, but also **(b)** to file a contract between the company and the members constituting the title of the allottees. This is because bonus shares, though not paid for with property, goods or services, are not paid for in 'cash' within the meaning of the section, for this expression is confined to cases where the member provides the company with further capital.

If the company fails to comply with s. 88, there is a fine on every officer in default, but the *validity of the allotments is not affected*. Thus whether or not they are irregular in any other way, the fact that no return of allotments is made will not render them void.

25. Summary of statutory provisions on allotment

The statutory provisions on allotment are so numerous that it is sometimes helpful to have a summary for easy reference, such as that given on the next page.

PUBLIC AND PRIVATE COMPANIES

SECTION		EFFECT OF CONTRAVENTION
s. 80	Company's authority required for allotment	Penalty on directors: s. 80 Allotment remains VALID: s. 80
ss. 89–96	Pre-emption rights	Company and officers liable to pay compensation: s. 92
s. 88	Return of allotments	Penalty on officers in default: s. 88 Allotment remains VALID

PUBLIC COMPANIES ONLY

SECTION		EFFECT OF CONTRAVENTION
s. 101	25% of nominal value to be paid before allotment	Penalty on company and officers in default: s. 114 Allottee liable to pay amount due: s. 101 Liability extended to all subsequent holders except purchasers for value without notice: s. 112
s. 102	Non-cash consideration to be transferred within 5 years of allotment	Same as for s. 101: ss. 102 and 112 + Relief from liability: s. 113
s. 103	Non-cash consideration to be valued by independent person	Same as for s. 102: ss. 103 and 112 + Relief from liability: s. 113
s.84	Disclosure in prospectus before allotment where issue not fully subscribed	Directors liable to pay compensation: s. 85 Allotment VOIDABLE: s. 85

10

Payment for shares

1. Methods of payment for shares

It is essential to understand at the outset that shares must always be paid for. The company cannot give them to the allottee, for the law always seeks to ensure that the company's actual capital is at least equal to the nominal value of its issued capital.

The basic rule at common law was that as long as the company received some consideration for the shares, it was immaterial whether they were issued for money, i.e. *cash*, or for property, goods or services, i.e. *consideration other than cash*.

This rule was given statutory form by the Companies Act 1980 and is now stated in s. 99 Companies Act 1985, which provides that shares allotted by a company may be paid up in *money or money's worth* (including goodwill and know-how). There are, however, the following limitations on it which are applicable only to *public* companies:

(a) Section 99 prohibits a public company from accepting payment for its shares, whether on account of the nominal value or of premium, by means of an *undertaking to do work or perform services* for the company.

The result of this prohibition is that shares in a public company must necessarily be paid up either in *cash* or in *non-cash assets*.

Section 738 provides that a share shall be taken to have been paid up in *cash* if the consideration is:

    (*i*) cash received by the company; *or*

    (*ii*) a cheque received by the company in good faith which the directors have no reason for suspecting will not be paid; *or*

    (*iii*) the release of a liability of the company for a liquidated sum; *or*

    (*iv*) an undertaking to pay cash to the company at a future date.

Section 739 provides that 'non-cash asset' means *any property or interest in property other than cash*.

Where a company contravenes s. 99 by accepting an undertaking for work or services in payment for its shares, the holder of those shares becomes liable to pay the amount of their nominal value, together with any premium, to the company, with interest at the appropriate rate.

Moreover, s. 112 applies here as it does to contravention of ss. 101–103 (*see* 9:**15–20**), with the result that where a person becomes liable through a contravention of s. 99 to pay an amount in respect of the shares, any subsequent holder also becomes liable, jointly and severally with him, to pay that amount unless either:

> (*i*) he is a purchaser for value without actual notice of the contravention at the time of the purchase; *or*
> (*ii*) he derived title to the shares from a person who acquired them after the contravention and was not himself so liable.

Section 113 again applies to any person liable under s. 99 (*see* 9:**17**).

(b) Section 106 requires shares issued by a public company to a subscriber to the memorandum in pursuance of his undertaking in it, together with any premium, to be paid up in *cash*.

2. The meaning of payment otherwise than in cash

If the allottee is simply buying the shares from the company and paying for them either on application (which is usual) or partly on application and partly when called upon later, no problems arise. The shares are either fully paid or partly paid according to their condition, and the only other relevant matters, namely premiums and discounts, are dealt with in this chapter.

If, however, he is providing the company with property, goods or services, there are two possible situations which should never be confused:

(a) *Where there is no express agreement to pay for the shares otherwise than in cash*:

It sometimes happens that a shareholder provides the company with property, goods or services for which he is owed a sum of money, and that at the same time he has taken shares in the company for which he owes a sum of money.

There are *two separate transactions* here, one under which the company is receiving some benefit for which it has agreed to pay, and another under which the allottee is receiving shares for which he must pay, and concerning which no agreement to pay otherwise than in cash has been made. There are therefore *two debts*, one from the company to the allottee, and another from the allottee to the company.

Clearly, if the two debts are for exactly the same amount of money, it would be unnecessarily complicated for the company to pay the sum owed only to receive it back again. Even if the two debts are not for exactly the same amount, it is still easier for the party who owes the bigger debt to pay the balance due after deducting the amount he is owed than for each party to pay the full amount. Consequently, provided the two debts are presently payable, the law permits them to be set off against each other. But since this arrangement is only a substitute for two cash payments, the shares issued to the allottee are still paid for in *cash*.

> Thus in *Spargo's Case* (1873), S bought shares from the company at the same time as he sold a mine to the company. The two debts were due on the two transactions at the same time, and one was set off against the other as described above. HELD: The shares were paid for in cash.

(b) *Where there is an express agreement to pay for shares otherwise than in cash*:
If in the first place the company agrees to allot shares to a person in return for property, goods or services, the shares are then said to be issued *otherwise than for cash*. There is *only one agreement* here, under which the shares are to be paid for with property, goods or services, and it will require to be registered under s. 88 (*see* 9:**24**).

Moreover, the limitations in respect of public companies mentioned in **1** must be borne in mind.

3. Inadequate consideration in private companies
It is no longer possible for consideration to be inadequate in a public company owing to the rules introduced by the Companies Act 1980. Shares in a public company must be paid for either in cash or in non-cash assets under s. 99, and non-cash assets must be valued by an independent person under s. 103. Neither of these safeguards, however, applies to a private company which may therefore lawfully accept work or services, or non-cash assets without a valuation, in payment for its shares.

In any such arrangement there is always the possibility that the property, goods or services received by the company will be over-valued, so that they will not in fact be equal to the nominal value of the shares issued in exchange. The consideration is real, but inadequate. One might expect this to be unlawful, for it has the effect of an issue of shares at a discount, but this is not the case. The law here preserves the normal contractual rule that each man is free to make a bad bargain. Consideration must be real, but need not be adequate, and as a rule the court will not inquire into the true value of the consideration received by the company in return for the shares issued.

There are, however, three cases where it will do so:

(a) where there is *fraud*;
(b) where it appears *on the face of the agreement* that the consideration is, or may be, inadequate;
(c) where the consideration is in fact entirely *illusory*, i.e. unreal.

> A good example of **(b)** occurred in *Hong Kong and China Gas Co.* v. *Glen* (1914), where the company agreed to allot *one-fifth of all future*

increases of capital fully paid in return for the consideration it had received from the allottee. HELD: The agreement could not be allowed to stand, since in time the number of fully paid shares issued to the allottee might obviously become wholly disproportionate to the consideration provided by him.

4. Issue of shares at a discount

So far we have seen two cases where shares may lawfully be issued at a discount, namely, under s. 97 by way of underwriting commission and, in a private company, where they are issued in exchange for over-valued consideration as described above.

Section 100 prohibits allotment at a discount in all other cases. Where shares are allotted in contravention of s. 100, the allottee remains liable to pay to the company an amount equal to the amount of the discount with interest at the appropriate rate. In such a case, as usual, any subsequent holder also becomes liable, jointly and severally with him, to pay that amount unless *either*:

(a) he is a purchaser for value without actual notice of the contravention at the time of the purchase; *or*
(b) he derived title to the shares from a person who acquired them after the contravention and was not himself so liable: s. 112.

Lastly, it should be noted that s. 100 applies only to shares and not to debentures which, as was pointed out in 8:4, are not part of the share capital and may therefore be issued at a discount whenever required.

5. Issue of shares at a premium

In contrast to an issue at a discount, an issue of shares at a premium, i.e. at a price *above* the par or nominal value, may be made whenever desired. In practice it is usual to issue shares at a premium.

The only statutory requirement here concerns the premium, i.e. the amount in excess of the par value. This must be transferred, under s. 130, to the *share premium account*, whether the company is issuing the shares for cash, or otherwise than for cash, i.e. for property, goods or services which are worth more than the nominal amount of the shares issued in exchange.

In two cases, however, the Act relieves the company from this requirement, namely in mergers and in group reconstructions. These are dealt with in **7** and **8** below.

6. The nature and uses of the share premium account

Section 130 makes it quite clear that the share premium account is to be regarded as *share capital* as far as reduction of capital is concerned, even though it is not, of course, divided up into shares. However, the section allows it to be used for *four specific purposes*:

(a) to pay up bonus shares to be issued as fully paid to members;
(b) to write off the preliminary expenses;
(c) to write off commissions or discounts, or the expenses of any issue of shares or debentures;
(d) to provide the premium payable on the redemption of debentures.

The share premium account is often called a *statutory capital reserve*, since it is regarded as part of the company's capital and its use is strictly controlled by the Act. It must be disclosed in the balance sheet. The provisions of s. 130 are very important, and they will be discussed again later in Chapter 11.

7. Relief from s. 130 for mergers

Section 131 gives relief in the case of a merger from the requirement in s. 130 to form a share premium account whenever shares are issued at a premium. Before looking at the provisions of the section, however, it is helpful to note that it introduces two technical expressions—'equity shares' and 'non-equity shares'. Section 131 defines 'equity shares' as meaning shares which form part of the company's equity share capital, while 'non-equity shares' means those which do not. This time one could almost have guessed as much!

Section 131, dealing with the circumstances in which the section applies, prescribes two conditions:

(a) There must be an arrangement under which one company (the issuing company) is allotting *equity shares* to the shareholders of another company in exchange for the issue or transfer of *equity shares* in that other company to itself, or for the cancellation of *equity shares* in that other company not held by itself.
(b) As a result of the arrangement the issuing company must have obtained at least a 90 per cent equity holding in the other company, although it need not have acquired the entirety of that holding by means of the arrangement. For instance, it might have had a small shareholding in the other company for many years and then decided to increase it.

Shares held by the issuing company's holding company, subsidiary or co-subsidiary in the other company must be regarded as held by the issuing company itself (*see* 13:**13, 14**).

Section 131 then provides that if, in these circumstances, the equity shares in the issuing company are issued at a premium, s. 130 will not apply.

Finally, s. 131 extends the relief to where the arrangement provides *in addition* for the allotment of *any* shares in the issuing company in exchange for the issue, transfer or cancellation of *non-equity shares* in the the other company.

8. Relief from s. 130 for group reconstructions

Section 132 gives relief in the case of a group reconstruction from the requirement in s. 130 to form a share premium account whenever shares are issued at a premium. Like s. 131, it includes two technical expressions which must be considered first—namely, 'the base value of the assets transferred' and 'the minimum premium value'.

'The base value of the assets transferred' is defined as:

(a) the cost of those assets to the company transferring them; *or*
(b) the amount at which those assets are stated in that company's accounting records immediately before the transfer;

whichever is the less.

'The minimum premium value' is defined as the amount, if any, by which the base value of the consideration for the shares allotted exceeds the nominal value of those shares.

Section 132 follows the same pattern as s. 131 and deals with the circumstances in which the section applies. There are, again, two conditions:

(a) The issuing company must be the wholly-owned subsidiary of another company (the holding company) (*see* 13:**13,14**).
(b) The issuing company must be allotting shares to its holding company or to a wholly-owned co-subsidiary in consideration for the transfer to it of assets, other than cash, of any company which is a member of the group of companies comprising the holding company and all its wholly-owned subsidiaries.

Section 132 then provides that if, in these circumstances, the shares in the issuing company are allotted at a premium, the company is not required by s. 130 to transfer any amount in excess of the minimum premium value to the share premium account.

11

Capital

1. The meaning of capital

The word 'capital' is as variable in meaning as the word 'company'. It means different things to different people, and in particular a lawyer will think of it in a different way from an accountant, and both of them will be perplexed by the economist. Since many students learn company law at the same time as accounting and economics, it is no wonder that they sometimes find definition impossible.

Most ordinary people — and lawyers, as far as accounting is concerned, are ordinary people — think of capital as *something the company has got*. It has got the money which it has raised by the issue of shares. It uses this money to buy the things which it needs, such as business premises and stock-in-trade, and these things are then called the *fixed* capital and the *circulating* capital respectively. Always the concept of capital is a *positive* one, based on the notion that what the company has obtained by issuing shares to members it must preserve at all costs.

There is nothing wrong with this idea and the lawyer survives happily until he looks at a company's balance sheet. Here he finds on the left-hand side clearly headed 'Liabilities' not only the share capital of the company, but also the debentures or 'loan capital' and, what is even worse, the trade creditors.

Slowly the truth begins to dawn upon him that the accountant thinks of capital in a *negative* way as *something the company owes*. The share capital is owed to the members, the loan capital is owed to the debenture-holders, and the trade debts are owed to the trade creditors. Almost certainly he will then wish that he knew some accounting principles, but when he asks an accountant for assistance he will probably be told that the idea of capital as a debt of the company flows directly from the law. Did not *Salomon* v. *Salomon & Co.* show that a company is a separate legal person from the members? Why, then, should the money contributed by the members to the company not be regarded as a debt due back to them? What could be more logical? The lawyer will be compelled to agree, but his viewpoint will have been disturbed. The accountant sounds as though he knows what he is talking about, and the lawyer has suddenly seen the picture from a new angle.

NOTE: The only advice which can safely be given to students on this point is to tread warily and always try to find out in what sense the book or the lecturer is using the word 'capital'. Unless the term is defined at the beginning, any subsequent discussion will be both useless and dangerous.

In this chapter it is used in the sense adopted by most legal textbooks and means *share capital*, i.e. the money raised by the issue of shares. Money raised by the issue of *debentures* is simply money which the company has *borrowed* at a fixed rate of interest and *is not capital in this sense*, though the confusing expression 'loan capital' is often used in books on business management and economics to mean money raised in this way.

2. The use of the word

There are many expressions involving the use of the word 'capital'. The *issued capital* of the company, for instance, means as a rule the share capital which has been allotted to members, although 'issue' is also a variable word and is not always used in this sense. The *paid-up capital* means that amount of the issued capital which has been paid up by members, so that if the shares are not fully paid this will leave the *unpaid capital* which is the amount still unpaid on the issued capital and which can be called up at any time that it is required. The issued capital can of course never exceed the *nominal* or *authorised* capital, i.e. the figure given in the capital clause of the memorandum of association, and if it is desired to issue more shares than the number authorised by this clause, then the nominal capital must be increased to cover the required amount. In this chapter the method of doing this and of making other alterations to capital will be discussed.

Section 351 provides that if there is a reference to the company's share capital on its business stationery or order forms, that reference must be to the *paid-up* share capital.

3. Reserve capital

Lastly, there is the *reserve capital*. This must never be confused with a *capital reserve*, which is entirely different. *Reserve capital can only be created under s. 120*, and if one turns to s. 120 the expression is clearly explained. Note that the margin of the Act refers to the reserve *liability*, while the section itself states how this reserve capital or liability is created. It provides that a company may determine by special resolution that its uncalled capital (i.e. the amount of the issued capital which is still unpaid and which has not yet been called up by the directors) may not be called up except on liquidation.

Once the company has created reserve capital in this way, it cannot charge it as it can the uncalled capital. (It will be seen later that a charge on uncalled capital is one of the types of registrable charge mentioned in s. 396: 21:22.) The reserve capital is not under the directors' control, and once the special resolution creating it has been passed, it cannot be revoked except under a scheme of arrangement with the consent of the court, for to do so would be a threat to the position of creditors who are relying on the existence of this fund of money. Reserve capital can, however, like all share capital, be reduced under s. 135 with the consent of the court.

Since it is possible to charge the uncalled capital, a difficult situation can arise if the company converts into reserve capital uncalled capital which has already been charged. In this case it would be injurious to the secured creditor with a charge on the uncalled capital if his charge could be destroyed by the simple expedient of converting the uncalled capital into reserve capital. The position here, therefore, is probably that the charge remains outstanding, although any further charges on what is now reserve capital are not permissible.

4. Provisions and reserves

As stated above, it is essential that the *reserve capital* should not be confused with a *capital reserve*. The meaning of the latter, however, becomes clear only if the term 'provision' is fully understood.

A provision is defined in para. 89 of Schedule 4 to the Act (*see* 18:**2, 11**) as 'any amount retained as reasonably necessary for the purpose of providing for any liability or loss which is either likely to be incurred, or certain to be incurred but uncertain as to amount or as to the date on which it will arise'.

Thus if a company owes *a precise sum of money* to a creditor, this is a *liability*, for the company knows that it owes a debt and it knows the exact amount of it. If it sets aside a sum of money to meet a debt which is merely *likely* to be incurred, or *uncertain* in amount or date, this is a *provision*. If it sets aside a sum of money simply out of prudence and not because it has a known or possible debt in mind, then this is a *reserve*. If this reserve is regarded as *free for distribution* to the members, it is a *revenue reserve*, and if not, it is a *capital reserve*.

5. Types of capital reserve

It is clear that a revenue reserve is profit retained in the business, but which is distributable to the members when desired. It is also clear that a *capital* reserve is a fund which is not regarded as distributable in this way. But in fact there are two types of capital reserve:

(a) Those the use of which is strictly controlled by the Act, which impliedly makes them non-distributable by stating the only purposes for which they may be used.

These are:
    (*i*) the share premium account: s. 130; *and*
    (*ii*) the capital redemption reserve: s. 170.

They are often termed the *statutory* capital reserves, since the Act controls both their creation and their use.

(b) Those the use of which is not controlled by the Act, and which are therefore often termed the *non statutory* capital reserves. Their only char acteristic is that they are *not regarded as free for distribution* to the members, but since they are not controlled by the Act in any way, they can in theory become regarded as free for distribution if desired and transferred to revenue reserve. This might be imprudent, but it would not be unlawful.

Non-statutory capital reserves can arise in several ways, e.g. where a fund is set aside out of profits to replace assets which are wearing out, such as heavy machinery. A well-managed company is one in which the directors plan for the future, and it would be imprudent not to provide for such demands on the company's resources.

> NOTE: In Chapter 20 we shall see that, provided the rules on dividends are observed, there is no *legal* bar to distribution of such funds to the members, though in most cases good management requires their retention in the company's hands. Accountants as a body tend to regard all capital reserves as non-distributable, and view the legal position with gloomy mistrust, but this is due to the belief characteristic of the members of that profession that caution is the greatest of all virtues.

6. Reserve fund
Students may be required to distinguish capital reserves from reserve capital, or be asked for examples of capital reserves, or for the meaning of the capital redemption reserve which will be explained later in this chapter. But the simple expression 'reserve fund' is normally used to mean a sum of money which the company has invested in a readily realisable asset so that it can be made available quickly when needed. It has no technical legal significance.

7. Types of share capital
The shares in any company may be all exactly alike, i.e. they may all carry the same rights to attend and vote at company meetings and to dividends. But often they are of different types with varying rights: in this case the company is said to have different *classes* of shares, and the rights attached to the different classes are called *class rights*. The class rights normally relate to voting, dividends or the return of capital in liquidation, and they will be set out either in the memorandum or articles of association of the company or in the terms of issue of the shares concerned. For a commentary on the different categories of class rights see Scott J. in *Cumbrian Newspapers Group Ltd* v. *Cumberland & Westmorland Herald Newspaper & Printing Co. Ltd* (1987) [B96].

Section 128 provides that any company allotting shares with rights which are *not* stated in the memorandum, the articles, or a resolution required to be filed with the registrar under s. 380 (*see* 15:**34**), and which are not uniform with shares previously allotted, must deliver to the registrar, within one month from the allotment, a statement containing particulars of those rights.

Similarly, where rights attached to shares are varied (*see* **13**), or a class of shares is given a name or other designation, *otherwise* than by an amendment of the memorandum or articles or a resolution required to be filed with the registrar under s. 380, a statement containing particulars of the variation, name or designation must be delivered to the registrar within one month.

These provisions ensure that in all cases, including that where the rights attached to shares are contained in or varied by an *ordinary* resolution, full details of the company's share capital reach the registrar who is then required, under s. 711, to publish his receipt of the statement in the *Gazette*.

There are the following types of share in existence:

(a) preference shares;
(b) ordinary shares;
(c) deferred shares.

8. Preference shares

The characteristic of the preference share is that it has a *preferred fixed dividend*, i.e. that the dividend payable on it is fixed at a certain figure, e.g. 7 per cent, and that this dividend must be paid *before* the ordinary shareholders receive anything.

It follows that preference shares are a safe, though far from stimulating, investment, and that when economic conditions are unstable they will be more in demand than when there is a period of prosperous growth or of inflation. On the other hand, nothing is more distressing than to own preference shares in a well-managed company which is making large profits. While the bulk of these profits will be distributed to the ordinary shareholders, whose shares will consequently rise on the market, the preference shareholder will continue to receive his modest fixed percentage. There are thus far more fluctuations in the market value of ordinary shares than of preference shares, providing more excitement to compensate for the greater risk.

Preference shares can be either:

(a) *Cumulative*, i.e. if the company is unable to pay a dividend in any particular year, it must *accumulate* the arrears of dividend on the preference shares from year to year until they are all paid, before the ordinary shareholders can receive any of the profits; *or*

(b) *non-cumulative*, i.e. if the company is unable to pay a dividend in any particular year, the preference shareholder will never receive any dividend for that year.

> NOTE: They are always *presumed to be cumulative* unless expressly described as non-cumulative.

Preference shares sometimes carry voting rights, but often carry different ones from those of the ordinary shares, or none at all.

Sometimes a company issues *participating* preference shares. These are preference shares which receive their fixed dividend, e.g. 6 per cent, in the normal way, but which then *participate further* in the distributed profits along with the ordinary shares after a certain fixed percentage has been paid on them as well. Note that a participating preference share will be part of the equity share capital unless it participates in profits only up to a further fixed percentage and there is also some restriction on its right to participate in surplus assets in a liquidation.

9. The rights attached to preference shares in a liquidation

In 1:**18** the order of distribution of assets in a liquidation was given. There it was seen that preference shares do not, contrary to popular belief, carry any priority to return of capital in a liquidation unless the memorandum or articles or the terms of issue confer it on them. Such a provision is, however, a common one and where it is made the preference shares *will not have any implied right to participate in the distribution of the surplus assets*. The right to receive the capital back in priority to the ordinary shareholders is said to be *exhaustive*, i.e. it implies that there is no right to receive anything more, and therefore if in such a case it is desired that the preference shares should also participate in the surplus assets, this right must be *expressly* given to them: *Scottish Insurance Corporation* v. *Wilsons and Clyde Coal Co.* (1949).

Difficulty sometimes arises over the payment of *arrears of dividend* on cumulative preference shares in a liquidation. Clearly, any dividend which has been declared must be paid, for it is a debt. But arrears of dividend, i.e. dividends which have *not* been declared, are not payable in a liquidation *unless the articles so provide*, for they do not constitute a debt. Moreover, the articles must provide for the payment of *arrears*. If they merely provide for payment of *arrears due*, the arrears of dividend will again not be payable unless they have been declared, since a dividend is not 'due' until it has been declared.

10. Ordinary shares

Ordinary shares normally carry the residue of distributed profits after the preference shares, if any, have received their fixed dividend. If the preference shareholders have priority as to return of capital in liquidation, the ordinary shares will then be entitled to all the surplus assets unless there are also deferred shares. Thus as a rule the ordinary shares are the *equity share capital* of the company.

(a) *Voting rights*: While preference shares often carry no voting rights, ordinary shares usually give the holder the right to vote; but this is not invariably the case. In some companies both voting and non-voting ordinary shares are issued, and this practice has been much criticised on several grounds. In principle, it is often thought to be wrong to divorce ownership from control so that those who may have invested the largest amount of money in the company may have no voice whatsoever in its management. Moreover, investors may not realise that their shares give them no voting rights until after they have bought them.

(b) *Control*: It is, however, always possible to keep control in the hands of a minority by the device of *weighted voting rights*, without issuing any non-voting shares, and it is sometimes desirable to be able to raise more capital without losing control.

11. Deferred shares

Deferred shares are not at all common. They usually give the holders the right to the residue of distributed profits after a certain fixed dividend has been paid on the ordinary shares. It follows that in such a case the deferred shares, not the ordinary shares, will constitute the equity share capital of the company.

Deferred shares may carry heavy voting rights as compared with the other shares in the company and may participate to a high degree in the surplus assets on the company's liquidation. For all these reasons they are normally issued to the promoters of the company, when they may be termed *founders' shares*, or to the directors, when they may be termed *management shares*.

12. No par value shares

So far all the types of share which we have considered have had a *par* or *nominal value*. This is because, as was explained in 2:**34**, shares with no par value cannot be issued in this country, though they exist in certain other countries, notably in the United States.

The rule that shares must have a par value is frequently criticised on two main grounds:

(a) The present form of balance sheet is linked to the figure of the nominal capital. This figure is almost certain to become entirely unrealistic in the course of time, for as the company's business expands and becomes more profitable, the market value of the shares will rise, bearing little or no relation to the original par value.

(b) Dividends are often declared in the form of a percentage of the nominal value. Thus a dividend of 25 per cent on shares with a par value of £1 but a market value of £5 gives the investor a yield of 5 per cent on his money, and although this is in fact a reasonable figure, it may not appear so to those who do not understand it.

13. Variation of rights

We have already seen in **7** that sometimes all the shares in a company are exactly alike, and sometimes they are divided up into different classes. We also saw that the rights attached to the shares are normally to be found in the memorandum, articles or terms of issue. These rights are described as 'class rights' only where there are different classes of shares in existence, in which case s. 128 ensures that the registrar receives particulars of them if they are not contained in a document already in his possession (*see* **7**). It is now necessary to consider how these rights can be altered and for this purpose to study each of the two possible situations separately.

Where all the shares in a company are *exactly alike*, the rights—which will not, of course, be class rights—may be specified either in the articles or in the memorandum. If specified in the articles, they may be altered in the same way as any other clause in the articles, i.e. by special resolution. If specified in the memorandum, however, the clause will be covered by s. 17.

This section, as we saw in **2:35**, covers with certain exceptions all the clauses in the memorandum other than the compulsory ones, and states that anything in the memorandum which could lawfully have been inserted in the articles instead can be altered by special resolution with the same provision for dissentients as is given by s. 5 for alterations of the objects clause.

Section 17, however, does not apply if the memorandum itself *stipulates a method* of altering the particular clause, in which case that method must be used. Nor does it apply if the memorandum *prohibits* alteration of the clause, in which case application must be made to the court under s. 425.

14. Variation of class rights

It must first be understood that s. 17 has no application here, for it expressly states that it does not apply to a variation of class rights (*see* **2:35**).

Such a variation is governed by s. 125 which lays down detailed rules. In an attempt to make these rules somewhat easier to learn, an initial distinction has to be drawn between those which apply where no provision for variation is contained in either the memorandum or the articles, and those which apply where such a provision exists.

(a) *Where there is no provision for variation in either the memorandum or the articles:*

    (*i*) Where the class rights are *specified in the memorandum*, any variation requires the consent of *all the members* of the company.

    (*ii*) Where the class rights are *specified elsewhere* (i.e. in the articles or terms of issue), any variation requires either the written consent of the *holders of three-quarters of the issued shares of that class*, or the sanction of an *extraordinary resolution* passed at a class meeting.

In addition, any other existing requirements for variation must also be observed, and s. 127, considered below, operates here to protect dissentients.

(b) *Where there is provision for variation in either the memorandum or the articles:*

    (*i*) Regardless of whether the class rights are specified in the memorandum or elsewhere, where the variation is connected with *either* the giving, variation, revocation or renewal of *the company's authority to the directors to allot shares* under s. 80, *or a reduction of capital* under s. 135, the rules for variation are *exactly the same as in* **(a)**(*ii*) above: s. 125.

    (*ii*) Where the class rights are *specified in the memorandum* and the articles contain a provision for variation which was included at the time of the company's incorporation, a variation may be made only in accordance with that provision (unless it falls under (*i*) above).

    (*iii*) Where the class rights are *specified elsewhere* and the articles contain a provision for variation, whenever it was first included, a variation may be made only in accordance with that provision (unless it falls under (*i*) above).

In *all three* of these cases s. 127 operates to protect dissentients. Thus the only time when s. 127 does *not* operate is in **(a)**(*i*) where no dissentients exist.

15. Protection of dissentients on variation of class rights

It will be clear from the wording of s. 127 that wherever there are class rights attached to shares in a company and *either the memorandum or the articles prescribe a method of variation* of those rights, the section operates to protect dissentients.

Section 127 also operates in one case where a method of variation is *not so* prescribed—namely, where the class rights are specified elsewhere than in the memorandum (*see* **14(a)**(*ii*)).

Section 127 allows the holders of 15 per cent of the shares of the class in question, who did not consent to the variation, to apply to the court within 21 days to have it cancelled. The court may then either cancel or confirm it.

Note that the required percentage of shareholdings by the applicants and the period for making the application are the same as under s. 5 regarding alterations of the objects clause and s. 17 regarding alterations of the non-compulsory clauses in the memorandum (i.e. 15 per cent and 21 days).

16. Further provisions on variation of class rights

Three further points are of importance when considering this topic:

(a) Section 125 provides that any *alteration* of a provision in the articles prescribing a method of variation of class rights, or the *insertion* of such a provision into the articles, is itself to be treated as a variation of those rights.

This brings into operation all the safeguards described above.

(b) Section 125 also provides that class meetings connected with a variation of class rights are governed by the normal rules relating to general meetings found in the Act, but lays down two special rules:

(*i*) The *quorum* at such a meeting, except an adjourned meeting, is at least two persons holding, or representing by proxy, one-third of the issued shares of the class in question; the quorum at an adjourned meeting is one person holding shares of the class in question, or his proxy.

(*ii*) Any holder of shares of the class in question present in person or by proxy may *demand a poll*.

(c) The Schedule to the Companies (Tables A–F) Regulations 1985 (SI 1985, No. 805) contains no provision for variation of class rights but the articles of many existing companies include such a provision since Table A in Schedule 1 to the Companies Act 1948 did so. Article 4 of that Table A provided that class rights might be varied with the written consent of the holders of three-quarters of the issued shares of that class, or the sanction of an extraordinary resolution passed at a class meeting.

Note that that article corresponded exactly with the requirements of s. 125: (*see* **14(a)**(*ii*)).

17. The meaning of variation

It is clear that if there are several classes of shares in a company, and the rights of one class are altered without the rights of the other class or classes being changed in any way, it is possible to change the *control* of the company. The voting rights attached to particular shares can be made quite ineffective by the giving of increased voting rights to another class, or by the issue of further shares of the same class.

In this context, however, the word 'variation' has a much more restricted meaning. It only covers *direct alterations*, i.e. if the rights attached to a particular class of shares are altered then that is a variation of rights, but the fact that the effect of the alteration is to remove control from another class of shareholders is immaterial, for this would merely be a consequential alteration. Of course the practical effect is to alter their rights, but this is not the meaning given by the law to the word 'variation'.

Section 125 provides, however, that in s. 125 and in any provision for variation of class rights contained in a company's memorandum or articles the word 'variation' includes *abrogation*. Similarly, s. 127 provides that 'variation' in s. 127 includes *abrogation*. However, satisfaction or fulfillment of a right, as by paying off the whole preference share capital, is not abrogation: *House of Fraser plc* v. *A.C.G.E. Investments Ltd* (1987) [B95].

> NOTE: A minority which can show that its interests are being *unfairly prejudiced* has, as will be seen later, a remedy under ss. 459–461. Furthermore, in *Clemens* v. *Clemens Bros Ltd* (1976), resolutions to increase the capital and issue the new shares in such a way as to deprive the plaintiff of her 'negative control' (i.e. diluting her voting power from 45 per cent to 24.6575 per cent) were set aside as having been passed by an inequitable use of the defendant's voting rights.

18. Alteration of capital

In Chapter 2 we considered the method of alteration of all the compulsory clauses in the memorandum except the capital clause. It must now be seen in what way this can be altered to suit the company's requirements.

Section 121 provides that a company may alter the capital clause of the memorandum, i.e. its nominal capital, in the following ways:

(a) It may increase the nominal capital by creating new shares.

(b) It may consolidate its existing shares into larger shares, e.g. by consolidating five 5p shares into one 25p share.

(c) It may subdivide its existing shares into smaller shares, but it must keep the proportion paid and unpaid on each share the same. (Shares are sometimes subdivided to make them more marketable, for investors tend to prefer a large number of 'cheap' shares to a few 'expensive' ones, ignoring the fact that the yield on their investment will be the same whatever the nominal value of the shares.)

(d) It may convert fully paid up shares into stock, or vice versa.

(e) It may cancel shares which have not been taken up, and diminish the amount of the nominal capital, by the number cancelled. (This is *not* a reduction of capital, for these shares have never been allotted to anyone. Section 121 makes this quite clear.)

In order to alter its capital clause in any of these ways, the company requires authority in its articles, but if the articles give no power to this effect it can be inserted. Since this involves altering the articles, a special resolution is required, and the same resolution may also be used to make the alteration of capital.

If, however, the articles already contain power to alter the capital an ordinary resolution will suffice to make the alteration, since s. 121 does not require a special one. The articles can, of course, prescribe a special resolution for this purpose, but Table A does not do so.

Section 123 provides that notice of any increase in the capital must be given to the registrar within 15 days.

Section 122 provides that notice of all alterations other than increases, including the redemption of redeemable shares under ss. 159–161 (*see* **24** below), must be given to the registrar within one month.

19. Stock

We have just seen that s. 121 allows the company to convert its fully paid up shares into stock, and it is therefore important to understand the nature of stock and any advantages which it may have.

Section 744, in defining a share, provides that 'share includes stock'. The *relationship* of a shareholder to the company is in no way altered if his shares are converted into stock and he becomes a stockholder. Section 370 covers the case where the articles make no provision for the voting rights attached to the stock, by providing that the member shall have one vote for each £10 of stock.

The provisions of s. 121, however, must be carefully observed. It only authorises the conversion of shares into stock if the shares are fully paid. Moreover, it expressly states that shares may be *converted* into stock, and from this it follows that a *direct issue* of stock is not lawful. An issue of *partly paid* stock or of *bonus* stock is therefore *ultra vires* and void, and in theory the same result should ensue from a direct issue of *fully paid* stock. In *Re Home and Foreign Investment Co.* (1912), however, it was held that a direct issue of *fully paid* stock could be validated by *lapse of time*.

Once shares are converted into stock, the stockholder owns, say, £100 of stock where formerly he held 100 £1 shares. Thus though his *relationship* with the company remains the same, his *interest* in it is described in a different manner. It is no longer divided up into shares with a nominal value. This raises the question of its divisibility and brings us to consideration of its *advantages:*

(a) In legal theory *stock is divisible into any amount required*. Thus it is possible to transfer £4.32 worth of stock, while it is never possible to transfer a fraction of a share.

In practice, however, this advantage seldom exists, since the articles usually prescribe the minimum amount of stock transferable.

(b) *Since stock is not divided up into units, it cannot be numbered.* Shares, on the other hand, must have a number and this causes a certain amount of administrative work. But this advantage of stock is offset to a certain extent by s. 182, which, while requiring shares to be numbered, makes an exception for fully paid shares ranking *pari passu* for all purposes.

20. Serious loss of capital by public company

Section 142 applies whenever the net assets of a public company fall to *half or less* of its called-up share capital.

In such a case the section requires the directors, not later than 28 days from the day on which that fact first becomes known to a director, to convene an extraordinary general meeting for a date not less than 56 days from that day.

The purpose of the meeting is to consider whether any, and if so what, steps should be taken to deal with the situation. It is likely that this will lead, in many cases, to a reduction of capital, the procedure for which is described below.

21. Reduction of capital

A reduction of capital is, of course, an *alteration* of capital, but is an alteration of such importance and of such potential danger to creditors that it is strictly controlled by the Act in s. 135, the requirements of which are far more stringent than those of s. 121 for other types of alteration.

Section 135 provides that with authority in its articles and the sanction of the court a company may by special resolution reduce its share capital in any way and make the necessary alteration to its memorandum. In particular, it may:

(a) extinguish or reduce the liability on unpaid share capital; *or*

(b) cancel paid-up capital which has been lost or is unrepresented by available assets; *or*

(c) pay off any paid-up share capital which is in excess of the company's wants.

NOTES: **(1)** *The section naturally applies to stock as well as shares*, except that there can be no liability on stock to be extinguished or reduced since, as we have seen, it must always be fully paid. Reserve capital too, it will be remembered, can be reduced under this section, although **(b)** and **(c)** would be inapplicable to it since they can apply only to paid-up capital.

(2) *If the articles do not give the necessary authority*, it is not possible here, as it was under s. 121, to insert the authority and alter the capital in a single resolution. Here a special resolution must first be passed to alter the articles, and then a second special resolution to reduce the capital, though both can be passed at the same meeting.

(3) Where the ground of reduction is that the capital has been lost, the loss must be a permanent loss so far as is at the time foreseeable and not merely a temporary fall in the value of some capital asset: *Re Jupiter House Investments (Cambridge) Ltd* (1985). However, the court may confirm a reduction where the loss is not shown to be permanent if the company gives an undertaking to safeguard creditors' interests: *Re Grosvenor Press plc* (1985).

(4) *When capital is to be returned to the shareholders*, as under (c), it is not simply handed back to them in proportion to their holdings. Their *class rights* will be considered, the court treating the reduction *as though it were a liquidation*. If, therefore, a certain class of shareholders would have priority to return of capital in liquidation, that class will also be the first to have the share capital returned to them in a reduction, and this is so even if they would prefer to remain members of the company: *Prudential Assurance Co. Ltd* v. *Chatterley-Whitfield Collieries Ltd* (1949).

22. Creditors' right to object to a reduction.
Section 136 gives the creditors of the company a right to object to the reduction in any case where their interests are threatened, i.e. where the liability on unpaid share capital is extinguished, or reduced, or where paid-up capital is returned to the shareholders. They can object in other cases if the court so directs.

The court settles the list of creditors entitled to object, as far as possible without requiring applications from creditors, and may publish notices fixing a day by which creditors not on the list must claim to be entered on it, or lose their right of objection.

If a creditor on the list does not consent to the reduction, the court may dispense with his consent if the company secures payment of his debt by appropriating to it, where it admits the debt, the full amount, and where it does not admit it, the amount fixed by the court.

Where a company owns leasehold properties, a list of landlords as creditors is not required if a sum sufficient to pay the rent is set aside or guaranteed. Ten years' rent will suffice for the court to dispense with the list, provided the leases are not onerous: *Re Lucania Temperance Billiard Halls (London)* (1966).

23. Confirmation and registration of reduction
Section 137 provides that if the court is satisfied either that the creditors entitled to object have consented to the reduction, or that their debts have been paid or secured, it may confirm the reduction. It may also direct that the words 'and reduced' be added to the company's name for a specified period, and that the company must publish the reasons for the reduction.

Section 138 provides that when the court order confirming the reduction is produced to the registrar, and a copy of it together with a minute giving the details of the company's share capital are delivered to him, he must register the order and the minute.

The minute specifies:

(a) the amount of the share capital;
(b) the number of shares into which it is to be divided;
(c) the amount of each share; *and*
(d) the amount paid up on each share.

The reduction takes effect on registration. The registrar must give a certificate of the registration of the order and minute, and this certificate is conclusive evidence both that the requirements of the Act have been complied with, and that the share capital is now as set out in the minute. The registered minute is deemed to be substituted for the corresponding part of the memorandum.

Section 139 contains special rules to apply where the court order confirming the reduction of the capital of a *public* company brings the nominal value of the company's allotted share capital *below the authorised minimum*. It prohibits the registrar from registering the order under s. 138 unless the court directs otherwise or the company is first *re-registered as a private company*.

The court, in these circumstances, may authorise the company to be re-registered as a private company under s. 53 (*see* 25:4) without its having passed the special resolution normally required for that operation. In these circumstances the court must then specify in its order the alterations to be made to the company's memorandum and articles connected with its re-registration.

24. Redeemable shares

In the normal way shares are not redeemable except on a reduction of capital effected with the consent of the court under s. 135, for if the company could give the members their money back at any time that it wished, the creditors could never rely on its having any money at all. For the same reason it is unlawful for a company to *convert* any of its share capital into redeemable shares and then redeem them.

Section 159, however, permits a company to issue shares which are redeemable at the option of either the company or the shareholder on compliance with the following conditions set out in ss. 159, 159A (inserted by s. 133 Companies Act 1989), 160 (as amended by s. 133 Companies Act 1989) and 170:

(a) There must be authority in the articles to make the issue: s. 159.
(b) There must be some non-redeemable issued shares in the company at the time: s. 159.

(c) The redeemable shares may be redeemable only if they are fully paid, and the terms of redemption must provide for payment on redemption: s. 159.

(d) The articles must specify the terms and conditions of redemption (date, other circumstances, amount payable, etc.): s. 159A

(e) The redeemable shares may be redeemed only out of distributable profits (*see* s. 181 and 20:**5–7**) or out of the proceeds of a fresh issue of shares made for the purpose: s. 160. This does not apply to private companies (*see* **33**).

(f) Any premium payable on redemption must be paid out of distributable profits: s. 160.

(g) Despite the rule in **(f)**, where the redeemable shares were *issued at a premium*, any premium payable on redemption may be paid out of the proceeds of a fresh issue of shares made for the purpose of the redemption, up to an amount equal to:

> (*i*) the aggregate premiums received by the company on the issue of the redeemable shares, *or*
>
> (*ii*) the current amount of the company's share premium account, including any sum transferred to that account in respect of premiums on the new shares,

whichever is the less: s. 160.

The company's share premium account must in either case then be reduced by the amount of the payment made out of the proceeds of the new issue.

(h) The shares redeemed must be treated as cancelled on redemption and the company's issued share capital is to be diminished by the amount of their nominal value. The company's authorised share capital, however, is not affected by the redemption: s. 160.

(i) Where a company is about to redeem shares it may issue new shares up to the nominal amount of the shares to be redeemed as if the latter had never been issued: s. 160.

(j) Where shares are redeemed out of profits a sum equal to the nominal amount of the shares redeemed must be transferred to the *capital redemption reserve*: s. 170.

> The capital redemption reserve, as explained in **5**, is a *statutory capital reserve* and s. 170 expressly states that it is to be treated as *share capital* for reduction proposes, although it may be used for paying up *bonus shares*.

Note how these rules maintain the capital of the company. If the redeemable shares are redeemed out of the proceeds of a fresh issue of shares, then the share capital is automatically replaced and no capital redemption reserve is required. If, however, they are redeemed out of distributable profits, then no shares are issued to replace them and a capital reserve must be formed in order to keep the total capital of the company constant. This capital reserve may be used for paying up bonus shares, but this merely converts it into share capital as opposed to a capital fund which is not divided into shares. The non-distributable funds are preserved throughout, for the total capital of the company does not alter (*see* 13:**20**).

Finally, s. 122 provides that notice of the redemption must be given to the registrar within one month. The registrar must then, under s. 711, publish his receipt of the notice in the *Gazette*.

25. Purchase by company of its own shares

It will be clear both from this chapter and from Chapter 13 that the preservation of a company's share capital is of fundamental importance. Not only the common law but also successive Companies Acts have developed this principle until it has now reached a highly sophisticated stage. It is all the more surprising, therefore, that the Companies Act 1985, in provisions derived from the Companies Act 1981, should appear to attack it by permitting companies to buy their own shares.

The attack is, however, more apparent than real, for when a company, in accordance with the Act, buys its own shares, all the safeguards which apply to the redemption of redeemable shares (*see* **24**) apply again. Private companies are permitted to buy their own shares out of capital, but only on certain conditions and with further safeguards. Moreover, even if the introduction of these rules is seen as a threat to the sanctity of share capital, there are a number of good reasons why it is justified. Thus a shareholder in a private company who wishes to sell his shares but cannot find a purchaser is now able to sell them to the company. An employee who has participated in an employees' share scheme can now sell his shares to the company if he ceases to be employed by it. A company which has issued redeemable shares can buy them back from the holder before the redemption date if the price is low, thus saving itself money—a practice which has always been possible in the case of debentures (*see* 21:**14**). There are many other ways in which the power of a company to buy its own shares may prove commercially useful without being dangerous.

The basic rule, which is of general application and therefore applies to every purchase by a company of its own shares, is found in s. 162. This permits a company to buy its own shares, including any redeemable shares (*see* **24**), if it is authorised to do so by its articles, *unless* as a result of the purchase there would no longer be any members of the company holding non-redeemable shares.

Where a company buys its own shares under s. 162, the provisions of both ss. 159–161 and s. 170 apply in exactly the same way as in the case of the redemption of redeemable shares (*see* **24**). This ensures the replacement of the share capital purchased by the company with either a fresh issue of shares or a capital redemption reserve.

26. Off-market purchase by company of its own shares

Although the general rule is given by s. 162, later sections contain additional rules which apply to particular situations and accordingly vary with the circumstances of the purchase. The first of these is in ss. 163 and 164, governing off-market purchases.

Under s. 163 an off-market purchase by a company of its own shares occurs if *either*:

(a) the shares are purchased otherwise than on a recognised investment exchange; *or*
(b) they are purchased on a recognised investment exchange but are not subject to a marketing arrangement on it.

> Such an arrangement exists if either the shares are listed under Part IV of the Financial Services Act 1986 or the company has been given facilities for them to be dealt in on that investment exchange without prior permission for individual transactions.

Section 164 permits a company to make an off-market purchase of its own shares only in pursuance of *a contract approved in advance* in accordance with the section or under s. 165 (*see* **27**). The rules prescribed by s. 164 are as follows:

(a) Before the company enters into the contract of purchase, its terms must be authorised by special resolution.
(b) The authority conferred by the special resolution may be varied, revoked or renewed by special resolution.
(c) In a *public* company the authority conferred by the special resolution must specify its date of expiry which may not be later than 18 months after the date on which the resolution is passed.
(d) No special resolution will be effective if any member who holds shares to which it relates exercises the voting rights attached to them and the resolution would not have been passed if he had not done so.
(e) No special resolution will be effective unless a copy of the contract of purchase or, if it is not in writing, a written memorandum of its terms, is available for inspection by members both:
   (*i*) at the registered office for at least 15 days ending with the date of the meeting at which the resolution is passed; *and*
   (*ii*) at the meeting itself.

> Any such memorandum must include the names of the members who hold the shares in question, while any copy of the contract must include them either in the contract itself or in an annexed memorandum.

27. Contingent purchase contracts

A similar set of additional rules are stated in s. 165 and apply to contingent purchase contracts.

Under s. 165 a contingent purchase contract is one which does not amount to a contract by the company to purchase its own shares, but under which it may, on some condition, become entitled or bound to purchase them.

In this case too such a purchase may be made only *if the contract is approved in advance*, and all the rules in s. 164 given in **26(a)–(e)** above apply again in exactly the same way.

28. Market purchase by company of its own shares

The third and last set of additional rules is found in s. 166 and governs market purchases. By s. 163 a market purchase is one made on a recognised investment exchange of shares which are either *listed* under Part IV of the Financial Services Act 1986 or in respect of which the company has been given *facilities for them to be dealt in* on that investment exchange without prior permission for individual transactions.

Section 166 prescribes the following rules for a market purchase by a company of its own shares:

(a) The purchase must first be authorised by a resolution of the company.

(b) The authority conferred by the resolution may be either conditional or unconditional and either general or limited to a particular class or type of share.

(c) The authority must:

(*i*) specify the maximum number of shares which may be acquired;

(*ii*) state the maximum and minimum price which may be paid for them; *and*

(*iii*) specify its date of expiry which may not be later than 18 months after the date on which the resolution is passed.

(d) The authority may be varied, revoked or renewed by resolution of the company.

(e) Any resolution must be filed under s. 380 (*see* 15:**34**).

This provision is necessary because the resolution is an *ordinary* one and there would not otherwise be any requirement to file it.

29. Assignment or release of company's right to purchase its own shares.

Section 167 provides that a company's rights under any contract approved under s. 164 or s. 165 (*see* **26, 27**) or authorised under s. 166 (*see* **28**) cannot be *assigned*.

Further, s. 167 provides that any agreement by a company to *release* its rights under a contract approved under s. 164 or s. 165 is *void* unless the release is approved in advance in accordance with the following rules:

(a) Before the company enters into the release agreement its terms must be authorised by special resolution.

(b) All the rules in s. 164 given in **26(a)–(e)** above apply again in exactly the same way.

30. Payments by company other than purchase price.
Section 168 applies where a company makes any payment in consideration of:

(a) *acquiring* a right under a contingent purchase contract;

(b) the *variation* of a contract for an off-market purchase or a contingent purchase contract; *or*

(c) the *release* of any of its obligations under a contract for an off-market purchase, a contingent purchase contract, or a contract for a market purchase.

In all three cases s. 168 requires the payment to be made out of the company's *distributable profits*.

If the company fails to comply with this rule any purchase of shares falling under **(a)** or **(b)** above will be unlawful and any release falling under **(c)** will be *void*.

31. Disclosure of purchases and authorised contracts
Section 169 requires a company to file with the registrar, within 28 days from the date on which any shares purchased were delivered to the company, a *return* stating:

(a) the number and nominal value of the shares purchased; *and*

(b) the date on which they were delivered to the company.

In the case of a *public* company, s. 169 requires the return to state also:

(a) the total amount paid by the company for the shares; *and*

(b) the maximum and minimum prices paid for the shares of each class purchased.

A company must keep for 10 years at its registered office:

(a) a copy of any contract approved under s. 164 or s. 165 or authorised under s. 166, if in writing, *or*

(b) if not in writing, a memorandum of its terms.

Every copy and memorandum must be open to inspection to any member of the company and, in the case of a public company, to the public. If inspection is refused, the court may order that it be allowed.

32. Effect of company's failure to redeem or purchase its own shares

Section 178 provides that where a company issues redeemable shares or agrees to purchase any of its own shares, it will not be liable in damages for failing to redeem or purchase them, as the case may be.

Any other rights which the shareholder may have are expressly preserved by the section, although his position is further weakened by the provision in s. 178 which prevents the court from granting an order for specific performance of the redemption or purchase terms if the company shows that it is unable to meet the cost of the redemption or purchase out of distributable profits.

33. Power of private company to redeem or purchase its own shares out of capital.

The rules contained in the Act as to the issue of redeemable shares and purchase by a company of its own shares are considerably less stringent in the case of private companies. Section 171 permits a private company, with authority in its articles, to make a payment in respect of a redemption of its shares under s. 160 (*see* **24**) or a purchase of its shares under s. 162 (*see* **25**) *otherwise* than out of its distributable profits or the proceeds of a fresh issue, i.e. the payment may be made out of *capital*.

The amount payable out of capital is termed the *permissible capital payment*. This is the amount which, together with any available profits and the proceeds of a fresh issue of shares made for the purpose of the redemption or purchase, is equal to the price of redemption or purchase, as the case may be. Thus it appears that if there are no available profits and no fresh issue is made, the *whole of* the price of redemption or purchase can be paid out of capital.

If the permissible capital payment is *less* than the nominal amount of the shares redeemed or purchased, the amount of the difference must be *transferred* to the capital redemption reserve. If it is *more*, the amount of the capital redemption reserve, share premium account or fully paid share capital (i.e. the capital in the legal sense: *see* **5**) and any amount representing unrealised profits arising on a revaluation of fixed assets (i.e. the revaluation reserve: *see* para. 34 of Schedule 4) may be *reduced* by the amount of the difference.

34. Procedure required for private company for redemption or purchase out of capital

Under s. 173 a private company may not take advantage of the privilege afforded to it by s. 171 unless it complies with the requirements of ss. 173–175. These are as follows:

(a) The payment out of capital must be approved by special resolution.

(b) The directors must make a statutory declaration specifying the amount of the permissible capital payment and stating that, after a full inquiry into the company's affairs and prospects, they have formed the opinion:

    (*i*) as regards its initial situation immediately after the date of the proposed payment, that there will be no grounds on which it could then be found unable to pay its debts; *and*

    (*ii*) as regards its prospects for the year following that date, that it will be able to carry on business as a going concern and pay its debts as they fall due throughout that year.

(c) The statutory declaration must contain the prescribed information with respect to the nature of the company's business and have annexed to it an auditor's report addressed to the directors stating that:

    (*i*) they have inquired into the company's state of affairs; *and*

    (*ii*) the amount specified in the statutory declaration as the permissible capital payment is in their view properly determined; *and*

    (*iii*) they are not aware of anything to indicate that the directors' opinion stated in the declaration is unreasonable.

(d) The resolution must be passed on the date on which the directors make the statutory declaration, or within the following week.

(e) The payment out of capital must be made not less than five nor more than seven weeks after the date of the resolution.

(f) No special resolution will be effective if any member who holds shares to which it relates exercises the voting rights attached to them and the resolution would not have been passed if he had not done so.

(g) No special resolution will be effective unless the statutory declaration and the auditors' report are available for inspection by members at the meeting at which the resolution is passed.

(h) Within a week after the date of the resolution the company must publish a notice in the *Gazette* stating:

    (*i*) that the company has approved a payment out of capital for the purposes of the redemption or purchase of its shares;

    (*ii*) the amount of the permissible capital payment and the date of the resolution;

    (*iii*) that the statutory declaration and the auditors' report are available for inspection at the registered office; *and*

    (*iv*) that any creditor of the company may at any time within the five weeks after the date of the resolution apply to the court under s. 176 (*see* **35**) for an order prohibiting the payment.

(i) Within a week after the date of the resolution the company must *either* publish a similar notice in an appropriate national newspaper *or* give notice in writing to that effect to each creditor.

(j) Not later than the first notice date the company must deliver a copy of the statutory declaration and the auditors' report to the registrar.

(k) The statutory declaration and auditors' report must be kept at the registered office from the first notice date until five weeks after the date of the resolution and must be open to the inspection of any member or creditor without charge.

If inspection is refused, the court may order that it be allowed.

35. Objections by members or creditors to redemption or purchase out of capital

Where a private company passes a special resolution approving a payment out of capital for the redemption or purchase of its own shares, s. 176 permits any member who did not vote in favour of the resolution and any creditor of the company to apply to the court within five weeks of the date when it was passed for its cancellation.

Those entitled to make such an application may appoint one or more of their number to make it on their behalf. If an application is made, the company must inform the registrar immediately and deliver to him an office copy of the court order within 15 days from when it was made.

The court may confirm or cancel the resolution or adjourn the proceedings in order that an arrangement may be made for the purchase of the interests of dissentient members or the protection of dissentient creditors: s. 177.

The court order may provide for the purchase by the company of the shares of any members and for the resulting reduction of capital. It can also make any alteration to the memorandum or articles which are thereby rendered necessary and prohibit the company from making subsequent alterations to these documents. The company may then make such alterations only with the leave of the court.

36. Liability of past members and directors in respect of redemption or purchase out of capital

Section 76 Insolvency Act 1986 provides that where a company is being wound up within a year from the date when it made a payment out of capital for the redemption or purchase of its own shares, and has not sufficient assets to pay its debts and the costs of winding up, the following persons are liable to contribute towards the deficiency:

(a) any person from whom the shares were redeemed or purchased; *and*
(b) any director who signed the statutory declaration, unless he can show that he had reasonable grounds for his opinion.

Under s. 76 of that Act a person falling under **(a)** above is liable to contribute to the company's assets up to the amount paid to him out of capital on his shares and the directors are jointly and severally liable with him. Finally, under s. 124 Insolvency Act 1986 any person who is liable under s. 76 of that Act to contribute to the company's assets in a winding up may petition the court for a winding-up order under s. 122 of that Act, in addition to any other right to petition which he may have as a contributory of the company in the usual sense (*see* 30:1, **4**).

12

Shares

1. The nature of a share

Section 182 provides that shares are personal property and that they are transferable in the manner laid down by the articles. Section 182, as was explained in 11:**19,** requires each share to be numbered, except where all the shares in a company, or all of those of a particular class, are fully paid up and rank *pari passu* for all purposes. The remainder of the sections on shares deal with transfer, share certificates and share warrants, and will be discussed later in this chapter.

None of these provisions is very helpful in telling us what a share is. It follows from s. 182, of course, that a share is a chose in action, since personal property consists of chattels real (leaseholds) and chattels personal, and chattels personal in their turn consist of choses in possession (tangible things such as goods) and choses in action (intangible things such as debts, contractual rights and patents). Clearly a share is intangible, its ownership being evidenced by a document called a *share certificate*. But if we were to try to describe it in these terms, no one would have much conception of what we were discussing. [The terminology of Scots law is different. A share is incorporeal moveable property, and ownership of it is evidenced by a document called a *share certificate*.]

Probably the best description of a share is not given in the Act at all, but in *Borland's Trustee* v. *Steel Brothers & Co. Ltd* (1901) [B108], by Farwell J.: 'A share is the interest of a shareholder in the company measured by a sum of money, for the purpose of liability in the first place, and of interest in the second'. This definition indicates the true position of the member: he is under a *liability* to the company, namely to pay for his shares on application, allotment, or when called upon to do so; but also he has an *interest* in the company which confers upon him certain rights, such as voting and dividend rights, and attendance at meetings. His interest is something he *owns*, so that he owns in reality a non-identified part of the company's undertaking. This is sometimes expressed by saying that the shareholders own the company, but of course no legal person can own another legal person. What the shareholders really own, collectively, is the entire undertaking of the company which, for convenience, is vested in the person of the company as soon as it is incorporated.

It will readily be seen why it is sometimes said that the company is the *agent* of the shareholders.

2. Transfer of shares

A transfer of shares is simply a *voluntary assignment* [in Scots law, *assignation*] and occurs, for example, where the shareholder sells his shares to another person or where he gives them away. Section 183 requires that a *proper instrument of transfer* must be delivered to the company. The word 'instrument' simply means a document, i.e. the transfer must be in writing. A deed is not necessary unless the articles require one, and Table A, Article 23, does not do so.

The effect of s. 183 is that an instrument of transfer is essential. An article, therefore, which attempts to provide for the *automatic* transfer of shares in the company to any particular person on the death of a member is illegal and void, for on death the legal ownership of the shares passes automatically to the personal representatives by transmission: *Re Greene* (1949). On the other hand an article which provides that on the death of a member his shares must be offered to certain other persons is valid, and will bind the personal representatives accordingly, for no avoidance of s. 183 is involved: *Jarvis Motors (Harrow) Ltd* v. *Carabott* (1964).

3. Form of transfer

At one time the instrument of transfer had to be executed both by the transferor and by the transferee and their signatures had to be witnessed. The Stock Transfer Act 1963, however, introduced a simplified 'stock transfer form' for fully paid shares. Such an instrument is signed by the transferor only, and need not be witnessed. The Act overrides any provision to the contrary in the company's articles.

Additional forms became permissible under the Stock Transfer (Addition of Forms) Order 1979 (SI 1979, No. 277), made under authority of the 1963 Act. These were introduced to facilitate the computerised 'Talisman' system of transfers on the stock exchange, and are the 'Talisman sold transfer' and the 'Talisman bought transfer'.

Section 207 Companies Act 1989 empowers the Secretary of State by regulations to make provision for the title to shares to be evidenced and transferred without a written instrument. This section enables advantage to be taken of modern systems of information technology. Regulations were made under s. 207 for the introduction of the TAURUS scheme of paperless transfers, but this scheme was abandoned in March 1993.

Table A, Article 24, provides that the directors may refuse to register a transfer unless:

(a) it is lodged at the registered office or at such other place as the directors may appoint;

(b) it is accompanied by the share certificate;

(c) it is in respect of only one class of share; *and*

(d) it is in favour of not more than four transferees.

Section 183 provides that on the application of the *transferor* of shares the company must enter the name of the transferee in the register of members in the same way as if the application for entry were made by the *transferee*.

4. Certification of transfers

Where a shareholder transfers only *some* of his shares in a company, it would be unsafe for him to part with the share certificate for his entire holding to the transferee. He therefore sends it to the company, which endorses the instrument of transfer with the words 'certificate lodged', returns it to the transferor, but retains the share certificate. This process is known as certification of the transfer.

The transferor then sends the certified instrument of transfer to the transferee, who applies to the company for registration. The company issues two new share certificates, one to the transferor to cover the shares which he continues to own, and one to the transferee to cover the shares he has acquired.

If the company is negligent and sends the transferor's original certificate for the entire holding back to him, it is not liable for any fraudulent act which he is able to do as a result, for that is *his* act and not that of the company.

5. The legal effect of certification

Section 184 provides that the certification of a transfer amounts simply to a representation by the company that documents have been produced to it showing that the transferor has a *prima facie* title to the shares. The section carefully amplifies this by going on to say what certification is *not*: it is not a representation that the transferor has a title.

Thus, when the certification of a transfer is effected, the company is merely saying that it has seen a share certificate which appears to be in order, though it is *not* saying that it is in order. For the company to guarantee the title of the transferor would be to put altogether too heavy a burden on it.

NOTE: Naturally, if the company makes a *fraudulent* certification, i.e. with the intention to deceive, it will be liable in damages. If however, it makes a false certification *negligently*, there was at one time no liability at common law for negligent mis-statements. Section 184 covers this possibility by providing that a company should be under the same liability for a negligent certification as for a fraudulent one. Possibly today this provision is no longer necessary, for it is arguable that the company and the transferee are in a 'special relationship' within the principle laid down in *Hedley Byrne & Co. Ltd* v. *Heller & Partners Ltd* (1964), and that the common law would now cover the position.

6. Restrictions on transfer

Subject to the articles, shares may be freely transferred to any person. For administrative convenience, however, the articles sometimes provide for the suspension of the registration of transfers for a short time each year in order to enable dividend lists to be prepared. Table A, Article 26, contains such a provision, which must necessarily be within the period laid down by s. 358, i.e. not more than 30 days in the year. But not all companies take advantage of s. 358, and there are many which do not close their books at all.

(a) *Private companies*: Before the Companies Act 1980 a company could not satisfy the definition of a private company unless its articles contained a restriction of some kind on the transfer of its shares. Even now it is probable that private companies will normally find it desirable to continue to include restrictions on the transfer of shares in their articles.

(b) *Public companies*: Often there are restrictions on transfer in *public* companies, although in this case the stock exchange will not grant a listing for the shares if they are fully paid. Table A, Article 24, provides that the directors may refuse to register the transfer of *partly paid* shares to a person of whom they do not approve. Were it not for such a restriction, a member could transfer his shares to a 'man of straw' simply for the purpose of avoiding liability for the next call on them. Article 24 also provides that the directors may refuse to register a transfer of any share on which the company has a lien. Where a company exercises its power of sale of shares over which it has a lien (*see* **30**), it is subject to the same restrictions on transfer as would have applied to the shareholder himself under the company's articles: *Champagne Perrier-Jouet S.A.* v. *H.H. Finch Ltd* (1982).

7. The exercise of the company's power to refuse registration

The company's power to refuse registration of a transfer is, under Article 24 of Table A, exercised by the board of directors, but unless they actively exercise it the transferee must be registered. Thus there must be a *majority* of the board *opposing* the registration in order to constitute exercise of the power.

It follows that if the board are evenly divided with no casting vote, the transfer must be registered: *Re Hackney Pavilion Ltd* (1924) and the Scottish decision *Shepherd's Trustees* v. *Shepherd* (1950). And if one of two directors intentionally fails to attend a board meeting so that the quorum of two will not be reached and accordingly transfers cannot be passed for registration, the transferee must, again, be registered: *Re Copal Varnish Co.* (1917). Moreover, the board's power to refuse registration of a transfer must be exercised within a reasonable time, or it will be lost: *Re Swaledale Cleaners Ltd* (1968).

So long as the directors act within the scope of the article, their decision cannot be challenged except on the grounds of bad faith: *Re Smith & Fawcett Ltd* (1942) [B11] Since the onus of proving bad faith rests on the plaintiff, the directors' refusal to register the transfer can seldom be successfully attacked, for while a state of mind may be a fact, it is a fact which is exceedingly difficult to prove.

> Thus in *Charles Forte Investments v. Amanda* (1964), the articles gave the directors power to refuse to register transfers 'in their absolute discretion and without assigning any reason'. They refused, giving no reason, to register a transfer by a former employee and minor shareholder who had quarrelled with one of the directors. He threatened to present a petition for winding up the company, whereupon the company applied for an injunction to prevent him from doing so. HELD: (*a*) the injunction should be granted, since the winding up would injure other members who were in no way responsible for the situation; (*b*) the directors were acting within the scope of the articles, unless bad faith could be proved, which it could not.

The articles may, of course, be more specific than they were in the *Forte* case; they may empower the directors to refuse to register transfers on certain specified grounds. The directors can then be interrogated as to the grounds for their refusal. But whether the article is widely phrased or narrowly expressed, they need show only that they were acting within its terms. They need give no reasons for their decision beyond this. If, on the other hand, they are foolish enough to give their reasons, then the court may consider whether those reasons were adequate. This is one of many legal situations in which the less that is said the less likelihood there is of liability.

A common form of restriction is a pre-emption clause in the articles by which, when shares are being sold by a member, the remaining members must first be given the opportunity to purchase them. The directors must then not register a transfer which is in breach of the pre-emption clause: *Tett* v. *Phoenix Property and Investment Co. Ltd* (1986) [B109].

Section 183 and Table A, Article 25, both provide that notice of a refusal to register a transfer must be sent to the transferee within two months from the date when the transfer was lodged with the company. If the transferee wishes to challenge the refusal, he should apply to the court for rectification of the register under s. 359.

8. Forged transfers

A forged document never has any legal effect. It can never move owner-ship from one person to another, however genuine it may appear. Thus a forged instrument of transfer leaves the ownership of the shares exactly where it always was: in the so-called transferor.

It follows that if the company registers a forged transfer, the true owner can apply to be replaced on the register. At the same time if the company has issued a new share certificate to a subsequent purchaser, it cannot, as will be seen later, deny his title to the shares, for the certificate estops [in Scots law bars] it from doing so. It will therefore be under a liability to compensate him for his loss: *Re Bahia and San Francisco Railway* (1868).

In order to avoid this result, companies normally notify the transferor of the transfer so that he can object if he wishes, but such a notification does not enable the company to escape liability if in fact it registers a forged transfer and causes loss to a transferee. Nor is it always of much use to the company, for the transferor may be abroad at the time, or not trouble to reply.

The Forged Transfers Acts 1891–2, however, permit the company to form a fund out of which to pay compensation for forged transfers, and it is always possible for a company to insure against the risk.

If the company is compelled to pay compensation, it can claim an indemnity from the person who sent the forged transfer, even though that person was unaware of the forgery: *Sheffield Corporation* v. *Barclay* (1905). Moreover, that person, however innocent, cannot rely on a share certifi-cate issued to him as an estoppel preventing the company from denying his title.

9. Share certificates

Section 185 provides that a company must have the share certificate ready for delivery within two months after the allotment or the lodging of the transfer, unless the terms of issue of the shares otherwise provide. It imposes no requirements as regards the form of the certificate. In the case of listed companies, stock exchange rules require certificates to be ready for delivery within two weeks.

Table A, Article 6, however, requires the certificate to be under seal and to specify both the shares to which it relates and the amount paid up on them. Article 7 provides that if a share certificate is defaced, worn-out, lost or destroyed, it may be renewed on such terms as to evidence and indemnity, and payment of expenses reasonably incurred by the com-pany in investigating evidence, as the directors may decide, but otherwise free of charge, and, in the case of defacement or wearing-out, on delivery up of the old certificate.

10. Legal effect of share certificates

Section 186, as amended by Schedule 17 Companies Act 1989 and Schedule 8 Law Reform (Miscellaneous Provisions) (Scotland) Act 1990, provides that a share certificate under the common seal of the company specifying the shares held by the member is in England and Wales *prima facie* evidence, and in Scotland sufficient evidence unless the contrary is shown, of his title to the shares. It is important to understand the legal effect of this provision:

(a) *A share certificate is not a negotiable instrument*, for its transfer from one person to another does not move the ownership of the shares. To move the ownership, as we have seen, an instrument of transfer must be completed, lodged with the company, and approved by the directors, after which the transferee must be entered on the register. It is this final act of entry on the register which completes the shift of ownership. The physical whereabouts of the share *certificate* is legally immaterial even though it may be administratively inconvenient. If lost, damaged, or destroyed, it must be renewed. But whatever has happened to it and wherever it is, the legal title to the shares is in the registered holder.

(b) *Evidence of title.* All that the share certificate amounts to, then, is a statement by the company that *at the moment when it was issued* the person named on it was the legal owner of the shares specified in it, and that those shares were paid up to the extent stated. It does not constitute title but is merely evidence of title. It is, however, a statement of considerable importance for it is made with the knowledge that other persons may act upon it in the belief that it is true, and this fact brings into operation the doctrine of *estoppel* [in Scots law the doctrine of personal bar].

(c) *Estoppel* [in Scots law *personal bar*] is not a principle of substantive law. It is a *rule of evidence which prevents a person from denying the legal implications of his conduct.* If he has behaved in a certain way, and if other persons have drawn certain natural and reasonable deductions from that behaviour as to his legal position, then he is not allowed to give evidence to show that his legal position is not in fact what it appeared to be. A company, therefore, is not allowed to deny the facts which it has stated to be true when it issued the share certificate.

This rule is expressed by saying that the share certificate acts as an estoppel against the company [in Scots law, bars the company] as regards:

(*i*) the title of the member: *Dixon* v. *Kennaway & Co* (1900); *and*

(*ii*) the amount paid up on the shares: *Bloomenthal* v. *Ford* (1897).

The company, once it has issued the certificate, may not deny these facts, except, as stated above, against a person who sent in a forged transfer, or where the certificate itself is a forgery: *Ruben* v. *Great Fingall Consolidated* (1906).

11. The rights of a transferee

It will be apparent from the preceding pages of this chapter that there is of necessity a certain interval of time between the *contract* to sell a shareholding and the *registration* of the transferee. During this period the transferee clearly has certain rights, but his exact legal position is far from clear. It can be most easily considered if a transfer is divided into stages.

The first stage in a sale of shares is the *contract of sale*. If the vendor breaks this contract, the would-be purchaser has a right to damages for breach of contract, calculated on the normal basis, wherever damages would be an adequate remedy. However, if he is trying to buy shares in a private company, or if the shares in question are not readily available on the market, damages will be quite useless. In this case he may seek a decree of specific performance: *Duncuft* v. *Albrecht* (1841). He is then often said to have an *equitable interest* in the shares and indeed he has an interest which equity protects; nevertheless, it is an equitable interest of a qualified nature, for the only right which it confers on the purchaser is the 'right to enforce the contract in proceedings for specific performance': *Oughtred* v. *Inland Revenue Commissioners* (1960). [In Scots law specific implement is similar to specific performance.]

The second stage in a sale of shares — and the first stage of a gift — is the completion of an instrument of transfer by the transferor. This in itself confers no further rights on a purchaser, at least where the vendor is still unpaid: *Musselwhite* v. *Musselwhite & Son Ltd* (1962). A donee has no rights at all.

The third stage in a sale — and the second stage of a gift — is the delivery of an executed instrument of transfer accompanied by the relevant share certificate to the purchaser or donee, as the case may be. At this point the transferor has done all that he can do. The only remaining thing to be done in order to perfect the transferee's title is an act of the *company*, not of the transferor — namely, the entry of the transferee's name in the register of members. It has been held that the completion of this stage is the true moment of gift: *Re Rose* (1951). From this moment onwards the transferee has a full beneficial interest in the shares and the transferor holds them on trust for him until registration is effected. Thus the benefits attached to the shares, such as dividends, belong in equity to the transferee, while the exercise of the transferor's voting rights are controlled by the transferee.

The parties to the transaction can of course modify these rules as they wish. They can, for instance, agree that the shares are to be sold 'cum' (with) dividend or 'ex' (without) dividend, and the price paid for the shares will vary accordingly. The vendor can also agree to sell 'with registration guaranteed', the effect of which is to make the eventual registration of the purchaser a *condition* of the contract, failure of which gives the purchaser the right to recover his money. If registration is not expressly guaranteed in this way, the purchaser has no remedy against the vendor if the company, under the appropriate provisions in its articles, lawfully refuses to register the transfer. He will simply continue to own the *equitable interest* in the shares while the *legal title* remains in the vendor. The rules concerning equitable interests are more fully explained later (see 14:**8–15**).

The final stage of a transfer, whether by sale or gift, is the company's entry of the transferee in its register of members. This is the moment at which the *legal title* to the shares passes from the transferor to the transferee, and the transaction is now complete.

12. The register of interests in shares

The register of interests in shares was introduced into company law by the Companies Act 1967. Far more detailed rules became applicable under the Companies Act 1981 and these now form Part VI (ss. 198–220) of the Companies Act 1985. Some amendments were made by s. 134 Companies Act 1989, particularly noteworthy being the Secretary of State's power to amend several of the provisions in Part VI of the 1985 Act by regulations: s. 210A Companies Act 1985.

Section 211 requires every *public* company to keep a register for the purposes of ss. 198–202 and, whenever it receives information under these sections, to inscribe it within three days in the register against the name of the person concerned, together with the date of the inscription. The same rule applies where a company is notified that a person has ceased to be a party to an agreement to which s. 204 applies (*see* **20**).

In computing the three days, Saturdays, Sundays and bank holidays are to be disregarded: s. 220.

Section 211 prevents the company from becoming concerned in any question regarding a person's rights relating to shares. The section is imposing merely an administrative duty and the company must be protected from further involvement.

The section requires the register to be made up so that the entries against each name are in chronological order. Unless it is already in the form of an index, the company must keep an index of the names inscribed in it which must indicate how the information with respect to each name may be readily found. Both the register and any index must be kept at the same place as the register of directors' interests (*see* 16:**13**) and, by s. 219, as amended by s. 143 Companies Act 1989, be open to the inspection of any person without charge.

Section 219 authorises any person to require a copy of the register, or any part of it, on payment of such fee as may be prescribed. The copy must be sent within 10 days. If inspection is refused, or a copy not sent within the 10 days, the court may order that inspection be allowed or the copy sent.

Finally, if a company ceases to be a public company and so is no longer governed by s. 211, it is required by s. 211 to keep the register and any index for six years.

13. Removal of entries from register of interests in shares

Section 218 prohibits a company from deleting any entry in its register of interests in shares unless it complies with the rules laid down in s. 217. If a company disregards this prohibition, the deleted entry must be restored to the register as soon as possible.

Under s. 217 a company may remove an entry from its register only when more than six years have elapsed since the date of its inscription, and *either*:

(a) it recorded the fact that the person in question had *ceased* to have a notifiable interest in the company's relevant share capital under Part VI; *or*

(b) it has been superseded by a later entry inscribed under s. 211 against that person's name.

In the case of **(a)** above, the company may remove from the register not only the entry, but also the person's name.

The section provides that where a person, in pursuance of a statutory obligation, gives a company the name and address of some other person as being interested in its shares, the company must within 15 days notify that other person that he has been so named and include:

(a) particulars of any entry made in the register as a result of the information given; *and*

(b) a statement informing him of his right to apply to have the entry removed in accordance with the section.

The application for removal must be in writing and the company must remove the entry if it is satisfied that the information on which it was based was incorrect.

Section 217 also deals with a person who appears in the register as a party to an agreement under s. 204 and who ceases to be such a party. He too may apply in writing for that fact to be recorded in the register and the company must comply.

If a company refuses an application under either of these two provisions the applicant is entitled to apply to the court for an order directing the company to remove the entry or record the information, as the case may be, and the court may make such an order if it thinks fit.

Lastly, where a person's name is removed from the register, any necessary alteration in the index must be made within 14 days.

14. Notifiable interests

It is clear from **12** above that certain interests in shares must be notified to the company and entered in its register.

Section 208 deals with the question of which interests are caught by the Act and are therefore notifiable.

The section shows that the scope of the provisions is intended to be very wide, for it provides that an interest *of any kind whatsoever* in shares is notifiable. Accordingly, while s. 209 excludes a person who is a *bare trustee* of an interest in shares, since he has no enjoyment of it, a *beneficiary* under the trust has, by s. 208, a notifiable interest.

Further, under s. 208, a person will be taken to have a notifiable interest in shares if:

(a) he enters into a contract to buy them; *or*

(b) although not the registered holder, he is entitled to exercise or control the exercise of any right conferred by the holding; *or*

(c) he has a right to call for their delivery to himself or to his order, whether absolute or conditional; *or*

(d) he has a right to acquire, or is under an obligation to take, an interest in them, whether absolute or conditional.

Finally, s. 208 provides that persons with a joint interest shall be taken each to have that interest, and that it is immaterial if the shares in which a person has an interest are unidentifiable.

15. Family and corporate interests

An interest may be notifiable not only when held by a particular person himself, but also when it is held by a member of his family or by a company which he controls.

Section 203 provides that a person must be taken to be interested in any shares:

(a) in which his spouse or infant child or step-child is interested; *or*

(b) if a company is interested in them *and*:

    (*i*) that company or its directors are accustomed to act in accordance with his directions; *or*

    (*ii*) he is entitled to exercise or control the exercise of one-third or more of the voting power at general meetings.

Section 203 goes even further along the same path, providing in effect that if Smith has one-third of the voting power in A Company and A

Company has one-third of the voting power in B Company, Smith is taken to be interested in shares held by B Company, as well as those held by A Company.

16. Meaning of 'relevant share capital'

Although, as explained in **14** and **15**, the word 'interest' is given a wide meaning by the Act so that any interest held by a person, his immediate family, or a company which he controls, will as a rule be notifiable, the duty to notify does not extend to interests in any type of share nor of any size. Section 199, as amended by s. 134 Companies Act 1989, imposes a duty to notify the company only where the interest is in *relevant share capital* and requires it to be at least 3 per cent of the nominal value of that share capital.

Section 198 defines *relevant share capital* as the issued share capital carrying the *right to vote* in all circumstances at general meetings.

Where the relevant share capital is divided into different classes of shares, s. 198 makes it clear that 3 per cent of any *class* will be a notifiable percentage, since the percentage is based on the nominal value of each class taken separately.

17. Obligation to notify known interests in voting shares

Section 198 imposes on a person with a notifiable interest in a notifiable percentage of the relevant share capital of a public company an obligation to notify the company. Under ss. 198 and 202, as amended by s. 134 Companies Act 1989, where he:

(a) knowingly acquires or ceases to hold such an interest; *or*
(b) becomes aware that he has acquired or has ceased to hold such an interest;

he must notify the company in writing within two days, specifying the share capital concerned, and *either* :

(a) stating the number of shares in which he knows he had an interest immediately after the obligation to notify arose; *or*
(b) stating that he has ceased to hold an interest.

In computing the period of two days, Saturdays, Sundays, and bank holidays are disregarded under s. 220 and the period runs, under s. 202, from the day after that on which the obligation to notify arose.

18 Particulars of registered holders

Further particulars which must be stated in any notification to the company under s. 198 are given in s. 202, as amended by s. 134 Companies Act 1989.

Section 202 requires the notification to include:

(a) the identity of each registered holder of any shares concerned;
(b) the number of those shares held by each registered holder; *and*
(c) the number of those shares in which the person making the notification is taken to have a notifiable interest under s. 208 (*see* **14**).

A person having a notifiable interest must also, under s. 202, notify the company within two days of any subsequent change in these particulars of which he becomes aware.

19. Notification of interests of persons acting together
Much criticism has long been levelled at persons who evade the disclosure rules by acquiring separately small quantities of shares, having previously agreed to combine their holdings at a suitable date. Such persons are often described as 'acting in concert' and the expression 'concert party' is used to indicate this type of agreement.

Sections 204–206 are directed at this kind of activity, the persons engaged in it being described as 'acting together'. An agreement is caught by s. 204 if it is made between two or more persons and:

(a) it includes provision for the acquisition by any of them of interests in shares in a particular public company, described as the *target company*;
(b) it imposes obligations or restrictions on any of them concerning the *use, retention or disposal* of those interests; *and*
(c) an interest in that company's shares is in fact acquired by any of them in pursuance of the agreement.

Section 204 provides that it does not apply to any agreement which is not legally binding, unless it involves *mutuality* in the undertakings, expectations or understandings of the parties. Underwriting agreements are also excluded from its scope.

Where an agreement is subject to the section, s. 205 applies, requiring any notification of his interest in shares in the target company made to that company under s. 198 by a person who is a party to the agreement to:

(a) state that he is such a party;
(b) include the names and, if known, the addresses of the other parties to the agreement; *and*
(c) state whether or not any of the shares mentioned in the notification are covered by the agreement and, if so, their number.

Conversely, if a person is making a notification to the company under s. 198 that he has *ceased* to have an interest in its shares owing to the fact that he or some other person has ceased to be a party to an agreement governed by s. 204, the notification must include a statement to that effect and, where applicable, the name and address of that other person.

20. Obligation of parties to a s. 204 agreement to notify each other.

Where a person who is a party to an agreement caught by s. 204 knows:

(a) that the target company is a public company;
(b) that the shares covered by the agreement are relevant share capital; *and*
(c) that the agreement is caught by s. 204;

he must within five days notify in writing every other party to it of any interest which he holds in the relevant share capital (*see* **16**) of the target company *independently of the agreement:* s. 206.

The notice must state:

(a) the number of shares in which he would be required to disclose his interest if it were notifiable under s. 198, apart from the agreement;
(b) particulars of the registered holders of those shares, if known to him; *and*
(c) particulars of the registered holders of any relevant share capital of the target company in which he has a notifiable interest apart from the agreement, and any change in them.

Further, s. 206 requires any party to a s. 204 agreement to notify in writing every other party of his current address and any change in it.

21. Power of company to require information concerning interests in its shares

Under s. 212 a *public* company may serve notice in writing on any person whom it knows, or has reasonable cause to believe, to hold or to have held at any time during the *last three years* an interest in the company's relevant share capital. The notice requires him either to confirm that fact or to indicate whether or not it is the case and, if it is, to give the following information in writing within a reasonable specified time:

(a) particulars of his own past or present interest held at any time during the three-year period;
(b) particulars of any other interest which exists or existed at any time as his own during the three-year period, in so far as he knows them; *and*
(c) where his interest is a past interest, the identity of the person who held it immediately after him, in so far as he knows it.

The particulars required by **(a)** and **(b)** above include the identity of persons interested in the shares and whether they were parties to an agreement governed by s. 204 (*see* **19**), or to any agreement concerning the exercise of the rights conferred by the shareholding (e.g. a voting agreement).

22. Registration of interests disclosed under s. 212

Section 213 provides that where a company receives any information in response to its notice, it must inscribe against the name of the registered holder of the shares in question, in a *separate part* of its register of interests in shares (*see* **12**), the following matters:

(a) the fact that it served a notice and the date when it did so; *and*

(b) any information received in response which relates to the *present* interests in the shares in question held by any person.

The section makes applicable by reference the provisions of s. 211 (*see* **12**), to this separate part of the register.

If a person on whom a notice is served fails to respond, the company may apply to the court under s. 216 for an order directing that the shares in question are to be subject to the restrictions imposed by Part XV (ss. 454–457) of the Act (*see* **22:12**). By s. 135 Companies Act 1989 the provisions of Part XV may be amended by regulations made by statutory instrument.

23. Exercise of company's powers under s. 212 on requisition

Section 214 provides that members of a company who hold *one-tenth or more of the paid-up voting share capital* may requisition the company to exercise its powers under s. 212.

The requisition must be signed by the requisitionists and deposited at the company's registered office, and must:

(a) state that they are requiring the company to exercise its powers under s. 212;

(b) specify the manner in which they require the powers to be exercised; *and*

(c) give reasonable grounds for so requiring.

As soon as the requisition is deposited at the registered office, the company is under a duty to comply with it.

By s. 215 the company must at the end of its inquiries prepare a report of the information received which must be available at the registered office within a reasonable time, not exceeding 15 days. If the inquiries are not concluded within three months from the day after that on which the requisition was deposited, an interim report must be prepared for each period of three months which elapses. Interim reports too must be available at the registered office within a reasonable time, not exceeding 15 days.

Within three days of making any report, final or interim, available at its registered office, the company must notify the requisitionists that it is there. All reports must be kept at the registered office for the ensuing six years and be available for inspection during that time in the same way as the register of interests in shares: s. 219.

24. Summary of statutory provisions on register of interests in shares

The Act contains such lengthy provisions on the register of interests in shares that a summary of the main points may perhaps be helpful:

(a) Only *public* companies are required to keep a register of interests in shares.

(b) 'Interest' is given a wide meaning in the expression 'notifiable interest'. Where there is a trust of shares, it includes an equitable interest but not the legal title of a bare trustee.

(c) The interests of a person's close family or of a company which he controls are regarded as his.

(d) An interest is not notifiable unless it comprises at least 3 per cent of the shares in question.

(e) An interest is not notifiable unless the shares in question are *voting* shares—the *relevant share capital*.

(f) Persons who agree to act in concert and then proceed to do so must notify the company of their agreement.

(g) They must also notify each other of their interests in the target company, whether notifiable to the company or not, which are independent of the agreement.

(h) A company may require information from a person regarding his interest in shares, and that of any other person, during the last three years.

(i) The holders of one-tenth or more of the paid-up voting share capital may requisition the company to exercise these powers of inquiry.

25. Share warrants

Section 188, as amended by Schedule 17 Companies Act 1989 and Schedule 8 Law Reform (Miscellaneous Provisions) (Scotland) Act 1990, permits a company limited by shares to issue share warrants provided:

(a) there is authority in the articles; *and*
(b) the shares are fully paid.

It also permits the company to provide for the payment of dividends on the shares included in the warrant by means of coupons.

A share warrant entitles the bearer to the shares specified in it, and the shares may be transferred by delivery of the warrant. It follows, therefore, that a share warrant, unlike a share certificate, *is a negotiable instrument*, and thus may be issued only by companies without restrictions on transfer in their articles.

Section 355 provides that on the issue of a share warrant the company must strike out of the register of members the name of the person who held the shares specified in the warrant, and enter in the register:

(a) the fact of the issue of the warrant;
(b) a statement of the shares included in the warrant, with distinguishing numbers, if any; *and*
(c) the date of the issue of the warrant.

The bearer of a share warrant is entitled to surrender it for cancellation and to have his name entered in the register in respect of the shares which were included in it.

The bearer of a share warrant may, if the articles so provide, be deemed to be a member of the company either to the full extent or for any purposes defined in the articles.

Section 291 provides that a share warrant will not constitute the share qualification of a director, where one is imposed by the articles.

Where a company has converted its shares into stock, stock warrants may be issued in exactly the same way. In practice neither share nor stock warrants are common.

26. Mortgage of shares

Shares, like any other form of property, may be mortgaged as security for a loan. The mortgage may be legal or equitable.

(a) *Legal mortgage*: Here the shares are actually transferred to the lender so that he becomes the registered holder with full membership rights. When the loan is repaid he transfers them back again to the borrower, with whom he has made an agreement to this effect.

Clearly this type of mortgage gives the lender complete security. He obtains the *legal* title to the shares, not merely an equitable interest in them. But it is cumbersome, and if the shares are only partly paid the lender becomes personally liable for calls while his name is on the register.
(b) *Equitable mortgage*: Here the shares are not transferred to the lender, but the share certificate is merely deposited with him, sometimes accompanied by a *blank transfer*, i.e. an instrument of transfer signed by the borrower but with the name of the transferee left 'blank'.

In this case the lender's security is not complete, for he has merely an *equitable* interest in the shares unless he fills in the blank transfer when the borrower defaults and becomes the registered holder. He cannot inform the company that he has an equitable interest in the shares, for

s. 360 provides that the company may not take notice of trusts. The only way in which he can protect his interest, then, is by serving a stop notice on the company.

Equitable mortgages are more common, however, than legal mortgages, for they do not have the same disadvantages.

[27. Assignation of shares in security

The term 'mortgage' is not properly a term of Scots law. In Scotland shares, like any other form of incorporeal moveable property, may be *assigned in security*. The procedure is for the shareholder to grant an assignation in security to his creditor and execute a transfer form. The creditor then becomes the registered holder of the shares. The position is comparable to that resulting from a legal mortgage under English law.

There is no effective 'equitable mortgage' in Scots law. The mere handing over by the shareholder to a creditor of a share certificate, with or without a blank transfer, gives the creditor no security.

Stop notices are not used in Scots law. If a company, when about to register a transfer, receives intimation from some person other than the transferee that the other person has an interest in the shares, the company is entitled to proceed to register the transfer unless the intimation is followed up by an interdict prohibiting the company from doing so.]

28. Calls

A call in the strict sense is a demand by the company for money due on the shares *excluding* the amounts payable on application, allotment or by instalments. Often the full amount of the share is payable on application, in which case the member is never liable to pay any more (with the exception of those rare cases when his liability can become unlimited). Sometimes a certain amount is payable on application and the balance on allotment or by instalments, i.e. at certain fixed dates. The date of a call, however, is not fixed until the call is made, and it will not be made until the company requires more capital.

Despite this distinction, Table A, Article 16, provides that for the purposes of Table A sums payable on allotment or at a fixed date, i.e. by instalments, shall be deemed to be calls, and all the provisions of the articles relating to calls apply to them as well.

The method of making calls depends entirely on the articles. Table A, Article 12, empowers the directors to make calls provided each member is given at least 14 days' notice of the time and place of payment. It also authorises the directors to revoke or postpone a call if they wish.

Table A, Article 15, provides that if the member does not pay the call he must pay interest on the sum due from the date fixed for payment until he actually pays it, though the directors may waive the payment of interest. Under s. 14, as was explained in 3:**10**, a call is in English law a specialty debt.

The directors' power to make calls must, like all their other powers, be exercised *bona fide* for the benefit of the company, and they may not abuse it. Thus they may not make calls on all the shareholders except themselves: *Alexander* v. *Automatic Telephone Co* (1900), nor on one particular shareholder alone because he happens to annoy them: *Galloway* v. *Hallé Concerts Society* (1915).

Section 119, however, permits a company, with authority in its articles, to arrange on the issue of the shares for a difference between the shareholders in the amounts and times of payment of calls, and Table A, Article 17, gives the necessary authority. It is important to remember, however, that such an arrangement must be made *on issue*, and so is a term of the contract between the shareholder and the company, and that even when it exists the directors cannot avoid their duty to act in *good faith*.

29. Payment of calls in advance
Section 119 also permits a company, with authority in its articles, to accept from a member the whole or part of the amount unpaid on his shares, even though it has not been called up. Table A, however, gives no such authority.

The advance payment, although in reality share capital, is treated as a *loan* to the company, for interest is a debt payable regardless of whether profits are available (*see* 20:**2**). Moreover, in liquidation (*see* 1:**18**) it must be repaid to the appropriate shareholders *after* the debts have been paid, but *before* the share capital is repaid to the shareholders generally. It cannot, however, be repaid to the shareholders while the company is a going concern, except under a reduction of capital complying with s. 135, so that in this respect it is treated as capital.

Where the articles authorise an advance payment they will also usually make it clear that the advance payment does *not* count as paid-up capital for dividend purposes. The reason for such a provision is, of course, that it would be inequitable if the advance payment carried a right to dividend as well as to interest. Once again, any power which the directors have to accept calls in advance must be exercised *bona fide*.

> In *Sykes' Case* (1872), the directors, who knew that the company was insolvent, paid up the amount unpaid on their own shares in advance, and then at once applied it in payment of their own fees.
> HELD: They were still liable for the amount unpaid on their shares.

30. Lien
A lien, like a mortgage or pledge, is a form of security. It can arise at common law, such as the possessory lien of a repairer on the article

repaired, or in equity, or under maritime law. The lien of a company on the shares of a member is an example of an equitable lien, giving the company an *equitable* interest in the shares of the member.

Apart from s. 150 (*see* below) the Act itself contains no reference to lien, but the articles of companies frequently give the company a lien on the shares of a member for money owed by him to the company. [In Scots law a company has at common law, without any provision in its articles, a lien on shares of a member for debts due by the member to the company.] Table A, Article 8, gives the company a lien on all *partly paid* shares in respect of *money due on the shares*. This lien extends to the dividends as well.

If the member does not pay the sum which he owes to the company, the lien can be enforced by applying to the court for an order for the sale of the shares. Possibly, in English law under the Law of Property Act 1925, this power of sale is exercisable without application to the court, but in any case the articles of the company usually give a power of sale in such circumstances. Table A, Article 9, accordingly gives the company *power to sell* any shares on which a lien exists provided:

(a) the sum in respect of which the lien exists is presently payable;

(b) written notice demanding payment has been given to the registered holder; *and*

(c) a period of 14 days after the notice has expired.

Article 10 permits the directors to authorise a transfer of the shares to the purchaser, who can then be registered in respect of them. His title is not affected by any irregularity in the proceedings.

Article 11 provides that the proceeds of the sale are to be applied in payment of the amount due to the company, the balance being paid to the original owner.

Since, as stated above, a lien gives the company an equitable interest, students should make sure that they fully grasp the rules relating to the priority of equitable interests explained in Chapter 14.

Section 150 greatly restricts the taking of a lien or other charge on its own shares by a *public* company. Such a lien or charge is *void* unless authorised by s. 150 which expressly permits a public company to take:

(a) a charge on its own *partly paid* shares for an amount payable in respect of them; *and*

(b) if it is a money-lending company, a charge on its own shares, *whether fully or partly paid,* as security in connection with a transaction entered into in the ordinary course of its business.

31. Forfeiture

When shares are forfeited the company *takes them away* from the member.

This is obviously a serious step to take, for not only does it deprive the shareholder of his property but, unless the shares are re-issued, it involves a *reduction of capital* without the consent of the court and is the only example of this apart from surrender.

It is unlawful to forfeit shares unless the articles authorise it. Table A, Article 18, authorises forfeiture for non-payment of calls and this includes, by Article 16, non-payment of sums payable at a fixed time, i.e by instalments. Forfeiture of shares for any debt which does not arise from the shares is invalid. Consequently it has a much narrower scope than a lien.

The procedure laid down in the articles, e.g. regarding notice, must be strictly followed: *Parkstone Ltd* v. *Gulf Guarantee Bank plc* (1990) [B113].

Article 18 empowers the directors to serve a notice on the defaulting member requiring him to pay the company. It provides that this notice must name a day at least 14 days ahead on or before which payment must be made, and must inform the member that unless he makes the required payment his shares will be liable to be forfeited. Article 19 empowers the directors to forfeit the shares concerned by resolution if the member does not comply with the notice.

Article 20 permits the directors to sell the forfeited shares or otherwise dispose of them as they wish. It also allows them to cancel the forfeiture up to the time when they have disposed of the shares. Where, for the purposes of its disposal, a forfeited share is to be transferred to any person, the directors may authorise some person to execute a transfer of the share to that person, who then becomes the registered holder and, by Article 22, is not bound to see to the application of the purchase-money; nor is his title affected by any irregularity in the proceedings. These provisions are similar to the provisions of Article 10 relating to sale of the shares on exercise of the company's lien.

As stated above, unless the shares are re-issued forfeiture results in a reduction of capital. Normally, therefore, the company re-issues them. It can re-issue at any price provided that the total of the *sum paid by the former holder* of the shares, together with the *amount paid on re-issue* and the *amount for which the purchaser is liable in the future*, is not less than the par value for, if it were, this would be an issue at a discount. Usually it is *more* than the par value, and the excess is of course a *premium* and must go into the share premium account.

The shares are forfeited in the condition in which they then are. Thus if they are £1 shares 50p paid up, and the shareholder is unable to pay a call of 25p, the shares will be re-issued 50p paid up, and the new holder becomes liable for the whole amount unpaid on the shares, including the call of 25p which resulted in the forfeiture. In this case the price the purchaser pays for the re-issued shares is a *premium*.

Meanwhile the original holder is discharged from all liability on the shares, except that he will be placed on the 'B' list if the company goes into liquidation within a year. To preserve his liability, an express provision in the articles is required, and Table A, Article 21, has this effect. Such an article makes him liable as *a debtor* for, as stated above, he is liable as a *contributory* in a liquidation in any case. The debt, as we have seen, is under s. 14 a specialty debt in English law, and accordingly he will be liable for 12 years: *Ladies' Dress Association* v. *Pulbrook* (1900).

32. Lien and forfeiture compared

Students are sometimes asked to compare the enforcement of the company's lien with forfeiture. The following points should then be borne in mind:

(a) A lien *never involves a reduction of capital*, for the shares are necessarily sold. Forfeiture *will involve a reduction of capital* unless the shares are re-issued.

(b) A lien is enforced by *sale*. Forfeiture is effected by *depriving the member of his shares*.

(c) Lien is a form of *security* for a debt. Forfeiture is a *penal proceeding*.

(d) In the case of lien, the liability of the former owner is only as a 'B' list *contributory* in a liquidation. After forfeiture an article similar to Table A, Article 21, can impose the liability of a *debtor* upon him.

(e) In the case of lien, the former owner *receives*, on the sale of the shares, the difference between *the amount received for them* and *the amount of his debt*. After forfeiture, he receives *nothing* and never recovers what he has already paid on the shares.

33. Surrender

The surrender of shares, like forfeiture, is lawful only where the articles authorise it, and Table A does not do so. Sometimes, however, a company's articles authorise the directors to accept a surrender of shares where it would be proper to do so.

Surrender is permissible only in two cases:

(a) as a short cut to forfeiture, to avoid the formalities;
(b) where shares are surrendered in exchange for new shares of the same nominal value (but with different rights).

Surrendered shares may be re-issued in the same way as forfeited shares, and if this is done no reduction of capital occurs in **(a)** above. In **(b)** there is of course no reduction because the capital is replaced.

34. Cancellation of shares after forfeiture or surrender

Section 146 gives two further rules applicable to *public* companies:

(a) Where shares are forfeited or surrendered, then unless the company has disposed of them (by re-issue) within the following three years, it must:

> (*i*) cancel them and diminish the amount of its share capital accordingly; *and*
>
> (*ii*) where the cancellation brings the nominal value of the allotted share capital below the authorised minimum, apply for *re-registration as a private company*.

Section 147 makes it clear that it is not necessary to comply with the rules in ss. 135 and 136 governing reduction of capital, although a board resolution altering the company's memorandum is required.

The board resolution must be filed with the registrar within 15 days in accordance with s. 380 (*see* 15:**34**).

(b) Section 146 prohibits the company from exercising any voting rights in respect of shares which have been forfeited or surrendered.

13

Membership

1. Methods of becoming a member

A person may become a member in the following ways.

(a) *Allotment*: Here the member takes the shares *directly from the company*. The statutory provisions on allotment have been fully discussed in Chapter 9.

(b) *Transfer*: Here the member acquires the shares *from an existing member* by sale, gift or some other transaction.

(c) *Transmission*: This is an involuntary transfer occurring on the *death* or *bankruptcy* of a member. Later it will be seen that the ownership in the shares then *automatically*, i.e. by operation of law, passes from the dead or bankrupt member to his personal representatives or trustee in bankruptcy, as the case may be, who may then be registered in respect of them. (The student who wrote that transfer was by act of parties, while transmission was by act of God, was somewhat overstating the divine responsibility.)

(d) *Subscribing the memorandum*: The subscribers must take their shares directly from the company, and not by transfer from another member.

Section 22 provides that the subscribers to the memorandum shall be deemed to have agreed to become members, and must be entered in the register of members.

(e) *Estoppel*: If a person's name is improperly placed on the register of members, and he knows and assents to it, he will then be *estopped from denying* that he is a member.

Estoppel is simply a *rule of evidence* which prevents a person from denying the legal implications of his conduct. Thus a man may behave as though he is a partner in a firm, and be 'held out' by the other partners as being one of their number: neither he nor they will then be allowed to deny that he is a partner, for they will be estopped from doing so. The same rule applies to a person who behaves as though he is a member of a company by allowing his name to be placed on the register.

[In Scots law the term corresponding to 'estoppel' is 'personal bar'.]

NOTE: Section 22 provides that every other person who agrees to become a member and whose name is entered on the register of members shall be a member. This clearly covers allotment, transfer, transmission and estoppel.

The phrase 'agrees to become a member' in s. 22 is satisfied where a person assents to become a member and it does not require a binding contract between the person and the company: the entry and consent are enough: *Re Nuneaton Borough Association Football Club Ltd* (1989).

2. The conditions of membership

It will be seen from the above that there are two conditions for member-ship:

(a) the *agreement* to become a member, either by subscribing the memo-randum, or by allotment or transfer, or after transmission has occurred, or as a result of estoppel [in Scots law, personal bar]; *and*
(b) the *entry on the register of members* of the shareholder's name.

Thus as a general rule all members are shareholders, and all sharehold-ers are members, so that the two words are synonymous. It has, however, been seen in Chapter 12 that there is an exception to this, namely, where share warrants have been issued. Also, in the case of death or bankruptcy, there will be a period of time when the person on the register no longer owns the shares, because he is either dead or bankrupt and transmission has occurred.

3. Joint holders

Where two or more persons own shares jointly, the *jus accrescendi* or right of survivorship applies. This means that on the death of any joint holder, the survivor or survivors simply *continue to own* the shares, which do not pass to the personal representatives of the deceased for distribution under the will or intestacy.

Joint holders may be entered on the company's register of members in any order which they desire, and the articles usually provide that the vote of the senior must be accepted to the exclusion of the votes of the others. Seniority is determined by the order in which the names stand in the register. Table A, Article 55, contains a provision to this effect.

Joint holders may require the company to split their holding equally among them. This will give them each a smaller holding but an equal number of votes. A similar result is obtained if their holding is split and their names in respect of each holding are placed in a different order. They will then all continue to own all the shares, but each will have the same voting rights as the others.

4. Methods of ceasing to be a member

There are a large number of ways in which a person may cease to be a member of a company, many of which are discussed in detail in other chapters:

(a) *Transfer*: Here the transferor ceases to be a member when the transferee is placed on the register.

(b) *Forfeiture*: The articles may provide that a member's shares may be forfeited for non-payment of calls.

(c) *Surrender*: This is a short-cut to forfeiture, in order to avoid the formalities.

(d) *Sale by the company under its lien*.

(e) *Transmission to personal representatives on death of member*: Later in this chapter we shall see that the dead member only ceases to be a member of the company when some other person is registered in his place.

(f) *Transmission to trustee in bankruptcy of member*: Here again the bankrupt member only ceases to be a member when some other person is registered in his place.

(g) *Disclaimer by trustee in bankruptcy of member*. [This does not apply to Scotland.]

(h) *Liquidation*: On liquidation the company will be dissolved and members will have their capital returned to them as far as possible. Since the existence of the company comes to an end, membership also ceases.

(i) *Issue of share warrants*: Under s. 355 a member is struck off the register on the issue of a share warrant, but it should be noted that s. 355 provides that the bearer of a share warrant may be deemed to be a member to the extent to which the articles provide.

(j) *Redemption of redeemable shares under s. 159.*

(k) *Purchase by company of its own shares under s. 162.*

(l) *Repudiation by minor.*

(m) *Rescission for misrepresentation in the prospectus.*

(n) *Court order:* For example, ss. 5, 54 and 459–461.

(o) *Section 428:* Where a 'take-over bid' is made, the shares of the dissenting minority may under certain conditions be bought by the offeror.

(p) *Sections 110 and 111 Insolvency Act 1986:* Where a liquidator is empowered to sell the company's property in return for shares in another company, those members who dissent from the arrangement can compel the liquidator either to abandon it or to buy their shares.

5. Legally abnormal persons

A *legally normal* person is any natural legal person of full age who is sane, sober and solvent.

Some legal persons are abnormal from their beginning, such as corporations which, as we have seen, are artificial legal persons. Others, whether by a disorder of their mind, body or finances, become abnormal in the course of their lives. Moreover, all normal persons are born: they are therefore minors, and legally abnormal for the first 18 years. They also die, creating a legal situation to which special rules apply.

It is now necessary to consider the rules which apply to legally abnormal persons as shareholders, i.e. to deal with minors, mentally disordered persons, personal representatives, trustees in bankruptcy and corporations. Drunkenness, though studied in the law of contract, does not affect shareholding unless of so persistent a nature that it leads to incapacity of mind, when the rules regarding lunacy will apply.

6. Minors

A minor may hold shares in a company, provided the company is willing to place his name on the register. Often the articles prohibit the transfer of shares to a minor, but even if they do not the company cannot be compelled to register him as a member.

(a) *A transfer to a minor is voidable.* If, therefore, the company has unknowingly registered a minor, it can still apply to the court to have the transfer set aside and the transferor put back on the register, but it must act promptly. If it acquiesces in the transfer, or delays too long before applying to have the register rectified, the minor shareholder will have to be recognised.

(b) *A minor shareholder may likewise repudiate his contract* either before attaining 18 years or within a reasonable time afterwards, and on doing so can avoid all future liability on partly paid shares. He cannot, however, recover money already paid on the shares unless there has been a total failure of consideration. If the shares have a market value, however small, the minor has received some consideration and therefore cannot recover his money: *Steinberg* v. *Scala (Leeds) Ltd* (1923).

(c) *A minor may subscribe the memorandum,* but can afterwards repudiate liability in the normal way.

(d) *A transfer of shares by a minor* is usually said to require an order from the court, though there is a conflict of opinion on the point.

[In Scotland, a person under the age of 16 may hold shares if the articles allow this; e.g. he may have received a gift of the shares. However, by the Age of Legal Capacity (Scotland) Act 1991, a person under 16 has no contractual capacity and so is unable to enter into any transaction to purchase shares.

Between the ages of 16 and 18 the young person has contractual capacity and so can transact with shares, but up to the age of 21 his transactions may be set aside by the court if they are prejudicial.]

7. Mentally disordered persons

A person declared mentally disordered by the court may be a shareholder, but his voting rights will be exercised by his receiver or other person appointed by the court to deal with his affairs [in Scots law, his *curator bonis*]. Table A, Article 56, specifically authorises this.

Such person may also be given authority to transfer the shares and to deal generally with the mentally disordered person's property.

8. Personal representatives

The expression 'personal representatives' covers both *executors*, who are appointed by the testator in his will, and *administrators*, who are appointed by the court when the testator fails to appoint an executor, or when the deceased has made no will. [In Scotland the term 'executors' is used, whether there is a will or not and whether they are appointed by the testator in his will or appointed by the court.]

It is essential to understand first that when a person dies, all his property vests at the moment of death in his personal representatives. This is known as *transmission*, or *transfer by operation of law*, or *involuntary assignment*, according to the context, but it can be expressed most simply by saying that because a deceased person cannot own anything, the ownership of all his property passes at the moment of death to those who *legally represent him. These persons, under the Administration of Estates Act 1925* (which applies to England and Wales only), *are his personal representatives.*

This raises no difficulties where the deceased has appointed an executor, but if he has not, there will be a period of time which must obviously elapse before the court makes the necessary appointment of an administrator. Nevertheless, the ownership of the property vests in the administrator, once he is appointed, *from the moment of death*, and his title *relates back* to the date when the deceased died.

Personal representatives, therefore, have in all cases the *legal* ownership of the deceased's property. But they are *trustees*: they hold the property *on trust* for those entitled to it under the will or the rules of intestacy. The position which arises where a person is a trustee of shares will be fully discussed later, but keep in mind these basic principles.

9. Provisions of the Act and Table A regarding personal representatives

There are two sections in the Act concerning personal representatives.

Section 187 states simply that the production to a company of any document which is by law sufficient evidence of probate of the will, or letters of administration of the estate, or confirmation as executor of a deceased person, must be accepted by the company as sufficient evidence of the grant, regardless of anything in the articles.

NOTE: This section does not make the personal representatives members of the company. The deceased is still on the register. But it impliedly recognises that the *ownership* in the shares has passed from the deceased to the personal representatives. Note here how membership is divorced from ownership, an exceptional position.

Section 183 proceeds further to implement this principle. It states that a transfer of the shares of the deceased made by a personal representative who is not a member of the company is as valid as if he were a member. Not only does he own the shares, but he may deal with them without his name being entered on the register of members.

Table A, Article 38, states that notice of meetings must be sent to the personal representative. But Article 31, while it gives him the right to dividends and other benefits attached to the shares, states that he shall not have any rights relating to meetings until his name is on the register of members. Thus while he receives the notice of a meeting, he will not be able to attend it or vote at it unless he has become registered as a member.

10. Registration of personal representatives as members

Unless the articles provide otherwise, personal representatives are entitled to be registered as members of the company if they wish, and may make their desire known to the directors by a *letter of request*. They may, however, prefer not to be registered but to transfer the shares to another person. Article 30 allows personal representatives to choose *either* to give notice to the company that they wish to be registered *or* to execute a transfer to another person, and provides that all the articles relating to transfer apply equally to the notice or to the transfer in this case.

If the shares are partly paid, personal representatives who are on the register of members are personally liable for calls, but they will have a right of indemnity against the deceased's estate for the amount paid. If they have not become registered as members, then the calls will be made on the estate and be payable out of it. Section 81 Insolvency Act 1986 provides that if the personal representatives default in paying the calls, the company itself may take administration proceedings in order to obtain the money due to it.

11. Trustees in bankruptcy

When a member of a company becomes bankrupt, the legal position is very similar to that arising on death. The debtor's name will be on the register of members, but he will no longer own the shares, for when he was made bankrupt the ownership passed by operation of law to his trustee in bankruptcy. Moreover, the title of the trustee in bankruptcy again *relates back* to a previous moment of time, namely the *commencement of the bankruptcy*, i.e. the date of the bankruptcy order made by the court.

NOTES: (1) *The trustee in bankruptcy*, though not on the register of members, becomes *entitled as owner of the shares* to deal with them, to control the debtor's vote, and to be registered as a member if he wishes. Article 38 provides that notice of meetings is to be sent to him, and Article 31 applies to him in the same way as to personal representatives.

(2) *If the shares are partly paid*, the company may prove in the bankruptcy both for calls in arrears and liability for future calls, but the trustee in bankruptcy may *disclaim* the shares under s. 315 Insolvency Act 1986 if they are onerous. If he disclaims, the company may prove for the damage resulting to it from the disclaimer, which will of course be the loss of the amount unpaid on the shares. The company may mitigate this damage by re-issuing the shares, as in the case of a forfeiture. [The term 'prove' is not used in Scotland for making a claim on a bankrupt estate. There is no right of disclaimer of onerous shares in Scots law.]

12. Corporations

A company may own shares in *another company*, and s. 375 then authorises it to appoint a person to act as its representative at meetings.

It is also lawful for two companies to own shares *in each other*, though when this position is carefully considered it will be seen that if the share capital of *both* companies is regarded *as a whole*, then *that capital is always reduced by the amount of the cross-holdings*.

Thus if Mr and Mrs Smith form Company A with a share capital of 100 £1 shares, taking 40 shares each, and then Company B with a share capital of 100 £1 shares, again taking 40 shares each, and if Company A then buys the remaining 20 shares in Company B, while Company B buys the remaining 20 shares in Company A, the combined issued share capital will be 200 £1 shares, though the actual cash in both companies together will be £160.

Nevertheless, there is nothing unlawful about this situation, with one important exception: cross-holdings are lawful *provided the companies involved do not constitute a group*.

It is therefore essential to know what a group is, and how it arises.

13. The nature of a group

A group exists wherever two or more companies are in the relationship of *holding* and *subsidiary* to each other. The Act gives an important definition of a subsidiary company in s. 736, as substituted by s. 144 Companies Act 1989.

The section provides that a company is a subsidiary of another company, its 'holding company', if *either* that other company:

(a) holds a majority of the voting rights in it; *or*
(b) is a member of it and has the right to appoint or remove a majority of its board of directors; *or*
(c) is a member of it and controls alone, pursuant to an agreement with other shareholders or members, a majority of the voting rights in it;

or it is a subsidiary of a company which is itself a subsidiary of that other company.

This definition must be studied with great care. An understanding of it is aided if 'H Ltd' is used of the holding company (described in the section as 'that other company'), and 'S Ltd' is used of the subsidiary. The final clause in the definition ('*or* S Ltd is a subsidiary of a company which is itself a subsidiary of H Ltd') shows that a subsidiary may not be directly below its holding company but may be several stages below it, provided that the relationship of holding company and subsidiary company is present at each stage in the chain.

The same section defines a 'wholly-owned subsidiary' by providing that a company is a 'wholly-owned subsidiary' of another company if it has no members except:

(a) that other company; *and*
(b) that other company's wholly-owned subsidiaries; *and*
(c) persons acting on behalf of either **(a)** or **(b)**.

The 1989 Act adds two further sections at this point — s. 736A and s. 736B.

Section 736A consists of provisions supplementing s. 736. These include the following:

(a) Rights held by a person in a fiduciary capacity (i.e. where the person is in the position of a trustee) are to be treated as not held by him.
(b) Rights held by a person as nominee for another are to be treated as held by that other; rights are held as nominee for another if they are exercisable only on his instructions or with his consent or concurrence.
(c) Rights attached to shares held by way of security are to be treated as held by the person providing the security if *either* the rights are exercisable only in accordance with his instructions *or* the shares are held in connection with the granting of loans as part of normal business activities and the rights are exercisable only in his interests.

Section 736B empowers the Secretary of State by regulations to amend ss. 736 and 736A so as to alter the meaning of the expressions 'holding company', 'subsidiary' or 'wholly-owned subsidiary'.

14. Size of groups

From these statutory provisions it will be seen that a group can be quite small, e.g. two companies, one of which is the holding company of the other, or very large, e.g. one holding company with 20 subsidiaries, which in turn have subsidiaries of their own. The chain can be very long; in theory it is infinite.

Often companies in a group are said to be similar to a family, and the holding company is referred to as the 'parent company'. The parent company in a group may itself be a subsidiary undertaking, and the group is then treated as a subsidiary of its parent company's parent company. The term 'fellow-subsidiary' is used of companies which have the same parent company

15. Unlawful cross-holdings

It will now be clear that in all cases where two companies are in a *direct* group relationship the holding company is a member of the subsidiary. If, therefore, the subsidiary company owns shares in the holding company, this will be a *cross-holding*, and it may here be affected by s. 23, as substituted in the 1985 Act by s. 129 Companies Act 1989. In fact, s. 23 is intended to cover *all* group relationships, even where they are *indirect* so that there is no cross-holding.

Section 23 provides that a subsidiary company cannot be a member of its holding company, and any allotment or transfer of shares in the holding company to its subsidiary is void.

The section was a new one in 1948, and therefore it was obvious that when the Act came into force there would be many groups in which the subsidiary owned shares in the holding company. This suddenly became unlawful. Consequently s. 23 carefully provides for these circumstances by stating that where a subsidiary company owned shares in the holding company *at the commencement of the Companies Act 1948*, it can continue to hold them, but cannot vote at meetings.

16. The exceptions to s. 23

Finally, there are three statutory exceptions to s. 23. The section expressly permits a subsidiary company to own shares in the holding company where it does so in the capacity of:

(a) personal representative (e.g. if the subsidiary is a banking company acting as executor to a deceased owner of shares in its holding company); *or*

(b) trustee, provided the equitable interest in the shares is owned by persons outside the group (e.g. if the subsidiary is a banking company appointed the trustee of a family settlement created by a settlor owning shares in the holding company); *or*

(c) a market maker, i.e. a person recognised by an investment exchange and holding himself out at all normal times as willing to buy and sell securities at prices specified by him.

As regards **(b)** above, there is one case where the equitable interest may be owned by a company within the group, namely, when it arises by way of security for a loan made by a money-lending company in the ordinary course of business (e.g. where the trustee wishes to raise a temporary loan, and mortgages the shares as security to a banking company within the group).

17. Disclosure in accounts of holding and subsidiary companies
Schedule 5 to the 1985 Act, as substituted by s. 6 of, and Schedule 3 to, the Companies Act 1989, lists the information which must be disclosed in notes to the accounts where there are related undertakings (*see* 18:**16**).

18. Associated companies
The expression 'associated companies' is a commercial one with no precise technical legal significance. It is normally used to indicate a shareholding of 10–50 per cent by one company in another, so that the two companies are not usually in the group relationship described in **13** above. Such a holding is often acquired for business reasons and may well lead to the formation of a group at a later date by the companies concerned.

The only recognition given by the Companies Act to this type of relationship between companies is in regard to group accounts. Schedule 4A to the 1985 Act, as inserted by s. 5 of, and Schedule 2 to, the 1989 Act, provides that an 'associated undertaking' means an undertaking in which an undertaking included in the consolidation has a participating interest and over whose operating and financial policy it exercises a *significant influence* and which is not:

(a) a subsidiary undertaking of the parent company; *or*
(b) a joint venture, as defined in Schedule 4A.

Where an undertaking holds 20 per cent or more of the voting rights in another undertaking, it is presumed to exercise a *significant influence* over it unless the contrary is shown.

19. Acquisition by company of its own shares
In **12** it was explained that a company may own shares in another company and that, with one exception, companies may own shares in each other.

A company may not, however, normally own shares *in itself*. This was formerly known as the rule in *Trevor v. Whitworth* (1887), where the articles authorised the company to buy its own shares, but were held illegal on the grounds that this would amount to a reduction of capital.

The rule is now given statutory form by s. 143 which, with one exception mentioned below, prohibits any limited company from acquiring its own shares, whether by purchase, subscription or otherwise. The Act imposes penalties on the company and every officer in default for contravention of the section and provides that any illegal acquisition of shares is *void*.

The single exception to the rule is that s. 143 expressly permits a company limited by shares to acquire any of its own *fully paid* shares *otherwise than for valuable consideration* (i.e. by way of gift). The exception is not new. A more limited version of it was formerly found in two well-known cases — *Kirby* v. *Wilkins* (1929) and *Re Castiglione's Will Trusts* (1958) — but it is helpful to have it in a broader statutory form.

It is clear, of course, that if a company has issued 100 £1 shares at par, and then uses £25 of that share capital to buy 25 shares from an existing member, it will still have an issued capital of 100 shares, but will have only £75 in cash. The capital of the company is reduced by the amount which it has used to buy its own shares.

If, however, a company has been in existence for some time, and has accumulated revenue reserves, and then uses those reserves to buy its own shares from an existing member, this is not a reduction of *capital* in the strict sense of the word. Nevertheless, it would still be unlawful, both at common law and under s. 143, for it has reduced the amount of the company's *assets*, and on liquidation there would be less available to meet the claims of creditors. Thus the rule seems to be based not so much on an illegal reduction of capital, as on an illegal use of the company's assets generally, by returning money to a shareholder and so potentially depriving creditors of that amount.

20. Cases falling outside s.143

Section 143 gives seven cases which fall outside the prohibition, despite the fact that in five cases out of the seven the company purchases its own shares.

These seven cases are:

(a) where the company redeems or purchases its own shares in accordance with the relevant provisions of the Act (*see* 11:**24, 25**); here, owing to the requirements of s. 170, no reduction of capital occurs;

(b) where the company acquires its own shares in a reduction of capital duly made;

(c) where the court makes an order for the purchase of shares in the company by the company under s. 5 (*see* 2:**27**);

(d) where the court makes an order for the purchase of shares in the company by the company under s. 54 (*see* 25:**5**);

(e) where the court makes an order for the purchase of shares in the company by the company under ss. 459–461 (*see* 23:**9**).

In these last three cases the court will also by order provide for the resulting reduction of the company's capital.

(f) where, under the company's articles, forfeiture of shares occurs (*see* 12:**31**);

(g) where the company accepts a surrender of shares in lieu of forfeiture (*see* 12:**33**).

21. Statutory extension of s. 143

Statutory rules which prohibited a company from giving financial assistance for the purchase of its own shares were formerly regarded as an extension of the common law rule in *Trevor v. Whitworth*. The rules are now in ss. 151–154 of the Act. Their effect is to broaden s. 143 in order to prevent attempted evasions of it.

Thus, if a company is approached by Smith and asked if it will *lend* him money in order to enable him to buy shares in that company, and it does so, then the company will have parted with some of its assets in return for a *debt* due to it from Smith. Probably Smith will repay it in due course, with interest, and the company may benefit from the arrangement. But possibly he will not. He might become bankrupt, or he might disappear. Then the loan will not be repaid and the company will have lost that amount of money.

Again, if Smith approaches the company saying that he wishes to buy shares in it, but has no cash available, and has therefore asked his bank manager for a loan which will be forthcoming provided the company acts as his *guarantor*, the same situation will result. Possibly Smith will repay the loan to the bank, and the company will never be liable on its guarantee, but possibly he will not, and the company may then have to pay to the bank the amount of the loan. There is a potential liability to the company here, a potential reduction of its assets.

Even if the company obliges Smith by providing *security* to his bank, e.g. by charging its assets in favour of the bank as security for the loan made to Smith, there is the same possibility that Smith will not repay the bank, which will then enforce its security. The company's assets will therefore be diminished by the value of that security.

Section 151 makes all these transactions illegal. It states the general rule that where a person is *either acquiring or proposing to acquire* any shares in a company, it is unlawful for the company or any of its subsidiaries to give *financial assistance*, directly or indirectly, for the purpose of that acquisition before or at the same time as the acquisition takes place. However, s. 153 provides that this general rule does not apply if:

(a) the acquisition is *either*:

    (*i*) not the company's principal purpose in giving such assistance; *or*

    (*ii*) merely an incidental part of some larger purpose of the company; *and*

(b) the assistance is given in good faith in the interests of the company.

For a transaction in which condition **(b)**, but not condition **(a)**, was held to have been satisfied see *Brady* v. *Brady* (1989) [B91].

Section 151 also deals with slightly different circumstances, providing that where a person *has already acquired* any shares in a company and a liability has been incurred, either by him or by some other person, for the purpose of that acquisition, it is not lawful for the company or any of its subsidiaries to give any *financial assistance*, directly or indirectly, for the purpose of reducing or discharging that liability. However, s. 153 provides that this does not prohibit a company from giving financial assistance if:

(a) the reduction or discharge of the liability is *either*:
    (*i*) not the company's principal purpose in giving such assistance; *or*
    (*ii*) merely an incidental part of some larger purpose of the company: *and*
(b) the assistance is given in good faith in the interests of the company.

By s. 152 the expression 'incurring a liability' includes a case where a person *changes his financial position*, no matter by what means. The restoration of his financial position to what it was before the acquisition took place falls within the prohibition.

It would seem that ss. 151–153 have given express statutory form to the decision in *Belmont Finance Corporation* v. *Williams Furniture Ltd* (1980). In that case it was held that there was a contravention of the general rule against financial assistance (then stated in s. 54 Companies Act 1948) where a company buys something from a vendor without regard to its own commercial interests, the purpose of the transaction being to provide the vendor with funds to buy shares in the company, and it was irrelevant that the price paid was a fair one.

Clearly the expression 'financial assistance' is of major importance and it is helpful to have it defined by the Act in considerable detail. This definition is considered in **22** below.

22. The meaning of 'financial assistance'

Section 152 defines 'financial assistance' as that given:

(a) by way of gift;
(b) by way of guarantee, security, indemnity, release or waiver;
(c) by way of:
    (*i*) a loan; *or*
    (*ii*) any other agreement under which any obligation of the person giving the assistance is to be fulfilled at a time when an obligation of some other party to the agreement remains outstanding; *or*
    (*iii*) the novation or assignment of any right arising under a loan or such other agreement; *or*

(d) in some other manner by a company the net assets of which are thereby reduced to a material extent, or which has no net assets.

'Net assets' here means the aggregate assets less the aggregate liabilities.

The section is silent, as was its predecessor, concerning the identity of the recipient of the financial assistance. However, in *Armour Hick Northern Ltd* v. *Whitehouse* (1980), it was held that the prohibition against financial assistance is not confined to that given to a purchaser, but extends to financial assistance *to whomsoever it is given* for the purpose of a purchase of the company's shares. Doubtless this rule still applies.

23. Transactions given unqualified exemption from the s. 151 prohibitions

Although the provisions of s. 151 mentioned above are widely worded, s. 153 exempts a large number of operations which fall outside their ambit and are therefore lawful. These are as follows:

(a) a distribution of a company's assets lawfully made by way of dividend or in the course of winding up;

(b) the allotment of bonus shares;

(c) a reduction of capital confirmed by order of the court under s. 137 (*see* 11:**21–23**);

(d) a redemption or purchase of any shares made in accordance with ss. 159–181 on redeemable shares and purchase by a company of its own shares (*see* 11:**24–35**);

(e) anything done in pursuance of an order of the court under s. 425 (compromises and arrangements with creditors and members) (*see* 32:**1–4**);

(f) anything done under an arrangement made in pursuance of s. 110 Insolvency Act 1986 (acceptance of shares by liquidator in winding up as consideration for sale of property) (see 29:**22**).

24. Transactions given qualified exemption from the s. 151 prohibitions

Section 153, as amended by s. 132 Companies Act 1989, also exempts three further operations from the prohibition in s. 151.

These are:

(a) The lending of money by the company in the *ordinary course of its business*, where it is a *money-lending company*.

In *Steen* v. *Law* (1964) it was held that this exception, which existed in identical terms under the earlier section, can apply only where the money lent is at the free disposition of the borrower so that he can do what he likes with it, and that it can never cover a loan made for the direct purpose of financing a purchase of the company's shares.

(b) The provision by a company, in good faith in the interests of the company, of financial assistance for the purposes of an employees' share scheme.

(c) The making of loans by a company to persons other than directors who are employed in good faith by the company with a view to enabling those persons to acquire fully paid shares in the company or its holding company to be held by themselves as beneficial owners.

These three exceptions differ from those in **23** above in that where the company in question is a *public* company they are subject to qualification. Section 154 permits a public company to give financial assistance of any of these three kinds only if:

(*i*) its net assets are not thereby reduced; *or*

(*ii*) to the extent that they are thereby reduced, the assistance is provided out of distributable profits.

25. The effect of contravention of s. 151

Section 151, taken along with Schedule 24, imposes criminal liability for breach of the section. If a company contravenes its provisions, the company is liable:

(a) on conviction on indictment, to a fine;

(b) on summary conviction, to a fine not exceeding the statutory maximum;

and any officer who is in default is liable:

(a) on conviction on indictment, to imprisonment not exceeding two years or a fine, or both;

(b) on summary conviction, to imprisonment not exceeding six months or a fine not exceeding the statutory maximum, or both.

With regard to civil liability, it would seem that the effect of contravention of the section is still uncertain. If, for instance, a company contravenes s. 151 by providing unlawful security, it might be expected that the transaction would be void for illegality. At the present time, however, its effect remains doubtful.

In *Victor Battery Co. Ltd* v. *Curry's Ltd* (1946) *security* given in breach of the equivalent provision in the Companies Act 1929 was held to be valid, while in *Selangor United Rubber Estates Ltd* v. *Cradock (No. 3)* (1968) a *loan* contravening s. 54 Companies Act 1948 was held to be void. In *Heald* v. *O'Connor* (1971) Fisher J. reviewed these decisions and held that a debenture giving a charge on the company's assets in breach of the section was void. According to the decision in the Privy Council case *Carney* v. *Herbert* (1985) the *whole transaction* of the purchase of the shares is not void if the unlawful elements in the transaction can be severed and eliminated.

The effect on the directors of the company is nevertheless quite clear. In *Wallersteiner* v. *Moir* (1974) Lord Denning M.R., with his customary lucidity, said:

> 'Every director who is a party to a breach of s. 54 [Companies Act 1948] is guilty of a misfeasance and breach of trust; and is liable to recoup to the company any loss occasioned to it by the default.'

Doubtless this statement can be applied in the same way to a breach of s. 151 Companies Act 1985.

26. Relaxation of the rules in s. 151 for private companies

It is already clear from **24** above that the Act treats private companies more favourably than public companies in relation to the rules laid down by s. 151. In ss. 155–158, however, it goes much further in this direction.

Section 155 removes the prohibitions in s. 151 in their entirety for a private company wishing to give financial assistance for the purpose of the acquisition of shares either in itself or, where its holding company is also a private company, in the holding company, provided that it complies with the rules laid down by ss. 155–158. The rules prescribe both conditions to be fulfilled and a procedure to be followed. They are set out below:

(1) The company's net assets must not be thereby reduced or, to the extent that they are reduced, the financial assistance must be provided out of distributable profits.

(2) Where the company is giving financial assistance for the purpose of the acquisition of shares in its holding company, it must not be a subsidiary of a public company which is itself a subsidiary of that holding company.

The situation envisaged here is that of the 'chain' explained in **13** and **14** above. The section is ensuring that the group chain consists entirely of private companies.

(3) Unless the company is a *wholly-owned subsidiary* (*see* **13**), the financial assistance to be given must be approved by a *special resolution*.

The resolution must be passed on the date when the directors make the statutory declaration mentioned below, or within the following week.

(4) Where the financial assistance to be given by the company is for the purpose of the acquisition of shares in its holding company, it must also be approved by a special resolution of that holding company and of any other holding company which is a subsidiary of that holding company, except in the case of a wholly-owned subsidiary.

The same provision applies to the special resolution here as applies to the special resolution under (3) above.

(5) Where any special resolution is passed by a company, an application for its cancellation may be made to the court by:

(a) the holders of not less than 10 per cent in nominal value of the company's issued share capital or any class of it; *or*
(b) if the company is not limited by shares, not less than 10 per cent of its members.

The application will be governed by the rules laid down in s. 54 (litigation to cancel resolution for re-registration of public company as private) (*see* 25: **5**).

(6) No special resolution will be effective:

(a) unless the statutory declaration and auditors' report mentioned below are available for inspection by members at the meeting at which the resolution is passed;
(b) if it is cancelled by the court on an application under (5) above.

(7) The directors of the company giving the financial assistance and, where the shares to be acquired are shares in its holding company, the directors of that holding company and of any other holding company which is a subsidiary of that holding company, must make a *statutory declaration* before the assistance is given, stating:

(a) the prescribed particulars of the assistance to be given, the company's business and the identity of the recipient;
(b) that they have formed the opinion that immediately after the date when the assistance is to be given there will be no ground on which the company could be found unable to pay its debts; and *either*:

(*i*) if it is intended to commence the company's winding up within 12 months of that date, that the company will be able to pay its debts in full within 12 months of the commencement of the winding up; *or*
(*ii*) if there is no such intention, that the company will be able to pay its debts as they fall due during the year immediately after that date.

(8) The statutory declaration must have annexed to it a *report* by the company's auditors, addressed to the directors, stating that they have inquired into the state of affairs of the company and are not aware of anything to indicate that the directors' opinion is unreasonable.

(9) The statutory declaration and auditors' report must be delivered to the registrar when the special resolution is filed under s. 380 (*see* 15:**34**) or, if no special resolution is required, within 15 days after the declaration is made.

(10) The financial assistance proposed must not be given:

(a) until four weeks have elapsed since the passing of any special resolution required or, if more than one, the last of them, unless every member of the company who is entitled to vote at general meetings voted in favour of it;

(b) until any application for cancellation of such a resolution under (5) above has been determined, unless the court orders otherwise;

(c) after eight weeks have elapsed since the date of the making of the statutory declaration or, if more than one, the earliest of them, unless the court, on any application for cancellation of the resolution, orders otherwise.

It will be seen from the above list that the technicalities prescribed by ss. 155–158 are distressingly detailed. For anyone who is compelled to commit them to memory, it may be helpful to suggest a simple framework in which they may be arranged. This might appear in the following form:

(a) the 'net assets' rule;
(b) the 'chain' rule;
(c) special resolution;
(d) statutory declaration;
(e) auditors' report;
(f) time limits.

For a transaction which was held by the House of Lords to fall within these requirements see *Brady* v. *Brady* (1989) [B91].

27. Acquisition of shares in company by the company's nominee

The prohibition imposed in s. 143 against a company's acquiring its own shares is fortified not only by the rules in ss. 151–158 as to financial assistance by a company for acquisition of its own shares, but also by ss. 144–149 concerning acquisition of shares in a company by the company's nominee. Fortunately the provisions of this section are less extensive.

Under ss. 144 and 145, where a limited company has a beneficial (i.e. equitable) interest in:

(a) shares which are issued, not to the company itself, but to its nominee; *or*

(b) partly paid shares which are acquired by the company's nominee from a third person;

the shares in question must be treated as held by the nominee on his own account and the company must be regarded as having no beneficial interest in them.

If he is called on to pay an amount in respect of them he must comply within 21 days. If he fails to do so, then:

(a) if the shares were issued to him as a subscriber to the memorandum, the *other subscribers*; or

(b) if not, the *directors* of the company at the time when he acquired them;

are jointly and severally liable with him to pay the amount in question.

28. Special rules applicable only to public companies

Section 146–149 impose stringent additional rules applying to *public companies only*. Section 146 gives four cases where these rules apply, the first of which has been considered in 12:**34** since it relates to forfeiture or surrender of shares.

The remaining three comprise cases where the company has a beneficial interest in its own shares and the shares in question were acquired:

(a) by the *company* otherwise than by any of the seven methods mentioned in s. 143 (*see* **20**);

(b) by the *company's nominee* from a third person *without* financial assistance from the company; or

(c) by *any person with* financial assistance from the company.

In each of these three cases s. 146 provides that the shares in question, or the company's interest in them, must, within three years from their acquisition in the case of **(a)** and **(b)** and within one year in the case of **(c)**, be either disposed of or cancelled by the company. If they are cancelled, the company's share capital must be diminished accordingly, and if in consequence it falls below the authorised minimum, the company must apply for re-registration as a private company.

By s. 147 the directors may take such steps as are necessary to enable the company to comply with s. 146 including the passing of a resolution to alter the company's memorandum. Any such resolution must be filed with the registrar within 15 days in accordance with s. 380 (*see* 15:**34**).

Thus in each of these cases the company's shareholding or interest will be purely temporary and the holder of the shares in question is meantime debarred by s. 146 from exercising any voting rights in respect of them.

Finally, s. 150 places strict limits on the cases where a public company may acquire an equitable interest in its own shares by way of security, e.g. a lien. This topic was discussed in 12:**30**.

14

The register of members

1. The sections to be studied

In 2:**16** the register of members was listed as one of the statutory books, and in 2:**15** as one of the registers and documents which the company must keep at its registered office. It must now be considered in detail.

The sections of the Act which are concerned with it range from ss. 352–361, but the student should commit to memory only the main points. These are given below, where it will be seen that s. 357 has been entirely omitted, while s. 355 relating to share warrants has been considered in an earlier chapter (*see* 12:**25**). The sections have not been dealt with in their statutory order, since s. 360 is of major importance and requires more lengthy explanation.

The provisions of s. 362 on overseas branch registers are also given in this chapter.

2. The contents of the register of members

Section 352 requires every company to keep a register of its members and to enter in it:

(a) the names and addresses of members, the shares held by each member distinguishing each share by its number and class, if any, and the amount paid up;
(b) the date of entry in the register;
(c) the date of cessation of membership.

Stock is entered instead of shares where appropriate.

Section 361 states that the register is *prima facie* evidence of the matters inserted in it while s. 352 permits any entry relating to a *former* member of the company to be removed from the register after the expiration of 20 years from the date on which he ceased to be a member.

Finally, s. 352 imposes a limitation period of 20 years on any liability incurred by the company through the making or deletion of an entry in the register.

By s. 352A, inserted by the Companies (Single Member Private Limited Companies) Regulations (SI 1992, No. 1699), if the number of members of a private limited company falls to one, there must be entered in the register of members, along with the name and address of the sole member, a statement that the company has only one member and the date on which the company became a one-member company. It is also provided that if the membership subsequently increases to two or more members, there must be entered in the register, along with the name and address of the former sole member, a statement that the company has ceased to have only one member and the date when that event occurred.

3. The place where the register of members must be kept
Section 353 requires the register of members to be kept at the registered office unless it is made up at another office of the company, when it may be kept there, or by some other person, when it may be kept at his office. It must never be kept outside the company's domicile.

Notice must be given to the registrar of where the register is kept, and of any changes, unless it has always been kept at the registered office.

4. The index of members
Section 354 requires every company with more than 50 members to keep an index, unless the register is already in the form of an index. It must alter the index within 14 days of altering the register.

The index must indicate how the account of each member may be readily found in the register of members.

The index must be kept at the same place as the register of members.

5. Inspection of the register of members and index
Section 356, as amended by s. 143 Companies Act 1989, provides that, except when closed under the provisions of the Act, the register of members and the index must be open to inspection by members free, and by other persons on payment of such fee as may be prescribed.

Any person may require a copy of the register, or any part of it, on payment of such fee as may be prescribed. The copy must be supplied within 10 days.

If inspection is refused, or a copy not sent within the 10 days, the court may order that inspection be allowed or that the copy should be sent.

Section 358, however, permits the company, on giving notice in a local newspaper, to close the register for not more than 30 days in each year.

6. Rectification of the register
Section 359 provides that if:

(a) the name of a person is entered in or omitted from the register of members without sufficient cause; *or*
(b) default or delay occurs in entering a cessation of membership;

the aggrieved person, or any member, or the company may apply to the court for rectification.

The court may either refuse the application, or may order rectification and payment by the company of damages for losses sustained by an aggrieved party.

The court also has power to decide questions of title (i.e. ownership of the shares) and any other necessary questions.

For the court to grant an order for rectification it is not necessary to prove any fault on the company's part: it is sufficient to show that the register is incorrect because of an error or omission: *Re Fagin's Bookshop* (1992) [B115].

The court must order that notice of any rectification shall be given to the registrar.

NOTE: This useful section deserves careful study, as much for its practical as for its academic importance. Note especially the three possible applicants, and the width of the powers given to the court. Often rectification proceedings provide the only remedy available to a person who thinks that he ought to be registered as a member, but who is rejected by the company.

7. Notice of trusts

Section 360 is a short section in simple language but with far-reaching consequences. It states merely that *no notice of any trust shall be entered on the register*, but many students find the concept of the trust difficult to understand and so do not entirely follow the meaning and purpose of the section.

An attempt, therefore, has been made to give a brief explanation of the trust before embarking on the effect of the section.

[Section 360 applies only to companies registered in England and Wales. It is competent for notices of trusts to be entered on the registers of companies registered in Scotland. The trustees are the members and personally liable as such: *Muir* v. *City of Glasgow Bank* (1879). The persons for whom the shares are held in trust are not members although their names may appear on the register: *Gillespie & Paterson* v. *City of Glasgow Bank* (1879). Trustees who have been held liable to calls are entitled to full relief from the trust estate.

The material on equitable ownership (**9–15**) is not applicable to Scotland.]

8. Legal ownership

In the normal way a person accepts the idea of *ownership* without question or analysis. If a student leaves a pen-knife behind after a class, and the lecturer asks to whom it belongs, he will reply: 'Me'. He seldom troubles to think of what he means because this one word, if true, gives him the right to pick it up and take it with him.

If, however, he is asked to think about it, he will readily agree that because he owns the knife he can carry it around with him, or keep it in his desk, or use it for its intended purpose of sharpening pencils, or its unintended purposes such as opening tins and bottles or slicing cucumber. He can sell it, or lend it to a friend, or hire it out to a friend at 10p per week, or pledge it to a pawnbroker. He can throw it in the dustbin or lose it without incurring liability to anyone. In fact, the only things which he may *not* do with it are *acts unlawful in themselves*, such as stabbing the lecturer or cutting the pages out of a library book.

Provided he is acting lawfully, then, the ownership of the knife gives him the right to do a very large number of things with it, and has therefore been described as 'a bundle of rights'. Intangible property, like shares, can be treated in the same way within the limits of its non-physical existence. Thus the owner of shares whose name, as we have seen, normally appears on the register of members, can deal with his shares in any lawful way, and can give them to a friend, sell them, mortgage them or dispose of them by will.

When we talk of ownership in this way, we are referring to a right, or a bundle of rights, recognised and protected by the *common law*. Common law ownership is often called *legal* ownership, to distinguish it from *equitable* ownership which arises under a *trust*.

A brief account of equitable ownership is given below.

9. The origin of equitable ownership

(a) The royal courts of common law had superseded the local and feudal courts and were giving general protection to litigants by the end of the thirteenth century. Their growth since the Conquest in 1066 had by this time led to jurisdiction in all types of case. It was only because the common law had severe disadvantages that the Chancellor, in his court of 'equity' or *natural justice*, started to protect a petitioner who could claim merely a *moral* or *equitable* right to property, and his jurisdiction in this field did not become comprehensive until at least a century later The first independent decree of the Chancellor in the Court of Chancery was given in 1474. Thus common law or legal ownership is historically earlier, and the idea of equitable ownership emerged afterwards to meet difficulties and defects.

(b) We cannot here consider all the disadvantages of the common law ownership of land, the most important type of property in mediaeval times. It is enough to know, for explanatory purposes, that a man could not devise his land by will at common law, and that all conveyances of land were required to be effected in public so that the ownership should never be in doubt. This latter rule was aimed mainly at preventing the evasion of the feudal incidents, i.e. the dues and other burdens which fell on the common law owner of land, whoever he might be. It is hardly surprising that the mediaeval landowner set out to improve his position in much the same way as the modern citizen wrestles with the Inland Revenue.

(c) Though the earliest examples of trusts of land appeared in the thirteenth century, it was not until the fourteenth century that it became a common practice for an owner of land to transfer it to a number of friends *on trust for himself*. By this device he had, *at common law*, no interest in the land at all, yet continued to enjoy it. As far as the common law courts were concerned, his friends owned it, and that was the end of the matter. They owned it as joint tenants, so that if any one of them died, the others merely continued as owners by the right of survivorship or *jus accrescendi*. As long as there were at least two of them, this avoided the worst of the feudal burdens, since these arose on the death of the landowner. If the original owner died, no dues became payable since at common law he was no longer connected with the land in any way. Moreover, he could dispose of the land by will by directing his friends to hold it on trust after his death for anyone he wished to name.

(d) Of course, at first a landowner who adopted this method of evading the disadvantages of common law ownership was taking the risk of his friends proving dishonest and taking advantage of their impregnable position at common law by depriving him of enjoyment. He had no remedy against them in that event, for at common law they were the owners and he was not. But from about the beginning of the fifteenth century the Chancellor, in the early court of equity, started to intervene to protect him.

(e) The Chancellor did this not by opposing the common law, but by ordering the defaulting friends to act equitably, and threatening them with imprisonment if they refused. In other words, he gave the petitioner a *remedy*, and where a court gives a remedy, the citizen has a *right*. The right here was merely in the Court of Chancery, but it was none the less effective against dishonest persons, and because it was recognised by the Chancellor in his equitable jurisdiction, it is called an *equitable right*, or, more usually, an *equitable interest*.

10. The enforceability of equitable interests

In the course of time the Chancellor protected the equitable interest of the petitioner not only against his defaulting friends, but against *any person to whom they should transfer the land* in breach of trust, with *one exception*: the petitioner *was never allowed to enforce his equitable interest against a person who took the land for valuable consideration and without notice of the equitable interest*.

From this development we can now see that there are *two essential rules* to remember:

(a) A legal or common law interest in property cannot be defeated by anyone.

At common law, with the exception of a sale in market overt, only the owner can deprive himself of ownership.

(b) An equitable interest in property can always be defeated by a *bona fide* purchaser for value of the legal interest in that property, though it cannot be defeated by anyone else.

Later these rules will be studied in relation to shares.

11. The nature of a trust

It will be seen from the above explanation that wherever there is an equitable interest in property, there is what is often called *duality of ownership*. By this expression we mean that one person is regarded as the owner of the property *at common law* (i.e. he is the *legal* owner), while another is regarded as the owner in *equity*.

Wherever this duality of ownership exists, there is a *trust*. The *legal* owner is the *trustee*, while the equitable owner is called the *beneficiary* or *cestui que trust*. There are many types of transactions which produce this duality of ownership, for the trust has developed enormously since mediaeval times, and is often said to be the most important feature of our law. An account of the occasions on which a trust arises is, however, outside the scope of this book and should be sought in manuals dealing with equity.

12. The purpose of s. 360

Let us now return to s. 360 which, as we have seen, states that *no notice of a trust shall be entered on the register of members*. It must be understood that the section does not say that there cannot be a trust of shares. It merely says that if there is a trust, it must not be entered on the register. We already know that the correct entry in the register is the name of the member, i.e. the person who *owns* the shares. This, of course, is the person who is the *legal* or *common law* owner, the *trustee* in the case of a trust. It is the *equitable* owner who must be kept off the register, whom the company must not recognise. Note that this is a purely *administrative* section. Its whole object is to simplify administration from the company's viewpoint.

There are in fact *two main reasons* for the section. First, it is possible for *several equitable interests* to arise in a single piece of property. Thus there can be several equitable interests in one holding of shares, while the legal ownership is in the member whose name is on the register. It is therefore possible for a dispute to arise among the owners of the equitable interests as to which of them has priority, i.e. the better claim to the shares.

If their names were to appear on the register, the company might be involved in this dispute, and therefore to prevent the company from being implicated in lengthy argument as to which owner of an equitable interest in the shares has priority, the section simply forbids the company from taking any notice of equitable interests at all. It is concerned solely with the *legal* owner, and if he happens to be a trustee and decides to commit a flagrant breach of trust, the company is not to blame unless it has actual knowledge not only of the trust, but also of the breach — a very unlikely circumstance.

> NOTE: An extreme example of the protection afforded to the company can be seen in *Simpson* v. *Molsons' Bank* (1895), where the company registered a transfer of shares by executors (who are trustees) in breach of the terms of the will of the deceased. The Act incorporating the company provided that it should not be bound to see to the execution of any trust to which its shares were subject. The company had a copy of the will in its possession and its president was one of the defaulting executors and the testator's brother. The company and the executors employed the same law agent. It was held that though the company knew that the shares in question were held by the executors in that capacity, it had no knowledge of their breach of trust, and the knowledge of the executor and law agent could not be imputed to the company so as to affect it with liability.

Without a statutory provision of this kind a company might never dare to register a transfer of shares at all, for fear that it might be party to a breach of trust. It already has been seen that equivalent provisions exist with regard to the register of interests in shares (12:**12**), and later it will be seen that equivalent provisions also exist with regard to the register of directors' interests (16:**17**). While equitable interests must be shown on both these registers, the company is protected from involvement.

Secondly, it is a rule of equity that anyone who meddles with trust property becomes himself a trustee. If the company, therefore, were able to recognise trusts it might become concerned with trust property and so become a trustee, with all the attendant duties and liabilities. This is hardly the proper function of a trading company, and so the section prevents this result from occurring by entirely precluding the company from recognising trusts.

13. Priority of equitable interests

Although s. 360 simplifies the position of the company, it is still sometimes necessary to know how the priority of equitable interests is regulated if there should be several in a single shareholding. There are *two basic rules* for this:

(a) If none of the owners of the equitable interests has succeeded in getting his name put on the company's register of members, then the person whose equitable interest is the earliest has priority.

This rule is often much more neatly expressed by the equitable maxim: *Where the equities are equal, the first in time prevails*. By 'equal' here is meant that the *moral* or equitable claims of the persons concerned are all equally good. Priority must obviously be regulated by something, so it is based on time.

> Thus in *Peat* v. *Clayton* (1906), C assigned his property, including some shares, to P who never obtained the share certificates and never became the registered holder, so that he had merely an equitable interest in them. C subsequently sold the shares to a purchaser who, under the contract of sale, also obtained an equitable interest in the shares. Before either party became registered, P started proceedings claiming that he had the prior equity and therefore the right to have the shares registered in his name. HELD: He was entitled to registration. (He had in fact notified the company of his equitable interest, but the notice was of course quite ineffective because of the section, and his priority depended simply on the rule given above.)

(b) If any one of the owners of the equitable interests succeeds in getting his name put on the register of members, so that he becomes the *legal* owner of the shares, the equitable interests of other persons, even though created earlier, will be destroyed provided he acted *bona fide*.

This rule is expressed by the equitable maxim: *Where the equities are equal, the law prevails*. By 'law' here is meant the *common law*, and we have already seen **(10)** that an equitable interest has a single but important weakness: it can be destroyed by what Maitland describes as that 'extremely rare and extremely lucky person' — the *bona fide* purchaser for value of the legal interest in the property.

The good faith of the person who succeeds in getting registered is an essential factor.

> Thus in *Coleman* v. *London County and Westminster Bank* (1916), a debenture-holder transferred some debentures to a trustee on trust for his own sons, but the transfer was never registered so that the legal interest remained in the original holder. One of the sons sold his equitable interest to a purchaser. Many years later the registered holder deposited the debentures with the bank as security, thus giving the bank an equitable interest in them. When the bank discovered that a purchaser of an equitable interest in the debentures already existed, it applied for registration and succeeded in becoming registered as the legal owner. HELD: It could not obtain priority over the earlier equitable interest in this way, for it was not acting *bona fide*. It *knew* that the earlier interest existed.

These rules are easy to apply provided they are carefully learnt. It cannot be sufficiently stressed that the priority of equitable interests in shares or debentures is regulated by time, but that all equitable interests can be destroyed by a *bona fide* purchaser for value of the legal interest in the property.

14. The stop notice

The student may at this stage feel that the owner of an equitable interest is in a very difficult position. He may not tell the company that he has such an interest, because if he does the company is simply not concerned with the information. Section 360 says so. Consequently he must remain in a precarious state: he has an interest in shares of which the registered holder is the legal owner. How can he protect himself against the holder's dishonesty? If he discovers that the holder is defrauding him, he can of course start legal proceedings. But how can he find out *in time*, i.e. before a *bona fide* purchaser for value has become the registered holder and so defeated his equitable interest entirely?

The answer is that there is a simple process by which he can compel the company to inform him of a pending transfer of the shares. This is to serve on the company a *stop notice* (formerly known as a notice in lieu of distringas), under Order 50, Rules of the Supreme Court 1965.

The effect of this notice is that the company becomes bound to inform the person serving it of any request to transfer the shares. Thus the owner of the equitable interest will be told of any impending threat to his position. He can then, if he likes, apply to the court within eight days for an injunction restraining the company from transferring the shares. If he does not do so, the company may register the transfer in the normal way.

> NOTE: The company is not concerned with the equitable interest; its sole duty is to inform the owner of an impending transfer of the shares. It is entirely up to him to protect his equitable interest by application to the court, and if he does not wish to do this the company is under no obligation to protect it for him.

15. Legal position where company acquires equitable interest

One final problem can arise where *the company itself* acquires an equitable interest in the shares of a member, e.g. under its lien. It has already been seen that where the articles of a company give it a lien on the shares of a member for money due in respect of them, the lien is an equitable interest (*see* 12:**30**).

If in such a case there were already earlier equitable interests in the shares, and if a dispute broke out between their owners and the company so that all claimed to be entitled to the legal ownership of the shares, it might be thought that s. 360 gives the company an unfair advantage in that it prevents the company from having notice of the equitable interests of other persons.

This is not so. The rule applying here is that *the company's equitable interest ranks after any prior equitable interest of which it knows, and it cannot rely on s. 360 to say that it does not know*. It must always be borne in mind that the purpose of s. 360 is administrative convenience, and not to place the company in a better legal position than the holders of other equitable interests.

> Thus in *Bradford Banking Co.* v. *Briggs* (1886), the articles gave the company a lien on the shares for the debts of a member. A member deposited his share certificate with the bank as security, thus giving the bank an equitable interest. The bank notified the company — a notice which in the normal way would be completely ineffective because of s. 360. The member then became indebted to the company, so that a second equitable interest in his shares was created under the company's lien. The question of the priority of the interests arose. HELD: The bank had priority, since s. 360 never operates to deprive the company of notice of an equitable interest *when the company itself is involved*. It gives no undeserved priority.

16. Overseas branch registers

Section 362 provides that a company with a share capital whose objects comprise the transaction of business in any of the countries or territories specified in Part I of Schedule 14 may cause to be kept in such a country or territory a branch register of members resident there, called an 'overseas branch register'.

Part II of Schedule 14 requires the company to give notice to the registrar of the office where any overseas branch register is kept, and of any changes in that office, and of the discontinuance of the register, within 14 days.

It also provides that an overseas branch register is deemed part of the company's principal register, and must be kept in the same manner as the principal register.

The company is required to:

(a) send to its registered office a copy of every entry in its overseas branch register as soon as possible; *and*

(b) keep a duplicate of its overseas branch register at the place where its principal register is kept.

15

Company meetings and the annual return

1. Types of company meeting

There are three types of meetings attended by shareholders

(a) annual general meetings;
(b) extraordinary general meetings;
(c) class meetings.

2. Annual general meetings

Section 366 requires every company in each year (i.e. calendar year) to hold a general meeting as its annual general meeting, and to specify it as such in the notices calling it. There must not be more than 15 months between the meetings.

If, however, the *first* annual general meeting is held *within 18 months of incorporation,* none need be held in the year of incorporation or the following year. Thus a company incorporated in September 1988 need not hold an annual general meeting in either 1988 or 1989, since it can hold its first annual general meeting early in 1990 without infringing the provisions of the Act.

Section 367 provides that if the company does not comply with s. 366, any member may apply to the Department of Trade and Industry, which may then itself call a general meeting and give such directions as it thinks fit, including a direction that *one member present in person or by proxy* shall be deemed to constitute a meeting.

Such a meeting is deemed to be an annual general meeting, but if it is not held in the year in which default occurred, it is not treated as the annual general meeting for the year in which it is actually held unless the company resolves that it be so treated.

3. Election by private company to dispense with annual general meeting.

By s. 366A, inserted in the 1985 Act by s. 115 Companies Act 1989, a private company may elect, by 'elective resolution' (*see* **37**), to dispense with the holding of annual general meetings.

An election has effect for the year in which it is made and later years, but does not affect any liability already incurred for default in holding an annual general meeting.

When an election has been made it may be readily cancelled, since s. 366A provides that any member may, by notice to the company not later than three months before the end of the year, require the holding of an annual general meeting in that year. The provisions of s. 366 as to the calling of the meeting and the consequences of default then again apply.

4 The business transacted at an annual general meeting.

The business usually transacted at an annual general meeting consists of:

(a) declaring a dividend;
(b) the consideration of the accounts, balance sheets, and directors' and auditors' reports;
(c) the election of directors; *and*
(d) the appointment and remuneration of the auditors.

Other business may also be transacted at the annual general meeting but it is in practice more usual to convene an extraordinary general meeting to deal with business other than that in **(a)** to **(d)** above.

5. The documents accompanying the notice of the annual general meeting.

As stated in **4** above, the annual general meeting is normally the occasion on which the directors lay before the company the profit and loss account and balance sheet.

Section 238 and 241 provide that a copy of the company's accounts (i.e. profit and loss account and balance sheet, the directors' report, the auditors' report and the company's group accounts if applicable) must, at least 21 days before the meeting, be sent to every member, every debenture-holder, and all other persons entitled to receive notice of general meetings.

If these documents are sent less than 21 days before the meeting, they are still deemed to have been duly sent if it is so agreed by all the members entitled to attend and vote: s. 238.

By s. 242 the directors must deliver a copy of the accounts to the registrar and if any document comprised in the accounts is in a language other than English must annex to the document a certified translation of it into English.

6. Extraordinary general meetings

All general meetings other than the annual general meeting are extraordinary general meetings. The directors may convene one whenever they wish.

Table A, Article 37, authorises the directors to call general meetings, and provides that if there are not within the United Kingdom sufficient directors to call a general meeting, any director or any member of the company may call a general meeting.

7. Convening of extraordinary general meeting on requisition

Section 368 provides that, despite anything in the articles, the directors *must* convene an extraordinary general meeting on the requisition of members holding *not less than one-tenth of the paid up capital carrying the right to vote* or, if the company has no share capital, members representing not less than one-tenth of the total voting rights.

The requisition must state the objects of the meeting, be signed by the requisitionists, and deposited at the registered office.

If the directors do not proceed to convene a meeting within 21 days from the deposit of the requisition, the requisitionists, or those representing more than half their total voting rights, may themselves convene a meeting. This meeting must not be held more than three months after the date of the deposit. It must be convened in the same manner as meetings convened by the directors.

Any reasonable expenses incurred by the requisitionists must be repaid to them by the company, and that sum must be retained by the company out of the remuneration due to the defaulting directors.

By an amendment of s.368 made by s. 145 and Schedule 19 Companies Act 1989, the directors are placed under an obligation to convene the meeting for a date not more than 28 days after the date of the notice convening the meeting. The purpose of this provision is to prevent the directors from fixing a date so far into the future that the value of the right to requisition a meeting will have, in effect, been lost.

The same purpose is served by the provision in Table A, Article 37, which requires the directors to convene a meeting held on requisition for a date not later than eight weeks after receipt of the requisition.

8. The business transacted at an extraordinary general meeting

This can comprise anything which under the Act or the articles is required to be done by the company in general meeting. Usually the business will be something other than the usual business of annual general meetings (*see* 4), e.g. it may be an alteration of the articles.

9. Provision enabling members to call a meeting

Section 370 provides that unless the articles otherwise provide, *two or more members holding not less than one-tenth of the issued share capital* (whether with voting rights or not), or if the company has no share capital, not less than 5 per cent of the members, may call a meeting.

10. Power of court to order a meeting

Section 371 provides that if for any reason it is impracticable to call or conduct a meeting, the court may, either of its own motion or on the application of any director or any member who would be entitled to vote, order a meeting to be called, held and conducted in such manner as the court thinks fit, and may give such directions as it thinks expedient, including a direction that *one member present in person or by proxy* shall be deemed to constitute a meeting.

Such a direction was given in *Re Opera Photographic Ltd* (1989) where one of the two shareholders refused to attend a meeting convened for the purpose of removing him from his directorship.

11. Class meeting

Sometimes a meeting of a particular class of shareholders is held. At a class meeting the holders of the remainder of the company's shares have no right to be present.

The usual business of a class meeting is to consider a variation of class rights. This topic has been extensively treated in Chapter 11.

12. The requisites of a valid meeting

For a meeting to be valid the following conditions must be satisfied:

(a) It must be properly convened. This means:

(*i*) that the persons entitled to attend must have been summoned by the proper authority, i.e. the board of directors, *and*

(*ii*) that proper and adequate notice must have been sent to all those entitled to attend.

In convening the meeting the directors must act at a valid board meeting, and in good faith in the interests of the company as a whole, as always. Thus they must not convene a general meeting at an unreasonable hour or inconvenient place, or with the deliberate intention of making it impossible for certain members to attend.

(b) It must be legally constituted. This means:

(*i*) that the proper person must be in the chair;

(*ii*) that the rules as to quorum must be observed; *and*

(*iii*) that the Act and the articles must be complied with.

(c) The business at the meeting must be validly transacted.

These three conditions are considered below.

13. Persons entitled to notice of meetings

Section 370 provides that unless the articles otherwise provide, notice of meetings must be served on *every member* in the manner required by the *Table A* which is at present in force (*see 3*: **6**).

Table A, Article 38, requires notice to be sent to:

(a) every member, except that, by Article 112, those who have neither got a registered address within the United Kingdom nor supplied the company with an address for the purpose are not entitled to receive any notice;

(b) the personal representative of a deceased member who, but for his death, would have been entitled to notice (13: **9**);

(c) the trustee in bankruptcy of a bankrupt member who, but for his bankruptcy, would have been entitled to notice (13: **11**);

(d) the directors and auditors.

At common law, notice of meetings may be excused if a person is beyond summoning distance or, perhaps, if he is too unwell to attend. But in the case of registered companies, this rule does not apply, for s. 372, considered below, allows members to appoint *proxies* to attend and vote on their behalf if they are unable to do so themselves. All members, therefore, should receive notice.

Again, at common law, failure to give notice, even if it is quite accidental, will invalidate the meeting. Nor can a member waive his right to notice by saying, for example, that he is unable to attend and therefore notice need not be served on him. Table A, Article 39, accordingly contains a provision which prevents this result, by stating that the accidental omission to give notice, or the non-receipt of notice, shall not invalidate the proceedings at the meeting.

Thus in *Re West Canadian Collieries* (1962) [B 217], in sending to members notice of a special resolution for a proposed reduction of capital, the company by an error omitted to send notice to nine of its members. The special resolution was passed at the meeting. The articles contained a clause identical with Article 39 above. HELD: The omission was 'accidental' within the article, and notice was deemed to have been duly given so that the proceedings were valid.

It should be noted under Table A, Article 38, *every member* is entitled to notice and therefore to attend the meeting. This is so even if he holds non-voting shares and thus cannot vote when he gets there. Probably a member without a vote would not be entitled to attend meetings unless the articles expressly provide to that effect: *Re Mackenzie and Co. Ltd* (1916).

14. Method of service of notice

Table A, Article 112, provides that notice may be given to any member either personally, or by sending it by post to him at his registered address or by leaving it at that address. If a member's registered address is not within the United Kingdom, he may give to the company an address within the United Kingdom at which notices are to be given to him, but otherwise he is not entitled to receive any notice.

Article 112 also provides that, in the case of joint holders, notice must be given to the joint holder whose name stands first in the register of members and that that is sufficient notice to all the joint holders.

By Article 115 proof that an envelope containing a notice was properly addressed, prepaid and posted is conclusive evidence that the notice was given. A notice is deemed to be given 48 hours after posting.

15. The contents of the notice

Table A, Article 38, provides that the notice must specify the time and place of the meeting and the general nature of the business to be transacted, and, in the case of an annual general meeting, must specify that the meeting is such a meeting.

A resolution which is not covered by the terms of the notice cannot validly be passed, and if it is an *extraordinary* or *special resolution the exact wording* of the resolution must be given.

> Thus in *Re Moorgate Mercantile Holdings Ltd* (1980) Slade J. held, with respect to a special resolution, that 'there must be absolute identity, at least in substance, between the intended resolution referred to in the notice and the resolution actually passed'.

Furthermore, s. 378 requires the notice to state that it is intended to propose the resolution as an extraordinary or special one, as the case may be.

Finally, s. 372 requires the notice to state that a member entitled to attend and vote is entitled to appoint a proxy to attend and vote instead of him, and that the proxy need not also be a member.

16. Statutory requirements as to length of notice

Articles may provide that the number of days' notice specified must be *clear days,* i.e. the number is exclusive of the day on which the notice is served and the day of the meeting. For instance, Table A, Article 38, requires 21 *clear days'* notice for an annual general meeting and for a special resolution or a resolution appointing a director. The Act contains important provisions on the number of days' notice required.

Section 369 provides that any article is *void* in so far as it provides for the calling of a meeting by a *shorter* notice than:

(a) 21 days' notice in writing for the annual general meeting;
(b) 14 days' notice in writing for all other meetings, except those for the passing of a special resolution.

Unless the articles otherwise provide by a clause which is not avoided by these provisions a meeting may be called:

(a) by 21 days' notice in writing for the annual general meeting;
(b) by 14 days' notice in writing for all other meetings, except those for the passing of a special resolution.

The effect of these two subsections is that the articles may provide for *longer* periods of notice than the stated 21 or 14 days, but may *not* provide for *shorter* periods.

The section does not state specifically the period of notice required when a special resolution is to be passed at a meeting other than the annual general meeting. The period is in fact 21 days, as is clear from s. 378 (*see* below).

Section 369 states when a *shorter* notice is permissible. It provides that a meeting shall be deemed to have been duly called, even though the period of notice is shorter than the required 21 or 14 days or the period required by the articles, if it is so agreed:

(a) in the case of the *annual general meeting*, by *all the members entitled to attend and vote*;
(b) in the case of *any other meeting*, by a *majority in number of* the members with the right to attend and vote *holding not less* than 95 per cent in nominal value of the shares giving the right to attend and vote.

If the company has no share capital, the majority must represent not less than 95 per cent of the total voting rights.

By an addition made to s. 369 by s. 115 Companies Act 1989 a private company may, by elective resolution (*see* **37**), substitute a percentage of not less than 90 per cent in place of 95 per cent in these provisions.

The consent to shorter notice may be given either at or before the meeting. It is usual to obtain it in writing by asking the shareholders to sign a form of consent, but presumably oral consent would suffice since s. 369 does not require it to be in writing.

The members cannot entirely dispense with notice: there must be some notice, however short. This follows from the wording of s. 369.

Section 378, mentioned above, provides that where a *special resolution* is to be passed, not less than *21 days' notice* of the meeting must be given, specifying the intention to propose the resolution as a special resolution. Shorter notice is again permissible here where agreed to by the same majority as required by s. 369, as amended by the 1989 Act, above.

17. Special notice

Certain *ordinary* resolutions require *special* notice, in which case s. 379 provides that such a resolution is not effective unless notice of the intention to move it has been given *to* the company at least *28 days before the meeting*.

The company must then give the members notice of the resolution at the same time and in the same manner as it gives notice of the meeting, or, if that is not practicable, by advertisement or in any other mode allowed by the articles, not less than 21 days before the meeting.

If a meeting is called for a date 28 days or less after the notice has been given, the notice, though not given within the time required by the section, is still deemed to have been properly given. This useful little provision is intended to defeat deliberately obstructive directors.

When a company receives special notice, it is not necessary to convene a meeting specially to enable the resolution to be considered. It can be deferred until the next annual general meeting or extraordinary general meeting which is convened.

It should also be noted that if the resolution is considered at an extraordinary general meeting, 14 days' notice is adequate provided it is given at the same time and in the same manner as the notice of the meeting.

The following are the resolutions requiring special notice:

(a) a resolution to remove a director: s. 303 (16: **23**);

(b) a resolution to appoint another director in his place: s. 303;

(c) a resolution appointing a director over the age limit: s. 293 (16: **19**);

(d) a resolution to appoint as auditor a person other than a retiring auditor: s. 391A (19: **14**);

(e) a resolution to fill a casual vacancy in the office of auditor: s. 388 (19: **11**);

(f) a resolution to reappoint as auditor a retiring auditor who was appointed by the directors to fill a casual vacancy: s. 388;

(g) a resolution to remove an auditor before the expiration of his term of office: s. 391A.

Students should be careful to observe that *special notice* (s. 379) has no connection whatever with *special resolutions* (s. 378). The terminology is confusing, but once it is understood that these two things are quite unconnected, there is less likelihood of error.

18. The chairman

Section 370 provides that unless the articles otherwise provide, *any member* elected by the members present at a meeting may be the chairman. Normally, however, the articles in fact provide otherwise, and Table A, Article 42, states that the *chairman of the board of directors* shall preside as chairman at every general meeting. It also states that if the chairman is not present within *15 minutes* of the time appointed for the commencement of the meeting, or is unwilling to act, the directors present must elect one of their number to be chairman.

Article 43 states that if no director is willing to act as chairman, or if no director is present within 15 minutes, the members present and entitled to vote must choose one of their number to be chairman.

At common law a chairman has no casting vote, but Table A, Article 50, gives him one in the case of an *equality of votes,* either on a show of hands or on a poll. If he is not also a shareholder in the company, this will be his only vote, and he is not bound to exercise it.

19. Duties of the chairman

The chairman's position is of great importance, and his duties include the following:

(a) He must act at all times *bona fide* and in the interests of the company as a whole.

(b) He must ensure that the meeting is properly convened and constituted, i.e. that proper notice has been given, that the rules as to quorum are observed, and that his own appointment is in order.

(c) He must ensure that the provisions of the Act and the articles are observed, that the business is taken in the order set out in the agenda, and that the business is within the scope of the meeting.

(d) He must preserve order.

(e) He must take the sense of the meeting by putting the motions in their proper form, and declare the result of the voting.

(f) He must exercise his casting vote, if any, *bona fide* in the interests of the company. This probably involves voting *against* the motion.

(g) He must exercise correctly his powers of adjournment and of demanding a poll.

20. Quorum

A quorum is the minimum number of persons whose presence is necessary for the transaction of business. At *common law, one* person cannot constitute a meeting, even though he holds proxies for several other persons, and the minimum quorum is therefore two persons entitled to vote and present in person: *Sharp* v. *Dawes* (1876).

In the case of registered companies s. 370 adopts the common law rule and states that, unless the articles otherwise provide, the quorum shall be *two members personally present.* Table A, Article 40, repeats this provision with recognition for proxies, stating that *two* persons, each being a member or a proxy for a member, shall be a quorum.

An interesting construction was put on an article which required *three members present in person* in the Scottish case of *Neil McLeod and Sons, Petitioners* (1967). There two shareholders attended the meeting, one of them in the dual capacity of individual and trustee. It was held that the required quorum was present. A different result might well have been reached in England where s. 360 applies (*see* 14: **12**).

Table A, Article 40, provides that no business shall be transacted at any meeting unless a quorum is present. This is in accordance with the common law, by which it is essential that the quorum remains present throughout the proceedings. If, however, the articles provide, as Table A in Schedule 1 to the 1948 Act provided, that no business shall be transacted unless a quorum is present *at the time when the meeting proceeds to business,* then the court may hold, as it did in *Re Hartley Baird Ltd* (1955), that a quorum need be present only when the meeting commences, it being immaterial that there is no longer a quorum present when a vote is taken.

Article 41 states that if within half an hour a quorum is not present, or if during a meeting a quorum ceases to be present, the meeting shall stand adjourned to the same day in the next week, at the same time and place, or to such time and place as the directors may determine.

21. Exceptions to the rule in *Sharp* v. *Dawes*

There are certain exceptional cases where, despite the rule in *Sharp* v. *Dawes, one* person may constitute a meeting. These are as follows:

(a) under s. 367 (*see* **2** above);

(b) under s. 371 (*see* **10** above);

(c) where there is a committee of one (*see* 16: **62**);

(d) where there is a class meeting of shareholders, and all the shares of that class are held by one person: *East* v. *Bennett Bros. Ltd* (1911);

(e) under Article 89, where the directors fix the quorum for board meetings at one.

(f) under s. 370A, inserted by the Companies (Single Member Private Limited Companies) Regulations 1992 (SI 1992, No. 1699), where a private limited company has only one member.

An instance of **(b)** is *Re Opera Photographic Ltd* (1989): A company had an issued share capital of 100 shares, of which A held 51 and B held 49. The quorum for shareholders' and directors' meetings was two persons. A and B fell out. A meeting was summoned under s. 368 (*see* **7**) by A to remove B from his directorship. As B did not attend, there was no quorum. A sought and obtained an order from the court under s. 371.

22. Adjournments

Table A, Article 45, provides that the chairman may, with the consent of any meeting at which a quorum is present, and shall if so directed by the meeting, adjourn the meeting.

Under such an article a chairman has no power to adjourn the meeting without its consent, unless there is disorder or he is for some other reason unable to ascertain the views of members (as where members were partly accommodated in overflow rooms and audio-visual links were not working: *Byng* v. *London Life Association Ltd* (1989)). He has a residual power to adjourn the meeting if the machinery of the articles breaks down, but if he wrongly adjourns it, the meeting may appoint another chairman and continue the business.

At *common law* no notice is required of an adjourned meeting unless the original meeting is adjourned *sine die* (without a day being fixed for the holding of the adjourned meeting) or unless *fresh business* is to be discussed. Articles often vary this rule, and Table A, Article 45, provides that no business shall be transacted at an adjourned meeting other than business which might properly have been transacted at the original meeting. Moreover, when the meeting is adjourned for 14 days or more, Article 45 requires at least seven days' notice of the adjourned meeting to be given.

A properly convened meeting *cannot be postponed* by subsequent notice to that effect. It should be held and then immediately adjourned without transacting any business.

23. Resolutions passed at adjourned meetings

Section 381 provides that resolutions passed at adjourned meetings are to be treated as having been passed on the date on which they were in fact passed.

This provision is necessary because in law an adjourned meeting is merely a continuation of the original meeting, so that a resolution passed at an adjourned meeting would otherwise take effect as if passed at the *original* meeting.

24. Voting

The common law method of taking a vote is on a *show of hands,* and this is adopted by registered companies.

Table A, Article 46, provides that a resolution shall be decided on a show of hands unless a poll is demanded by the proper persons, and Article 54 states that on a show of hands *every member present shall have one vote*. It follows that under Article 54 *proxies* cannot vote on a show of hands.

Section 372 provides that unless the articles otherwise provide, a proxy is not entitled to vote on a show of hands, but even where the articles confer this right, a member present who holds proxies for several other absent members still has only one vote.

Section 375 provides that a representative appointed by a corporation to attend and vote at meetings of a company of which it is a member or creditor has the same powers as it would have if it were an individual. Thus he can vote on a show of hands, and is not a proxy.

Section 378 provides that at a meeting at which an extraordinary or special resolution is to be passed, a declaration by the chairman that it is carried is, unless a poll is demanded, conclusive evidence of that fact without proof of the number of votes recorded for or against the resolution. Table A, Article 47, contains an even stronger provision to the same effect, stating that unless a poll is demanded, a declaration by the chairman that a resolution has been carried, or carried unanimously, or by a particular majority, or lost, or not carried by a particular majority and an entry in the minutes to that effect, is conclusive evidence of the fact without proof of the number of votes recorded for or against the resolution.

NOTE: Article 31 (13:**9**), Article 55 (13:**3**), and Article 56 (13:**7**) are all relevant here, but have already been discussed. Article 57 provides that a member may not vote unless all calls or other sums presently payable by him in respect of his shares have been paid. Lastly, Article 58 provides that no objection may be raised to the qualification of any voter *except at the meeting* or adjourned meeting at which the vote objected to is given, and every vote not disallowed at such meeting is valid. Any objection made in due time must be referred to the chairman, whose decision is final.

25. Voting on a poll

Voting on a show of hands ceases to have any effect once a poll has been properly demanded; indeed, a poll can be demanded without going through the formality of a show of hands at all: *Holmes* v. *Keyes* (1959). The chairman must then allow a poll and decide when and where it is to be taken.

Table A, Article 51, provides that a poll demanded on the *election of a chairman* or on a *question of adjournment* must be taken forthwith. A poll demanded on *any other question* must be taken either forthwith or within the next 30 days at such time and place as the chairman directs, and meanwhile any other business may be proceeded with.

On a poll, members have the number of votes attached to their shares. Table A, Article 54, provides that a member has one vote for each share, and s. 370 provides that unless the articles otherwise provide, every member has one vote for each share or each £10 of stock. Article 59 provides that on a poll votes may be given either *personally* or *by proxy*.

Section 374 provides that on a poll, a member entitled to more than one vote need not use all his votes, nor cast all those used in the same way. This enables a nominee shareholder holding shares on trust for more than one beneficial owner to exercise the votes as the beneficial owners direct.

If the chairman decides that a poll should be taken at some future date, the question arises as to whether proxies lodged between the date of the meeting and the date of the poll can be accepted. A poll is an enlargement or *continuation* of the meeting at which it was demanded, and *not an adjournment* of it, so that in *Shaw* v. *Tall Concessions Ltd* (1913), where the articles allowed lodgment of proxies 48 hours before a *meeting or any adjournment thereof*, it was held that fresh proxies could *not* be lodged between the meeting and the poll.

Table A, Article 62, however, resolves this difficulty by providing that proxies must be lodged at least 48 hours before the time of the meeting or any adjournment of it, or, in the case of a poll taken more than 48 hours after it is demanded, at least 24 hours before the time appointed for the taking of the poll. In the case of a poll not taken forthwith but taken within 48 hours after it is demanded, the proxy must be delivered at the meeting at which the poll is demanded to the chairman or to the secretary or to any director. Thus, if the poll is not taken within the next 48 hours, fresh proxies can under this article be accepted between the date of the meeting and that of the poll.

26. The right to demand a poll

The right to demand a poll is a *common law* right which normally may be excluded by the regulations of any association. In the case of registered companies, however, s. 373 gives members a *statutory right* to demand a poll on any question *except*:

(a) the election of the chairman; *and*
(b) the adjournment of the meeting.

This statutory right cannot be excluded by the articles.

Section 373 provides that an article which *makes ineffective* a demand for a poll by any of the following is *void*:

(a) by five or more members having the right to vote;
(b) by members having at least one-tenth of the total voting rights of members having the right to vote at the meeting;
(c) by members holding voting shares on which one-tenth of the sum paid up on all voting shares has been paid up.

Students often find this provision difficult, especially **(a)**. Perhaps this can be more simply expressed by saying that *any five or more members have a right to demand a poll, no matter what the articles may say*. In fact, Table A, Article 46, gives *wider rights* than the section, for it states that a poll may be demanded by:

(a) the chairman; *or*
(b) at least two members having the right to vote; *or*

(c) members representing at least one-tenth of the total voting rights of all members having the right to vote at the meeting; *or*

(d) members holding voting shares on which one-tenth of the total sum paid up on all voting shares has been paid up.

It is important to understand that there is no conflict between s. 373 and Article 46. The Act is merely ensuring that the articles do not insist on a poll being demanded by, for example, 20 persons before the demand is valid. There is nothing to prevent the articles from stating that a poll may be validly demanded by *one* member, if this is thought desirable.

Section 373 also provides that an instrument appointing a proxy to vote is deemed also to confer authority to demand a poll, and Table A, Article 46, contains a provision to the same effect.

Finally, Article 48 provides that a demand for a poll may, before the poll is taken, be withdrawn, but only with the consent of the chairman.

27. Proxies

The term 'proxy' covers not only the *person* who is appointed to act on behalf of a member at a meeting, but also the *instrument* by which the appointment is made. There is no right to appoint a proxy at *common law*, but s. 372 gives members a statutory right to do so.

That section provides that any member entitled to attend and vote is entitled to appoint another person (*whether a member or not*) as his proxy to attend and vote instead of him. In a *private* company a proxy also has the same right as the member to *speak*.

However, unless the articles otherwise provide:

(a) that provision applies only to companies with share capital;

(b) a member of a *private* company may appoint only one proxy on each occasion;

(c) a proxy may vote only on a poll.

Any provision in the articles is *void* if it requires the instrument appointing the proxy to be received by the company more than 48 hours before a meeting or adjourned meeting. Table A, Article 62, specifies the maximum period permitted by the Act, i.e. 48 hours.

A member who has appointed a proxy, however, may still attend the meeting and exercise his vote if he wishes, though this will revoke his proxy. Proxies may also be revoked by notice to the company at any time before they are acted upon, or by the death of the member. Accordingly Table A, Article 63, provides that a vote of a proxy is valid despite the termination of the proxy's authority unless notice of the termination has been received by the company before the commencement of the meeting.

28. Specified proxies

Many companies send along with the notice of the meeting a form of proxy in favour of the directors. Members who cannot attend the meeting merely have to complete the form and send it back to the company. These proxy forms may be sent at the expense of the company, but some control is obviously necessary to prevent the directors sending them only to persons who will support their policy.

Section 372 accordingly provides that if invitations to appoint as proxy a person *specified in the invitations* are issued at the company's expense to *some only* of the members, every officer who knowingly and wilfully authorises their issue is liable to a fine, unless he does so at the written request of the member, and the form would be available to every member on his written request.

29. Form of proxy

Table A, Article 60, provides that the instrument appointing a proxy shall be in writing executed by or on behalf of the appointor. *A proxy need not be a member*: s. 372.

Two forms of proxy are in use:

(a) The *ordinary* form, as shown in Table A, Article 60, which simply authorises the proxy to *vote on behalf of the member* (a *general* proxy).

(b) The *two-way* form, as shown in Table A, Article 61, which directs the proxy to *vote for or against the resolution*; here only if the member fails to give the proxy express directions how to vote may he exercise his discretion (a *special* proxy).

30. Minutes

In 2:**16** we saw that s. 382 requires every company to keep minutes of the proceedings at both general and board meetings.

Minutes, if signed by the chairman of the meeting or the next succeeding meeting, are evidence of the proceedings. They are normally only *prima facie* evidence, though Article 47 (*see* **24**) gives an exception to this.

Section 382 provides that where minutes have been made in accordance with the section, the meeting is deemed duly held and convened, the proceedings duly had, and appointments of directors or liquidators valid, until the contrary is proved.

By s. 382A, inserted by s. 113 Companies Act 1989, written resolutions by private companies under s. 381A (*see* **36**) must also be entered in a book in the same way as minutes of a general meeting, and the record, if signed by a director or by the company secretary, is *prima facie* evidence that the requirements of the Act with regard to the proceedings in agreeing to the resolution have been complied with.

By s. 382B, inserted by the Companies (Single Member Private Limited

Companies) Regulations 1992, where a private limited company has only one member and he takes any decision which may be taken by the company in general meeting, then (unless the decision is taken by way of a written resolution) he must provide the company with a written record of the decision. A sole member failing to comply with this provision is liable to a fine, but the validity of the decision is not affected.

Section 383, as amended by s. 143 Companies Act 1989, requires the minute books of proceedings at general meetings to be kept at the registered office (*see* 2:**15**), and to be open to inspection to any member free. Any member is entitled, on payment of such fee as may be prescribed, to a copy of the minutes within seven days, and the court has power to order inspection or the provision of copies if the company fails to comply with the section.

31. Resolutions

There are three types of resolutions: ordinary (passed by a simple majority), extraordinary (passed by a majority of 75 per cent) and special (passed by a majority of 75 per cent on 21 days' notice). In all cases, the majority is of those members present and voting, i.e. absentees and abstentions are not counted. It is important to understand that unless an Act or the articles expressly require a special or extraordinary resolution, an ordinary resolution will suffice.

It is therefore essential to know the occasions on which an Act requires a special or extraordinary resolution.

32. Purposes for which a special resolution is required

A special resolution is required:

(a) under s. 4, to alter the objects clause of the memorandum;

(b) under s. 9, to alter the articles;

(c) under s. 17, to alter any condition in the memorandum other than the compulsory clauses and class rights;

(d) under s. 28, to change the name of the company;

(e) under s. 35, as substituted by s. 108 Companies Act 1989, to ratify an act done by directors which is beyond the company's capacity;

(f) under s. 43, to re-register a private company with a share capital as a public company;

(g) under ss. 43 and 48, to re-register an unlimited private company as a public company;

(h) under s. 51, to re-register an unlimited (private) company as limited;

(i) under s. 53, to re-register a public company as a private company;

(j) under s. 95, to withdraw or modify the statutory pre-emption rights;

(k) under s. 120, to create reserve capital;

(l) under s. 135, to reduce capital, with the consent of the court;

(m) under s. 155, to approve the giving of financial assistance by a private company for the acquisition of shares in itself;

(n) under s. 173, to approve a payment out of capital by a private company for the redemption or purchase of its own shares;

(o) under s. 307, to make the liability of the directors unlimited;

(p) under s. 308, to approve the assignment of office by a director;

(q) under s. 84 Insolvency Act 1986, to wind up voluntarily;

(r) under s. 110 Insolvency Act 1986, to sanction the sale of the company's property by the liquidator in a members' voluntary winding up for shares in another company;

(s) under s. 122 Insolvency Act 1986, to effect a winding up by the court.

33. Purposes for which an extraordinary resolution is required

An extraordinary resolution is required:

(a) under s. 125, at a class meeting to sanction a variation of class rights in certain circumstances;

(b) under s. 84 Insolvency Act 1986, to wind up the company voluntarily because it cannot continue its business owing to its liabilities;

(c) under s. 165 and Schedule 4 Insolvency Act 1986, in a members' voluntary winding up, to sanction the exercise by the liquidator of the following powers:

    (*i*) to pay any class of creditors in full;

    (*ii*) to make a compromise or arrangement with creditors;

    (*iii*) to compromise all calls, debts and claims between the company and a contributory or other debtor.

34. The filing of resolutions

Section 380, as amended by s. 116 Companies Act 1989, requires a copy of the following resolutions or agreements to be sent to the registrar within 15 days:

(a) *special* resolutions;

(b) *extraordinary* resolutions;

(c) an *elective* resolution or a resolution revoking such a resolution (*see* **37**);

(d) resolutions or agreements which have been agreed to by *all the members,* but which would not otherwise have been effective unless they had been passed as special or extraordinary resolutions;

(e) resolutions or agreements which have been agreed to by *all the members of some class* of shareholders, but which would not otherwise have been effective unless passed by some *particular majority* or in some *particular manner,* and all resolutions or agreements which *bind all the members of a class* of shareholders though not agreed to by all of them;

(f) a resolution passed by the *directors* to comply with a direction under s. 32 (change of name on Secretary of State's direction) (*see* 2:**13**);

(g) a resolution passed under s 80 (authority conferred on directors for certain allotments) (*see* 9:**9**);

(h) a resolution of the *directors* passed under s. 147 (alteration of memorandum on company ceasing to be a public company, following acquisition of its own shares) (*see* 12:**34** and 13:**28**);

(i) a resolution passed under s. 166 (authority conferred for market purchase of company's own shares) (*see* 11:**28**);

(j) a resolution for voluntary winding up passed under s. 84 Insolvency Act 1986, when the period fixed by the articles for the company's duration expires.

Further, by s. 111 there must also be delivered to the registrar within 15 days:

(k) a resolution passed under s. 104 (transfer to public company of non-cash asset in initial period) (*see* 6:**5**).

Section 380 provides that where articles have been registered, a copy of every resolution and agreement to which the section applies must be embodied in or annexed to every future copy of the articles. By s. 18 where any resolution or agreement sent to the registrar makes an alteration in the memorandum or articles (other than an alteration of objects) the company must send with it a printed copy of the memorandum or articles as altered.

Section 380 provides that where articles have not been registered, a copy of every resolution and agreement to which the section applies must be sent to any member at his request, on payment of a small fee.

Finally, s. 711 requires the registrar to publish in the *Gazette* a copy of any resolution or agreement to which s. 380 applies and which:

(a) states *the rights attached to any shares in a public company*, other than shares which are in all respects uniform with those previously allotted;

(b) *varies rights* attached to any shares in a public company; *or*

(c) *assigns a name or other designation*, or a new name or designation, to any class of shares in a public company.

35. Circulation of members' resolutions
Section 376 provides that on the requisition in writing of:

(a) *any number of members* representing *at least one-twentieth of the total voting rights* of all the members with a right to vote at the date of the requisition, *or*

(b) *at least 100 members* (whether entitled to vote or not) who have *paid up* on their shares *an average sum of at least £100 per member*, the company must, at the requisitionists' expense unless the company otherwise resolves, give members entitled to receive notice of the next *annual* general meeting notice of any resolution which may properly be moved and is intended to be moved at that meeting.

It must also circulate to members entitled to notice of *any* general meeting any statement of not more than 1000 words concerning the subject-matter of any proposed resolution or the business to be dealt with at that meeting.

The notice of the resolution must be given, and the statement must be circulated, in the same manner and, as far as is practicable, at the same time as the notice of the meeting, though under s. 377 the company need not circulate any statement if, on the application of the company or any aggrieved person, the court is satisfied that these rights are being abused to secure *needless publicity for defamatory matter.*

Section 377 provides that a company need not comply with s. 376 unless:

(a) a copy of the requisition signed by the requisitionists is deposited at the registered office:

(*i*) in the case of a requisition requiring notice of a resolution, at least *six weeks* before the meeting, *and*

(*ii*) in the case of any other requisition, at least *one week* before the meeting; *and*

(b) there is deposited or tendered with the requisition a sum reasonably sufficient to meet the company's expenses.

However, s. 377 also provides that if after a copy of a requisition requiring notice of a resolution has been deposited at the registered office, an annual general meeting is called for a date six weeks or less afterwards, the copy is still deemed to have been properly deposited.

36. Written resolutions of private companies

In accordance with the trend to de-regulate private companies s. 113 Companies Act 1989 inserts in the 1985 Act ss. 381A–381C enabling private companies to dispense with the formalities of meetings and notice of meetings and have instead written resolutions complying with ss. 381A–381C.

Section 381A is the leading provision. It makes it clear that the provisions apply to class meetings as well as to general meetings and to all types of resolutions.

The written resolution must be signed by or on behalf of *all the members entitled to attend and vote at the date of the resolution.*

Schedule 15A, however, inserted in the 1985 Act by s. 114 Companies Act 1989, makes two exceptions: written resolutions cannot be used:

(a) under s. 303 to remove a director before the expiration of his period of office; *or*

(b) under s. 391 to remove an auditor before the expiration of his term of office.

In addition, Schedule 15A lists a number of provisions of the Act which are to be applied with specified adaptations when a resolution is a written one instead of being passed at a meeting. The general purpose of the adaptations is that members, before signing the written resolution, must be made aware, by the issue to them of documents, of the same information as would have been available at the meeting if a meeting had been held.

The provisions listed are:

(a) s. 95 (disapplication of pre-emption rights);

(b) s. 155 (financial assistance for purchase of company's own shares or those of holding company);

(c) ss. 164, 165 and 167 (authority for off-market purchase or contingent purchase contract of company's own shares);

(d) s. 173 (approval for payment out of capital);

(e) s. 319 (approval of director's service contract); *and*

(f) s. 337 (funding of director's expenditure in performing his duties).

Section 381B provides that a copy of any written resolution must be sent to the company's auditors, and that if the resolution concerns the auditors as auditors, they may within seven days of receiving the copy give notice to the company that the resolution should be considered by a meeting. A written resolution does not have effect unless:

(a) the auditors notify the company that the resolution does not concern them as auditors; *or*

(b) the seven days expire without any notice having been given; *or*

(c) the auditors notify the company that the resolution does concern them as auditors but need not be considered at a meeting.

Section 381C provides that ss. 381A and 381B have effect in spite of any provision in the memorandum or articles.

37. Elective resolutions of private companies

In accordance with the same trend for de-regulation of private companies, the 1989 Act permits a private company to dispense with certain statutory requirements. It is for the company to choose or 'elect' in each case whether it will take advantage of the permission which the Act makes available. The procedure involves the passing of an 'elective' resolution under s. 379A, inserted in the 1985 Act by s. 116 Companies Act 1989.

The following are the provisions of the 1985 Act, as amended by the 1989 Act, under which an elective resolution is permitted:

(a) under s. 80A (election as to duration of authority to allot shares);
(b) under s. 252 (election to dispense with laying of accounts and reports before general meeting);
(c) under s. 366A (election to dispense with holding of annual general meeting);
(d) under s. 369 or 378 (election as to majority required to authorise short notice of meeting); *and*
(e) under s. 386 (election to dispense with appointment of auditors annually).

The Secretary of State may add further provisions by regulations.
An elective resolution is not effective unless:

(a) at least 21 days' notice in writing is given of the meeting, stating that an elective resolution is to be proposed and stating the terms of the resolution; *and*
(b) the resolution is agreed to at the meeting, in person or by proxy, by all the members entitled to attend and vote at the meeting.

The company may revoke an elective resolution by passing an ordinary resolution to that effect.
An elective resolution ceases to have effect if the company is re-registered as a public company.
Elective resolutions are available to a private company in spite of any contrary provision in its memorandum or articles.

38. The duty to make the annual return

The provisions as to a company's annual return are in ss. 363, 364, 364A and 365, all as substituted in the 1985 Act by s. 139 Companies Act 1989.
Section 363 provides that every company must deliver to the registrar successive annual returns, each of which is made up to a date not later than the company's 'return date', i.e.:

(a) the anniversary of the company's incorporation; *or*
(b) if the company's last return was made up to a different date, the anniversary of that date.

Each return must be in the prescribed form, be signed by a director or the secretary and be delivered to the registrar within 28 days after the date to which it is made up.

39. The contents of the annual return

Section 364 lists the information which must be given in all annual returns, while s. 364A applies to a company which has a share capital and lists the particulars of share capital and shareholders which must be contained in the annual return of such a company.

The following is a list in outline of the information which s. 364 requires to be contained in every annual return:

(a) the address of the registered office;

(b) the type of company it is and its principal business activities;

(c) the name and address of the company secretary;

(d) the name, address, and nationality of every director and particulars of other directorships as contained in the company's register of directors;

(e) the address where the registers of members and debenture-holders are kept, if not kept at the registered office;

(f) if the company has elected to dispense, under s. 252, with the laying of accounts and reports before the company in general meeting or has elected to dispense, under s. 366A, with the holding of annual general meetings, a statement of that fact.

By s. 364A the annual return of a company with a share capital must contain the following information as to its share capital and shareholders:

(a) the total number of issued shares and their aggregate nominal value;

(b) the nature of each class of shares, and the total number and aggregate nominal value of each class;

(c) the names and addresses of persons who are members on the date to which the return is made up and of persons who have ceased to be members since the date of the last return, with an index of names where necessary;

(d) the number of shares of each class held by each member and the number transferred since the date of the last return with the dates of registration of the transfers.

Where the company has converted any of its shares into stock, the return must give the corresponding information as to stock.

As regards **(c)** and **(d)** above, a complete list is required only every third year; in the intervening years only changes need be given.

By s. 365 the Secretary of State has power to make further provision by regulations as to the information to be given in annual returns. Such regulations may amend or repeal the provisions of ss. 364 and 364A.

40. Destruction of old records

Section 707A, inserted in the 1985 Act by s. 126 Companies Act 1989, provides that the originals of documents delivered to the registrar in legible form must be kept by him for 10 years, after which they may be destroyed.

Directors and secretary

1. Definition of a director

Section 741 defines a director as including 'any person occupying the position of director, by whatever name called'. This is a definition based purely on *function*: a person is a director if he does whatever a director normally does. But the Act gives little guidance on the function and duties of a director.

A director is an *officer* of the company, for s. 744, as we saw in 2:**10**, states that officer 'includes a director, manager or secretary'. He is also an *agent* of the company, though the Act does not say so. But he is *not an employee* and is therefore not entitled to preferential payment when the company goes into liquidation.

2. Shadow directors

Several provisions of the Act relating to directors are made applicable also to 'shadow directors', e.g. s. 309, which requires directors to have regard to the interests of the company's employees, and s. 319, which relates to a director's contract of employment for more than five years.

The term 'shadow director', by s. 741, means 'a person in accordance with whose directions or instructions the directors are accustomed to act'. However, a person is not deemed to be a shadow director merely because the directors act on advice given by him in a professional capacity.

3. The number of directors required

Section 282 states that every public company must have at least two directors, and every private company must have at least one.

The Act also contains a number of provisions designed to ensure that the offices of director and secretary do not fall into the same hands in companies with only one director.

Thus s. 283 provides that every company must have a secretary, but then provides that a sole director may not be the secretary. Of course, if there are two or more directors, one of them may be the secretary and in practice often is.

In order to prevent evasion of the provision mentioned by using the device of the corporate person, s. 283 further provides that where two companies have the same person as sole director, neither company may be the secretary of the other, and that where the same person is sole director of X company and secretary of Y company, X company may not be the sole director of Y company.

Finally, s. 284 provides that anything which must be done by the secretary and a director must be done by *two separate individuals*, and not by one person acting in both capacities.

4. Appointment of the first directors

Section 13 provides that the persons named in the statement required by s. 10 (*see* 4:1) as the directors of the company shall, on incorporation, be deemed to have been appointed the first directors. In practice, the articles often name the first directors, but s. 10 invalidates any such appointment unless the persons mentioned have also been named as directors in the statement.

5. Subsequent appointments

Table A, Article 73, provides that at the first annual general meeting all the directors retire, and at every subsequent annual general meeting one-third, or the number nearest one-third, retire. This is *retirement by rotation*.

Article 74 provides that those to retire are those who have been longest in office, but if they all took office on the same day, those to retire must (unless they otherwise agree among themselves) be determined by lot.

Article 80 provides that retiring directors are eligible for re-election.

Article 75 provides that if the company, at the meeting at which a director retires by rotation, does not fill the vacancy the retiring director shall be *automatically re-elected*, unless:

(a) it is resolved not to fill the vacancy; *or*

(b) a resolution for his re-election is lost.

Article 76 provides that if it is desired to propose a person other than a director retiring by rotation or a person recommended by the directors for election as a director, then at least 14 and not more than 35 clear days before the meeting a written notice must be left at the registered office. It must be signed by a member entitled to attend and vote, and give notice of his intention to propose that person for election. It must be accompanied by that person's written consent to stand.

6. Appointment of directors to fill casual vacancies

Article 79 states that if a vacancy on the board occurs in between two annual general meetings, the remaining directors may appoint a person to fill it. It also authorises the directors to appoint additional directors, so long as the maximum number permitted by the regulations is not exceeded.

In both cases the directors so appointed hold office only until the next annual general meeting. They are then eligible for re-election, but are not taken into account in determining those who are to retire by rotation at that meeting.

7. Voting on the appointment of directors

Section 292 provides that in a *public* company (*see* 25:**6**) directors must be elected *individually*, unless the meeting has first resolved *nem. con. (nemine contradicente* = with no vote cast *against* the resolution) to vote on them together.

The purpose of this section is to ensure that the will of the meeting is expressed on each director as an individual. If two or more directors could be elected by a single resolution, this would be impossible. Accordingly s. 292 invalidates any resolution which contravenes the section by attempting to apply to more than one director.

8. Permanent directors

Sometimes the articles appoint a person a permanent director, i.e. for life. In such a case it is not necessary to re-elect him, and the articles usually expressly exclude him from the operation of the clauses relating to retirement by rotation. He is normally given wide powers of management, and in practice he will probably be a major shareholder in the company.

It should not, however, be thought that he is truly 'permanent'. He is, like any other director, removable under s. 303, the provisions of which will be discussed later in this chapter. It follows that unless he has voting control, he can be removed at any time. We have already seen (*see* 3:**10**) that the articles never constitute a *contract* between the company and any person in a capacity other than that of *member*. But even if a permanent director has taken care to see that, quite apart from the appropriate clause in the articles, he has entered into a valid service contract with the company as, for example, its managing director, he can still be removed. He will in this case have a right of action for breach of contract, but no right to continue in office.

9. Assignment of office by directors

If the articles or any agreement empower a director to assign his office to another person, s. 308 provides that the assignment will be void unless approved by a special resolution of the company.

10. Alternate directors

Alternate directors are entirely different from assignees of office, and are not affected by s. 308. The main distinction between them is that in the case of alternate directors there is only a *temporary* delegation of authority and function.

An alternate director cannot be appointed unless there is authority in the articles to that effect. Most articles nowadays contain the necessary authority.

Table A, Article 65, provides that any director may appoint any other director, or any other person approved by resolution of the directors, to be an alternate director. By Article 66 an alternate director is entitled to receive notices of all directors' meetings, to attend and vote at such meetings and generally to perform all the functions of his appointor, but he is not entitled to receive any remuneration from the company for his services as an alternate director. Article 67 provides that an alternate director ceases to be an alternate director if his appointor ceases to be a director. By Article 68 the procedure for appointment or removal of an alternate director is by notice to the company, signed by the director making or revoking the appointment, or any other procedure approved by the directors. Most important is Article 69 which provides that an alternate director is to be alone responsible for his own acts and defaults and is not to be deemed to be the agent of the director appointing him. (If the alternate director were the agent of his appointor, the appointing director would be responsible for all acts done by the alternate.)

Most of the statutory provisions apply to alternate directors in the same way as to ordinary directors. Thus ss. 285 (validity of acts of directors), 288–289 (register of directors and secretaries) and 291 (share qualification of directors) are applicable. So also are ss. 305 (directors' names on company correspondence, etc.), 314–316 (disclosure of payment for loss of office) and 317 (disclosure of interest in contracts). All these sections are considered later in this chapter. Section 282, however, requiring a minimum of two directors in a public company, is not satisfied by the company having one director with his alternate, for an alternate director is essentially a *substitute*.

11. The register of directors and secretaries

Section 288 requires every company to keep a register of its directors and secretaries at its registered office (*see* 2:**15,16**).

Section 289, as amended by s. 145 and Schedule 19 Companies Act 1989, provides that this register must contain the following particulars with respect to each director:

(a) his name and former name, if any;
(b) his address;
(c) his nationality;
(d) his business occupation, if any;

(e) particulars of any other directorships held by him or formerly held by him within the last five years, with two exceptions mentioned below;
(f) his date of birth.

Where the director is a corporation or Scottish firm, the register must specify its corporate or firm name and its registered or principal office.

NOTES: (1) *Particulars of other directorships.* The exceptions to **(e)** mentioned above relate to:

    (*i*) directorships of *dormant* companies (*see* 18:**33**); *and*
    (*ii*) directorships of a company grouped with the company keeping the register.

For the purpose of (*ii*), the Act gives a meaning of 'grouped with' which is difficult to understand unless specific companies are inserted as follows: A company (A Ltd) is regarded as being grouped with another (B Ltd) if:

(a) B Ltd is a wholly-owned subsidiary of A Ltd; *or*
(b) A Ltd is a wholly-owned subsidiary of B Ltd; *or*
(c) A Ltd is a wholly-owned subsidiary of C Ltd *and* B Ltd is a wholly-owned subsidiary of C Ltd.

The underlying purpose of these complicated statutory provisions is to make it unnecessary, where there is such a closely-knit group, to include in the register of directors of any one company the directorships held by the directors in other companies within the same group.

(2) *Notification to registrar, publication and inspection of register.* Section 288 requires the company to notify the registrar of any change among its directors or in its secretary, or any change in the particulars contained in the register, within 14 days. Any notification of a person having become a director or secretary must contain a signed consent by that person to act in the relevant capacity.

Section 711 requires the registrar to publish in the *Gazette* the receipt by him of any notification of a change among its directors. If the change was not officially notified by the registrar at the material time and if the company cannot show that it was known at the time to the person concerned, then the company cannot rely on the change against that person: s. 42.

Finally, s. 288, as amended by s. 143 Companies Act 1989, requires the register to be kept open for inspection to members free, and to other persons on payment of such fee as may be prescribed.

12. Particulars of directors on documents

Section 305, as amended by s. 145 and Schedule 19 Companies Act 1989, prohibits a company from stating, in any form, the name of any of its directors (except in the text of the letter or as a signatory) on any business letter on which the company's name appears, unless it also states the name of every director who is an individual and, in the case of a corporation or Scottish firm, the corporate or firm name. The provisions extend to shadow directors.

13. Directors' interests in shares or debentures

Section 324, taken along with Schedule 13, requires a director within five days to notify the company in writing of his interests in shares or debentures of the company or any other company within the group, giving particulars of the amount of shares or debentures of each class held by him.

He is also required within five days to notify the company in writing of any of the following events:

(a) an event as a result of which he becomes, or ceases to be, interested in such shares or debentures;
(b) the making by him of a contract to sell such shares or debentures;
(c) the assignment by him of any right granted to him by the company to subscribe for shares or debentures;
(d) the grant to him by any other company within the group of a right to subscribe for shares or debentures of that company, and his exercise or assignment of it.

In each case the amount and class of shares or debentures involved must be stated.

In computing the five days, Saturdays, Sundays and bank holidays must be disregarded.

The provisions apply to shadow directors but there is no duty to disclose interests in shares in a company which is the wholly-owned subsidiary of another company.

14. Extension of s. 324 to spouses and children

Section 328 extends the application of s. 324 by providing that an interest of a director's spouse or infant child in shares or debentures must be treated as being the director's interest.

A contract, assignment or right of subscription exercised or made by a director's spouse or infant child must be treated as having been exercised or made by the director, and a grant made to a director's spouse or infant child must be treated as having been made to the director.

A director must within five days notify the company in writing of the occurrence of either of the following events:

(a) the grant by the company to the director's spouse or infant child of a right to subscribe for shares or debentures of the company; *and*
(b) the exercise of that right by the director's spouse or infant child.

15. Duty of company to notify investment exchange of directors' interests

Section 329 provides that whenever a *listed* company is notified by a director under s. 324 or 328 of any matter relating to *listed* shares or debentures, it must, before the end of the following day, notify the investment exchange which may publish the information received.

16. The nature of an interest

Part I of Schedule 13 explains what constitutes an interest within ss. 324 and 328. The provisions of the Schedule include the following:

Where shares or debentures are held on trust, any *beneficiary under that trust* (including discretionary trusts) shall be taken to have an interest within ss. 324 and 328, while a person who is a *bare trustee* of shares or debentures shall be treated as having none.

A person is taken to have an interest in shares or debentures if:

(a) he enters into a contract to buy them, whether for cash or other consideration; *or*
(b) although not a registered holder, he is entitled (other than as a proxy or corporation representative) to exercise or control the exercise of any right conferred by the holding.

A person is taken to be interested in shares or debentures if a *company* is interested in them and:

(a) that company or its directors are accustomed to act according to his instructions; *or*
(b) he exercises or controls the exercise of *one-third or more* of the voting power at general meetings of that company.

The rule in **(b)** applies even if a person exercises the control through another company. Thus if Smith controls one-third of the voting power in X Company and X Company controls one-third of the voting power in Y Company, Smith will be taken to control one-third of the voting power in Y Company.

A person is taken to have an interest in shares or debentures if (otherwise than through an interest under a trust):

(a) he has a right to call for delivery of them; *or*
(b) he has a right to acquire or an obligation to take an interest in them.

It is immaterial whether the right or obligation is conditional or absolute. However, rights or obligations to *subscribe* for shares or debentures are expressly excluded.

Finally persons with a joint interest are deemed each to have that interest, and it is immaterial if the shares or debentures in which a person has an interest are unidentifiable.

17. The register of directors' interests

Section 325, which is to be taken along with Part IV of Schedule 13, as amended by s. 143 Companies Act 1989, requires every company to keep a register for the purpose of recording the information furnished under ss. 324 and 328 (*see* **13** and **14**). Whenever it obtains such information, it must within three days inscribe it in the register against the name of the director concerned, together with the date of the inscription. In computing the three days, Saturdays, Sundays and bank holidays are to be disregarded.

Section 325, with Schedule 13, Part IV, requires every company:

(a) whenever it *grants to a director a right to subscribe* for shares or debentures of the company, within three days to inscribe in the register against his name:

(*i*) the date on which the right is granted;

(*ii*) the period during which it is exercisable;

(*iii*) the consideration for the grant, or, if none, that fact;

(*iv*) *the description of the shares or debentures involved;*

(*v*) the amount of shares or debentures involved; *and*

(*vi*) the price to be paid for them;

(b) whenever a *right to subscribe* for shares or debentures of the company is *exercised* by a director, within three days to inscribe in the register against his name:

(*i*) the fact that the right was exercised;

(*ii*) the amount of shares or debentures involved;

(*iii*) if they were registered in his name, that fact, and if not, the name of the registered holder.

Other requirements are as follows:

The register must be made up so that the entries against each name appear in chronological order.

The company is not affected with notice of, or put upon inquiry as to, the rights of any person in relation to any shares *or debentures (cf.* s. 211 (*see* 12:**12**) and s. 360 (*see* 14:**12**)).

The register must be kept at the registered office or at the same place as the company's register of members (*see* 14:**3**), and be open to the inspection of any member without charge, and of any other person on payment of such fee as may be prescribed. Any person may require a copy of the register, or any part of it, on payment of such fee as may be prescribed. The copy must be supplied within 10 days.

The company must notify the registrar of the place where the register is kept, unless it has at all times been kept at the registered office.

The register must be produced at the company's annual general meeting, and remain open and accessible during the meeting to any person attending it.

Section 326 of the Act provides that if inspection is refused or a copy not sent within the 10 days, the court may order that inspection be allowed or that the copy be sent.

18. Qualification shares

There is a widespread misconception that a director is necessarily a member of the company. This is not so. The Act imposes no share qualification on the directors, so that unless the company's *articles* contain a requirement to that effect, a director need not be a shareholder unless he wishes. While the articles of many companies provide that the directors must hold a specified number of shares in the company, those of many other companies do not. Table A, for instance, does not require any share qualification for directors.

If the articles impose a share qualification on the directors, s. 291 applies. It requires them to obtain their share qualification within a maximum period of two months after appointment. The articles may fix a shorter period. The section provides that the holding of a *share warrant* will not suffice for this purpose, and that if a director fails to obtain his share qualification within the specified time after his appointment, or at any time after appointment ceases to hold it, he vacates office.

> NOTE: Care must be taken in computing the period of time when a poll is demanded on the election of a director and there is an interval between the taking of the poll and the declaration of the result. The period of time is calculated as running from the date when the result of the poll is *ascertained*, not from the earlier date when the votes were cast: *Holmes* v. *Keyes* (1959).

Where a share qualification is imposed by the articles, a joint holding will suffice unless the articles provide otherwise. The holding of stock instead of shares is also permissible. The shares or stock need not necessarily have been allotted to the director by the company; he may have acquired them by transfer from another member. Moreover, as long as his name appears on the register of members as the holder of the shares, it is immaterial that he is a mere trustee and does not own the *equitable* interest in them. This is so even where the articles provide, as they sometimes do, that he shall own them 'in his own right', though this curious expression has been held not to cover the case where a director held the shares as liquidator of another company.

19. The age limit for directors

Section 293 contains provisions regarding age limit. It applies only to *public* companies and to private companies which are *subsidiaries of public companies.*

A person cannot be appointed a director of such a company if he has attained the age of 70. Further, an existing director of such a company must vacate office at the end of the next annual general meeting held after he attains the age of 70.

These stringent provisions, however, are rendered considerably less harsh by the remainder of the section. The articles may alter or entirely remove the age limit, and a director may be appointed at any age if the appointment is approved by the company in general meeting, so long as *special notice* of the resolution is given, stating his age. It also contains a similar provision regarding existing directors who attain the age of 70.

Section 294 requires any person who is appointed, or is proposed to be appointed, director of such a company to give notice of his age to the company when he has attained the age limit either under the Act or under the company's articles.

20. Disqualification orders

A disqualification order is an order made by a court forbidding a person, without leave of the court, from being:

(a) a director of a company; *or*
(b) a liquidator or administrator of a company; *or*
(c) a receiver or manager of a company's property; *or*
(d) in any way, directly or indirectly, concerned in the promotion, formation or management of a company.

The provisions of the Companies Act 1985 on this subject were strengthened by the Insolvency Act 1985, and these two sets of provisions were consolidated in the Company Directors Disqualification Act 1986. *References in the rest of this paragraph are, therefore, unless the contrary is indicated, to that Act of 1986.*

The Act deals with the grounds of disqualification under three headings:

(a) *Disqualification for general misconduct in connection with companies*:

By s. 2 the court may make a disqualification order where the person is convicted of an indictable offence in connection with the promotion, formation, management or liquidation of a company, or with the receivership or management of a company's property.

The maximum period of disqualification in this case is 15 years.

By s. 3 the court may make a disqualification order where it appears that the person has been persistently in default in delivering returns, accounts or other documents to the registrar. 'Persistent' default is conclusively proved if it is shown that in the five previous years he has been 'adjudged guilty' of three or more defaults. The phrase 'adjudged guilty' involves either a conviction for an offence or a default order under one of the following provisions:

(*i*) s. 242 Companies Act 1985 (order requiring delivery of company accounts);

(*ii*) s. 713 Companies Act 1985 (enforcement of company's duty to make returns);

(*iii*) s. 41 Insolvency Act 1986 (enforcement of receiver's or manager's duty to make returns); *or*

(*iv*) s. 170 Insolvency Act 1986 (corresponding provision for liquidator in winding up).

The maximum period of disqualification under s. 3 is five years.

By s. 4 the court may make a disqualification order if in the course of winding up it appears that the person:

(*i*) has been guilty of an offence for which he is *liable* (whether he has been convicted or not) under s. 458 Companies Act 1985 (fraudulent trading); *or*

(*ii*) has otherwise been guilty, while an officer (including a shadow director) or liquidator of the company or receiver or manager of its property, of any fraud in relation to the company or of any breach of his duty.

The maximum period of disqualification under this section is 15 years.

Section 5 relates to convictions for summary offences consisting of failure to deliver a return, account or other document to the registrar. The court convicting the person of the offence may, if it is at least his third offence within five years, make a disqualification order for a maximum period of five years.

(b) *Disqualification for unfitness*:

By s. 6 the court *must* make a disqualification order against a director (including a shadow director) if it is satisfied:

(*i*) that he is or has been a director of a company which has at any time become insolvent (whether while he was a director or subsequently); *and*

(*ii*) that his conduct as a director makes him unfit to be concerned in the management of a company.

A company becomes insolvent for the purposes of this section if:

(*i*) the company goes into liquidation at a time when its assets are insufficient for the payment of its debts and other liabilities and the expenses of the winding up; *or*

(*ii*) an administration order is made in relation to the company; *or*

(*iii*) an administrative receiver of the company is appointed.

The minimum period of disqualification is two years and the maximum period is 15 years.

Examples of s.6 orders are *Re T. & D. Services (Timber Preservation &*

Damp Proofing Contractors) Ltd (1990) [B148] and *Re Sevenoaks Stationers (Retail) Ltd* (1991) [B149].

Section 7 contains the following further provisions relating to a disqualification order under s. 6:

(*i*) An application for such an order may be made by the Secretary of State if it appears to him that such an order is expedient in the public interest. Alternatively, if the company is being wound up by the court in England and Wales, the application may be made by the official receiver on the Secretary of State's direction.

(*ii*) The application must be made within two years of the company's having become insolvent, unless the court grants leave for the application to be made later.

(*iii*) The office-holder responsible (i.e. the official receiver in the case of a winding up by the court in England and Wales, the liquidator in any other mode of winding up, the administrator if an administration order is in force, or the administrative receiver if such has been appointed) if it appears to him that the conditions for the making of a s. 6 order are satisfied must immediately report the matter to the Secretary of State.

(*iv*) The Secretary of State or the official receiver may require the liquidator, administrator or administrative receiver to furnish him with information concerning any person's conduct as a director and to produce books, papers and other records relevant to such conduct.

By s. 8 if it appears to the Secretary of State from a report made by inspectors under s. 437 Companies Act 1985 or from information or documents obtained under ss. 447 or 448 of that Act, that it is expedient in the public interest that a disqualification order should be made against a director or shadow director, he may apply to the court for an order, and the court may make an order if it is satisfied that the person's conduct in relation to the company makes him unfit to be concerned in the management of a company.

The maximum period of disqualification under this section is 15 years.

It should be noted that for both an order under s. 6 and an order under s. 8 the court must be satisfied that the person's conduct as a director or shadow director makes him unfit to be concerned in the management of a company. This is enlarged on by Schedule 1 which consists of a list of specific instances indicating unfitness, and by s. 9 the court must have particular regard to that list. The Schedule may be modified by statutory instrument.

(c) *Other cases of disqualification:*

Section 10 is linked to ss. 213 (fraudulent trading) and 214 (wrongful trading), Insolvency Act 1986, which provides that if in the course of winding up it appears that there has been fraudulent or wrongful trading within the meaning of these sections (*see* 31:**14**), the liquidator may apply to the court for a declaration that persons who were knowingly parties to the fraudulent or wrongful trading are to be liable to make such contributions to the company's assets as the court thinks proper. Section 10 Company Directors Disqualification Act 1986 enables the court also to make a disqualification order against the person concerned.

The maximum period of disqualification is 15 years.

By s. 11 it is an offence for a person who is an undischarged bankrupt to act as director of, or directly or indirectly to take part in or be concerned in the promotion, formation or management of, a company, except with the leave of the court.

Section 12, which does not apply to Scotland, relates to the situation where a person fails to make any payment which he is required to make by an administration order under Part VI of the County Courts Act 1984, and the court, under s. 429 Insolvency Act 1986, revokes the administration order. Section 12 Company Directors Disqualification Act 1986 provides that such a person must not, except with the leave of the court, act as director or liquidator of, or directly or indirectly take part or be concerned in the promotion, formation or management of, a company.

Penalties are imposed by s. 13 for contravention of any of the above-mentioned provisions of the Act, and in addition, by s. 15, the person contravening becomes personally responsible for all the debts and other liabilities of the company incurred when he was involved in its management.

21. The register of disqualification orders

Section 18 Company Directors Disqualification Act 1986 requires officers of courts to furnish the Secretary of State with prescribed particulars of cases in which a disqualification order is made or, by action taken by the court, is varied or ceases to be in force, or in which leave is granted by the court for a person who is subject to an order to do anything which otherwise the order prohibits him from doing.

From the particulars so furnished the Secretary of State must maintain a register of orders, which is open to inspection on payment of a prescribed fee. The Secretary of State must delete an entry from the register when the order ceases to be in force.

22. Vacation of office

Apart from the sections mentioned above, and s. 303 which is discussed in the next paragraph, the articles usually contain a clause setting out the events which will cause a director to vacate office.

Thus Table A, Article 81, provides that the office of director shall be vacated if:

(a) he ceases to be a director by any provision of the Acts or becomes prohibited by law from being a director; *or*

(b) he becomes bankrupt or makes any arrangement with his creditors generally; *or*

(c) he suffers from mental disorder; *or*

(d) he resigns office by notice to the company; *or*

(e) he is absent for more than six consecutive months, without permission of the directors, from meetings of directors *and* the directors resolve that his office be vacated.

23. Removal of directors

Section 303 gives the company its ultimate power of control over the directors. While they are in office there is very little which the company can do to influence the way in which the directors choose to manage the company's affairs. But if the company disapproves strongly enough of the method of management, it can resort to removing the board under this section. The only time this will be impossible is where the directors themselves have voting control.

The section does not, however, prevent the company from weighting the votes, i.e. attaching greater voting rights to certain shares for certain matters, e.g. to directors' shares on any resolution for their removal: *Bushell* v. *Faith* (1970) [B145].

Section 303 provides that a company may by ordinary resolution remove a director before the expiration of his period of office and despite anything in the company's articles or in any agreement between the company and the director. There is one exception for certain directors of private companies (*see* 25:6).

The intention of the section is clear: the shareholders must have power to remove the board. But the director so removed is not without his remedy. The section does not deprive him of his right to sue for damages for breach of contract, if in fact he has one.

Section 303 requires *special notice* to be given of any resolution to *remove a director*, or to *appoint another director in his place*.

By s. 304, the company, on receiving notice of an intended resolution to remove a director under s. 303, must immediately send a copy of the notice to the director and he is entitled to be heard on the resolution at the meeting. The director may also make written representations to the company (not exceeding a reasonable length) and request that they be notified to members. The company must then, unless the representations are received too late:

(a) in the notice of the resolution given to members state the fact that representations have been made; *and*

(b) send a copy of the representations to every member to whom notice of the meeting is sent.

If a copy is not sent out in this way because the representations were received too late or because of the company's default, then the director may require them to be read out at the meeting.

It may perhaps occur that a director reacts sharply to the copy of the special notice of the resolution to remove him, and makes a statement in his own defence which is highly defamatory of some other person. Section 304 provides for this situation by stating that copies of the representations need not be sent out, nor need the representations be read out, if the company or any aggrieved person applies to the court and the court thinks that the director is abusing his rights *to secure needless publicity for defamatory matter*. Moreover the court may order that the company's costs on such an application shall be paid by the director.

> NOTE: These provisions in s. 304 concerning the written representations are *exactly the same as those in s. 391A* relating to auditors. Once learnt, they apply to both directors and auditors alike.

Finally, it should be noted that difficulties may arise regarding the use of the provisions of s. 303. It appears from *Pedley* v. *Inland Waterways Association Ltd* (1977) that an *individual* member has no right to compel the inclusion of a resolution in the agenda of a company meeting unless the provisions of ss. 376 and 377 (*see* 15:**35**) have also been complied with. He can serve special notice under s. 379, but that is as far as he can go. If this decision represents the law, it would appear that the same problem would arise with the procedure for the removal of an auditor which, as stated above, is exactly the same.

24. Validity of directors' acts
Section 285 provides that the acts of a director are valid despite any defect which may afterwards be discovered in his appointment or qualification. Table A, Article 92, repeats this provision.

The effect of this section must not be over-stated. It does *not* permit an improperly appointed or unqualified director to do whatever he likes. It simply means that provided the director's act is in other respects *a proper act*, the mere fact that he has not been properly appointed or is not qualified is immaterial and does not invalidate that act. This can be clearly seen in *Craven-Ellis* v. *Canons Ltd* (1936), the facts of which are given in 3:**14**, and where the act which the improperly qualified directors were trying to do, namely to appoint another improperly qualified director, was an *improper act* in itself and therefore not protected by what is now s. 285 of the 1985 Act.

The section is stating in a narrow form what is really a well-known and fundamental rule of *agency*, namely, that a principal is always bound by the act of his agent provided the agent is acting within the scope of his *actual or apparent authority*. This rule applies to companies and their agents in the same way as it applies to natural legal persons and their agents, and has been enunciated in the famous decision in *Royal British Bank* v. *Turquand* (1856).

25. The rule in *Royal British Bank* v. *Turquand*

The rule in *Turquand's* case is historically important in company law. It qualified the doctrine of constructive notice, by which every person was deemed to have read the company's public documents (including the company's memorandum and articles and special and extraordinary resolutions).

> In *Royal British Bank* v. *Turquand* (1856) [B80], the company's deed of settlement (corresponding to a modern memorandum and articles) empowered the directors to borrow such sums as were authorised by an *ordinary* resolution of a general meeting. The directors issued a bond to T, from whom they borrowed money. The bond was under the company's seal, but no resolution was passed by the company authorising it. HELD: The company was bound.

It should be remembered that a third party has no means of knowing whether an *ordinary* resolution has been passed by the company. He can read the public documents and discover whether a *special* or *extraordinary* resolution has been passed, but he cannot know, unless he has been told, whether an ordinary resolution such as was required in this case has been passed by a general meeting. The loan was clearly within the *capacity* of the company. It was also clear from the articles that the directors could have had the necessary *authority*. A third party did not need to go further: he did not need to make sure that the rules of *internal management* had been observed.

The rule in *Turquand's* case is in accordance with the ordinary rules of agency. If a principal places *secret* restrictions on the apparent authority of his agent, they do not affect the third party; unless his suspicions are aroused, the third party need not take steps to ensure that there are no such restrictions, for this would make the carrying on of business a practical impossibility.

The difficulty which arose in the application of these ordinary rules to company law resulted from the doctrine of constructive notice, by which the third party was assumed to know of all the restrictions which could be discovered by his reading of the public documents—a step which in the ordinary course of business it was impracticable for the third party to take.

The position was changed by s. 9 European Communities Act 1972, which, on consolidation, was re-enacted by the Companies Act 1985. The present provisions are to be found in s. 35A inserted in the 1985 Act by s. 108 Companies Act 1989, and s. 711A, inserted in the 1985 Act by s. 142 Companies Act 1989.

The leading provision in s. 35A is that in favour of a person dealing with a company in good faith, the power of the board of directors to bind the company, or authorise others to do so, is to be deemed to be free of any limitation under the company's constitution (*see* 2:20).

Section 711A provides that a person is not to be taken to have notice of any matter merely because of its being disclosed in any document kept by the registrar (and thus available for inspection) or made available by the company for inspection. A person may still be affected by notice of any matter where he has failed to make such inquiries as he ought reasonably to have made.

26. Remuneration of directors

We have already seen in 1 that directors are officers and agents, but not servants. They have not, as directors, any contract with the company and are not employed by it, though often they are employed by it in another capacity and are then termed 'service directors'.

As directors, they accordingly have no right to remuneration. The articles, however, normally make provision for them, and Table A, Article 82, states that the directors shall be entitled to such remuneration as the company may by ordinary resolution determine. Article 83 allows them travelling and hotel expenses for meetings and for other expenses properly incurred by them in connection with the discharge of their duties: these would not otherwise be allowed. The articles are not, of course, a contract, but they make it proper for the company to make such payments as are authorised by them.

Section 311 makes it unlawful for a company to pay a director his remuneration tax-free, and provides that if a provision for tax-free payment is made, it will take effect as if the *net* sum payable were a *gross* sum subject to tax.

As stated in 1, a director is not entitled to preferential payment when the company goes into liquidation, for he is not an 'employee' within s. 386 and Schedule 6 Insolvency Act 1986.

27. Apportionment of directors' remuneration

The Apportionment Act 1870 provides that all salaries are apportionable, but it is undecided whether this Act applies to directors. If it does not, and the articles provide for payment 'at the rate of' a certain sum per annum, or are expressed in such a way as to indicate that the annual sum is to be apportioned, then a director who holds office for less than a year is entitled to a proportion of that annual sum. If, however, the articles provide for payment of an annual sum on an annual basis, the remuneration is not apportionable. Table A, Article 82, provides that, unless the resolution provides otherwise, the remuneration shall *accrue from day to day*, making the position quite clear wherever Table A is applicable.

Probably, however, the Apportionment Act applies, so that the wording of the articles is immaterial.

28. Right of inspection of directors' service contracts

In the case of a 'service director' (*see* **26**) s. 318, as amended by s. 143 Companies Act 1989, gives the members of the company a right to inspect any director's contract of service. A shadow director (*see* **2**) must be treated as a director for the purposes of this section.

Section 318 requires every company to keep at an appropriate place:

(a) in the case of a director whose contract of service is in writing, *a copy of the contract*;
(b) in the case of a director whose contract of service is not in writing, *a written memorandum* setting out its terms; and
(c) in the case of a director employed under a contract of service with a *subsidiary* of the company, *a copy of the contract* or, if it is not in writing, *a written memorandum* setting out its terms.

All the copies and memoranda must be kept at the same place.

The following places are appropriate:

(a) the registered office;
(b) the place where the register of members is kept, if elsewhere;
(c) the principal place of business.

Every company must give notice to the registrar of the place where the copies and memoranda are kept, and of any change in that place, except where they have always been kept at the registered office.

Every copy and memorandum must be open to the inspection of any member without charge.

If inspection is refused, the court may by order compel an immediate inspection.

Finally, there are two provisions which apply in special circumstances. First, the section does not apply where the unexpired term of the contract is *less than a year*, or when the contract can be terminated by the company within the next year without payment of compensation. Secondly, the section does not apply if the director's contract requires him to work wholly or mainly *outside the United Kingdom*. Instead, the company must keep a *memorandum* which sets out:

(a) the *name* of the director;

(b) the provisions of the contract relating to its *duration*; *and*
(c) in the case of a contract of service with a *subsidiary* of the company, the *name and place of incorporation* of that subsidiary.

29. Directors' contracts of employment exceeding five years

Section 319 requires long-term contracts of employment of directors to be approved by the company in general meeting. It should be noted that the meaning of 'contract of employment' is somewhat wider than 'contract of service' since it includes a *contract for services*, e.g. a consultancy agreement. A shadow director is treated as a director for the purposes of s. 319.

Section 319 applies to any term by which a director's employment with the company of which he is a director or, where he is the director of a holding company, his employment within the group, is to continue for a period of *more than five years* during which it:

(a) cannot be terminated by the company by notice; *or*
(b) can be so terminated only in special circumstances.

A company is prohibited from incorporating such a term in any agreement unless it is first approved by a resolution of the company in general meeting and, in the case of a director of a holding company, by a resolution of the holding company in general meeting as well. The only exception to this rule is in the case of a wholly-owned subsidiary where no approval by its members is required.

The resolution may not be passed unless a *written memorandum* setting out the proposed agreement incorporating the term is available for inspection by members of the company both:

(a) at the registered office for not less than 15 days ending with the date of the meeting; *and*
(b) at the meeting itself.

If a term is incorporated in an agreement in contravention of the section, it is *void* and the agreement, the rest of which remains valid, is deemed to contain a term entitling the company to terminate it at any time by giving reasonable notice.

30. Connected persons

The Act contains a number of provisions which refer to a person being 'connected' with a director and to a director being 'associated with' or 'controlling' a body corporate. The meaning of these words is found in s. 346 and should be borne in mind whenever the expression appears.

The section provides that, unless a person is himself a director of the company, he is *connected* with a director if he is:

(a) that director's *spouse, child* or *step-child* (including illegitimate children but not any person over 18 years of age);

(b) a *body corporate* with which the director is associated;

(c) a person acting in his capacity as the *trustee* of any trust under which the beneficiaries include the director or any person falling under **(a)** or **(b)** above; or

(d) a person acting in his capacity as *partner* of that director or of any person falling under **(a)**, **(b)** or **(c)** above.

Section 346 provides that a director is *associated* with a body corporate if he and the persons connected with him together are *either*:

(a) interested in at least one-fifth in nominal value of its equity share capital; or

(b) entitled to exercise or control the exercise of more than one-fifth of the voting power at any general meeting.

References to voting power the exercise of which is controlled by a director include references to voting power the exercise of which is controlled by a *body corporate* controlled by that director (a neat example of 'veil-lifting' (*see* 1:**23**)).

Section 346 provides that a director is deemed to *control* a body corporate if:

(a) he or a person connected with him is interested in any part of its equity share capital or is entitled to exercise or control the exercise of any part of the voting power at any general meeting; *and*

(b) he, the persons connected with him, and the other directors of the company together are interested in more than half the equity share capital or are entitled to exercise or control the exercise of more than half of that voting power.

31. Substantial property transactions involving directors

Section 320 is in principle very much the same as s. 319. It too requires the approval by the company in general meeting—this time where a director acquires substantial non-cash assets from the company, or vice versa (*see* 10:**1**).

The section prohibits a company from making any arrangement by which a director of the company or of its holding company, or a person connected with such a director (*see* **30**), is to acquire *a non-cash asset of the requisite value* from the company, or vice versa, unless that arrangement is first approved by a resolution of the company in general meeting. If the director or connected person is a director of the holding company or a person connected with such a director, approval by a resolution in general meeting of the holding company is required as well.

By s. 320 a non-cash asset was of the requisite value if its value exceeded £50,000 or 10 per cent of the amount of the company's net assets normally determined by reference to the last annual accounts, and was not less than £1000. These amounts, however, can be increased at any time by order of the Secretary of State under s.345, and were increased to £100,000 and £2000 respectively, by the Companies (Fair Dealing by Directors) (Increase in Financial Limits) Order 1990 (SI 1990, No. 1393).

By s. 321, in the case of a wholly-owned subsidiary no approval by its members is required.

32. Effect of contravention of s. 320

Section 322 deals with the effect of contravention of s. 320. Any unlawful arrangement, and any transaction entered into in pursuance of it, is *voidable by the company* unless:

(a) *restitution* of the subject-matter is *impossible; or*
(b) the company has been *indemnified* (*see* below) for the loss suffered; *or*
(c) *rights acquired by a third party bona fide*, for value, and without notice of the contravention would be affected by the avoidance; *or*
(d) the arrangement is, within a reasonable time, *affirmed* by the company in general meeting and, where applicable, by a resolution of its holding company in general meeting as well.

Contravention of s. 320 not only has an effect on the arrangement or transaction in question but, under s. 322, it renders the director, any person connected with him and any other director of the company who authorised it liable:

(a) to *account to the company for any gain* which he made by it, directly or indirectly; *and*
(b) jointly and severally with any other person liable, to *indemnify the company* for any resulting loss.

Whether or not the unlawful arrangement or transaction has been avoided under s. 322 is immaterial.

Where an unlawful arrangement is made by a company and a person connected with a director, that director will not be liable if he shows that he took all reasonable steps to secure the company's compliance with s. 320, while the connected person and the other directors who authorised it can escape liability if they can show that at the time it was made, they did not know of the contravention.

33. Arrangements exempted from s. 320

Section 321 entirely exempts from the provisions of s. 320 three types of arrangements:

(a) any arrangement for the acquisition of a non-cash asset by a holding company from any of its wholly-owned subsidiaries or vice versa, or by one wholly-owned subsidiary from another wholly-owned subsidiary of the same holding company;

(b) any arrangement entered into by a company which is being wound up (unless the winding up is a members' voluntary winding up); *and*

(c) any arrangement by which a member acquires an asset from a company and which is made with him in his character of member.

34. Legislation on loans to directors

Before embarking on the highly technical and sophisticated rules in ss 330–346, which deal with loans to directors, including shadow directors, it is essential to understand the meaning given by the Act to three expressions:

(a) a relevant company;

(b) a quasi-loan;

(c) a credit transaction.

35. Meaning of 'relevant company'

Section 331 is the interpretation section of ss. 330–346. It provides that 'relevant company' means a company which:

(a) is a public company; *or*

(b) is a subsidiary of a public company; *or*

(c) is a subsidiary of a company which has as another subsidiary a public company; *or*

(d) has a subsidiary which is a public company.

The gist of this definition is that a relevant company is *either*:

(a) a public company; *or*

(b) a private company which forms part of a group containing a public company.

36. Meaning of 'quasi-loan'

Section 331 defines a quasi-loan as a transaction under which one party ('the creditor') pays or agrees to pay a sum for another ('the borrower'), or reimburses or agrees to reimburse expenditure incurred by another party for another ('the borrower'):

(a) on terms that the borrower will reimburse the creditor; *or*

(b) in circumstances giving rise to a liability on the borrower to reimburse the creditor.

An example of a quasi-loan is where the company pays a debt which is owed by a director to a third party on terms that the director will pay the company over a period of time at his convenience.

37. Meaning of 'credit transaction'

Section 331 defines a credit transaction as a transaction under which one party ('the creditor'):

(a) sells any land or supplies any goods under a hire-purchase or conditional sale agreement;
(b) leases or hires any land or goods in return for periodical payments;
(c) otherwise disposes of land or supplies goods or services on the understanding that payment (however made) is to be deferred.

38. Loans to directors

Section 330 provides that, with certain exceptions, no company may:

(a) make a *loan* to any of its directors or to any director of its holding company;
(b) enter into any *guarantee* or provide any *security* in connection with a loan made by any other person to such a director.

This comprehensive prohibition applicable to all companies is followed by one which applies to *relevant companies* (*see* **35**).

The provision is that, again with certain exceptions, no *relevant company* may:

(a) make a *quasi-loan* to any of its directors or to any director of its holding company (*see* **36**);
(b) make a *loan or quasi-loan* to a person connected with such a director (*see* **30**);
(c) enter into a *guarantee* or provide any *security* in connection with a loan or quasi-loan made by any other person for such a director or connected person;
(d) enter into a *credit transaction* as creditor for such a director or connected person (*see* **37**);
(e) enter into any *guarantee* or provide any *security* in connection with a credit transaction made by any other person for such a director or connected person.

39. Extension of prohibitions in s. 330 to indirect arrangements

Section 330 extends to indirect arrangements by which a company may try to evade the rules stated above.

It provides that no company may arrange for the assignment to it of rights, or the assumption by it of obligations, under a transaction which would have contravened the provisions of s. 330 if it had been entered into by the company itself.

No company may take part in any arrangement by which another person:

(a) enters into a transaction which would have contravened the provisions of s. 330 if it had been entered into by the company itself; *and*
(b) obtains a benefit from the company or any company within the group.

40. General exceptions to s. 330

Sections 332–338 give a large number of exceptions to the rules laid down in s. 330. The exceptions in ss. 332–335 are exceptions to specific provisions within s. 330, whereas the exceptions in ss. 336–338 are general exceptions in the sense that they exclude *all* the provisions of s. 330 in particular situations. It is simplest to start with this latter category of exceptions.

There are four cases where s. 330 does not apply at all:

(a) A *loan* or *quasi-loan* by a company to its *holding company*, or a *guarantee* or *security* given by a company in connection with a loan or quasi-loan made by any other person to its holding company: s. 336.
(b) A company's entering into a *credit transaction* as creditor for its *holding company*, or giving a *guarantee* or *security* in connection with any credit transaction made by any other person for its holding company: s. 336.
(c) A company's doing anything to provide any of its directors with funds to meet *expenditure incurred for the purposes of the company* or to enable him *properly to perform his duties as an officer*, or anything to enable any of its directors to avoid incurring such expenditure, provided *either*:
  (*i*) that thing is done with the *prior approval of the company in general meeting* at which all the details are disclosed; *or*
  (*ii*) it is done on the condition that if the approval of the company is not so obtained at or before the next annual general meeting, the loan will be repaid or the liability discharged *within six months* from the end of that meeting: s. 337.

Even if one of these conditions is satisfied, the exception is subject to a financial limit in the case of any *relevant company*. Such a company may not enter into any transaction under **(c)** if the *aggregate of the relevant amounts* exceeds £20,000 (substituted for former £10,000 by the Companies (Fair Dealing by Directors) (Increase in Financial Limits) Order 1990 (SI 1990, No. 1393)).

(d) A loan or quasi-loan made by a *money-lending company* to any person, or a guarantee given by a money-lending company in connection with any other loan or quasi-loan, provided:

(*i*) the loan or quasi-loan is made, or the guarantee given, in the *ordinary course of its business; and*

(*ii*) the amount of the loan, quasi-loan or guarantee is not greater, and the terms not more favourable, than the company could reasonably be expected to offer to a person of the *same financial standing but unconnected with the company*: s. 338.

Even if these two conditions are satisfied, this exception is also subject to a financial limit in the case of *any relevant company which is not a banking company* (i.e. by s. 744, a company which is authorised under the Banking Act 1987). Such a company may not enter into any transaction under **(d)** if the *aggregate of the relevant amounts* exceeds £100,000: s. 338, as amended by the Banking Act 1987 and by s. 138 Companies Act 1989.

The second condition, however, is itself subject to an exception regarding a *dwelling-house*. Section 338, as amended by s. 138 Companies Act 1989, provides that **(d)**(*ii*) above does not prevent a company from making a loan to one of its directors or a director of its holding company:

(*i*) for the purpose of the *purchase of a dwelling-house*, together with any land to be occupied with it, for use as that director's *only or main residence,*

(*ii*) for the purpose of *improving* such a dwelling-house or land,

(*iii*) in substitution for any loan made by any other person for either of the above purposes,

if loans of that description are ordinarily made by the company to its employees on terms which are no less favourable, and if the aggregate of the relevant amounts does not exceed £100,000.

41. Exception for small loans

Section 334, as amended by s. 138 Companies Act 1989, gives a special exception for small loans.

The section provides that s. 330 (*see* **38**) does not prohibit a company from making a loan to any of its directors or to any director of its holding company, provided the *aggregate of the relevant amounts* does not exceed £5,000.

42. Exceptions for short-term quasi-loans and inter-company loans

This paragraph deals with exceptions in ss. 332 and 333.

The prohibition of quasi-loans in s. 330, which in any case applies only to *relevant companies*, does not prevent such a company from making a quasi-loan to any of its directors or to any director of its holding company if:

(a) the quasi-loan contains a term requiring the director to reimburse the creditor within two months; *and*

(b) the aggregate of the amount of that quasi-loan and the amount outstanding on any others does not exceed £5,000: s. 332, as amended by s. 138 Companies Act 1989.

Section 333 gives an exception to inter-company loans in the same group.

Where a *relevant company* is a member of a group of companies, the prohibitions in s. 330 do not prevent it from:

(a) making a loan or quasi-loan to another company in that group; *or*
(b) giving a guarantee or security in connection with a loan or quasi-loan made by any other person to another company in that group;

merely because a director of one company within the group is associated with another (*see* **30**).

43. Exception for minor and business transactions

Section 335 gives an exception to the prohibitions of credit transactions in s. 330 (*see* **38(d)** and **(e)** above). These prohibitions, which again apply only to relevant companies, do not prevent such a company from entering into any transaction for any person if:

(a) the *aggregate of the relevant amounts* does not exceed £10,000 (substituted for former £5,000 by the Companies (Fair Dealing by Directors) (Increase in Financial Limits) Order 1990 (SI 1990 No. 1393)); *or*
(b) (*i*) the company enters into the transaction in the *ordinary* course of its business; *and*
(*ii*) the value of the transaction is not greater, and its terms not more favourable, than the company could reasonably be expected to offer to a person of the *same financial standing, but unconnected with the company*.

44. Relevant amounts

When considering the rules on loans it should be borne in mind throughout that any of the amounts specified in the statutory provisions on this topic can be increased at any time by order of the Secretary of State under s. 345.

In several of the rules governing the exceptions, however, the expression 'aggregate of the relevant amounts' appears, namely in ss. 334 (*see* **41**), 335 (*see* **43**), 337 (*see* **40**) and 338 (*see* **40**). Its meaning is given in s. 339 but unfortunately, again, not without tears. Before 'relevant amounts' can be understood, it is necessary to understand the meaning of 'relevant arrangement' and 'relevant transaction'.

A *transaction* is relevant if it was made:

(a) for the director for whom the proposed transaction or arrangement is to be made, or for any person connected with him; *or*

(b) where the proposed transaction or arrangement is to be made for a person connected with a director, for that director or any person connected with him.

An *arrangement* is relevant if it relates to a relevant transaction.

The *relevant amounts* in relation to a proposed transaction or arrangement are:

(a) the value of the *proposed transaction or arrangement*;
(b) the value of any *existing relevant arrangement* falling under one of the indirect arrangements to which s. 330 extends (*see* **39**) but covered by one of the exceptions;
(c) the amount outstanding under *any other relevant transaction* covered by one of the exceptions.

The amounts to be included under **(b)** and **(c)** comprise not only those provided by the company, but also those provided by any of its subsidiaries or, where the proposed transaction or arrangement is to be made for a director of its holding company or a person connected with him, by that holding company or any of its subsidiaries.

45. Civil remedies for breach of s. 330
The provisions of s. 341 regarding the effect of contravention of s. 330 on the transaction or arrangement in question are, with one exception, *exactly the same* as those relating to substantial property transactions involving directors which are described in **31** above.

The single difference is that the provision regarding affirmation by the company (*see* **(d)** in **32**) does not appear in s. 341.

46. Criminal penalties for breach of s. 330
Section 342, which deals with the penalties for contravention of s. 330, applies only to *relevant companies*.

A *director* of a relevant company who authorises or permits the company to enter into a transaction or arrangement, knowing or having reasonable cause to believe that the company was thereby contravening s. 330, is guilty of an offence.

A *relevant company* which enters into a transaction or arrangement for one of its directors or for a director of its holding company in contravention of s. 330 is also guilty of an offence, unless it shows that at the time the transaction was entered into it did not know the relevant circumstances.

A *person* who *procures* a relevant company to enter into a transaction or arrangement, knowing or having reasonable cause to believe that the company was thereby contravening s. 330, is guilty of an offence.

Finally, s. 342, taken along with Schedule 24, states the penalties. A director, company or other person guilty of an offence under the section is liable:

(a) on conviction on indictment, to imprisonment not exceeding two years or a fine, or both;

(b) on summary conviction, to imprisonment not exceeding six months or a fine not exceeding the statutory maximum, or both.

47. Summary of statutory provisions on loans to directors

It can be seen from **34–46** above that the rules relating to loans by a company to its directors are not easy to master. It is probably best to acquire a thorough knowledge of **38** and then, given a transaction which appears to be prohibited by it, see which, if any, of the exceptions are applicable.

To assist the student in this exercise this approach is adopted below.

(1) First make sure that you have read and understood the definition in s. 331 of the terms: 'quasi-loan' and 'credit transaction'.

(2) Then be quite clear on what is meant in s. 331 by: 'relevant company', i.e. a company which is *either*:

(a) a *public* company; *or*

(b) in the *same group* as a public company.

(3) Now make sure that the transaction in question *falls within one of the prohibitions in s. 330.*

Notice that while *all* companies are caught by the prohibitions on *loans* in s. 330, *only relevant companies are caught by the prohibitions on quasi-loans* and *credit transactions* in s. 330.

(4) Once you are sure that the transaction in question is caught by s. 330, see if it can be saved by any of the following exceptions:

LAWFUL LOANS TO DIRECTORS

ALL COMPANIES

Section 334	Section 336**(a)**, **(b)**	Section 337
Loan to director of the company or of its holding company.	Loan, quasi-loan or credit transaction for *holding company*.	*Anything done* to provide a director with funds to meet expenditure incurred for the purposes of the company, or to enable him properly to perform his duties as an officer.
Limit: £5,000	Guarantee or security for loan, quasi-loan or credit transaction by any other person for *holding company.*	*Requirements: Either:* prior approval of company in general meeting; *Or:* thing done on condition that, if not approved at or before the next AGM, loan must be repaid or liability discharged within six months from end of AGM.
		Limit: £20,000 in the case of a relevant company.

Section 333	Section 332	Section 335
Loan or quasi-loan to another company in same group	*Quasi-loan* to director of the company or of its holding company.	*Credit transaction* for director or connected person.
Guarantee or security for loan or quasi-loan by any other person to another company in same group.	*Requirements:* Term for reimbursement within two months. *Limit:* £5,000	Guarantee or security for credit transaction made by any other person for director or connected person. *Requirements:* (1) in ordinary course of company's business; and (2) on usual commercial terms. *Limit:* £10,000

MONEY-LENDING COMPANIES ONLY
(Section 338)

Loan or quasi-loan to any person.
Guarantee of any loan or quasi-loan.

Requirements:
(1) in ordinary course of company's business; and
(2) on usual commercial terms.

Limit: £100,000 in the case of a *relevant company other than a banking company under the Banking Act 1987.*

Dwelling-House

Requirement (2) above (usual commercial terms) *does not apply* to loan to director of the company or of its holding company for *purchase* or *improvement of dwelling-house* provided two conditions are satisfied:
(a) loans of that kind are normally made by the company to its employees on the same terms; and
(b) loan does not exceed £100,000.

48. Disclosure in accounts of transactions involving directors

There are detailed provisions in s. 232 and Schedule 6, both as amended by s. 6 and Schedule 4 Companies Act 1989, concerning disclosure, in *notes to the accounts,* of loans and other transactions favouring directors and officers.

Section 232, taken along with Schedule 6, requires a note to the accounts of *any company other than a holding company* to contain *specified particulars* (*see* **49**) of:

(a) any transaction or arrangement *of a kind described in s. 330* entered into by the company for any of its directors, or a director of its holding company, or for any person connected with such a director;

(b) an agreement by the company to enter into any such transaction or arrangement; *and*

(c) any other transaction or arrangement with the company in which any of its directors, or a director of its holding company, had, directly or indirectly, *a material interest.*

Similarly, group accounts of a holding company (or if it is not required to prepare group accounts, its individual accounts) must disclose in a note to the accounts specified particulars of the same transactions or arrangements, except that those entered into by any subsidiary of the company must also be included.

Schedule 6 enlarges on **(c)** above, stating that:

(a) a transaction or arrangement between a company and any of its directors, or a director of its holding company, or a person connected with such a director, must be treated, if it would not otherwise be so, as one in which that director is interested; *and*

(b) an interest is not 'material' if it is not material in the opinion of the majority of the directors, other than that director, of the company which is preparing the accounts in question.

49. The specified particulars

Schedule 6 gives details of the specified particulars which are to be disclosed. It provides that these consist of particulars of the *principal terms* of the transaction, arrangement or agreement including:

(a) a statement of the fact that it either was made or subsisted during the financial year in question;

(b) the name of the person for whom it was made and, where that person is connected with a director of the company or of its holding company, the name of that director;

(c) the name of any director with a material interest and the nature of that interest;

(d) in the case of a loan, agreement for a loan, or an indirect arrangement within s. 330 relating to a loan (*see* **39**):

(*i*) the amount of the liability of the person to whom the loan was made or agreed to be made, in respect of principal and interest, at the beginning and at the end of the financial year in question;

(*ii*) the maximum amount of that liability during that financial year;

(*iii*) the amount of any interest which has fallen due but not been paid; *and*

(*iv*) the amount of any provision made in respect of any failure by the borrower to repay the loan or any interest on it;

(e) in the case of a guarantee, security, or an indirect arrangement within s. 330 relating to a guarantee or security (*see* **39**):

(*i*) the amount for which the company or its subsidiary was liable both at the beginning and at the end of the financial year in question; (*ii*) the maximum amount for which the company or its subsidiary may become so liable; *and*
(*iii*) any amount paid or liability incurred by the company or its subsidiary in fulfilling the guarantee or discharging the security; *and*
(f) in the case of any other transaction, arrangement or agreement, the value of the transaction or arrangement in question.

50. Types of transactions excluded from s. 232
Certain types of transactions are excluded from the disclosure requirements of s. 232. In Schedule 6 these are stated to be:

(a) a transaction, arrangement or agreement between one company and another in which a director of the first company, or of its subsidiary or holding company, is interested only by virtue of his being a director of the latter;
(b) a contract of service between a company and any of its directors or a director of its holding company, or between a director of a company and any of its subsidiaries;
(c) a transaction, arrangement or agreement which was not entered into during the financial year in question and which did not subsist at any time during that year.

51. Exclusion of small transactions from s. 232
There are further exclusions in Schedule 6 for small transactions. No disclosure is required if:

(a) the transaction is made by a company or its subsidiary for a person who at any time during the financial year in question was a director of the company or of its holding company, or connected with such a director; *and*
(b) *either:*
(*i*) it is a *credit transaction*, agreement to enter into a credit transaction, a guarantee or security given in connection with a credit transaction, or an indirect arrangement within s. 330 (*see* **39**) relating to a credit transaction, and the *outstanding aggregate values* of each such transaction made for that person did not at any time during that year exceed £5,000; *or*
(*ii*) it is a transaction or arrangement with the company or any of its subsidiaries in which a director of the company or of its holding company had a *material interest*, and the *outstanding aggregate values* of each such transaction made for that person did not at any time during that year exceed £1,000, or, if more, did not exceed £5,000 or *1 per cent of the company's net assets*, whichever is the less.

The amounts specified above can be increased at any time by order of the Secretary of State under s. 345 as applied by Schedule 6.

52. Disclosure in accounts of transactions involving officers other than directors

Section 232, taken along with Schedule 6, also applies to officers of the company other than directors. The accounts must contain, by way of notes to the accounts, a *statement* relating to transactions, arrangements and agreements made by the company or a subsidiary of it for persons who at any time during the financial year were *officers but not directors*.

The statement must give details of the aggregate amounts outstanding at the end of the financial year under specified transactions, and the number of officers for whom such transactions were made.

The Schedule lists the transactions in question as consisting of *loans, quasi-loans and credit transactions*, guarantees and securities relating to them, indirect arrangements within s. 330 (*see* **39**) relating to them, and agreements to enter into any of these transactions or arrangements.

The Schedule exempts transactions from such disclosure if the aggregate amount outstanding does not exceed £2,500.

53. Duty of auditors regarding non-compliance with disclosure requirements

Section 237, as substituted by s. 9 Companies Act 1989, provides that if a company fails to comply with the requirements of Schedule 6 regarding disclosure in the accounts, the auditors must include in their report a statement giving the required particulars, in so far as they are reasonably able to do so.

54. Compensation for loss of office

Section 312 provides that it is not lawful for a company to pay a director compensation for loss of office or to make any payment to him in connection with his retirement, unless the amount of the proposed payment is disclosed to the members and approved by the company. If it is not so disclosed and approved the directors responsible for making it are liable to the company for misapplication of the company's funds: *Re Duomatic* (1969) [B133].

Section 313 contains an exactly similar provision regarding payments to directors when the undertaking or property of the company is being transferred. If such an illegal payment is in fact made, the director must hold the amount which he received in trust for the company.

Section 314 requires the amount of the payment to be stated in any notice given to shareholders of an offer for their shares wherever a transfer of all or any of the shares in the company results from:

(a) an offer to the general body of shareholders;

(b) an offer by some other company with a view to making the company its subsidiary;

(c) an offer by an individual with a view to his acquiring at least one-third of the voting power; *or*

(d) any other offer conditional on acceptance to a given extent (i.e. the offer stands *provided* a specified fraction of the members accept it).

Offers for the shares of a company often result in its directors being virtually paid to go quietly, and the Act is merely making sure that the members know what is happening.

Section 315 further provides that if s. 314 is not complied with, the director must hold the amount which he has received in trust for any persons who have sold their shares as a result of the offer.

> NOTE: The provisions of these three sections are also very important and must be studied carefully. It should be noted, however, that they apply only to payments *which the company is not legally obliged to make*. Payments made in fulfilment of the terms of a service contract are thus not subject to the requirement of approval by the company: *Taupo Totara Timber Co. Ltd* v. *Rowe* (1978).
>
> Similarly, it is clear from s. 316 that a *bona fide* payment to a director by way of damages for breach of contract or pension for past services is also outside the scope of the sections.

55. Disclosure in accounts of payments to directors

Section 232 and Schedule 6, both as amended by s. 6 and Schedule 4 Companies Act 1989, require a note to the company's accounts to show:

(a) the aggregate amount of the directors' emoluments, distinguishing between those received by him *qua director* and those received *qua employee* if in fact he has a service contract with the company;

(b) the aggregate amount of directors' or past directors' pensions; *and*

(c) the aggregate amount of any compensation to directors or past directors for loss of office.

Section 232 requires a director to disclose to the company all the information necessary for the purposes of these provisions of Schedule 6.

With the exception mentioned below, Schedule 6 requires a note to the accounts to show also the *emoluments of the chairman*, and of the most highly paid director if he is paid *more than the chairman*. In addition, it must show the number of directors who received £5,000 or less. It must then proceed to show the number of directors receiving more than £5,000 but not more than £10,000, the number receiving more than £10,000 but not more than £15,000, and so on up a scale of multiples of £5,000. The Schedule requires a note to the accounts to show the number of directors who have *waived* their rights to emoluments, and the aggregate amount of the emoluments concerned.

These provisions with regard to the emoluments of the chairman and of the directors do not apply to any company which is neither a holding nor a subsidiary company if the amount shown in the note to its accounts under **(a)** above does not exceed £60,000.

56. The legal position of directors

We have already seen that directors are officers of the company and agents of it. All the normal rules of agency apply, e.g. a director may not make a *secret profit*.

Sometimes, however, the directors are in the position of agents of *the shareholders* as well. This can arise where the shareholders *expressly appoint* them to act as their agents: *Briess* v. *Woolley* (1954), or where by their own *behaviour* they render themselves agents for the shareholders: *Allen* v. *Hyatt* (1914). But this is not the normal legal position and arises only in exceptional circumstances.

Directors are also sometimes said to be *trustees* for the company, but this is not truly the case. A trustee is the *legal owner* of property which he holds on trust for a beneficiary; a director does not hold property on trust for the company, for the company itself is the legal owner. Moreover, the duties of a trustee are well defined by law, e.g. under a will or a settlement, but a director's duties are not capable of precise definition.

On the other hand a director, like a trustee, is in a *fiduciary relation* towards the company. He is, of course, in a fiduciary relation towards the company in any case where he is acting as the company's agent, for an agent is always in a fiduciary relation with his principal. But the fiduciary relation of the director towards the company covers not only his activities as its agent, i.e. the making of contracts on its behalf, but the entire field of operation. There is nothing he can do in his capacity of director which is *not* required to be done *in good faith*, for the *benefit of the company as a whole*. The care and control of its assets, the making of calls, the forfeiture of shares, the approval of transfers—all these things and any other things which are done by the directors as directors must be done in good faith. It is this that is meant when they are said to be trustees of their powers.

57. Directors' duties of good faith and care

These can best be summed up by saying that a director is permitted to be very stupid so long as he is honest. In fact, if one were to draw any conclusions from the state of the law, one would imagine that the business world was full of honest, stupid men.

The courts have imposed two duties upon directors:

(a) the *fiduciary* duty; *and*

(b) the duty of *care*.

Statute law is almost silent concerning both, so that the source of all but one of the following rules is the decided cases.

(a) *The fiduciary duty*: We have already seen in **56** that directors must always act *bona fide* for the benefit of the company as a whole. Acting in this way may justify the directors in no longer observing an agreement previously made, e.g. an agreement to recommend acceptance of a take-over bid as in *Dawson International plc* v. *Coats Patons plc* (1989) [B153]. However, here there are a number of points which must be borne in mind:

(*i*) The directors owe their duty to the *company*, not to individual members.

Thus in *Percival* v. *Wright* (1902), the directors bought some shares in the company from a member who wished to sell them. The directors knew at the time that negotiations were in progress for the sale of all the shares in the company at a higher price than they were paying, but they did not disclose this fact to the member. HELD: The sale should not be set aside. The directors owed no duty to that individual member.

It should be borne in mind, however, that today the directors in question would have committed a criminal offence under the 'insider dealing' rules (*see* Chapter 24).

(*ii*) Their duty to the company as *directors* does not prevent them from voting as *members* at general meetings in any way that they wish: *North-West Transportation Co. Ltd* v. *Beatty* (1887).

They may not, however, use their voting control to ratify their own fraud: *Cook* v. *Deeks* (1916) [B163].

(*iii*) They must exercise their powers not only in good faith, but for a proper purpose: *Hogg* v. *Cramphorn Ltd* (1967) [B177].

Thus in *Howard Smith Ltd* v. *Ampol Petroleum Ltd* (1974) [B161], where the directors of R.W. Miller (Holdings) Ltd issued shares to Howard Smith with a view to diluting the majority voting power of two large existing shareholders, Ampol and Bulkships, and so facilitating a take-over bid from Howard Smith, the Privy Council dismissed Howard Smith's appeal from the decision of the Supreme Court of New South Wales setting aside the issue. The directors had used their fiduciary power 'solely for the purposes of shifting the power to decide to whom and at what price shares are to be sold', and this could not be 'related to any purpose for which the power over the share capital was conferred on them'.

See also *Rolled Steel Products (Holdings) Ltd* v. *British Steel*

Corporation (1986) [B154] so far as it relates to the exercise of directors' powers; the directors were held to have been in breach of their fiduciary duty in granting a guarantee and debenture for a purpose which was not authorised by the memorandum. (Note, however, that this case was concerned with a transaction which took place before any change had been made on the *ultra vires* doctrine.)

However, the company in general meeting may choose to ratify an act done by directors for an improper purpose provided it is within the company's powers: *Bamford* v. *Bamford* (1970).

(*iv*)   They must not place themselves in a position where their interests conflict with their duty without making full disclosure to the general meeting. If they fail to make full disclosure, any contract made in these circumstances may be *voidable* by the company; and the director will be accountable to the company for any profits made out of the transaction: *Aberdeen Railway Co.* v. *Blaikie Bros.* (1854) [B165]; *Guinness plc* v. *Saunders* (1990) [B166]; *Movitex Ltd* v. *Bulfield* (1986) [B167]; and *Lee Panavision Ltd* v. *Lee Lighting Ltd* (1992) [B168].

The liability to account for the profit to the company 'arises from the mere fact of a profit having been made': *Regal (Hastings) Ltd* v. *Gulliver* (1942) [B170]. It is irrelevant that the profit could not have been obtained by the company; thus in *Industrial Development Consultants Ltd* v. *Cooley* (1972) where Cooley obtained for himself the benefit of a contract which could not have been obtained by the company, but failed to make any disclosure to the company although he was a director at the time, he was held accountable for the profit.

(*v*)   They must have regard in the performance of their functions to the interests of the company's *employees* in general, as well as those of the members.

This is the single statutory rule in the midst of well-developed case-law relating to fiduciary duties. It is found in s. 309 and the section makes it clear that, like any other fiduciary duty, the duty of directors to consider the employees is owed to the *company* and thus enforceable by the company alone. The provision has been much criticised as being ineffective and indeed is illustrative, along with certain other sections of the Act, of the truth of the ancient proverb that barking dogs seldom bite.

(b)   *The duty of care:* This was considered at length by Romer J. in *Re City Equitable Fire Insurance Co. Ltd* (1925) [B172] where the following propositions were stated:

(*i*)   'A director need not exhibit in the performance of his duties a greater degree of skill than may reasonably be expected from a person of his knowledge and experience'.

He may, however, have no knowledge of the company's business, and little experience, so that a reasonable standard of skill may be a very low one.

(*ii*) 'Directors are not liable for mere errors of judgment'. Brett L.J. had stated many years earlier in *Marzetti's Case* (1800). 'Mere imprudence is not negligence. Want of judgment is not.'

(*iii*) 'A director is not bound to give continuous attention to the affairs of his company'. He is not bound to attend all (board) meetings, though he ought to attend whenever he is reasonably able to do so.

(*iv*) 'In respect of all duties that . . . may properly be left to some other official, a director is, in the absence of grounds for suspicion, justified in trusting that official to perform such duties honestly'.

It is clear that the standard of care required from a director is *subjective*, i.e. it is a variable standard depending on the skill and knowledge of the particular director in question. In law a director may safely be ignorant, inexperienced and lacking in judgment so long as he is honest and careful.

In *Dorchester Finance Co. Ltd* v. *Stebbing* (1989) [B175], where all three directors were accountants, no distinction was made between executive and non-executive directors in relation to the duty of care. The two non-executive directors were held to be negligent in failing to carry out their duties and in signing blank cheques, which allowed the executive director to act as he pleased.

A statutory explanation of a director's duty of care occurs in s. 214 Insolvency Act 1986 in connection with wrongful trading. The section provides that the liquidator of a company which has gone into insolvent liquidation may apply to the court for a declaration that a director is to be liable to make such contribution to the company's assets as the court thinks proper. Before making such an order the court must be satisfied that:

(a) at some time before the commencement of the winding up of the company, the director *knew or ought to have concluded* that there was no reasonable prospect that the company would avoid going into insolvent liquidation; *and*

(b) the director did not take *every step with a view to minimising the potential loss to the company's creditors that he ought to have taken.*

The section provides that for the purposes of the words in italics the standard to be applied is that of a reasonably diligent person who has both:

(*i*) the general knowledge, skill and experience reasonably to be expected of a person carrying out the same functions as are carried out by, or entrusted to, that director in relation to the company; *and*

(*ii*) the general knowledge, skill and experience which that director has.

An illustration is *Norman* v. *Theodore Goddard (a firm)* (1991) [B176]: A director who was a chartered surveyor with no knowledge of company law was held to have acted reasonably in accepting information from a senior partner in an eminent firm of city solicitors and acting on it without further enquiry.

58. Disclosure by directors of interests in contracts

Section 317 requires a director who is in any way interested in a contract with the company to declare the nature of his interest at a *board meeting*. Unless the articles state otherwise, this duty to disclose to the board is in addition to, and not instead of, the duty to disclose to the general meeting imposed by the rules of equity considered in **57** and expressly preserved by s. 317.

The section provides that the declaration must be made at the board meeting at which the question of entering into the contract is first considered, or, if the director was not interested in it at that date, at the next board meeting held after he became interested. If he became interested in the contract only after it was made, he must declare his interest at the first board meeting held after he became so interested.

If a director gives a *general notice* to the board that he is a member of a specified company or firm and is to be regarded as interested in any contract which is made with it, this is a sufficient declaration of interest. Such a notice, however, must either be given at a board meeting, or brought up and read at the next board meeting after it is given.

If proper disclosure as required by the section is not made, the director is liable under the section, taken along with Schedule 24, to a fine of an unspecified amount on conviction on indictment, and on summary conviction to a fine not exceeding the statutory maximum.

The articles often exclude the equitable duty to disclose an interest to the general meeting provided the director complies with s. 317. This is the effect of Article 85 of Table A, but see also Article 94, which restricts the interested director's right to vote, and Article 95, which provides that a director not entitled to vote cannot be counted in the quorum.

It should be noted that the meaning of the word 'contract' in s. 317 is extended to include any transaction or arrangement, whether constituting a contract or not. Moreover a transaction or arrangement within s. 330 (*see* **38** and **39**) made by a company for any of its directors, or for a person connected with such director, must be treated, for the purposes of s. 317, as one in which that director is interested.

Lastly, s. 317 applies to a *shadow director (see* **2**) in the same way that it applies to a director, except that a shadow director must declare his interest, not at a board meeting, but by a *written notice* to the directors which is *either*:

(a) a *specific* notice given before the meeting at which, if he had been a director, the declaration would be required to be made; *or*

(b) a sufficient *general* notice.

For the purpose of minutes, the declaration is treated as if it had formed part of the proceedings at the meeting in question.

The requirement of s. 317 is to declare the interest at a meeting of the whole board: it is not sufficient to declare it to a directors' committee: *Guinness plc* v. *Saunders* (1990) [B166].

59. Dealings in options by directors

Section 323 prohibits a director from purchasing any option, whether a 'call' option, a 'put' option or a 'double' option, with regard to shares or debentures of the company or any other company within the group if a stock exchange listing has been granted in respect of them. The prohibition applies to a shadow director as to a director.

Section 323 nevertheless permits him to buy an option to *subscribe* for the shares or debentures of a company, or to buy debentures entitling the holder to subscribe for shares or convert the debentures into shares.

Section 327 extends the application of s. 323 to a director's spouse or infant child, though it is a defence for such a person to prove that he had no reason to believe that his spouse or parent, as the case may be, was a director of the company in question.

60. Liability for acts of co-directors and relief from liability

A director is the agent of the *company* and not of the other members of the board. It follows that nothing done by the *board* can impose liability on a director who did not know of their action and did not participate in it, even if he attends the subsequent board meeting at which the minutes recording the wrongful action of the earlier meeting are confirmed. To incur liability he must either be a party to the wrongful act, or later acquiesce in it.

Where the directors have misappropriated the company's money, any director against whom an action is brought is entitled to *contribution* from as many of his co-directors as were parties to the misapplication.

Finally, in relation to a director's liability, note should be taken of the provisions of ss. 310, as amended by s. 137 Companies Act 1989, and 727. These sections apply not only to directors but to other officers and to auditors.

Section 310 states that any provision in the articles or in any contract exempting such persons from, or indemnifying them against, liability for negligence or breach of duty towards the company is *void*. Thus it is impossible for a director to limit or exclude liability for negligence by the terms of his contract.

If, however, the court thinks that, though liable, the director has acted honestly and reasonably and ought fairly to be excused, it may, under s. 727, relieve him from liability on such terms as it thinks fit. Further, s. 310 as amended provides that it does not prevent a company from:

(a) purchasing and maintaining for any director insurance against such liability; *or*
(b) indemnifying any director against any liability incurred by him in defending any civil or criminal proceedings in which judgment is given in his favour.

61. Powers of directors

The directors' powers are normally set out in the articles. Once these powers are vested in the directors, only they may exercise them. Thus the shareholders cannot control the way in which the directors choose to act, provided their actions are within the scope of the powers given to them. If the shareholders disapprove of the board's actions strongly enough, they can alter the articles to restrict the board's powers, or they can remove the directors under s. 303, but they cannot themselves try to perform the very functions which they have entrusted to the directors: *Quin & Axtens Ltd* v. *Salmon* (1909), applied in *Breckland Group Holdings Ltd* v. *London and Suffolk Properties Ltd* (1989).

Table A, Article 70, provides that the business of the company shall be managed by the directors, who may exercise all the powers of the company subject to the provisions of the Act, the memorandum and articles and any direction given by a special resolution.

The effect of this article is to vest in the directors all the powers *except* those which the Act or the memorandum and articles or a special resolution specifically state must be exercised by the company in general meeting. It could not, therefore, be more widely expressed.

62. Delegation of directors' powers

The maxim *'delegatus non potest delegare'* applies to directors in the same way as to all agents. A person to whom a function has been delegated may not himself delegate it further without the consent of his principal.

Table A, Article 72, however, specifically permits delegation, stating that the directors may delegate any of their powers to committees consisting of such member or members of their body as they think fit. Thus a committee may consist of a single director under this article.

63. The managing director

The directors may not appoint a managing director unless the articles authorise them to do so. Table A, Article 72, empowers them to delegate to any managing director such of their powers as they consider desirable to be exercised by him. The delegation may be made subject to conditions and may be revoked or altered.

The managing director is normally a service director with a contract setting out his powers and duties and terms of employment. He has a dual capacity — that of director and that of employee: *Anderson* v. *James Sutherland (Peterhead) Ltd* (1941) [B132].

If he has a service contract, the revocation of his appointment by the directors under Article 72, or an alteration of the articles, or his removal under s. 303 from the office of director, cannot deprive him of his right to damages for breach of contract, if indeed a breach has been committed. But it is for him to prove that his dismissal was contrary to the terms of his service agreement: *Caddies* v. *Harold Holdsworth & Co. (Wakefield) Ltd* (1955).

Where the articles include a power to appoint a managing director, a person who acts as a managing director, though not expressly appointed, has ostensible authority to bind the company: *Freeman & Lockyer* v. *Buckhurst Park Properties (Mangal) Ltd* (1964) [B139] and *Allison* v. *Scotia Motor and Engineering Co. Ltd* (1906) [B143].

64. The secretary

A secretary, as we have already seen in **1**, is an officer of the company under s. 744, and s. 283 (*see* **3**) requires every company to have one.

Nevertheless, until recently, his important status was not recognised by the courts. In 1887 Lord Esher said: 'A secretary is a mere servant; his position is that he is to do what he is told, and no person can assume that he has any authority to represent anything at all': *Barnett, Hoares & Co.* v. *South London Tramways Co.* (1887) [B186]. In 1902 Lord Macnaghten described his duties as 'of a limited and of a somewhat humble character': *George Whitechurch Ltd* v. *Cavanagh* (1902).

In *Panorama Developments (Guildford) Ltd* v. *Fidelis Furnishing Fabrics Ltd* (1971), [B187], however, the Court of Appeal were of the opinion that times had changed. The secretary was no longer a mere clerk, but the chief administrative officer of the company, and as regards *matters of administration* (e.g. hiring of cars) had ostensible authority to sign contracts on behalf of the company.

This change in the secretary's status is reflected in s. 286 which has its origin in the Companies Act 1980 and which deals with his qualifications. The section provides that in a *public* company it is the directors' duty to take all reasonable steps to secure that the secretary is a person who appears to them to have the requisite *knowledge and experience* to discharge his functions *and*:

(a) held office as secretary, assistant secretary, or deputy secretary of the company when the 1980 Act came into operation; *or*

(b) for at least three out of the five years immediately preceding his appointment as secretary held office as secretary of a public company; *or*

(c) is a member of any of the bodies listed in the section, (i.e. the Institutes of Chartered Accountants, the Chartered Association of Certified Accountants, the Institute of Chartered Secretaries and Administrators, the Chartered Institute of Management Accountants, and the Chartered Institute of Public Finance and Accountancy); *or*

(d) is a barrister, advocate or solicitor; *or*

(e) is a person who, by virtue of his having held some other position or being a member of some other body, appears to the directors to be capable of discharging those functions.

Board meetings

1. The holding of board meetings

Table A, Article 88, provides that, subject to the provisions of the articles, the directors may regulate their proceedings as they think fit. Questions shall be decided *by a majority of votes*, and the chairman has a *casting vote*. A director may, and the secretary at the request of a director shall, at any time call a meeting. It is not necessary to give notice of a meeting to a director who is absent from the United Kingdom.

2. Notice of board meetings

Board meetings are often held regularly on the same day in each week or month, and in such cases notice is not required though it may be given in practice. If they are not held regularly in this way, then either *the period of notice prescribed by the articles* or, if none, *reasonable* notice must be given. Table A does not specify any particular period.

The notice need not be in writing, and oral notice will therefore suffice. If all the directors are assembled together and no one objects, no notice at all is necessary and a meeting may be held then and there, but it is essential that they all consent to the holding of the meeting.

> Thus in *Barron* v. *Potter* (1914), B and P, who were both directors of the company, disliked each other and refused to meet at board meetings. One day they met by chance at Paddington station, whereupon P insisted on holding a board meeting on the spot, claiming that he had proposed a motion and carried it with his chairman's casting vote.

> HELD: B had not consented to the holding of the meeting, and his mere physical presence without consent did not constitute a valid meeting.

3. The chairman of board meetings

Table A, Article 91, provides that the directors may appoint one of their number to be the chairman of the board of directors and may at any time remove him from that office. If there is no director holding that office, or if the director holding it is unwilling to preside or is not present *within five minutes* after the time appointed for the meeting, the directors present may appoint one of their number to be chairman of the meeting.

This article may be compared with Article 42 (*see* 15: **18**) which contains a similar provision but requires less promptitude.

4. Quorum at board meetings

Table A, Article 89, states that the quorum necessary for the transaction of business may be fixed by the directors, and unless so fixed shall be two (*see* 15: **21(e)**).

If the articles *empower the directors* to fix the quorum, but fail to specify what the quorum shall be if they do not fix it, then the *number of directors who usually act* will form the quorum. If the articles make no provision concerning quorum at all, then the *majority* of the directors must be present to constitute a valid meeting.

The quorum at a board meeting must be a *disinterested quorum*. This means that directors who are disqualified from voting on a resolution because they have an interest in it (*see* 16:**58**) must not be counted in ascertaining whether a quorum is present, though they cannot be excluded from the meeting. Articles 85, 94 and 95 should be re-read at this point.

Table A, Article 90, permits the continuing directors to act in spite of any vacancies on the board so long as there are enough of them to form a quorum. Once, however, their number falls below that required for a quorum, *they may act only for two purposes*:

(a) to fill vacancies; *and*
(b) to call a general meeting of the company.

5. Power to dispense with board meeting

Table A, Article 93, states that a resolution in writing signed by all the directors entitled to receive notice of a board meeting shall be as valid as if it had been passed at a board meeting. The same applies to a meeting of a committee of directors.

18

The accounts

1. The statutory provisions on accounts

The statutory provisions on company accounts are contained in Part VII (consisting of ss. 221–262) of the 1985 Act and in Schedules 4 to 10 to that Act. In order to comply with the Seventh European Company Law Directive, it was necessary to make substantial amendments of these provisions and this was accomplished by the Companies Act 1989, as stated in s. 1 Companies Act 1989, by:

(a) inserting new provisions in place of the existing ss. 221–262 of the 1985 Act (including some new sections, e.g. ss. 245A, 245B and 245C to follow s. 245); and

(b) amending or replacing Schedules 4 to 10 to that Act and inserting new Schedules.

References in this chapter are therefore to ss. 221–262 of the *1985 Act as substituted by the 1989 Act*, and references to Schedules 4 to 10 are similarly to be understood as being references to Schedules 4 to 10 to the *1985 Act as amended or substituted by the 1989 Act*.

2. Content of the Schedules

The Schedules which concern the accounting provisions are:

(a) Schedule 4 to the 1985 Act (form and content of company accounts), as *amended* by s. 4 and Schedule 1 Companies Act 1989;

(b) Schedule 4A to the 1985 Act (form and content of group accounts), *inserted* by s. 5 and Schedule 2 Companies Act 1989;

(c) Schedule 5 to the 1985 Act (disclosure of information: related undertakings), as *substituted* by s. 6 and Schedule 3 Companies Act 1989;

(d) Schedule 6 to the 1985 Act (disclosure of information: emoluments and other benefits of directors and others), as *amended* by s. 6 and Schedule 4 Companies Act 1989;

(e) Schedule 7 to the 1985 Act (matters to be included in directors' report), as *amended* by s. 8 and Schedule 5 Companies Act 1989;

(f) Schedule 8 to the 1985 Act (exemptions for small and medium-sized companies), as *substituted* by s. 13 and Schedule 6 Companies Act 1989;

(g) Schedule 9 to the 1985 Act (special provisions for banking and insurance companies and groups), as *amended* by s. 18 and Schedule 7 Companies Act 1989;

(h) Schedule 10 to the 1985 Act (directors' report where accounts pre pared in accordance with special provisions for banking or insurance companies or groups), as *substituted* by s. 18 and Schedule 8 Companies Act 1989;

(i) Schedule 10A to the 1985 Act (parent and subsidiary undertakings: supplementary provisions), *inserted* by s. 21 and Schedule 9 Companies Act 1989.

3. Power to alter accounting requirements

The provisions comprising Part VII of the Act and its associated Schedules, as now amended by the Companies Act 1989, present the student with a great mass of detail. Full treatment of the various requirements is well beyond the scope of this book.

It is important, moreover, to note that alteration of the requirements does not necessarily require a further Act of Parliament, since by s. 257 the Secretary of State has power to modify the provisions of Part VII by regulations made by statutory instrument.

4. Parent and subsidiary undertakings

Frequent mention will be made in this chapter of parent and subsidiary undertakings. It is, therefore, appropriate to note at this preliminary stage the meaning of these terms for the purposes of Part VII of the Act.

By s. 258 an undertaking is a parent undertaking in relation to another undertaking (a subsidiary undertaking), if:

(a) it holds a majority of the voting rights in the undertaking; *or*

(b) it is a member of the undertaking and has the right to appoint or remove a majority of its board of directors; *or*

(c) it has the right to exercise a dominant influence over the undertaking:

(*i*) by virtue of provisions contained in the undertaking's memorandum or articles; *or*

(*ii*) by virtue of a control contract; *or*

(d) it is a member of the undertaking and controls alone, pursuant to an agreement with other shareholders or members, a majority of the voting rights in the undertaking.

Section 258 further provides that an undertaking is also a parent undertaking in relation to another undertaking (a subsidiary undertaking), if it has a *participating interest* in the undertaking and:

(a) it actually exercises a dominant influence over it; *or*

(b) it and the subsidiary undertaking are managed on a unified basis.

A parent undertaking may be more than one remove away from its subsidiary undertakings; for example, to take the simplest case, a parent undertaking is treated as the parent undertaking not only of its own immediate subsidiary undertakings but also of undertakings which are the subsidiary undertakings of its own immediate subsidiary undertakings.

It will be noted that the term used is not 'company' but 'undertaking'. By s. 259 'undertaking' for the purposes of Part VII of the Act means:

(a) a body corporate or partnership; *or*
(b) an unincorporated association carrying on a trade or business, with or without a view to profit.

The expression 'participating interest' used in s. 258 also calls for explanation. By s. 260 'participating interest' means an interest held by an undertaking in the shares of another undertaking which it holds on a long-term basis for the purpose of securing a contribution to its activities by the exercise of control or influence arising from or related to that interest. A holding of 20 per cent or more of the shares of an undertaking is presumed to be a participating interest unless the contrary is shown.

More detailed matter on the meaning of 'parent undertaking' and 'subsidiary undertaking' is included in ss. 258–260 and in addition there are supplementary provisions on these expressions in Schedule 10A to the Act.

5. Keeping accounting records

By s. 221 every company must keep accounting records which are sufficient to show and explain the company's transactions and are such as to disclose with reasonable accuracy the company's financial position and enable the directors to ensure that the company's annual accounts comply with the Act.

By the same section the accounting records must in particular contain:

(a) entries from day to day of receipts and payments;
(b) a record of assets and liabilities; *and*
(c) if the company's business involves dealing in goods, statements as to stock and stocktakings.

The accounting records must, by s. 222, be kept at the registered office or such other place as the directors think fit, and must at all times be open to inspection by the company's officers. It is also provided that if accounting records are kept at a place outside Great Britain, accounts and returns must be sent to, and kept at, a place in Great Britain and be likewise open to inspection by officers.

If a company fails to comply with any of these provisions in ss. 221 and

222, every officer who is in default is guilty of an offence unless he shows that he acted honestly and that in the circumstances in which the company's business was carried on the default was excusable: ss. 221 and 222.

6. Preservation of accounting records
Section 222 further provides that the accounting records must be preserved in the case of a private company for three years and in the case of a public company for six years, and that an officer is guilty of an offence if he fails to take all reasonable steps for securing compliance by the company with this provision or intentionally causes any default by the company under it.

7. A company's financial year
Section 223 states how a company's 'financial year' is determined.

Its first financial year begins with the first day of its first 'accounting reference period' and ends with the last day of that period (or such other date, not more than seven days before or after the end of that period, as the directors may determine).

Subsequent financial years begin with the day immediately following the end of the company's previous financial year and end with the last day of its next 'accounting reference period' (or such other date, not more than seven days before or after the end of that period, as the directors may determine).

Section 223 further provides that the financial year of a subsidiary undertaking must coincide with the parent company's own financial year except where in the opinion of the directors of the parent company there are good reasons against it.

8. The accounting reference period
Section 223, on the company's financial year, leads on to section 224 which deals with the company's accounting reference period and its accounting reference date.

Section 224 permits a company to give notice to the registrar within nine months after incorporation specifying a date on which, in each calendar year, the accounting reference period of the company is to end. That specified date is then the company's 'accounting reference date'.

If the company gives no such notice to the registrar, the company's reference date is:

(a) in the case of a company incorporated before s. 3 Companies Act 1989 came into force, 31 March; *and*
(b) in any other case, the last day of the month in which the anniversary of its incorporation falls.

A company's first accounting reference period is the period of more than six months, but not more than 18 months, beginning with the date of its incorporation and ending with its accounting reference date.

Its subsequent accounting reference periods are successive periods of 12 months beginning immediately after the end of the previous accounting reference period and ending with its accounting reference date.

9. Alteration of accounting reference date
Section 225 makes it permissible for a company to alter its accounting reference date in two situations.

First, a company may by notice in the prescribed form given to the registrar specify a new accounting reference date which will take effect for the company's *current* accounting reference period *and subsequent* periods.

Secondly, a company may by such a notice specify a new accounting reference date which will take effect for the company's *immediately previous* accounting reference period *and subsequent* periods if:

(a) the company is a subsidiary undertaking or parent undertaking of another company and the alteration will make the accounting reference dates of the two companies coincide; *or*
(b) an administration order under the Insolvency Act 1986 is in force (*see* 27:1).

10. Duty to prepare individual company accounts
Section 226 requires the directors of every company to prepare for each financial year of the company a balance sheet as at the last day of the year and a profit and loss account. These accounts are referred to as the company's 'individual accounts'.

The balance sheet must give a true and fair view of the state of affairs of the company as at the end of the financial year, while the profit and loss account must give a true and fair view of the profit or loss of the company for the financial year.

11. Form and content of individual accounts
A company's individual accounts must, by s. 226, comply with the provisions of Schedule 4 as to the form and content of the balance sheet and profit and loss account and additional information to be provided by way of notes to the accounts.

The overriding principle is that the accounts must give a true and fair view. Section 226 accordingly provides that where compliance with Schedule 4, and the other provisions of the Act as to matters to be included in a company's individual accounts or in notes to those accounts, would not be sufficient to give a true and fair view, the necessary additional information must be given in the accounts or in a note to them.

Further, s. 226 provides that if in special circumstances compliance with any of the statutory provisions is inconsistent with the requirement to give a true and fair view, the directors must depart from that provision to the extent necessary to give a true and fair view; and particulars of any such departure, the reasons for it and its effect must be given in a note to the accounts.

12. Duty to prepare group accounts

By section 227, if at the end of a financial year a company is a parent company, the directors must, as well as preparing individual accounts for the year, prepare group accounts.

The group accounts must be consolidated accounts comprising:

(a) a consolidated balance sheet dealing with the state of affairs of the parent company and its subsidiary undertakings; *and*
(b) a consolidated profit and loss account dealing with the profit and loss of the parent company and its subsidiary undertakings.

The accounts must give a true and fair view of the state of affairs as at the end of the financial year, and the profit or loss for the financial year, of the undertakings included in the consolidation as a whole, so far as concerns members of the company.

13. Form and content of group accounts

A company's group accounts must, by s. 227, comply with the provisions of Schedule 4A as to the form and content of the consolidated balance sheet and consolidated profit and loss account and additional information to be provided by way of notes to the accounts.

The overriding principle is again that the accounts must give a true and fair view, and s. 227 includes the same provisions as s. 226 (*see* **11**) in support of this principle.

14. Exemption for parent companies included in larger groups

Section 228 provides that a company is exempt from the requirement to prepare group accounts if it is itself a subsidiary undertaking and its immediate parent undertaking is established under the law of a member state of the EC and if *either*:

(a) the company is a wholly-owned subsidiary of that parent undertaking; *or*
(b) that parent undertaking holds more than 50 per cent of the shares in the company *and* notice requesting the preparation of group accounts has not been served on the company by shareholders holding in aggregate:

(*i*) more than half of the remaining shares in the company; or

(*ii*) five per cent of the total shares in the company.

The notice must be served not later than six months after the end of the financial year before that to which it relates.

The exemption in s. 228 is conditional upon compliance with all of the following conditions:

(a) the company is included in consolidated accounts for a larger group drawn up to the same date, or to an earlier date in the same financial year, by a parent undertaking established under the law of a member state of the EC;

(b) those accounts are drawn up and audited, and that parent undertaking's annual report is drawn up, according to that law, in accordance with the Seventh Directive;

(c) the company discloses in its individual accounts that it is exempt from the obligation to prepare and deliver group accounts;

(d) the company states in its individual accounts the name of the parent undertaking which draws up the group accounts and the country of its incorporation (or, if it is unincorporated, the address of its principal place of business);

(e) the company delivers to the registrar, within the period allowed for delivering its individual accounts, copies of those group accounts and of the parent undertaking's annual report, together with the auditors' report on them; and

(f) a translation into English of any document in **(e)** above which is not in English is annexed to the copy delivered.

The exemption does not apply to a company any of whose securities are listed on a stock exchange in any member state of the EC.

15. Exclusion of subsidiary undertakings from consolidation

Section 229 provides for some exceptions to the general rule that all the subsidiary undertakings of the parent company must be included in the consolidation.

In any of the following cases a subsidiary undertaking *may* be excluded from consolidation:

(a) if its inclusion is not material for the purpose of giving a true and fair view (but two or more undertakings may be excluded *only if* they are not material when taken together);

(b) where severe long-term restrictions substantially hinder the exercise of the rights of the parent company over the assets or management of the undertaking;

(c) the information necessary for the preparation of group accounts cannot be obtained without disproportionate expense or undue delay;

(d) the interest of the parent company is held exclusively with a view to subsequent resale and the undertaking has not previously been included in consolidated group accounts prepared by the parent company.

Subsidiary undertakings *must* be excluded from consolidation where the activities of one or more subsidiary undertakings are so different from those of undertakings to be included in the consolidation that their inclusion would be incompatible with the obligation to give a true and fair view.

Where all the subsidiary undertakings of a parent company fall within the above exclusions, no group accounts are required at all.

16. Disclosure required in notes to accounts

Schedules 5 and 6 to the Act specify information which must be given in notes to a company's annual accounts: ss. 231, 232.

Schedule 5, which deals with related undertakings, is divided into two Parts. Part I is applicable where the company is not required to prepare group accounts, while Part II is applicable where the company is required to prepare group accounts: s. 231.

The information required by Schedule 5 need not be disclosed with respect to an undertaking which:

(a) is established under the law of a country outside the UK; *or*

(b) carries on business outside the UK;

if in the opinion of the directors of the company the disclosure would be seriously prejudicial to the business of that undertaking, or to the business of the company or any of its subsidiary undertakings, *and* the Secretary of State agrees that the information need not be disclosed: s. 231.

Section 231 also provides that if the directors of the company are of the opinion that the number of undertakings about which the company is required to disclose information under Schedule 5 would result in information of excessive length being given, the information (with some exceptions) need only be given in respect of:

(a) the undertakings whose results or financial position, in the opinion of the directors, principally affected the figures shown in the company's annual accounts; *and*

(b) undertakings excluded from consolidation under provisions of s. 229 (*see* **15**).

The full information must, however, be annexed to the company's next annual return: s. 231.

Schedule 6, on disclosure in notes of emoluments and other benefits of directors and others, has three Parts. Part I relates to the emoluments of directors, pensions of directors and past directors, compensation for loss of office to directors and past directors and sums paid to third parties in respect of directors' services, Part II relates to loans, quasi-loans, and other dealings in favour of directors and connected persons and Part III relates to transactions, arrangements and agreements made by the company or a subsidiary undertaking for officers of the company other than directors: s. 232.

17. Approval and signing of accounts

By s. 233 a company's annual accounts must be approved by the board of directors and signed on behalf of the board by a director.

The signature must be on the company's balance sheet, and every copy of the balance sheet which is laid before the company in general meeting, or which is in any other way circulated, published or issued, must state the name of the person who signed. The copy of the balance sheet which is delivered to the registrar must be signed on behalf of the board by a director.

Section 233 also provides that if annual accounts are approved which do not comply with the above requirements, every director who is party to their approval and who knows that they do not comply or is reckless as to whether they comply is guilty of an offence and liable to a fine. For this purpose every director of the company at the time when the accounts are approved is taken to be a party to their approval unless he shows that he took all reasonable steps to prevent their being approved. If a copy of the balance sheet is laid before the company, or in any other way circulated, published or issued without the balance sheet having been duly signed or without the signatory's name being included or if a copy of the balance sheet is delivered to the registrar without being duly signed, the company and every officer of it who is in default is guilty of an offence and liable to a fine.

18. Directors' report

Section 234 requires the directors for each financial year to prepare a report containing a fair review of the development of the business of the company and its subsidiary undertakings during the financial year and of their position at the end of it. The report must state:

(a) the amount (if any) which the directors recommend should be paid as dividend;

(b) the amount (if any) which they propose to carry to reserves;

(c) the names of the persons who, at any time during the financial year, were directors of the company; *and*

(d) the principal activities of the company and its subsidiary undertakings in the course of the year and any significant change in those activities in the year.

The report must also comply with Schedule 7 as regards the disclosure of the matters mentioned in that Schedule.

The Schedule is divided into five Parts, the contents of which, in outline, are:

Part I: matters of a general nature, including changes in asset values, directors' shareholdings and other interests and contributions for political and charitable purposes;

Part II: the acquisition by a company of its own shares or a charge on them;

Part III: the employment, training and advancement of disabled persons;

Part IV: the health, safety and welfare at work of the company's employees; and

Part V: the involvement of employees in the affairs, policy and performance of the company.

Failure to comply with the statutory provisions as to the preparation and contents of the report makes every person who was a director of the company immediately before the end of the period for laying and delivering accounts and reports for the financial year in question (*see* **25**) guilty of an offence and liable to a fine. It is, however, a defence for the director to prove that he took all reasonable steps for securing compliance with the requirements in question.

By s. 234A the directors' report must be approved by the board of directors and signed on behalf of the board by a director or the secretary of the company, and every copy of the report which is laid before the company in general meeting, or which is otherwise circulated, published or issued, must state the name of the person who signed it on behalf of the board. The copy of the report which is delivered to the registrar must be signed on behalf of the board by a director or the secretary of the company. Failure to comply with these provisions as to signature etc, makes the company and every officer who is in default guilty of an offence and liable to a fine.

19. Auditors' report

Sections 235–237 deal with the auditors' report.

Section 235 provides that the auditors must make a report to the members on all annual accounts of which copies are to be laid before the company in general meeting.

The report must state whether in the auditors' opinion the accounts have been properly prepared in accordance with the Act, and in particular whether a true and fair view is given:

(a) in the case of an individual balance sheet, of the state of affairs of the company as at the end of the financial year;

(b) in the case of an individual profit and loss account, of the profit and loss of the company for the financial year;

(c) in the case of group accounts, of the state of affairs and the profit or loss of the undertakings included in the consolidation as a whole, so far as concerns members of the company.

The auditors must consider whether the information given in the directors' report is *consistent* with the accounts. If they think that it is not, they must state that fact in their report.

By s. 236 the auditors' report must state the names of the auditors and be signed by them, and every copy which is laid before the company in general meeting or otherwise circulated, published or issued, and the copy which is delivered to the registrar, must state the names of the auditors. The copy delivered to the registrar must also be signed by them.

Section 237 requires the auditors, in preparing their report, to carry out such investigations as will enable them to form an opinion as to:

(a) whether proper accounting records have been kept by the company, and adequate returns have been received from branches not visited by them; *and*

(b) whether the company's individual accounts agree with the accounting records and returns.

If they think that this is not the case, they must state that fact in their report.

If the auditors fail to obtain all the information and explanations which, to the best of their knowledge and belief, are necessary for the purposes of their audit, then, by s. 237, they must state that fact in their report.

It is further provided in s. 237 that if the requirements of Schedule 6 (on disclosure of emoluments and other benefits of directors and others) are not complied with, the auditors must include in their report, so far as they are reasonably able to do so, a statement giving the required particulars.

20. Persons entitled to receive copies of accounts and reports
By s. 238 a copy of the company's annual accounts, together with a copy of the directors' report for that financial year and of the auditors' report on those accounts, must be sent to:

(a) every member of the company;
(b) every debenture-holder; *and*
(c) every person who is entitled to receive notice of general meetings;

not less than 21 days before the date of the meeting at which copies of those documents are to be laid in accordance with s. 241 (*see* **23**).

Copies need not be sent to a person who is not entitled to receive notices of general meetings or to a person whose address is not known to the company.

If copies are sent less than 21 days before the date of the meeting, they may still be deemed to have been duly sent if that is agreed to by all the members entitled to attend and vote at the meeting.

If default is made in complying with s. 238, the company and every officer of it who is in default is guilty of an offence and liable to a fine.

21. Right to demand copies of accounts and reports

Section 239 provides that any member and any debenture-holder is entitled to be furnished, on demand and without charge, with a single copy of the company's last annual accounts and directors' report and a copy of the auditors' report on those accounts. This is in addition to any copy to which the person may be entitled under s. 238 (*see* **20**).

If such a demand is not complied with within seven days, the company and every officer of it who is in default is guilty of an offence and liable to a fine and, for continued contravention, to a daily default fine.

22. Publication of accounts

By s. 240 if a company publishes any of its statutory accounts, they must be accompanied by the relevant auditors' report.

Further, a company which is required to prepare group accounts for a financial year must not publish its statutory individual accounts for that year without also publishing with them its statutory group accounts.

A company may publish non-statutory accounts but only under certain restrictions imposed by s. 240; for example, it must publish with them a statement indicating that they are not the company's statutory accounts and whether the auditors' report on the statutory accounts was qualified.

Publishing for the purposes of s. 240 extends to making a document available in any way for public inspection in a manner calculated to invite members of the public generally, or any class of members of the public, to read it.

To contravene any provision in s. 240 is an offence, making the company and any officer of it who is in default liable to a fine.

23. Laying of accounts and reports before the general meeting

Section 241 provides that the directors must in respect of each financial year lay before the company in general meeting copies of the company's annual accounts, the directors' report and the auditors' report on those accounts.

If these requirements are not complied with before the end of the period allowed for laying and delivering accounts and reports (*see* **25**), every person who immediately before the end of that period was a director is guilty of an offence and liable to a fine and, for continued contravention, to a daily default fine. It is, however, a defence for a person charged with such an offence to prove that he took all reasonable steps for securing that the requirements were complied with in due time; it is not a defence to prove that the documents in question were not in fact prepared as required by the Act.

24. Delivery of accounts and reports to the registrar

By s. 242 the directors must in respect of each financial year deliver to the registrar a copy of the annual accounts together with a copy of the directors' report and a copy of the auditors' report on those accounts.

If any document in the accounts or reports is in a language other than English, the directors must annex a translation into English.

If these requirements of s. 242 are not complied with before the end of the period allowed for laying and delivering accounts and reports (*see* **25**), every person who immediately before the end of that period was a director is guilty of an offence and liable to a fine and, for continued contravention, to a daily default fine.

Further, by the same section, if the directors fail to make good the default within 14 days after the service of a notice on them requiring compliance, the court may, on the application of any member or creditor of the company or of the registrar, make an order directing the directors (or any of them) to make good the default within the time specified in the order. The court's order may direct that all costs of the application shall be borne by the directors.

It is a defence for a person charged with an offence under s. 242 to prove that he took all reasonable steps for securing that delivery of the accounts and reports to the registrar would be made in due time.

It is not a defence in any proceedings under s. 242 to prove that the documents in question were not in fact prepared as required by the Act.

In addition to any liability of the directors under s. 242, there is imposed by s. 242A a civil penalty for failure to deliver the accounts and reports in due time. The penalty is imposed on the company, and its amount depends on whether the company is a public or a private company and on the length of time for which the non-compliance lasts, e.g. if the length of the period is more than 12 months, the amount of the civil penalty is £5000 in the case of a public company and £1000 in the case of a private company.

The penalty may be recovered by the registrar and he must then pay it into the Consolidated Fund.

It is not a defence in proceedings under s. 242A to prove that the documents in question were not in fact prepared as required by the Act.

25. Period allowed for laying and delivering accounts and reports
Section 244 provides that the period allowed for laying and delivering accounts and reports is:

(a) for a private company, 10 months after the end of the accounting reference period; *and*
(b) for a public company, seven months after the end of that period.

If the accounting reference period is the company's first and is a period of more than 12 months, the period allowed is:

(a) 10 months or seven months, as the case may be, from the first anniversary of the company's incorporation; *or*
(b) three months from the end of the accounting reference period;

whichever last expires.

Section 244 also provides that where a company carries on business, or has interests, abroad, the directors may, by giving notice to the registrar, extend these periods for a further three months.

Further, if for any special reason the Secretary of State thinks fit, he may, on an application made before the expiry of the period otherwise allowed, by notice in writing to a specified company extend that period by a further period specified in the notice.

26. Voluntary revision of accounts and directors' report
By s. 245, if it appears to the directors that any annual accounts or directors' report did not comply with the Act, they may prepare revised accounts or a revised report.

The Secretary of State has power to make regulations as to how the provisions of the Act on this matter are to be applied.

27. Secretary of State's notice in respect of accounts
Section 245A provides that where copies of the annual accounts have been sent out under s. 238 (*see* **20**), or a copy of the accounts has been laid before the company in general meeting or delivered to the registrar, and it appears to the Secretary of State that there is, or may be, a question whether the accounts comply with the Act, then the Secretary of State may give notice to the directors indicating the respects in which it appears to him that such a question arises or may arise.

The notice will specify a period of not less than one month for the directors to give him an explanation of the accounts or prepare revised accounts, and if at the end of the specified period it appears to the Secretary of State that no satisfactory explanation of the accounts has been given and that the accounts have not been revised so as to comply with the Act, he may, if he thinks fit, apply to the court.

28. Application to court in respect of defective accounts

By ss. 245B and 245C an application may be made to the court for a declaration that the annual accounts of a company do not comply with the Act and for an order requiring the directors to prepare revised accounts.

Section 245B provides that the application may be made by:

(a) the Secretary of State, after he has complied with s. 245A (*see* **27**); *or*
(b) a person authorised by the Secretary of State.

For the purposes of (b), it is provided in s. 245C that the Secretary of State may authorise any person who appears to him:

(a) to have an interest in, and to have satisfactory procedures directed to securing, compliance by companies with the accounting requirements of the Act;
(b) to have satisfactory procedures for receiving and investigating complaints about the annual accounts of companies; *and*
(c) otherwise to be a fit and proper person to be authorised.

By s. 245B notice of the application, along with a general statement of the matters at issue in the proceedings, must be given by the applicant to the registrar for registration.

On the conclusion of the court proceedings, the applicant must give to the registrar for registration an office copy of the court order or, as the case may be, notice that the application has failed or been withdrawn: s. 245B.

29. Exemptions for small and medium-sized companies

Section 246 provides that a company which qualifies as a small or medium-sized company is exempt from some of the accounting requirements of the Act. The exemptions are detailed in Schedule 8, which is divided into three Parts—Part I relating to small companies, Part II relating to medium-sized companies and Part III containing supplementary provisions.

The general effect of the provisions in Part I is that a small company may, in respect of the delivery of accounts and reports to the registrar under s. 242 (*see* **24**), deliver only an abbreviated version of the full balance sheet without a copy of the profit and loss account, and is exempt from many of the requirements as to information to be given in notes to the accounts.

A medium-sized company's exemptions are fewer: it may deliver a less detailed profit and loss account, and is exempt from giving particulars of turnover in notes to the accounts.

In Part III of Schedule 8 it is provided that where the directors take advantage of the exemptions in Part I or Part II of the Schedule, the balance sheet must contain a statement of the grounds on which, in the directors' opinion, the company is entitled to those exemptions, and the accounts delivered must be accompanied by a special report of the auditors stating that in their opinion the company is entitled to the exemptions claimed and that the accounts delivered are properly prepared in accordance with Schedule 8.

It should be noted that the exemptions apply only to delivery of accounts to the registrar and have no application to the duty to lay accounts before the general meeting (*see* **23**).

30. Companies not entitled to exemptions as small or medium-sized

By s. 246 a company is *not* entitled to the exemptions available to small or medium-sized companies if it is, or was at any time within the financial year to which the accounts relate:

(a) a public company;
(b) a banking or insurance company;
(c) an authorised person under the Financial Services Act 1986; *or*
(d) a member of an ineligible group.

A group is 'ineligible' for the purpose of this section if any of its members is:

(a) a public company or a body corporate other than a company which may offer its shares or debentures to the public;
(b) an authorised institution under the Banking Act 1987;
(c) an insurance company to which Part II of the Insurance Companies Act 1982 applies; *or*
(d) an authorised person under the Financial Services Act 1986.

It is further provided by s. 246 that a parent company must not be treated as qualifying as a small or medium-sized company unless the group headed by it qualifies as a small or medium-sized group, respectively (*see* **32**).

31. The qualifying conditions as to size

Section 247 provides that a company qualifies as small or medium-sized in relation to a financial year if the 'qualifying conditions' are met:

(a) in the case of the company's first financial year, in that year; *and*
(b) in the case of any subsequent financial year, in that year and the preceding year.

The section also provides that a company shall be *treated* as qualifying as small or medium-sized in relation to a financial year if *either*:

(a) it qualified in relation to the previous financial year as small or medium-sized; *or*

(b) it was treated as qualifying in relation to the previous financial year under (a) and the 'qualifying conditions' are in fact met in the year in question.

The effect of these provisions is that (with the exception of the company's first year) one must look at two consecutive years in order to discover whether the small or medium-sized company can avail itself of the exemptions, but that once the status of small or medium-sized has been obtained, it continues to be enjoyed by the company until for two consecutive years the company is no longer qualified as small or medium-sized.

The 'qualifying conditions' referred to in the above provisions are, by s. 247, met by a company if it satisfies *two or more* of the following requirements:

Small company

1. Turnover	Not more than £2 million
2. Balance sheet total	Not more than £975,000
3. Number of employees	Not more than 50

Medium-sized company

1. Turnover	Not more than £8 million
2. Balance sheet total	Not more than £3.9 million
3. Number of employees	Not more than 250

32. Exemption for small and medium-sized groups

Section 248 provides that a parent company need not prepare group accounts for a financial year in relation to which the group headed by that company qualifies as a small or medium-sized group and is not an ineligible group.

A group is 'ineligible' for the purposes of this section if any of its members is:

(a) a public company, or a body corporate other than a company which may offer its shares or debentures to the public;

(b) an authorised institution under the Banking Act 1987;

(c) an insurance company to which Part II of the Insurance Companies Act 1982 applies; *or*

(d) an authorised person under the Financial Services Act 1986.

The auditors' report must state that in their opinion the company is entitled to the exemption, and that report must be attached to the individual accounts of the company.

The qualifying conditions for small and medium-sized groups are set out in s. 249. They are the same as those for small and medium-sized companies (*see* 31) with the necessary modification that in this case the figures are aggregate figures.

33. Unaudited accounts of dormant companies

Section 250 provides that in certain circumstances a dormant company may pass a special resolution making itself exempt from the provisions in Part VII of the Act relating to the audit of accounts.

A company is 'dormant' for the purposes of this provision if during the period in question no significant accounting transaction occurs, i.e. no transaction which is required by s. 221 (*see* 5) to be entered in the company's accounting records. A company ceases to be 'dormant' when such a transaction occurs.

The circumstances in which such a special resolution may be passed are:

(a) where the company has been dormant from the time of its formation and the special resolution is passed before the first general meeting of the company at which annual accounts are laid;

(b) where the company has been dormant since the end of the previous financial year, is entitled to exemptions as a small company and is not required to prepare group accounts and the special resolution is passed at a general meeting of the company at which the annual accounts for that year are laid.

These provisions do *not* apply to:

(a) a public company;
(b) a banking or insurance company; *or*
(c) an authorised person under the Financial Services Act 1986.

34. Summary financial statement to shareholders in listed public companies

Section 251 provides that a public company whose shares are listed need not always send copies of all the accounts and reports to members of the company, but may instead send them a summary financial statement. 'Listed' here means admitted to the Official List of The International Stock Exchange of the United Kingdom and the Republic of Ireland Ltd.

The circumstances in which this exception is available and the form and content of the summary depend on regulations made by the Secretary of State by statutory instrument.

Copies of the full documents from which the summary financial statement is derived must always be sent to any member who wishes to receive them.

Every summary financial statement must contain a statement by the company's auditors of their opinion as to whether it is consistent with the full accounts and the directors' report, and give further information about the auditors' report on the full accounts.

35. Private company's election to dispense with laying of accounts and reports

By s. 252 a private company may elect to dispense with the laying of accounts and reports before the company in general meeting. The election has effect in relation to the financial year in which it is made and subsequent financial years.

The procedure for making the election is for the company to pass an 'elective resolution' in accordance with s. 379A (*see* 15:**37**).

If an election ceases to have effect, the requirement to lay accounts and reports before the general meeting under s. 241 will again apply for the financial year in which the election ceases to have effect and for subsequent years.

By s. 253, where an election under s. 252 is in force, the copies of the accounts and reports must be sent out not less than 28 days before the end of the period allowed for laying and delivering them (*see* **25**), and they must be accompanied by a notice informing the member of his right to require the laying of the accounts and reports before a general meeting.

Within the 28-day period, any member or auditor may by notice in writing deposited at the registered office require that a general meeting be held for the purpose of laying the accounts and reports before the company. The directors must then within 21 days from the date of the deposit of the notice proceed to convene a meeting for a date not more than 28 days after the date of the notice convening it. If the directors do not do so, then the person who deposited the notice may convene the meeting himself, with reasonable expenses being made good to him by the company and recouped by the company out of remuneration due to those directors who were in default.

36. Exemption of unlimited companies

By s. 254 the directors of an unlimited company are not required to deliver accounts and reports to the registrar.

It is a condition of this exemption that at no time during the accounting reference period in question:

(a) has the company been, to its knowledge, a subsidiary undertaking of a limited undertaking; *or*

(b) have there been to its knowledge, exercisable by two or more limited undertakings, rights which if they had been exercisable by one of them would have made the company a subsidiary undertaking of it; *or*

(c) has the company been a parent company of a limited undertaking.

The exemption does not apply to a company carrying on business as the promoter of a trading stamp scheme under the Trading Stamps Act 1964.

37. Special provisions for banking and insurance companies and groups

Section 255 provides that a banking or insurance company may prepare its individual accounts in accordance with Part I of Schedule 9 rather than Schedule 4, and s. 255A provides that the parent company of a banking or insurance group may prepare group accounts in accordance with Part VII of the Act as modified by Part II of Schedule 9.

Where accounts are prepared in accordance with these special provisions for banking and insurance companies and groups, then by s. 255B the disclosure requirements in Schedule 5 (related undertakings) and in Schedule 6 (emoluments and other benefits of directors and others) are modified by Part III and Part IV, respectively, of Schedule 9, and similarly s. 255C, taken along with Schedule 10, modifies the provisions as to the directors' report.

19

Auditors

1. The statutory provisions on auditors

The statutory provisions relating to company auditors are to be found in two Parts of the Companies Act 1989.

Part II of that Act, headed 'Eligibility for Appointment as Company Auditor' and consisting of ss. 24–54, enacts the provisions necessary to implement the Eighth European Company Law Directive on regulation of auditors.

In Part V of the same Act, headed 'Other Amendments of Company Law', the opportunity was taken to re-enact, with amendments, the other provisions relating to auditors, formerly in the Companies Act 1985.

It follows that in this chapter:

(a) in **2–10** references to sections are to sections of the 1989 Act, being sections which fall within Part II of that Act, and references to Schedules are to Schedules to the 1989 Act; *and*

(b) in the remainder of the chapter references to sections are to sections of the 1985 Act, *as inserted in that Act by provisions in Part V of the 1989 Act.*

2. Eligibility for appointment

The main purposes of Part II of the 1989 Act are to secure that only persons who are properly supervised and appropriately qualified are appointed as company auditors, and that audits are carried out properly and with integrity and with a proper degree of independence: s. 24.

Section 25 provides that a person is eligible for appointment as company auditor only if he:

(a) is a member of a recognised supervisory body; *and*
(b) is eligible for the appointment under the rules of that body.

The auditor may be either an individual or a firm.

3. Supervisory bodies

By s. 30 'supervisory body' means a body established in the UK (whether a body corporate or an unincorporated association) which maintains and enforces rules as to:

(a) the eligibility of persons to seek appointment as company auditors; *and*

(b) the conduct of company audit work.;

which are binding on persons seeking appointment or acting as company auditors either because they are members of that body or because they are otherwise subject to its control.

Schedule 11 sets out the details as to recognition of supervisory bodies. In particular, a supervisory body may apply to the Secretary of State for an order declaring it to be a recognised supervisory body (a 'recognition order'). Such an order may be revoked by the Secretary of State by giving notice with reasons stated and even without such notice if he considers that step to be essential in the public interest.

To obtain recognition, the body must, by Schedule 11, have rules stating that a person is not eligible for appointment as a company auditor unless:

(a) in the case of an individual, he holds an appropriate qualification;

(b) in the case of a firm:

(*i*) the individuals responsible for company audit work on behalf of the firm hold an appropriate qualification; *and*

(*ii*) the firm is controlled by qualified persons.

4. Meaning of 'appropriate qualification'

The only persons who are regarded as holding an 'appropriate qualification' are those who satisfy the provisions of s. 31.

For the full understanding of s. 31 it is necessary to look back to s. 389 Companies Act 1985—a section repealed by the 1989 Act. That section provided that a person was not qualified as auditor unless *either*:

(a) he was a member of a body of accountants established in the UK and for the time being recognised by the Secretary of State (i.e. the Institute of Chartered Accountants in England and Wales, the Institute of Chartered Accountants of Scotland, the Chartered Association of Certified Accountants and the Institute of Chartered Accountants in Ireland); *or*

(b) he was authorised by the Secretary of State, as having similar qualifications obtained outside the UK.

The leading provision in s. 31 of the 1989 Act is that a person holds an appropriate qualification if:

(a) he was, as being a member of a body recognised for the purposes of s. 389 Companies Act 1985, qualified as auditor under that section immediately before 1 January 1990 and immediately before s. 25 above came into force;

(b) he holds a recognised professional qualification obtained in the UK; *or*

(c) he holds an approved overseas qualification under s. 33 (*see* **6**).

Section 31, as can be seen by looking back to s. 389 Companies Act 1985, includes as having an appropriate qualification existing auditors who are members of the bodies mentioned. The 1989 Act is less generous to existing auditors who were under the 1985 Act merely authorised by the Secretary of State as having similar qualifications obtained outside the UK. Section 31 provides that a person who immediately before 1 January 1990 and immediately before s. 25 came into force was qualified as auditor under s. 389 Companies Act 1985 without being a member of one of the recognised bodies is to be treated as holding an appropriate qualification only for 12 months from the date on which s. 25 came into force. If he wishes to retain the benefit of his qualification for the future, he must within that period give written notice and information to the Secretary of State.

A transitional provision in s. 31 for persons training in accountancy is that a person who:

(a) began before 1 January 1990 a course of study or practical training leading to a professional qualification in accountancy offered by a body established in the UK; *and*

(b) obtained that qualification on or after that date and before 1 January 1996;

is treated as holding an appropriate qualification if the qualification is approved by the Secretary of State for this purpose. The Secretary of State must be satisfied that the body concerned has adequate arrangements to ensure that the qualification is awarded only to persons educated and trained to a standard equivalent to that required in the case of a recognised professional qualification.

5. Professional qualifications

Schedule 12 sets out the details on recognition of a professional qualification.

A qualifying body may apply to the Secretary of State for an order declaring a qualification offered by it to be a recognised professional qualification. By s. 32 'qualifying body' means a body established in the UK (whether a body corporate or an unincorporated association) which offers a professional qualification in accountancy.

The provisions on the manner of application made to the Secretary of State are in Schedule 12. The Secretary of State may grant or refuse recognition. He may also revoke a recognition order. Schedule 12 also specifies the requirements for entry, education, examination, training and experience which must be satisfied by the body seeking recognition.

6. Approval of overseas qualifications

By s. 33 the Secretary of State may declare that persons who:

(a) are qualified to audit accounts under the law of a specified country or territory outside the UK; *or*

(b) hold a specified qualification in accountancy recognised under the law of a country or territory outside the UK;

are to be regarded as holding an appropriate overseas qualification.

The Secretary of State must be satisfied that the qualification in question affords an assurance of professional competence equivalent to that afforded by a recognised professional qualification (*see* **5**).

The Secretary of State may also require a person holding an approved overseas qualification to hold additional educational qualifications ensuring that the person has an adequate knowledge of the law and practice of the UK on audit of accounts.

7. Ineligibility owing to lack of independence

By s. 27 a person is ineligible for appointment as company auditor if he is:

(a) an officer or employee of the company; *or*

(b) a partner or employee of such a person, or a partnership of which such a person is a partner;

or if he is ineligible under **(a)** or **(b)** for appointment as company auditor of any associated undertaking.

In this context 'associated undertaking' means:

(a) a parent undertaking or subsidiary undertaking of the company; *or*

(b) a subsidiary undertaking of any parent undertaking of the company.

Other connections between a person and the company or any associated undertaking may also be a ground of ineligibility if so specified in regulations authorised to be made by the Secretary of State under s. 27.

By s. 28 if a company auditor becomes ineligible during his term of office, he must immediately vacate office. It is an offence for him not to do so.

Section 29 provides that where a company auditor was, for any part of the period of the audit, ineligible for that office, the Secretary of State may direct the company to have the relevant accounts audited again by an eligible person.

8. The register of auditors

Under s. 35 regulations made by the Secretary of State require the keeping of a register of:

(a) the individuals and firms eligible for appointment as company auditor; and

(b) the individuals holding an appropriate qualification who are responsible for company audit work on behalf of such firms.

9. Information about firms to be available to public

Under s. 36 regulations made by the Secretary of State require recognised supervisory bodies to keep and make available to the public the following information about the firms eligible under their rules for appointment as a company auditor:

(a) in relation to a body corporate, the name and address of directors and shareholders;

(b) in relation to a partnership, the name and address of each partner;

and such other information as is specified in the regulations.

10. Delegation of Secretary of State's functions

The Secretary of State had many new functions conferred on him by Part II of the 1989 Act, some of which have been indicated above.

In addition, by ss. 37 and 38, he has wide-ranging powers to require a recognised supervisory or qualifying body to give him such information as he may reasonably require for the exercise of his functions under Part II of the Act.

Section 46 provides that the Secretary of State may by a 'delegation order' establish a body corporate to exercise many of his functions under Part II. The constitution, proceedings and functions of such a body are detailed in Schedule 13 to the Act.

11. Appointment of auditors

At this stage we turn to the provisions of the 1985 Act as replaced by Part V of the 1989 Act.

Section 384 provides that every company must appoint an auditor or auditors. This provision is subject to the exception that a dormant company (*see* 18:**33**) is exempt from the obligation to appoint auditors: s. 388A.

Section 385 deals with appointment at the general meeting at which accounts are laid. It, therefore, applies to:

(a) every public company; *and*

(b) a private company which has not elected to dispense with the laying of accounts (*see* 18:**35**).

A company in either of these categories must, at each general meeting at which accounts are laid, appoint auditors to hold office from the conclusion of that meeting until the conclusion of the next general meeting at which accounts are laid.

Also by s. 385 the first auditors may be appointed by the directors at any time before the first general meeting at which accounts are laid, and such auditors hold office until the conclusion of that meeting. If the directors fail to exercise this power, the company in general meeting may exercise the power.

Section 385A applies to a private company which has elected under s. 252 (*see* 18:**35**) to dispense with the laying of accounts before the company in general meeting. It provides that auditors must be appointed by the company in general meeting within 28 days after copies of the accounts have been sent to members under s. 238 (*see* 18:**20**). The provisions of s. 385A as to appointment of the first auditors are to the same effect as the corresponding provisions of s. 385 above.

By s. 386 a private company may elect, by elective resolution under s. 379A (*see* 15:**37**), to dispense with the obligation to appoint auditors annually. The auditors are then deemed to be re-appointed for each succeeding financial year on the expiry of the time for appointing auditors for that year, unless:

(a) the company has passed a special resolution under s. 250 making itself a dormant company; *or*
(b) a resolution has been passed under s. 393 (*see* **16**) to the effect that their appointment should be brought to an end.

Section 387 provides that if in any case no auditors are appointed or deemed to be re-appointed, the Secretary of State may appoint a person to fill the vacancy.

When a casual vacancy occurs, then, by s. 388, the directors, or the company in general meeting, may fill the vacancy, but while the vacancy continues, the surviving or continuing auditor, if any, may continue to act. Special notice (*see* 15:**17**) is required for a resolution at a general meeting:

(a) filling a casual vacancy; *or*
(b) re-appointing as auditor a retiring auditor who was appointed by the directors to fill a casual vacancy.

On receiving notice of such an intended resolution, the company must immediately send a copy of it:

(a) to the person proposed to be appointed; *and*
(b) if the casual vacancy was caused by the resignation of an auditor, to the auditor who resigned.

12. Rights of auditors
By s. 389A the auditors have a right of access at all times to the company's

books, accounts and vouchers, and are entitled to require from the company's officers such information and explanations as they think necessary for the performance of their duties as auditors. An officer is guilty of an offence if knowingly or recklessly he makes an oral or written statement to the auditors which is misleading, false or deceptive in a material particular. The auditors of a parent company have also the right to require information and explanations from a subsidiary undertaking and its auditors.

Additional rights for auditors are dealt with in s. 390. The auditors are entitled to:

(a) receive all notices of any general meeting which a member of the company is entitled to receive;
(b) attend any general meeting; *and*
(c) speak at any general meeting on any part of the business which concerns them as auditors.

A further provision in s. 390 is that, where it is proposed that a written resolution be agreed to by a private company under s. 381A (*see* 15:**36**), the auditors are entitled:

(a) to receive all the communications relating to the resolution as are required to be supplied to a member;
(b) to give notice that the resolution concerns them as auditors and should be considered by the company in general meeting;
(c) to attend any such meeting; *and*
(d) to speak at the meeting on any part of the business which concerns them as auditors.

13. Remuneration of auditors
Section 390A provides that the remuneration of auditors appointed by the company in general meeting is fixed by the company in general meeting or in such manner as the company in general meeting may decide. The remuneration of auditors appointed by the directors or by the Secretary of State must be fixed by the directors or the Secretary of State, as the case may be.

The amount of the remuneration must be stated in a note to the company's annual accounts.

It can happen that auditors (or their associates) perform other services for the company apart from auditing the accounts, and for these other services they will receive remuneration, distinct from their remuneration as auditors. Section 390B empowers the Secretary of State to make regulations containing disclosure provisions for this other remuneration also; the definition of 'associate' in this context depends on the regulations.

14. Removal of auditors

Section 391 provides that a company may by ordinary resolution at any time remove an auditor from office, in spite of anything in any agreement between it and him. The company must within 14 days give notice to the registrar of such a resolution. By the same section, an auditor who has been removed is still entitled to the rights under s. 390 (*see* **12**) in respect of any general meeting:

(a) at which his term of office would otherwise have expired; *or*
(b) at which it is proposed to fill the vacancy caused by his removal.

Section 391A provides that special notice is required for a resolution at a general meeting:

(a) removing an auditor before the expiration of his term of office; *or*
(b) appointing as auditor a person other than a retiring auditor.

On receiving notice of such an intended resolution the company must immediately send a copy of it to the person proposed to be removed or, as the case may be, to the person proposed to be appointed and to the retiring auditor.

The auditor proposed to be removed or the retiring auditor, as the case may be, may make representations in writing to the company and ask members to be notified of them. The company must then (unless they are received too late) send a copy of them to every member to whom notice of the meeting is, or has been, sent. If they are not sent out the auditor may require them to be read out at the meeting. It is, however, provided that copies need not be sent out and the representations need not be read out if the company or any person aggrieved applies to the court and satisfies the court that these rights are being abused to secure needless publicity for defamatory matter.

15. Resignation of auditors

Section 392 provides that an auditor may resign his office by depositing a notice to that effect at the company's registered office. In order to be effective, the notice must be accompanied by a statement complying with s. 394 (*see* **17**).

The company must within 14 days of the deposit of the notice send a copy of it to the registrar of companies: s. 392.

A resigning auditor has certain rights under s. 392A. The section applies where an auditor's notice of resignation is accompanied by a statement of circumstances which he considers should be brought to the attention of members or creditors of the company. He may deposit with the notice a signed requisition calling on the directors to convene an extraordinary general meeting to receive and consider an explanation of the circumstances connected with his resignation. He may request the company to circulate to members a written statement of the circumstances. The same statutory provisions then apply to this statement as apply to the representations made by an auditor under s. 391A (*see* **14**).

16 Termination of appointment of auditors not appointed annually

Section 393 deals with the situation where an election has been made under s. 386 by a private company to dispense with annual appointment of auditors (*see* **11**).

Any member may deposit notice at the company's registered office proposing that the appointment of the company's auditors be brought to an end. No member may deposit more than one such notice in any financial year.

If a notice is deposited, it is the duty of the directors to convene a general meeting to be held within the next 28 days and to propose at that meeting a resolution as to whether the appointment of the auditors should be brought to an end. If the decision of the company at the meeting is that the appointment of the auditors should be brought to an end, the auditors are no longer deemed to be re-appointed when next they would have been.

17. Statement by person ceasing to hold office as auditor

Section 394 provides that where an auditor ceases for any reason to hold office, he must deposit at the company's registered office a statement of any circumstances connected with his ceasing to hold office which he considers should be brought to the attention of the members or creditors of the company, or, if he considers that there are no such circumstances, a statement that there are none.

If the statement is of circumstances which the auditor considers should be brought to the attention of the members or creditors, the company must within 14 days of the deposit *either*:

(a) send a copy of it to every person entitled to be sent copies of the accounts; *or*
(b) apply to the court and notify the auditor of the application.

In relation to **(b)**, if the court is satisfied that the auditor is using the statement to secure needless publicity for defamatory matter, it directs that copies need not be sent out, but if, on the other hand, the court is not so satisfied, then the company must within 14 days of the court's decision send out copies and notify the auditor of the court's decision.

Where the company does not apply to court and also where it applies to court and the court's decision is that copies should be sent out, the auditor has a duty to send a copy of the statement to the registrar of companies.

18. Legal position of auditors

An auditor is not an officer of the company within s. 744, which defines an officer as including a director, manager or secretary. He is, however, an officer for the purposes of certain sections, e.g. ss. 206–211 Insolvency Act 1986, which impose criminal liability on officers of companies in liquidation, and s. 212 Insolvency Act 1986, dealing with misfeasance by officers of companies which comes to light in liquidation.

He is for certain purposes an agent of the company, e.g. s. 434, dealing with an investigation of the company's affairs by the Department of Trade and Industry. He is not, however, an agent of the company for the purposes of acknowledging a debt on its behalf within the Limitation Act 1980 when he signs his report on the balance sheet.

19. Auditors' liability for negligence

An auditor is naturally liable to the *company* for loss occasioned by breach of his duty of care, i.e. negligence, for he is in a contractual relationship with it.

> Thus in *Re Thomas Gerrard and Son Ltd* (1968), a director of a company falsified the company's accounts by fraudulent entries, *inter alia*, regarding stock. The auditors were suspicious and asked him for an explanation, but made no further investigation. As a result their estimate of the company's profits was wrong and the company declared dividends which it would not otherwise have done, paying tax which would not otherwise have been payable. The company went into liquidation and the liquidator took misfeasance proceedings against the auditors under s. 333 Companies Act 1948 (now s. 212 Insolvency Act 1986). HELD: The damages recoverable by the liquidator included the dividends, the costs of recovering the tax, and any tax not recoverable.

The further question can arise of whether an auditor can be held liable for negligence to persons with whom he has no contractual relationship.

On the one hand, the decision of the House of Lords in *Hedley Byrne & Co. Ltd* v. *Heller & Partners Ltd* (1964) established that a person may be liable for a negligent mis-statement even when there is no contractual relationship between him and the party to whom he makes it, *provided there is some 'special relationship' between them, and provided he does not expressly disclaim responsibility*. The House of Lords did not define the expression 'special relationship', but thought that it arose wherever one person relied on the skill or knowledge of another who was using it responsibly, though gratuitously, to assist him. It seemed that this would cover an auditor who, for example, made a negligent mis-statement to a potential investor.

This view must now yield to the greater authority of the decision of the House of Lords in *Caparo Industries plc* v. *Dickman* (1990) [B199] a case specifically on the auditor's liability to existing and prospective individual shareholders. This case has established that the extent of the 'special relationship' was not to be extended beyond the actual limits fixed in the *Hedley Byrne* case.

> The *Caparo* case involved a successful take-over bid by Caparo Industries plc of F. plc. After the take-over bid Caparo brought an action against the auditors of F. plc, alleging that the accounts of F. plc were inaccurate and misleading in that they showed a profit of £1.2m when in fact there had been a loss of over £400,000, that the auditors had been negligent, that Caparo had purchased further shares and made the take-over bid in reliance on the audited accounts and that the auditors owed them a duty of care either as potential bidders or as existing shareholders of F. plc interested in buying more shares.
>
> The House of Lords held that for a duty of care to exist there were three criteria: (1) foreseeability of damage, (2) proximity of relationship and (3) the reasonableness or otherwise of imposing a duty. In applying these criteria the House of Lords concluded that an auditor of a public company's accounts owed no duty of care to a member of the public who relied on the accounts to buy shares, because there was no relationship of proximity between the auditor and a member of the public. Further, an auditor owed no duty of care to an individual shareholder who wished to buy more shares, because he was in no better position than a member of the public, the auditor's statutory duty being owed to *the body of shareholders as a whole*, to enable them to control their company and not to enable individual shareholders to buy more shares with a view to profit.
>
> In *Al Saudi Banque* v. *Clark Pixley (a firm)* (1990) [B201] Millett J. held that auditors owed no duty of care to a bank which lent money to a company in reliance on the company's audited accounts which the bank alleged did not reflect a true and fair view of the company's affairs.

20. Duties of auditors

(a) *An auditor must act honestly*, and with *reasonable skill, care and caution*.
(b) *He must show the true financial position as shown by the books.* If proper accounting records have not been kept, or they do not, in his opinion,

show a true and fair view of the company's affairs, he must state that fact in his report and even refuse to certify the accounts and resign.

(c) *He must know his duties* under the articles and the Companies Acts, and in particular his report must comply with s. 235 (*see* 18:**19**).

(d) *He must verify the existence of the company's securities* and see that they are in safe custody. Thus he should actually see the securities unless they have been deposited with a third party with whom securities would normally be deposited in the ordinary course of business, e.g. a bank.

(e) He must check the *cash in hand* and *the bank balance*.

(f) *He is not concerned with policy or management*. He must simply state the effect of what has been done, and the remedy for bad management will lie with the shareholders, who can remove the directors or at least raise the matter at a meeting.

(g) *He is not under a duty to take stock*, unless there are suspicious circumstances, but he should make sure that the amount of stock stated to exist is a reasonably probable figure. In practice, an auditor often thinks it prudent to exceed his legal duty with regard to stock-taking.

(h) *A watchdog but not a bloodhound*. Although the famous words of Lopes L.J. in *Re Kingston Cotton Mill Co. Ltd (No. 2)* (1896) [B193] that an auditor 'is a watch-dog but not a bloodhound' are invariably remembered by students and are often the only remark which they can make when asked for the duties of an auditor, constant repetition of even such a delightful phrase tends to depress the examiner. Lopes L.J. also said that 'an auditor is not bound to be a detective', which is another way of expressing the same idea and at least makes a change.

(i) It was observed by Woolf J. in *Lloyd Cheyham & Co. Ltd* v. *Littlejohn & Co.* (1987) [B207] that while Statements of Standard Accounting Practice are not rigid rules, they are very strong evidence as to what is the proper standard to be adopted, and that, unless there is some justification, a departure from them will be regarded as a breach of duty. This observation would apply equally to the more recent Financial Reporting Standards.

21. Relief from liability

Section 310 applies not only to officers of the company but also to auditors. It states that any provision in the articles or in any contract exempting them from, or indemnifying them against, liability for negligence or breach of duty towards the company is *void*. Thus it is impossible for an auditor to limit or exclude liability for negligence by the terms of his contract.

If, however, the court thinks that, though liable, the auditor has acted honestly and reasonably and ought fairly to be excused, it may, under s. 727, relieve him from liability on such terms as it thinks fit.

Further, s. 310, as amended by s. 137 Companies Act 1989, provides that s. 310 does not prevent a company from:

(a) purchasing and maintaining for the auditor insurance against such liability; *or*

(b) indemnifying the auditor against any liability incurred by him in defending any civil or criminal proceedings in which judgment is given in his favour.

22. Share valuations by auditors

The valuation of shares is not an easy matter. It is not just a question of valuing the entire undertaking of the company and then dividing the figure reached by the number of shares issued, i.e. estimating what is called the 'break-up' value. A share in a going concern will be affected by many factors: the dividend yield, the number of times the dividend was covered, the marketability of the shares, the existence of reserves, the possibility of expansion and the making of 'rights' issues, and the hope of a take-over bid.

Auditors, therefore, are often required to make such valuations under the articles of a private company where there are no dealings in the shares and some price must be attached to them. When they perform this function they must of course act honestly, but they *need not give reasons for their valuation*. Indeed, the less said the better, for if they give reasons the court can inquire into the accuracy of the valuation and set it aside: *Burgess* v. *Purchase & Sons (Farms) Ltd* (1983). Their position here is similar to that of directors who refuse to register a transfer of shares under an article conferring on them an unrestricted discretion.

In valuing shares an auditor is not normally acting in a judicial or arbitral capacity and is therefore not entitled to the immunity from liability for negligence possessed by a judge or arbitrator. He is exercising a professional function, not settling a dispute, and will therefore be liable to the person who employs him for any loss caused to the person by his negligence: *Arenson* v. *Casson Beckman Rutley and Co.* (1977).

The machinery in articles for the valuation of shares by the auditor enables the valuation to be done quickly, and the auditor is not expected to use the standard of care expected of a specialist valuer; the standard required is merely that of a reasonably competent accountant acting as auditor: *Whiteoak* v. *Walker* (1988).

The auditor will, of course, also be liable for fraud or collusion if he acts dishonestly.

20

Dividends

1. The nature of a dividend

A company pays *dividends* to its members, *interest* to its debenture-holders. It is important to distinguish between these two types of payment.

A dividend is a *proportion of the distributed profits* of the company. It may be a *fixed* annual percentage, as in the case of preference shares, or it may be *variable* according to the prosperity of the company, as in the case of ordinary shares, but since it is payable only out of the distributed profits, it follows that if no profits are made, or if none are distributed, no dividend will be declared.

The shareholder cannot insist on the company declaring a dividend, for this is a matter which is at the discretion of the directors. It is the directors who control the management and financial policy of the company, and it is they who recommend the amounts of dividend to be paid. If, therefore, the members do not approve the directors' policy, their proper remedy is to make appropriate changes to the board.

The articles normally contain provisions on payment of dividends. Before the Companies Act of 1980 and 1981, there was only one statutory provision. It is now in s. 119 of the 1985 Act and provides that a company, with authority in its articles, may pay dividends in proportion to the amount paid up on the shares where a larger amount is paid up on some shares than on others. Table A, Article 104, gives this authority.

2. The nature of interest

The payment of interest is in no way dependent on the existence of profits. Interest is a *debt*. It is payable whether profits are available or not, and may therefore lawfully be paid either out of capital or out of revenue.

In accounting, debenture-holders' interest and the dividends of preference shareholders are often collectively referred to as *prior charges*. This term simply indicates that both these types of payment must be made before the ordinary shareholders receive anything. It is a mistake to think that they are in any way similar in law; even though the debenture-holder is a creditor of the company to the extent of the sum which he has lent and the interest on it, while the shareholder, as we have seen in Chapter 11, is regarded in accounting as a creditor to the extent of the capital which he has invested, the *funds out of which they may be paid are different*. The debenture-holder may lawfully be paid his interest out of *any of the company's funds*, including capital. The shareholder, whether he holds preference or ordinary shares, may lawfully be paid dividends *only if profits are available*. Furthermore, while interest on a loan will accrue at the agreed rate per annum and will automatically become a debt, a dividend is not a debt until it is declared, and there is no obligation to declare it.

Thus there are two fundamental distinctions between interest and dividends:

(a) *They are payable out of different funds*, interest being payable out of any of the company's moneys, while dividends are payable only out of profits.
(b) *Interest is a debt, while a dividend is not a debt until it is declared*. Even then, under s. 74 Insolvency Act 1986, in a liquidation it is not payable until *after* the company's debenture-holders and trade creditors have been paid, for it is a debt payable to a member in his capacity of member (*see* 1:**18**).

3. Meaning of distribution, profits and losses

There was formerly little difference between funds which were legally distributable and the concept of 'profits'. All 'profits' were normally distributable so long as the articles did not contain restrictive provisions and the fixed assets as a whole were maintaining their value. Thus the mere description of funds as 'profits' indicated that the company had almost complete freedom to use them as it desired.

These lenient rules for distribution were often criticised as a potential danger to creditors for they went far beyond the limits of prudence. It was, for instance, permissible to make a distribution on the strength of an unrealised accretion to a fixed asset: *Dimbula Valley (Ceylon) Tea Co. Ltd* v. *Laurie* (1961). [The position in Scotland was to the contrary: *Westburn Sugar Refineries Ltd* v. *Inland Revenue* (1960).] There are now, however, provisions in the Act (derived from the Companies Act 1980) which, while leaving the concept of 'profits' unchanged, lay down stringent rules regarding dividends which considerably restrict the funds out of which they may lawfully be paid. In other words, not all 'profits' are now legally distributable.

Before considering these rules it is essential to grasp the meaning given by the Act to the words 'distribution', 'profits' and 'losses'.

Section 263 provides that 'distribution' means every description of distribution of a company's assets to its members, whether in cash or otherwise, *except* those made by way of:

(a) an issue of fully or partly paid bonus shares;
(b) the redemption or purchase of any of the company's own shares out of capital (including the proceeds of any fresh issue of shares) or out of

unrealised profits in accordance with the provisions of the Act concerning redeemable shares and purchase by the company of its own shares;
(c) the reduction of share capital by extinguishing or reducing the liability of members in respect of unpaid share capital or by paying off paid- up share capital; *and*
(d) a distribution of assets to members on winding up.

Section 280 explains that the word 'profits' in the Act refers to *both revenue and capital profits*, while the word 'losses' refers to *both revenue and capital losses*.

4. Restriction on distribution of assets by public companies

Not only are there now more stringent rules regarding dividends in general but there is also an additional restriction on distributions of assets applicable only to public companies. By s. 264 a public company may make a distribution only:

(a) if the amount of its net assets at the time is not less than *the aggregate of its called-up share capital and its undistributable reserves; and*
(b) if, and to the extent that, the distribution does not reduce the amount of the net assets to less than that aggregate.

The undistributable reserves, for the purpose of this provision are:

(a) the share premium account;
(b) the capital redemption reserve;
(c) the amount by which the company's accumulated *unrealised* profits exceed its accumulated *unrealised* losses; *and*
(d) any other reserve which the company is prohibited from distributing by any other enactment or by its memorandum or articles.

An example of **(d)** is found in s. 148 which provides that where a public company or its nominee acquires shares or an interest in shares in the company, and those shares or that interest appear in the balance sheet as an asset, then an amount equal to their value must be transferred out of distributable profits to a *reserve fund* which is not available for distribution.

5. Profits available for distribution

With the provisions of ss. 263 and 264 in mind, the general rules for the payment of dividends can be considered. (The special rules applying to investment companies and contained in s. 265 have been omitted here.)

The basic rule is found in s. 263 which prohibits any company, public or private, from making a distribution except out of *profits available for the purpose*. These are stated to be a company's *accumulated realised profits less its accumulated realised losses*.

This strict rule is fortified by the further provision in s. 263 which prohibits a company from applying an *unrealised* profit in paying up debentures or amounts unpaid on issued shares. It also destroys, with a single statutory blow, all the former leniency of English rules on dividends.

6. Revaluation of fixed assets and provisions

Section 275 appears to throw a bone to the corporate dog by providing that if an unrealised profit is made on the revaluation of a fixed asset, and the sum allowed for depreciation after revaluation exceeds the sum which would have been allowed had no such profit been made, an amount equal to the amount of the extra depreciation is to be treated as *realised profit*. Without such a rule directors might be discouraged from effecting revaluations of the company's assets, since depreciation is normally charged against distributable profits.

Revaluation clearly raises difficulties where the cost of an asset is unknown. Accordingly s. 275 thoughtfully provides that where there is no record of the original cost, or one cannot be obtained without unreasonable expense or delay, the cost of an asset must be taken to be the value ascribed to it in the earliest available record made after the company acquired it.

Finally, s. 275 provides that a *provision* (*see* 11:4) must be treated as a *realised loss*, except where it is in respect of a diminution in value of a fixed asset appearing on a revaluation of all the fixed assets of the company, or all of them other than goodwill. Under s. 275 any consideration by the directors of the value of a fixed asset must be *treated* as a revaluation for the purposes of this exception. If, however, this results in assets being treated as re-valued when this is not in fact the case, the exception applies *only* if the directors are satisfied that their value is not less than the amount at which they are stated in the accounts.

7. Development costs and distributions in kind

Two further sections, derived from the Companies Act 1981, deal with development costs and distributions in kind.

Firstly, s. 269 provides that where *development costs* are shown as an asset in the accounts (which is not the usual procedure) the amount shown in respect of them must be treated, for the purposes of s. 263, as a *realised loss*.

Secondly, s. 276 states that where a company makes a distribution of any *non-cash asset*, any part of the amount at which that asset is stated in the accounts representing unrealised profit must be treated as *realised profit*.

8. Legality of distribution

Section 270 provides that the question whether a company may make a distribution without contravening s. 263 or s. 264, as well as the amount of the distribution, must be determined by reference to the *relevant accounts, i.e. normally the last annual accounts*. The distribution will be unlawful unless the requirements of s. 271 concerning those accounts are complied with.

The requirements are:

(a) The accounts must have been properly prepared.

(b) The auditors must have made a report in respect of them under s. 236.

(c) If, because of something referred to in it, their report is *not unqualified*, they must have stated in writing whether, in their opinion, that thing is *material* for the purpose of determining whether the distribution is unlawful.

(d) A copy of any such statement must have been laid before the company in general meeting.

An 'unqualified report' is a report without qualification to the effect that in the auditors' opinion the accounts have been properly prepared. It has been held that, since the requirement for an auditors' written statement under **(c)** above is designed for the protection of creditors, it is not a procedural matter which can be waived with the unanimous agreement of all members voting at meetings: *Precision Dippings Ltd* v. *Precision Dippings Marketing Ltd* (1986) [B103].

9. Restrictions in memorandum or articles

Section 281 makes it clear that all the above rules apply without prejudice to any further restrictions on distributions which may appear in the company's memorandum or articles. Thus the articles may stipulate that dividends may be paid only out of 'trading profits' or 'the profits of the business', in which case realised profits on fixed assets (capital profits) could not be used for this purpose. They may be even more restrictive, stating that dividends may be paid only out of 'the profits of the business for the year', in which case revenue reserves could not be used. For a dividend held to be unlawful where it was, contrary to the company's memorandum, paid out of a realised capital profit on the sale of assets, see *Re Cleveland Trust plc* (1991) [B104].

It is accordingly important always to look carefully at a company's articles on this point. Table A, however, does not contain any further restrictions.

10. The declaration of dividends

Under the articles of most companies, it is the company which *declares* the dividend, but the directors who recommend its *amount*. The articles usually provide that the dividend shall not exceed the amount recommended by the directors and Table A, Article 102, does this, so that while the share-holders can reduce the amount of the dividend, they cannot increase it.

Unless the company takes advantage of s. 119 (*see* 1) and inserts a clause similar to Table A, Article 104, in its articles, dividends are declared either as a percentage based on the nominal value of the shares, or, with increasing frequency, as a specific sum per share. The amount paid up on the shares is irrelevant.

NOTES: (1) *Debt*: Once declared by the company, the dividend becomes a debt due to the members. It has been held in England that it is not a specialty debt and the period of limitation is thus the normal one of six years: *Re Compania de Electricidad de la Provincia de Buenos Aires Ltd* (1978). [In Scotland the prescriptive period is five years (Prescription and Limitation (Scotland) Act 1973).] Unclaimed dividends, however, may give rise to practical problems. It was held in *Jones* v. *Bellgrove Properties Ltd* (1949), that a statement of a debt in the balance sheet of a company signed by the company's officers constituted a written acknowledgment of that debt and prevented it from becoming statute-barred under the Limitation Act 1939. The point was further clarified in *Re Gee & Co (Woolwich) Ltd* (1975), where it was held that a balance sheet duly signed by the directors was an effective acknowledgment of the state of indebtedness as at the date of the balance sheet, so that the cause of action was deemed to have accrued at that date. However, in *Re Compania de Electricidad de la Provincia de Buenos Aires Ltd* (1978) mentioned above, Slade J. further held that a written acknowledgment is not effectively made to a creditor within the Limitation Act unless it actually reaches him.

(2) *Interim dividends*: Sometimes the articles authorise the directors to pay *interim* dividends to the members, i.e. dividends which are paid in between two annual general meetings, usually six months after the final dividend. Table A, Article 103, gives the directors this power. Some companies apply the main part of their distributable profits towards the final dividend, so that the interim dividend is comparatively small. Others aim at making half-yearly dividend payments of approximately the same size.

Where a *public* company proposes to pay an interim dividend which would be unlawful if paid on the basis of the last annual accounts, *interim accounts* will be necessary to show that it is justified: ss. 270 and 272. These too must be properly prepared and a copy of them delivered to the registrar of companies, but they do not have to be audited.

(3) *Method of payment of dividends*: Table A, Article 106, states that dividends may be paid by cheque sent through the post to the registered address of the holder, or to such person as the holder may direct. Many shareholders require the company to send their dividends to their bank, which then informs them of the amount. Article 107 provides that dividends shall not bear interest, and Article 108 provides that any dividend which has remained unclaimed for 12 years shall, if the directors so resolve, be forfeited and cease to remain owing by the company.

(4) *Payment in cash*: Since a shareholder has a right to receive his dividend in *cash* unless there is a provision in the articles authorising payment in some other way, Table A, Article 105, empowers the company, on the recommendation of the directors, to direct that the dividend be satisfied wholly or partly by the distribution of assets.

11. Consequences of unlawful distribution

We have already seen that dividends may be paid only out of profits available for distribution. If, however, other funds of the company are wrongly used for dividend purposes, s. 277 makes all shareholders who, when they received the improper dividend, knew or had reasonable ground for believing that it was paid out of undistributable funds, liable to repay it to the company.

Presumably where the shareholders are entirely innocent of the illegality, the directors will be liable to replace the funds improperly used, as was the case before there was any statutory provision on the matter.

12. The creation of reserves

As was stated earlier, the directors cannot be compelled to recommend a dividend. They may think it prudent to put all the profits for that year to reserve, and articles usually give them power to do this.

13. Capitalisation issues

Section 280 provides that the expression 'capitalisation' in relation to the profits of a company means:

(a) applying profits in wholly or partly paying up unissued shares to be allotted to members as fully or partly paid *bonus shares; or*
(b) transferring profits to the capital redemption reserve.

The first of these operations, described in **(a)** above, is normally and correctly termed a *capitalisation issue*. It is often called a *bonus issue* which is equally correct, but wrongly gives the impression that the shares are 'free' when in fact they have been paid for out of funds which could instead have been distributed to shareholders by way of dividend. Another term for the same operation is *scrip issue* — an expression commonly used by brokers.

In the case of a capitalisation issue the new shares are allotted to members in proportion to their existing holdings fully, or occasionally partly, paid up. The members thus receive shares on which all or some of the money payable has been already paid out of profits retained by the company and on which there is no, or only a partial, further liability. Since this issue of shares is an addition to capital, the shareholder will not pay income tax on it.

NOTES: (1) *Effect of bonus issue*: Such an issue increases the company's capital, and often entails increasing the nominal capital under s. 121. A company may wish to bring its issued capital more into line with the true worth of its undertaking, and the bonus issue frequently achieves this. On the other hand, the increase in the issued capital causes an immediate fall in the market value of the shares of the company, since the cake is now divided up into a larger number of slices each of which must necessarily be smaller than before. The fall in the market price gives investors a good opportunity to buy the company's shares at a low price, for often it is accentuated by shareholders selling their bonus shares as soon as they receive them.

(2) *Authority in articles and funds available for a bonus issue*: In order to make a bonus issue, a company must have authority in its articles. Table A, Article 110, gives it, allowing a company to use for this purpose any amount standing to the credit of any of its reserve accounts or its profit and loss account which is *available for distribution*. Such funds may also be used under the article to pay up any partly paid shares *already held* by members, which would not, of course, result in any increase in the issued share capital although the shares so treated would have a bonus element.

In addition, Article 110 permits a company to apply its share premium account and its capital redemption reserve to pay up unissued shares to be allotted to members credited as fully paid shares. In either of these cases there is no true capitalisation issue, for these funds are already, in law, capital and not profits (*see* 11:5).

Finally, Article 110 authorises a company to use any profits *not available for distribution* to pay up unissued shares to be allotted to members credited as fully paid shares, e.g. an unrealised profit on a fixed asset.

14. Rights issues

A capitalisation issue must not be confused with a rights issue. Here the company wishes to raise more share capital, and having effected any necessary increase in its nominal capital proceeds to issue new shares. These it first offers to its existing members, on favourable terms, in proportion to their existing holdings. The members may then subscribe for the shares and so increase their holdings, or sell their 'rights' on the market. If a large number of 'rights' are sold, this again may be a good opportunity for an investor to buy shares in the company while they are easily available and the price temporarily depressed.

In reality there is no bonus element in a rights issue, but the members of the company are often pleased to subscribe for more shares at a figure below the market price, and this advantage is often loosely referred to as the bonus element. Payment for the new shares, however, is made entirely by shareholders subscribing fresh capital and not, as in the case of a bonus issue, by the company applying its profits or reserves for that purpose.

It should be noted that where the statutory pre-emption rights apply, an issue of shares will necessarily be a rights issue (*see* 9:**10**).

Debentures

1. The nature of a debenture

The statutory definition of a debenture in s. 744 is very wide. The Act here states that debenture includes debenture stock, bonds, and any other securities of a company whether constituting a charge on the assets or not.

The definition is juristically confused, for a debenture is strictly speaking a *document*, while debenture stock is not. The word 'securities' also sometimes misleads students here. It is used to mean the *undertaking to repay* the money borrowed, and the definition goes on to state that this undertaking may or may not be accompanied by a charge on the company's assets. Thus a mortgage of the company's property to a single individual as security is a debenture within the definition. ['Mortgage' is not a term of Scots law. Security over a company's heritable property (i.e. land and buildings) is in Scotland created by a 'standard security' under the Conveyancing and Feudal Reform (Scotland) Act 1970.]

Usually, however, a debenture is *one of a series* issued to a number of lenders. It is often accompanied by a charge on the assets which may be either fixed or floating (*see* 7). But sometimes no charge is given, and then the debenture is described as 'naked' or 'unsecured'. Moreover, the term 'mortgage debenture' is restricted by the Stock Exchange to debentures with *fixed* charges, although its legal meaning would appear to cover charges of both types.

Shares and debentures are commonly mentioned, even in the Act, as though they were similar, but their legal nature is entirely different. *A share is in England a chose in action* [*in Scotland incorporeal moveable property*], *evidenced by a document* called a share certificate. *A debenture is a document which is evidence in England of a chose in action* [*in Scotland of ownership of incorporeal moveable property*], i.e. the debt. *Debenture stock*, however, is similar to *stock*, for it is evidenced by a document called a *debenture-stock certificate*, while stockholders receive a *stock certificate*. Moreover, a debenture can be transferred only *as a whole*, i.e. if it is evidence of a debt from the company of £500, then the *whole debt* must be transferred. Debenture stock, on the other hand, is *divisible* into any amounts required, in the same way as stock.

Sometimes the debenture holders are given a right, by the terms of the debenture, to convert their debentures into shares at some future date. Such debentures are called *convertible*, and if the holders exercise their right of conversion they cease to be lenders to the company and become members instead. The convertible debentures cannot, however, be issued at a discount entitling the holder to exchange them immediately for shares of the same par value, as this would be an indirect method of issuing shares at a discount and therefore unlawful under s. 100: *Mosely* v. *Koffyfontein Mines Ltd* (1904) [B223].

2. Power of company to borrow

The power of a company to borrow money is implied in the case of all trading companies. Non-trading companies, however, must be expressly authorised to borrow by their memorandum.

A power to borrow money, whether express or implied, includes the power to charge the assets of the company by way of security to the lender (*see* 6 and 7). The company can charge any type of property which it happens to own. It can also charge its uncalled capital, though not its reserve capital (*see* 11:3).

Borrowing powers are not exercisable until the company can *commence business*. Public companies, therefore, must first obtain their trading certificate by complying with the requirements of s. 117 which are set out in 5:2 Moreover, the memorandum may restrict the amount of money which the company may borrow.

3. Authority of directors to borrow

The power of the company to borrow is exercised by the directors. While the company's power to borrow relates to the company's *capacity*, the exercise of the company's power by the directors relates to the directors' *authority*.

It can happen that the power of the company to borrow is unrestricted, but the authority of the directors, acting as the agents of the company, is limited to a certain figure. For instance, the articles may prohibit (as Table A in Schedule 1 to the Companies Act 1948 did) the directors from borrowing a sum which exceeds the nominal amount of the issued share capital unless they first obtain the sanction of a general meeting of the company. There is, however, no restriction in Table A in the Companies (Tables A–F) Regulations 1985.

4. Company's capacity and directors' authority before the European Communities Act 1972

Formerly it was very important to distinguish between:

(a) borrowing which was *ultra vires* the company, i.e. outside the capacity of the company; *and*

(b) borrowing which was *intra vires* the company, i.e. within the capacity of the company, but beyond the scope of the directors' authority.

The position was substantially altered by s. 9 European Communities Act 1972, which implemented the First EC Directive of 1968, and further alterations were made by the Companies Act 1989. It is necessary to say something about the original position before turning to the present position. The intermediate position, which existed between the 1972 and the 1989 Acts need not now concern us.

Originally, any act which was *ultra vires* the company was void, and the behaviour of the directors, as the company's agents, could have no effect whatsoever on the validity of the loan, for no agent can ever have more capacity than his principal. If, therefore, the borrowing was *ultra vires* so that the company had no *capacity* to undertake it, the lender could have no right of action against the company in respect of it, nor could he enforce any security granted to him. This was so even where the company's memorandum empowered it to borrow if the loan, to the lender's knowledge, was to be used for an *ultra vires* purpose: *Introductions Ltd* v. *National Provincial Bank Ltd* (1969).

On the other hand, borrowing which was *intra vires* the company, but beyond the directors' authority was governed by the principles of the law of agency. The company had the power to borrow; there was no lack of *capacity*. It had, however, restricted the *authority* of its agent to a certain sum which was not to be exceeded. The company could, if it wished, ratify its agent's unauthorised act, and, if it did so, the loan bound both the lender and the company as if it had been made with the company's authority in the first place.

If the company declined to ratify the directors' act, then, according to the normal principles of agency, the lender's rights depended on whether or not he knew that the director was exceeding his authority. To his actual knowledge, there had to be added his deemed knowledge of all the public documents of the company. If he knew in either way of the restriction, he had no right of action against the company. On the other hand, however, the third party was not affected by *secret* restrictions on the directors' authority, and so, if the lack of authority was not clear from the public documents and the lender did not know of it from some other source, the company was bound (*see* 16:**24, 25**).

5. Company's capacity and directors' authority after the Companies Act 1989

The leading provision in s. 35, as substituted in the 1985 Act by s. 18 Companies Act 1989, is that the validity of an act done by a company is not to be called into question on the ground of lack of capacity by reason of anything in the company's memorandum. This protects a third party who has lent money to a company where the company has no relevant borrowing power in its memorandum. The third party is, by s. 35B, inserted in the 1985 Act by s. 108 of the 1989 Act, not bound to enquire as to whether the transaction is permitted by the company's memorandum or not.

The authority of directors to bind the company is dealt with in s. 35A, inserted in the 1985 Act by s. 108 of the 1989 Act. The leading provision of s. 35A is that in favour of a person dealing with a company in good faith, the power of the board of directors to bind the company, or authorise others to do so, is to be deemed to be free of any limitation under the company's constitution. Again, by s. 35B, the third party is not bound to enquire as to any limitation on the powers of the board of directors to bind the company or authorise others to do so.

On these provisions, *see* further 2:**19–21.**

6. Types of security

Before further consideration of debentures it is appropriate to look at the nature of security in general and in particular at security given by companies.

When a person owes money to another, either because he has borrowed it or for any other reason, the sum owed is a *debt*. This debt can be either *unsecured* or *secured*.

When the debt is unsecured, the creditor has only one remedy: to sue for the amount owed, i.e. a right of action. He is not, therefore, at all safe if the debtor goes bankrupt or disappears. He has no security. Ordinary trade debts are usually unsecured, as is money borrowed from a friend when a person unexpectedly finds that he has not enough money in his pocket for his fare home.

A wise creditor, therefore, will demand security, i.e. a right over the debtor's *property* which is *in addition* to his right of action. A bank overdraft, for instance, is often secured by a deposit of the title deeds of the borrower's house (a mortgage), or of his share certificates (*see* 12:**27**) [In Scotland the mere deposit of title deeds or of share certificates creates no valid security. For the creation of a valid security over the borrower's house a standard security must be recorded in the Register of Sasines or registered in the Land Register of Scotland. For the creation of a valid security over shares the borrower must transfer his shares to the lender and the lender's name must be entered in the register of members.] An unpaid seller of goods who is still in possession of them has a lien on those goods for the price, under the Sale of Goods Act 1979. An unpaid repairer of goods, e.g. a cobbler, has a lien at common law on the goods he has repaired, i.e. he can retain them until he is paid the amount owed to him. A bank may ask a customer who wishes to borrow money whether he can find another person of means to guarantee his overdraft, i.e. someone who is willing to undertake to repay the bank if the borrower does not do so. And a pawnbroker or pledgee has possession of the goods pledged to him. Thus a mortgage [in Scotland a standard security], a charge, a lien, a guarantee and a pledge are all *types of security*, i.e. methods by which a creditor's position is made safer.

7. Security given by companies

A company, like any other person, can give its creditors security. Often it mortgages or charges its property to its *debenture holders*, i.e. the persons who have lent money to it. These persons will then not only be able to sue the company for the amount of money which they have lent to it, but they will be able to enforce their security, i.e. claim that the property charged belongs to them. The charges given by the company fall into two categories:

(a) *Fixed or specific charges*: These are charges on definite or specific property of a permanent nature, e.g. land or heavy machinery, and may be either legal or equitable (*see* 14:**8–10**). [In Scots law there is no distinction between legal and equitable charges, and the term 'securities' is more commonly used than 'charges'.]

(b) *Floating charges*: By the common law of England these are charges which do not initially attach to the property charged and are thus necessarily equitable. They are useful when the assets to be charged are of the kind turned over in the course of trade, e.g. stock, for the company may continue to deal in the usual way with the property charged without the consent of the creditor. The classic description is to be found in *Re Yorkshire Woolcombers Association Ltd (Illingworth* v. *Houldsworth)* (1903) [B224].

A floating charge will attach to the particular property then in the company's possession if:

    (*i*) the company goes into liquidation; *or*

    (*ii*) the company ceases to carry on business; *or*

    (*iii*) the debenture holders take steps to enforce their security, e.g. by appointing a receiver (*see* **15**).

It is then said to become fixed or to crystallise.

[Floating charges were not recognised by the common law of Scotland. They were introduced by the Companies (Floating Charges) (Scotland) Act 1961, an Act which made no provision for the appointment of receivers. A further Act in 1972, the Companies (Floating Charges and Receivers) (Scotland) Act, as well as re-enacting with amendment the provisions on floating charges of the 1961 Act, introduced receivers. These provisions are now in ss. 462–487 of the 1985 Act, provisions applicable to Scotland only. By s. 463 on the commencement of the winding up, a floating charge attaches to the property then owned by the company, and by ss. 53 and 54 Insolvency Act 1986 on the appointment of a receiver by the holder of the floating charge or by the court, respectively, the floating charge attaches to the property which is then subject to the charge, and that attachment has effect as if the floating charge were a fixed security. The term 'crystallise' is not used in the statutory provisions.]

NOTE: Section 411, inserted in the 1985 Act by s. 101 Companies Act 1989, requires *all* charges given by a company to its creditors to be shown in the company's register of charges kept at the company's registered office. Each entry in that register must contain:

(1) a short description of the property charged;
(2) the amount of the charge; and
(3) the names of the persons entitled to the charge.

A copy of every instrument creating a charge must also be kept at the same place.

8. Trust deeds

When a *series of debentures* is issued to numerous debenture holders, a trust deed is normally drawn up. Under the terms of the deed the company undertakes to pay the debenture holders their principal and interest, and normally charges its property to the trustees (usually a trust corporation) as security. If under English law the charge is to be a *legal fixed* charge such a deed is essential, for a legal estate in land cannot be owned by more than four persons, and therefore could not be granted to a large number of debenture holders.

The deed usually empowers the trustees to appoint a receiver to protect the property charged if the company defaults in payment of the principal or interest, and may contain other provisions concerning meetings of the debenture holders, supervision of the assets charged, and the keeping of a register of debenture holders.

A similar deed can be drawn up for debenture stock.

9. Advantages of a trust deed

A trust deed has two main advantages:

(a) As stated above, it makes it possible for the company to give the debenture holders (through the trustees) a *legal fixed charge* [in Scotland a *fixed security*] over property of a permanent nature such as land.
(b) The rights of the debenture holders and the company's covenants for payment of principal and interest and for the care and insurance of the property charged to them can be enforced by the trustees against the company.

It would be much more difficult for a large and fluctuating body of individual debenture holders to do this.

The Act does not impose any specific statutory duties on the trustees, but s. 192 renders *void* any provision in the trust deed exempting them from, or indemnifying them against, liability for breach of trust.

10 Forms of debenture

A debenture may be either:

(a) a registered debenture; *or*
(b) a bearer debenture.

It is usually, though not necessarily, under the company's seal if the company has a seal.

11. Registered debentures

These are subject to many of the same rules as shares. A register of debenture holders is kept in the same way as a register of members, and must under s. 190 normally be kept at the registered office of the company (*see* 2:**15**). Section 191 imposes a limitation period of 20 years on any liability incurred by the company through the making or deletion of any entry in the register, as in the case of the register of members (*see* 14:**2**). Section 183 applies to debentures as well as to shares, requiring a *proper instrument of transfer* to be delivered to the company before a transfer can be registered. Section 185 applies to debentures and debenture-stock certificates in the same way as it applies to share certificates (*see* 12:**9**) and so also does s. 183 concerning notice of the company's refusal to register a transfer (*see* 12:**7**).

The debenture itself consists of two parts:

(a) the covenants by the company to pay the principal and interest; *and*
(b) the endorsed conditions, i.e. the terms of the loan.

The endorsed conditions vary, but they normally contain a provision that the debenture is one of a series all ranking *pari passu*. This is necessary because without such a clause the debentures would rank *in the order of issue* regarding the assets charged by the company, and if a large issue of debentures is made it is obviously essential that the debenture holders should all have the same rights as regards security.

Another usual endorsed condition in an English debenture is a provision keeping trusts off the register. This is required because s. 360 (*see* 14:**7**) applies only to the register of members and not to the register of debenture holders. [In Scotland there would be no corresponding desire to exclude trusts from the register. Section 360 does not apply to Scotland.]

12. Bearer debentures

Bearer debentures are similar to share warrants in that they too are negotiable instruments, transferable by delivery. The interest on them is paid by means of attached coupons, as are dividends on share warrants (*see* 12:**25**).

13. Perpetual debentures

As a general rule when a mortgage is made by an individual, *equity will not permit it to be irredeemable*. The purpose of the transaction has been to borrow money: anything therefore, which prevents the borrower from repaying the loan and recovering his security will be void in equity. This will be the position right up to the moment when the mortgagee has obtained an order for the sale or foreclosure of the mortgaged property, even if the legal or contractual right to redeem has long since expired. Equity expresses this rule in the maxim: 'Once a mortgage, always a mortgage'.

Thus the mortgagor normally has a *legal or contractual* right to repay the loan and redeem his property on the date specified in the contract of loan. Once this date has passed, he has an *equitable* right to redeem his property on payment of the loan and accrued interest. From the moment the mortgage is created, he has an *equitable interest* in the mortgaged property which remains in him so long as the mortgage endures, and which is called the *equity of redemption*. Equity will hold invalid any provision which 'clogs' the equity of redemption, i.e. fetters the rights of the mortgagor, and his most important right is his equitable right to redeem.

This rule, however, is subject to an exception in the case of companies. Section 193 expressly states that a condition in a *debenture* is *not invalid* on the grounds that the debenture is *irredeemable* or *redeemable only* on the occurrence of an event, however remote, or on the expiration of a period of time, however long. It follows that debentures can be made *perpetual*, i.e. the loan is repayable only on winding up, or after a long period of time.

14. The company's power to re-issue redeemed debentures

Although in the last paragraph we saw that debentures may be perpetual or irredeemable, they are, unlike shares, normally redeemable at a certain specified future date. The company may then lawfully effect an economy by redeeming them, i.e. buying them back from any willing seller, *before* the specified redemption date has arrived.

When debentures are redeemed they are, at common law, extinguished and the company would therefore be unable to re-issue them were it not for the provisions of s. 194. This section permits the company to re-issue them, or to issue others in their place, *with the priority of the original series* provided:

(a) there is no provision to the contrary, express or implied, in the articles or in any contract made by the company; *and*

(b) the company has not shown an intention to cancel them, e.g. by passing a resolution to that effect.

15. The remedies of debenture holders

The remedies of a debenture holder vary according to whether he is secured or unsecured. He will naturally have wider protection in the former case.

An *unsecured* debenture holder is in exactly the same position as an ordinary trade creditor. The fact that his debt arises from a loan to the company rather than the supply of goods to it or the performance of services for it is quite immaterial. He is owed money and he has no security. Like any other unsecured creditor, therefore, he has *only three remedies*:

(a) He can *sue* for his principal and interest, obtain judgment, and, if the judgment debt is not paid, levy execution against [in Scotland, do diligence against] the company's property.

(b) He can apply to the court for the court to make an administration order under ss. 8 and 9 Insolvency Act 1986 on the ground that the company is or is likely to become unable to pay its debts.

(c) He can, if he wishes, *petition under s. 124 Insolvency Act 1986 for a winding up* of the company by the court on the ground specified in s. 122 of that Act, namely, that the company is unable to pay its debts.

A *secured* debenture holder has *each of the above remedies*, but in addition he also has the following courses open to him:

(d) He can *exercise any of the powers* which are given to him by the *debenture or the trust deed*, as the case may be, without applying to the court. Usually these include a power to appoint a receiver, and a power to sell the company's property.

(e) He can *apply to the court* for the appointment of a *receiver* or for an order for the *sale or foreclosure* of the property.

When the company defaults in payment of principal or interest, any debenture holder may sue, but he normally brings the action on behalf of himself and the other debenture holders of the same class. This is known as a *debenture-holders' action*, and if several individuals start to sue separately, the court can consolidate their actions into one.

16. Receivers

The statutory provisions on receivers are divided into two groups in the Insolvency Act 1986. Sections 28–49 apply to England and Wales, and ss. 50–71 apply to Scotland. Major points of difference are that there is no person in Scotland corresponding to the official receiver in England and Wales, and no distinction is made in Scotland between a receiver and an administrative receiver.

A receiver may be appointed:

(a) by the court; *or*

(b) under the terms of the debenture or the trust deed.

In England and Wales s. 30 Insolvency Act 1986 disqualifies a corporation from appointment as a receiver, and s. 31 of that Act disqualifies an undischarged bankrupt unless he is acting under a court order. [Similarly in Scotland s. 51 disqualifies a corporation and an undischarged bankrupt, and it also disqualifies a Scottish firm.] Moreover, a receiver is caught by the provisions of the Company Directors Disqualification Act 1986, so that a disqualification order may be made against him by the court (*see* 16:**20**). In England and Wales if the company is in compulsory liquidation when the debenture holders apply to the court to appoint a receiver, s. 32 Insolvency Act 1986 provides that the official receiver may be appointed. [There is no corresponding provision applicable to Scotland, since there is no official receiver in Scotland.]

Once the appointment is made, every invoice, order for goods or business letter on which the company's name appears is required by s. 39 [for Scotland s. 64] Insolvency Act 1986 to contain a statement that a receiver has been appointed.

17. A receiver appointed by the court

In England and Wales, when a receiver is appointed by the court, he is not the agent either of the debenture holders or of the company, but is an *officer of the court*. He must therefore act according to the court's directions. He is personally liable on contracts, but has a right of indemnity out of the company's assets. His remuneration is fixed by the court.

[In Scotland, by s. 57 Insolvency Act 1986 a receiver is deemed to be the agent of the company in relation to the property attached by the floating charge. He is personally liable on any contract entered into by him, except in so far as the contract otherwise provides, and has a right of indemnity out of the property attached by the floating charge. His remuneration is decided by agreement between him and the holder of the floating charge but if there is any dispute it is fixed instead by the Auditor of the Court of Session.]

In England and Wales, it has been decided that the court may appoint a receiver:

(a) if the principal or interest is in arrears; *or*

(b) if the security is in jeopardy, i.e. where the company or its other creditors are about to take steps which will put the assets charged beyond the reach of the debenture holders; *or*

(c) if the company is being wound up.

[In Scotland, s. 52 Insolvency Act 1986 specifies the circumstances which justify the appointment of a receiver by the court as being:

(a) the occurrence of any event which by the provisions of the instrument creating the floating charge, entitles the holder to make that appointment; *or*

(b) the court is satisfied that the position of the holder of the charge is likely to be prejudiced if no appointment is made; *or*

(c) the expiry of 21 days after the making of a demand for payment of the whole or any part of the principal, without payment having been made; *or*

(d) the expiry of two months during the whole of which interest has been in arrears; *or*

(e) the making of an order or the passing of a resolution for winding up.

[Circumstances **(b)** to **(e)** justify appointment only where the instrument creating the charge does not provide otherwise.]

18. A receiver appointed under a power in the debenture or trust deed

In England and Wales, when a receiver is appointed under the terms of the debenture or trust deed, he would naturally be the agent of the *debenture holders*, if it were not for the terms of the debenture itself and of the Insolvency Act 1986. In fact, however, the debenture or trust deed normally provides that he shall be the agent of the *company* and s. 44 Insolvency Act 1986 provides that an 'administrative' receiver (i.e., by s. 29 of that Act, a receiver of the whole (or substantially the whole) of a company's property) is deemed to be the company's agent unless and until the company goes into liquidation, while ss. 37 and 44 of the same Act make any receiver personally liable on any contract entered into by him but entitled to an indemnity out of the company's assets.

[For Scotland, s. 57 Insolvency Act 1986 provides that a receiver is deemed to be the agent of the company in relation to the property attached by the floating charge. He is personally liable on any contract entered into by him except in so far as the contract otherwise provides but entitled to be indemnified out of the property attached by the floating charge. The term 'administrative receiver' does not appear in the Scottish provisions.]

Section 35 [for Scotland, s. 63] Insolvency Act 1986 entitles the receiver to apply to the court for directions whenever he wishes so that as a result his legal position is equivalent to that of a receiver appointed by the court.

The receiver's remuneration is fixed by agreement except that the court may fix it if the company goes into liquidation and the liquidator applies to the court for that purpose under s. 36 of the 1986 Act. [In Scotland, s. 58 provides that the receiver's remuneration is decided by agreement between the receiver and the holder of the floating charge, and that if there is a dispute it may be fixed instead by the Auditor of the Court of Session on an application being made to him by:

(a) the receiver;

(b) the holder of any floating charge or fixed security over all or any of the company's property;

(c) the company; *or*

(d) the liquidator of the company.]

The powers conferred on an administrative receiver in England and Wales by the debentures under which he was appointed are, by s. 42 Insolvency Act 1986, deemed to include the 23 powers listed in Schedule 1 to that Act except in so far as these are inconsistent with any of the provisions of the debentures. A person dealing with an administrative receiver in good faith and for value is not concerned to inquire whether the receiver is acting within his powers.

[Similarly in Scotland, by s. 55 Insolvency Act 1986, a receiver has in addition to the powers given by the instrument creating the floating charge the 23 powers listed in Schedule 2 to that Act except so far as these are inconsistent with any provision contained in the instrument. All the receiver's powers, however, are restricted by:

(a) the rights of any person who has 'effectually executed diligence' on any property of the company prior to the appointment of the receiver; *and*

(b) the rights of any person holding over any part of the property a fixed security or a floating charge ranking prior to or *pari passu* with the floating charge in question.

The phrase 'effectually executed diligence' in **(a)** above, has been considered in several cases: in *Lord Advocate* v. *Royal Bank of Scotland* (1977) an arrestment standing by itself and not followed by a decree of furthcoming was held not to be an 'effectually executed diligence' but this case was distinguished in *Iona Hotels Ltd* v. *William Craig* (1990) [B228] where there was an arrestment on the dependence of an action prior to the creation of the floating charge.

Section 55 also provides that a person dealing with a receiver in good faith and for value is not concerned to inquire whether the receiver is acting within his powers.]

Section 43 Insolvency Act 1986 enables an administrative receiver to apply to court for authority to dispose of property which is subject to a security. He must satisfy the court that a disposal of the property would be likely to promote a more advantageous realisation of the company's assets than would otherwise be effected. The secured creditor who is thus deprived of his security is entitled to the net proceeds of the disposal together with any amount necessary to bring that amount up to the net amount which would have been realised if the property had been sold in the open market by a willing seller.

[For Scotland, there are corresponding provisions in s. 61 Insolvency Act 1986.]

19. Provisions as to information when receiver is appointed

The Insolvency Act 1986 requires certain information, prescribed in greater detail by regulations made under that Act, to be given by a receiver appointed under a power in the debenture or trust deed. In England and Wales, the requirements are more elaborate in the case of administrative receivers than in the case of other receivers. [The Scottish provisions make no distinction between administrative receivers and other receivers. The provisions are in line with those applicable to administrative receivers in England and Wales.]

By s. 38 Insolvency Act 1986 in England and Wales a receiver other than an administrative receiver must deliver to the registrar an account of his receipts and payments. The time allowed for delivery of such accounts is one month (or such longer period as the registrar may allow) after the expiration of 12 months from the date of the receiver's appointment and of every later period of six months and also within one month after he ceases to act as receiver. The accounts take the form of an abstract showing receipts and payments during the relevant period of 12 or six months as the case may be, except that in the case where the receiver ceases to act the period may be less in duration, but there must also be shown the aggregate amount of receipts and payments during all the preceding periods since the receiver's appointment.

A receiver who makes default in complying with s. 38 is liable to a fine and, for continued contravention, to a daily default fine.

[For Scotland, there is no provision corresponding to s. 38.]

The more stringent provisions applicable to administrative receivers are to be found in ss. 46–49 Insolvency Act 1986. [There are corresponding provisions for Scottish *receivers* in ss. 65–68. The term 'administrative receiver' is not applicable to Scotland.]

By s. 46 [for Scotland, s. 65] where an administrative receiver is appointed he must:

(a) immediately send to the company and publish in the prescribed manner a notice of his appointment; *and*

(b) within 28 days after his appointment, unless the court otherwise directs, send such a notice to all the creditors of the company, so far as he is aware of their addresses.

By s. 47 [for Scotland, s. 66] an administrative receiver must immediately after his appointment require some or all of the company's officers and employees (including persons who have been its officers or employees within the preceding year) to submit to him a statement in a prescribed form showing:

(a) particulars of the company's assets, debts and liabilities;
(b) the names and addresses of its creditors;
(c) the securities held by each of them;
(d) the dates when each of the securities was given; *and*
(e) any other information which is prescribed.

The statement must be submitted to the administrative receiver within 21 days, except that the administrative receiver, or, failing him, the court, may extend the period or may release a person altogether from the obligation to submit the statement.

Section 48 [for Scotland, s. 67] deals with an administrative receiver's report. Within three months (or such longer period as the court may allow) after his appointment the administrative receiver must send to the registrar, to any trustees for secured creditors and (so far as he is aware of their addresses) to all secured creditors [and in Scotland also to the holder of the floating charge] a report as to:

(a) the events leading up to his appointment, so far as he is aware of them;
(b) the disposal or proposed disposal by him of any property of the company and the carrying on or proposed carrying on by him of any business of the company;
(c) the amounts of principal and interest payable to the debenture holders by whom or on whose behalf he was appointed and the amounts payable to preferential creditors (*see* **20**); *and*
(d) the amount, if any, likely to be available for the payment of other creditors.

The administrative receiver must also, within three months (or such longer period as the court may allow) after his appointment, *either*:

(a) send a copy of the report (so far as he is aware of their addresses) to all unsecured creditors; *or*
(b) publish in the prescribed manner a notice stating an address to which unsecured creditors should write for copies of the report to be sent to them free of charge.

In either case (unless the court directs otherwise) he must lay a copy of the report before a meeting of unsecured creditors summoned for the purpose on not less than 14 days' notice.

Where the company goes into liquidation the receiver must send a copy of his report to the liquidator within seven days of the liquidator's nomination or appointment.

The administrative receiver's report must include a summary of the statement of affairs submitted to him under s. 47 [for Scotland, s. 66] and a summary of any comments made by him upon that statement.

The report need not include any information the disclosure of which would seriously prejudice the carrying out by the administrative receiver of his functions.

If the administrative receiver fails without reasonable excuse to comply with ss. 46–48 [or, in Scotland, ss. 65–67], he is liable to a fine and, for continued contravention, to a daily default fine.

Section 49 provides that where a meeting of creditors is summoned under s. 48 [or, in Scotland, s. 67], the meeting may, if it thinks fit, establish a committee ('the creditors' committee'), and that that committee may require the administrative receiver to attend before it and furnish it with information relating to the carrying out by him of his functions.

20. Priority of preferential debts
Where any receiver is appointed on behalf of the holders of debentures secured by a floating charge and the company is *not in liquidation*, s. 40 [for Scotland, s. 59] Insolvency Act 1986 requires him to pay all preferential debts of the company (money due to the Inland Revenue for income tax deducted at source, VAT, betting and gaming duties, social security and pension scheme contributions, remuneration, etc. of employees, as listed in Schedule 6 to the 1986 Act) out of the assets in his hands before meeting any claim for principal or interest in respect of the debentures.

(Note that if the company *is in liquidation*, the priority of the preferential debts is preserved by s. 175 Insolvency Act 1986 (*see* 1:**18**).)

21. Registration in the companies charges register
Quite apart from the company's own register of charges which it has created over its property (*see* **7**), the registrar must keep another register of charges for each company.

Part XII of the 1985 Act contains the provisions as to registration of charges. Originally it was divided into two chapters — Chapter I (ss. 395–409) applicable to England and Wales and Chapter II (ss. 410–424) applicable to Scotland. There was a widespread demand for improvements to the registration system, and in 1989 Professor Aubrey Diamond, as part of his general review of security interests in property for the Department of Trade and Industry, made a number of proposals for urgent legislation on company charges.

Effect was substantially given to Professor Diamond's recommendations by Part IV of the Companies Act 1989. The provisions of Part IV (ss. 92–107) of that Act amend the provisions of the 1985 Act by inserting new provisions in Part XII of the 1985 Act: s. 92 Companies Act 1989. There are no longer separate provisions for Scotland.

It should be noted that by s. 413 of the 1985 Act, inserted by s. 102 Companies Act 1989, the Secretary of State has a wide-ranging power to make regulations as to the provisions of Part XII in relation to charges of any description specified in the regulations.

In the remainder of this chapter, references to sections are to sections of the 1985 Act as inserted by Part IV of the Companies Act 1989.

22. Charges requiring registration

Section 396 lists the charges requiring registration:

(a) a charge on land or any interest in land, other than a charge for rent or such other periodical sum;

(b) a charge on goods or any interest in goods, other than a charge under which the chargee is entitled to possession either of the goods or of a document of title to them;

(c) a charge on intangible movable property [in Scotland, incorporeal moveable property] of any of the following descriptions:

(*i*) goodwill;

(*ii*) intellectual property;

(*iii*) book debts (whether book debts of the company or assigned to the company);

(*iv*) uncalled share capital of the company or calls made but not paid;

(d) a charge for securing an issue of debentures; *and*

(e) a floating charge on the whole or part of the company's property.

'Intellectual property' in **(c)**(*ii*) means *either* any patent, trade mark, service mark, registered design, copyright or design right *or* any licence under any such right.

The Secretary of State may amend the above provisions by regulations made by statutory instrument.

23. The companies charges register

By s. 397 the registrar must keep for each company a register, in such form as he thinks fit, of charges on property of the company. The register must consist of a file containing particulars of each charge and the other information delivered to him under Part XII.

By the same section any person may require the registrar to provide a certificate stating the date on which particulars etc. were delivered to him. The certificate must be signed by the registrar or authenticated by his official seal.

The certificate is *conclusive evidence* that the particulars etc. were delivered to the registrar no later than the date stated in the certificate; and it is *presumed*, unless the contrary is proved, that they were not delivered earlier than that date.

24. Company's duty to deliver particulars for registration

Section 398 provides that it is the duty of a company which creates a charge or acquires property subject to a charge to deliver the prescribed particulars of the charge to the registrar within 21 days after the date of the charge's creation or the date of the acquisition of the property, as the case may be.

However, s. 398 also provides that particulars may be delivered by any person interested in the charge, and in that case the person concerned is entitled to recover from the company the amount of any fees paid by him to the registrar in connection with the registration.

If the particulars are not delivered by the company or by anyone else, the company and every officer of it who is in default are liable to fines.

By the same section the registrar must file the particulars in the register and make a note of the date on which they were delivered to him. He must then send to the company and to the person who appears from the particulars to be the chargee, and, if the particulars were delivered by another person interested in the charge, to that person, a copy of the particulars filed and of the note made as to date.

25. Effect of failure to deliver particulars for registration

Section 399 provides that where a charge is created by a company and no particulars are delivered for registration within the 21-day period, the charge is void against:

(a) an administrator or liquidator of the company where insolvency proceedings begin after the creation of the charge; *and*
(b) any person who for value acquires an interest in or right over property subject to the charge, where the acquisition takes place after the creation of the charge.

These provisions of s. 399 are modified by s. 400 in the case where particulars are delivered late, i.e. more than 21 days after the charge's creation. Section 400 provides that the charge will not be void if the insolvency proceedings in **(a)** above or the acquisition in **(b)** above occurs after the particulars are in fact registered.

This modification is in its turn subject to an exception. By s. 400 where the company is at the date of delivery of the particulars unable to pay its debts (or later becomes unable to pay its debts as a result of the transaction under which the charge is created) *and* insolvency proceedings begin before the end of the relevant period, the charge is still void as against the administrator or liquidator. In this context the phrase 'unable to pay its debts' has the same meaning as in s. 123 Insolvency Act 1986 (*see* 30:2) and 'relevant period' is:

(a) two years in the case of a floating charge created in favour of a person connected with the company;
(b) one year in the case of a floating charge created in favour of a person not connected with the company; *and*
(c) six months in any other case (i.e. when the charge is not a floating charge).

26. Delivery of further particulars
By s. 401 further particulars of a charge, supplementing or varying the registered particulars, may be delivered to the registrar at any time. They must be signed by or on behalf of both the company and the chargee. The registrar then files them in the register, makes a note of the date of their delivery and sends to the company, to the chargee and, if the particulars were delivered by some other interested person, to that person a copy of the further particulars filed and of the date on which they were delivered.

27. Effect of omissions and errors in registered particulars.
Just as complete failure to deliver particulars makes a charge void (*see* 25), so also, by s. 402, is a charge void where the registered particulars are not complete and accurate, but there are two modifications in this case.

First, the charge will be void only to the extent that rights which have not been disclosed ought to have been disclosed.

Secondly, the chargee may make an application to the court for an order that the charge is effective. The court must be satisfied, in the case of an administration order or a liquidation:

(a) that the omission or error is not likely to have misled materially to his prejudice any unsecured creditor of the company; *or*
(b) that no person became an unsecured creditor while the registered particulars were incomplete or inaccurate.

In the case of a person acquiring an interest in or right over property subject to the charge, the court must be satisfied that he did not rely on registered particulars which were incomplete or inaccurate.

28. Memorandum of charge ceasing to affect company's property
Section 403 provides that where a charge ceases to affect the company's

property, a memorandum to that effect, signed by or on behalf of both the company and the chargee, may be delivered to the registrar. This is then filed by the registrar and the date of its delivery noted. The registrar must send to the company, to the chargee and, if the memorandum was filed by another interested person, to that person a copy of the memorandum and of the date on which it was delivered.

If a memorandum is delivered in a case where the charge in fact continues to affect the company's property, the charge is void for the future, to the same extent as is explained in **25** above.

29. Additional information to be registered

Sections 408–410 specify additional information which must be registered and then filed by the registrar.

By s. 408, where particulars of a charge for securing an issue of debentures have been delivered to the registrar, then it is the duty of the company to deliver also particulars of the date and amount, when debentures of that issue are taken up, and to do so within 21 days after the date on which they are taken up.

By s. 409, where a receiver or manager of the company's property is appointed, he must, within the next seven days, give notice of that fact to the registrar. If he ceases to act, he must also give notice of that fact.

Section 410 empowers the Secretary of State by regulations to require notice of further matters to be given to the registrar, e.g. notice of an event causing a floating charge to crystallise. [Regulations under this section do not apply to Scottish floating charges.]

Investigations and inspection of documents

1. Part XIV Companies Act 1985

There are three types of investigation which can be carried out by the Secretary of State for Trade and Industry under Part XIV (i.e. ss. 431–453) Companies Act 1985 as amended by Part III (i.e. ss. 55–91) Companies Act 1989. These are:

(a) an investigation of the company's *affairs*;
(b) an investigation of the company's *ownership*;
(c) an investigation of *share dealings*.

Part XIV of the Act and this chapter also deal with the Secretary of State's power to make:
(d) an inspection of the company's *documents*.

Despite the wide powers conferred on the Secretary of State, s. 452 provides safeguards for privileged information in relation to all four types of investigation. Thus no disclosure is required:

(a) by any person of any information which he would in an action be entitled to refuse to disclose on grounds of legal professional privilege except, if he is a lawyer, the name and address of his client;
(b) by a banker unless:
    (*i*) the person to whom the obligation of confidence is owed is the company under investigation;
    (*ii*) the person to whom the obligation of confidence is owed consents to the disclosure; *or*
    (*iii*) the requirement is authorised by the Secretary of State.

The general effect of the amendments made by the 1989 Act was to increase the Secretary of State's control over investigations, e.g. in relation to dispensing with final reports and publication of reports in certain cases.

Investigation of affairs

2. Power to investigate affairs of company

Section 431 provides that the Secretary of State *may* appoint inspectors to investigate and report on a company's affairs:

(a) in the case where it has a share capital, on the application of:

    (*i*) at least 200 members; *or*

    (*ii*) members holding at least one-tenth of the shares issued;

(b) in the case where it has no share capital, on the application of at least one-fifth of the members; *and*

(c) in any case, on the application of the company.

The section provides that the application must be supported by such evidence as the Secretary of State may require, showing good reason for the investigation. The Secretary of State may also require security for costs not exceeding £5000 from the applicants.

Section 432 provides that the Secretary of State *may* appoint inspectors to investigate the company's affairs if it appears:

(a) that its affairs are being or have been conducted:

    (*i*) with intent to defraud creditors; *or*

    (*ii*) for some other fraudulent or unlawful purpose; *or*

    (*iii*) in a manner unfairly prejudicial to any of its members; *or*

(b) that any actual or proposed act or omission of the company is or would be unfairly prejudicial to any of its members; *or*

(c) that the company was formed for a fraudulent or unlawful purpose; *or*

(d) that the persons concerned with formation or management have been guilty of fraud, misfeasance or other misconduct towards the company or its members; *or*

(e) that its members have not been given all the information about its affairs which they might reasonably expect.

By an amendment to s. 432 made by s. 55 Companies Act 1989 it may be a term of the inspectors' appointment that their report is not for publication.

Section 432 provides that the power of the Secretary of State is exercisable even if the company is in voluntary liquidation, and that the word 'member' in **(a)** above includes a person who is not a member but to whom shares have been transferred or transmitted by operation of law (e.g. a personal representative).

3. Duty to investigate affairs of company

Section 432 provides that the Secretary of State *must* appoint inspectors to investigate and report on a company's affairs if the court declares that its affairs ought to be investigated.

4. Investigation into affairs of connected companies

Section 433 provides that if an inspector appointed under either s. 431 or s. 432 thinks it necessary, he may also investigate and report on the affairs of any other company which is or has been within the same group.

Note that this section provides an example of 'lifting the veil of incorporation', for, in order to discover whether or not a group exists, it is essential to establish the identity of the *members*.

5. Powers of the inspector

Section 434, as amended by s. 56 Companies Act 1989, requires all officers and agents of the company and of any other company within the group to produce to the inspectors all documents in their custody or power relating to the company, or to a company within the group, to attend before them and to give them all the assistance that they reasonably can. An auditor is an agent for this purpose, and 'documents' include information recorded in any form.

This provision also extends to any other person who, in the inspectors' opinion, has or may have information about the company's affairs.

Section 434 empowers the inspector to examine any person on oath.

Moreover, by s. 436, as amended by s. 56 Companies Act 1989, the inspector may certify any obstruction to the court, and the offender then becomes punishable as if guilty of contempt of court.

6. The inspectors' report

Section 437 provides that the inspectors may, and, if directed to do so by the Secretary of State, must make interim reports to the Secretary of State, and at the end of the investigation must make a final report. Reports must be either written or printed, as the Secretary of State directs.

Section 437 requires the Secretary of State, where the inspectors were appointed under s. 432 in pursuance of a court order, to furnish a copy of their report to the court.

Additions made to s. 437 by s. 57 Companies Act 1989 provide that if it appears to the Secretary of State that matters have come to light in the course of the investigation which suggest that a criminal offence has been committed, and those matters have been referred to the appropriate prosecuting authority, he may direct the inspectors to take no further steps or only such further steps as he directs. In such a case the inspectors do not make a final report to the Secretary of State unless they were appointed in pursuance of a court order or the Secretary of State directs them to make a final report.

Under s. 437 the Secretary of State may, if he thinks fit:

(a) forward a copy of any report to the company's registered office;
(b) provide a copy on request and payment of the prescribed fee to:
  (*i*) any member of the company or any other company which is the subject of the report;
  (*ii*) any person whose conduct is mentioned in the report;
  (*iii*) the auditors of the company or any other company which is the subject of the report;
  (*iv*) the applicants for the investigation;
  (*v*) any other person whose financial interests appear to the Secretary of State to be affected by the matters dealt with in the report, whether as a creditor of such company or other company, or otherwise; *and*
(c) cause the report to be printed and published.

Section 441 provides that a copy of any inspectors' report certified by the Secretary of State to be a true copy is admissible in any legal proceedings as evidence of the inspectors' opinion concerning anything in it.

7. Powers of the Secretary of State arising from investigation

Section 124A Insolvency Act 1986, added to that Act by s. 60 Companies Act 1989, provides that if it appears to the Secretary of State from any inspectors' report or from information obtained under Part XIV of the Companies Act 1985 that it is expedient in the public interest that the company should be wound up, he may, unless the company is already being wound up by the court, *present a petition for it to be so wound up* if the court thinks it just and equitable.

Section 460 provides that if it appears to the Secretary of State from any inspectors' report or from information or documents obtained under s. 447 or 448 that there is any ground for a petition by a member under s. 459, he may, as well as or instead of presenting a winding-up petition, present a petition for an *order under s. 459* (*see* 23:**6–10**)

Finally, s. 438, as amended by s. 58 Companies Act 1989, empowers the Secretary of State himself to bring *civil proceedings* in the name of any company if, from any report made or information obtained under Part XIV of the Act, it appears to him in the public interest to do so.

Investigation of ownership

8. Power to investigate ownership of company

Section 442 provides that where there appears to be good reason to do so, the Secretary of State *may* appoint inspectors to investigate and report on the membership of any company in order to determine the true persons financially interested in its success or failure, or able to control or materially influence its policy.

9. Duty to investigate ownership of company

Section 442, as amended by s. 62 Companies Act 1989, provides that where members qualifying within s. 431 as to numbers or shareholdings (*see* 2) apply to the Secretary of State for the appointment of an inspector to make an investigation of ownership, he *must* appoint an inspector unless the application is vexatious or he thinks that an investigation under s. 444 (*see* 11) would be sufficient.

Students should note carefully, when they have learnt the figures relating to the applicants under s. 431, that while s. 431 gives the Secretary of State a *power* to appoint an inspector, s. 442 imposes on him a *duty* to do so. This is an important practical and academic distinction which, if not accurately made, leads to confused answers to examination questions.

10. Powers of inspector in an investigation of ownership

Section 442 empowers the inspector to investigate arrangements which, though not legally binding, are observed in practice.

Under s. 443, the provisions of ss. 433 (investigation into affairs of connected company), 434 (production of documents and evidence to inspectors), 436 (obstruction of inspectors treated as contempt of court) and 437 (inspectors' reports) also apply to an investigation of ownership. In an investigation of ownership, however, if the Secretary of State thinks that there is good reason for not divulging any part of a report, he may disclose the report under s. 437 with that part omitted.

11. Power to require information

Section 444 applies where it appears to the Secretary of State that the ownership should be investigated, but that it is unnecessary to appoint an inspector. It empowers the Secretary of State to require any person whom he has reasonable cause to believe to have or to be able to obtain any information as to the present or past interests in the shares or debentures of the company to give such information to him.

12. Power to impose restrictions on shares or debentures

Where the Secretary of State makes an investigation under either s. 442 or s. 444 and finds difficulty in obtaining information, s. 445 and Part XV (i.e. ss. 454–457), as amended by s. 145 and Schedule 19 Companies Act 1989, empower him to impose restrictions on the shares or debentures as follows:

(a) Any transfer of shares or debentures or, if unissued, any transfer of the right to be issued with them, shall be void.
(b) Voting rights shall not be exercisable.
(c) No further rights issues may be made (*see* 20:**14**).
(d) No payment, either of capital or otherwise, shall be made of any sums due from the company on the shares or debentures, except in a liquidation: ss. 445 and 454.

Where shares or debentures are subject to the restrictions in **(a)** above, any *agreement* to transfer them or, if they are unissued, the right to be issued with them, is *void*, unless it is made in pursuance of a court order for transfer. The same rule applies to agreements to transfer rights falling under **(c)** or **(d)** above.

Section 456 authorises any person who is aggrieved by the restrictions imposed to apply to the court for an order directing that the shares or debentures shall cease to be subject to them. An order of the court or the Secretary of State lifting the restrictions may be made only if:

(a) the court or the Secretary of State, as the case may be, is satisfied that the relevant facts about the shares or debentures have been disclosed to the company and that no unfair advantage has accrued to any person as a result of the earlier failure to make that disclosure; *or*
(b) the shares or debentures are to be transferred for valuable consideration and the court or Secretary of State approves the transfer.

Despite this rule, however, the court may always, on the application of either the Secretary of State or the company, order the shares or debentures to be sold and at the same time lift the restrictions on them.

The proceeds of the sale, less the costs, must be paid into court for the benefit of those entitled to them: s. 457.

Investigation of share dealings

13. Power to investigate share dealings
Section 446 authorises the Secretary of State, if circumstances suggest that contravention of ss. 323 (directors dealing in share options) (*see* 16:**59**), 324 (duty of directors to disclose shareholdings) (*see* 16:**13**), or 328 (extension of s. 324 to spouses and children) (*see* 16:**14**) has occurred regarding a company's shares or debentures, to appoint an inspector to investigate in order to establish whether this is the case, and to report the result of the investigation to him.

For the purposes of such an investigation, ss. 434, 436 and 437 (*see* **5, 6**) apply.

Inspection of company's documents

14. Inspection of company's documents

Section 447, as amended by s. 63 Companies Act 1989, empowers the Secretary of State if he thinks there is good reason to do so, to require the production of any specified documents from the company or from any person who appears to be in possession of them, without prejudice to that person's lien on them, if any. 'Documents' include information recorded in any form.

The power conferred by the section includes power:

(a) if the documents are produced:
    (*i*)　to take copies of or extracts from them; *and*
    (*ii*)　to require the person producing them, or any employee, or past or present officer of the company in question, to explain them;
(b) if they are not produced, to require the person required to produce them to state, to the best of his knowledge and belief, where they are.

Section 451 states that if such person gives an explanation or makes a statement which he *knows to be false in a material particular*, or gives a false explanation or makes a false statement *recklessly*, he is guilty of an offence.

Section 448, as substituted by s. 64 Companies Act 1989, authorises a justice of the peace, if satisfied by the Secretary of State that there are reasonable grounds for suspecting that there are on any premises documents which have been required but not produced, to issue a warrant authorising any constable, along with any other person named in the warrant, to enter (using such force as is reasonably necessary) and search the premises, and:

(a) to take possession of the documents;
(b) to take copies of them;
(c) to take any other steps necessary for preserving them or preventing interference with them; *and*
(d) to require any person named in the warrant to provide an explanation of them or to state where they may be found.

15. Security for information

Section 449, as amended by s. 65 Companies Act 1989, provides that no information or document obtained under s. 447 shall be published or disclosed without the company's previous consent in writing, except to a competent authority, unless publication or disclosure is required for any of a list of criminal, investigatory or disciplinary proceedings under the Act and other Acts.

For the purposes of s. 449 the following are among the 'competent authorities':

(a) the Secretary of State;
(b) an inspector;
(c) the Treasury;
(d) the Bank of England;
(e) the Director of Public Prosecutions [for Scotland, the Lord Advocate]; *and*
(f) any constable.

16. Destruction of documents

Section 450, as amended by s. 66 Companies Act 1989, makes it an offence for an officer of a company to destroy, mutilate or falsify a document relating to the company's property or affairs, or to make a false entry in it, unless he proves that he did not intend to conceal the state of affairs or defeat the law.

It is also an offence for him fraudulently to part with, alter or make an omission in any such document.

17. Investigation of overseas companies

Section 453, as substituted by s. 70 Companies Act 1989, provides that Part XIV applies to companies incorporated outside Great Britain which carry on business in Great Britain, but with some exceptions, adaptations and modifications.

The following provisions do *not* apply:

(a) s. 431 (investigation on application of company or its members);
(b) s. 438 (power to bring civil proceedings on the company's behalf);
(c) ss. 442–445 (investigation of company ownership etc.); *and*
(d) s. 446 (investigation of share dealings).

The other provisions of Part XIV apply with such adaptations and modifications as may be specified in regulations.

Majority rule and minority protection

1. The rule in *Foss* v. *Harbottle*

Next after *Salomon* v. *Salomon & Co. Ltd* (1897) the most fundamental case in company law is *Foss* v. *Harbottle* (1843) [B239]. This case is usually considered in textbooks in connection with meetings. Strictly speaking, however, it relates, like Salomon's case, to the theory of the corporate personality. The facts were as follows:

> The minority shareholders brought an action against the directors to compel them to make good losses incurred by the company owing to the directors' fraud. HELD: The action failed, for the proper plaintiff for wrongs done to the company is the company itself, and the company can act only through its majority shareholders.

[Instances in Scots law include *Lee* v. *Crawford* (1890), which was an action against a director for payment to the company of funds alleged to have been illegally lent to company officials, and *Brown* v. *Stewart* (1898), which was an action against directors for damages on the ground that they had been reckless in commencing business when too few shares had been applied for.]

The decision in *Foss* v. *Harbottle* is the logical result of the principle that a company is a separate legal person from the members who compose it. Once it is admitted that the company is a legal person, it follows that if a wrong is done to it, the company is the proper person to bring an action. This is a simple rule of *procedure* which applies to all wrongs; only the injured party may sue. If, for instance, A intentionally pushes B down the stairs because he does not like him, and B breaks his leg in consequence, it is no use if C, who has seen the whole incident, brings an action against A. C has not been hurt: he is not the injured party; he is the wrong plaintiff. The right plaintiff is B, or, sometimes, persons who are injured by having been deprived of B's services. But if a person has not been injured, he cannot sue.

Of course, as applied to companies, the rule appears a little more complicated. After all, the directors who have been fraudulent have injured the *company*. The company is composed of *members*. Losses to the company affect *all the members*, not simply the majority or the minority or any particular member. Why, then, should an individual member not sue, since he has been injured?

The answer is that injury is not enough. The plaintiff must show that the injury has been caused by a *breach of duty* to him. In the course of existence a person suffers many injuries for which no action can be brought, for no duty to him has been broken; and individual shareholders, or even the minority shareholders as a body, who try to show that the directors owe a duty to *them personally* in their management of the company's assets will assuredly fail. The directors owe no duty to the individual members, but only to *the company as a whole*. A company is a person, and if it suffers injury through breach of a duty owed to it, then the only possible plaintiff is the company itself acting, as it must always act, through its majority.

> NOTE: *Foss* v. *Harbottle* concerned a wrong done to the company by the *directors*, but it is immaterial by whom it was done. In *Leon* v. *York-O-Matic Ltd* (1966), it was stated that for wrongs done by a *liquidator*, such as selling the company's assets at an undervalue, the proper plaintiff would have been the *company*, and not a creditor or a director.

2. Advantages of the rule in *Foss* v. *Harbottle*

There are two main advantages of the rule in *Foss* v. *Harbottle*, of a purely practical nature:

(a) Clearly, if every individual member were permitted to sue anyone who had injured the company through a breach of duty, there could be as many actions as there are shareholders. Legal proceedings would never cease, and there would be enormous wastage of time and money.

(b) If an individual member could sue a person who had caused loss to the company, and the company then ratified that person's act at a general meeting, the legal proceedings would be quite useless, for a court will naturally hold that the will of the majority prevails.

3. Apparent exceptions to the rule in *Foss* v. *Harbottle*

There are a number of occasions on which an *individual member may bring an action*, and these are as follows:

(a) Where the act done is *illegal*.

> However, in *Smith* v. *Croft (No. 3)* (1987) [B254] an individual shareholder was held not to have a right to bring an action to recover money spent by directors, in breach of s. 151 (prohibition of financial assistance for acquisition of a company's own shares). Knox J. considered that the fact that a majority of the shareholders

did not wish the action for recovery to be brought was a sufficient reason for disallowing the action.

(b) Where the act can validly be done only by a special or extraordinary resolution, but in fact has been done by a simple majority: *Edwards* v. *Halliwell* (1950) [B257].

(c) Where the majority are committing a fraud on the minority.

> In *Prudential Assurance Co. Ltd* v. *Newman Industries Ltd* (*No.2*) (1981) [B260] Vinelott J. held that dicta in *Foss* v. *Harbottle* indicated that an action might be brought not only where the wrongdoers were a majority with voting control, but also where they 'were able . . . by manipulation of their position in the company to ensure that the action is not brought by the company' i.e. where they had merely *de facto control* and the interests of justice would be defeated if an action were not allowed. He further stated that the 'fraud' lies in the controllers' 'use of their voting power, not in the character of the act or transaction giving rise to the cause of action' — a useful and penetrating distinction.
>
> The Court of Appeal, however, while observing that it could not properly decide the scope of the exception to *Foss* v. *Harbottle* in this case because Vinelott J. had already permitted the action to proceed, disapproved his view that there is an exception to the rule in *Foss* v. *Harbottle* whenever the justice of the case so requires. The court was 'not convinced that this is a practical test'.
>
> More recently, in *Estmanco* (*Kilner House*) *Ltd* v. *GLC* (1982) the Vice-Chancellor, Sir Robert Megarry, held that 'no right of a shareholder to vote in his own selfish interests or to ignore the interests of the company entitles him with impunity to injure his voteless fellow shareholders by depriving the company of a cause of action and stultifying the purpose for which the company was formed'. Accordingly, he allowed a voteless shareholder to bring a derivative action (*see* 4) since in his judgment 'the exception usually known as "fraud on the minority" is wide enough to cover the present case'.

(d) Where a minority shareholder has no other remedy and the directors are using their powers, either fraudulently *or negligently*, in a manner which benefits themselves at the expense of the company: *Daniels* v. *Daniels* (1978).

(e) Where the *personal* rights of the *individual member* have been infringed e.g. voting rights: *Pender* v. *Lushington* (1877) [B263].

(f) Where a company meeting cannot be called in time to be of practical effect: *Hodgson* v. *National and Local Government Officers Association* (1972).

These six occasions are often said to be exceptions to the rule in *Foss* v.

Harbottle — exceptions which, to quote the incisive Lord Lloyd of Kilgerran, 'have taken the matter into the realms of near incomprehensibility'. If, however, they are considered carefully it appears that five of them are unconnected with it and based not so much on legal logic as on common sense. In the first four, the wrongful act is done not so much *to* the company as *by* it. If the majority act illegally, or alter the objects clause by ordinary resolution, or oppress the minority, it is the *company* who is doing these things. One cannot say that the majority constitutes the company for one purpose and not for another. And if the company is doing these things, who is to stop it except for the minority? Thus the law permits the minority to sue and, since the decision of the Court of Appeal in *Wallersteiner* v. *Moir (No.2)* (1975), to be indemnified by the company against all costs reasonably incurred in the proceedings.

The fifth occasion is of an entirely different nature. Here the wrong has been done to the individual member *as such*. His dividend has been withheld, or his vote disallowed. The company's duty to him has been broken, and he is injured thereby. Naturally in such a case he is not merely the proper plaintiff, but the only possible one, for he has contractual rights against the company, and injury has been caused to him by their breach. Thus here we have not so much an exception to *Foss* v. *Harbottle* as an example of the very principle which *Foss* v. *Harbottle* enunciates.

Only in the sixth occasion, therefore, do we have a genuine and entirely proper exception.

4. Derivative and representative actions distinguished

On all the occasions mentioned above in **3** with the exception of **(e)**, where the individual member is bringing his own action, the minority shareholders are bringing *the company's* action, since it is the company which has been injured. Because their right of action is *derived* from the company, the proceedings are known in English law as a *derivative action* and the damages payable, if any, will be paid to the *company*. [In Scotland, the minority shareholders would require to proceed in their own names.]

It may well be, however, that in addition to the company's cause of action each of a number of shareholders has a separate claim in tort [Scots law, delict] for injury caused to him. Because the injury to each of them will have been caused by the same illegal conduct, it is sufficient in English law if one of them brings a *representative* action on behalf of himself and all other members who have been similarly injured. This avoids the necessity of repeatedly proving the illegal conduct before the court. [In Scotland, the minority shareholders would require to proceed in their own names.]

In a representative action the successful plaintiff will normally obtain only *declaratory* relief, i.e. the court will hold that the illegal conduct has been satisfactorily proved. The plaintiff can then go on to claim damages on the basis of the declaration and the other injured members can do likewise.

In *Prudential Assurance Co. Ltd* v. *Newman Industries Ltd* (*No.2*) (1981) [B260] Vinelott J. held that the two claims were not mutually exclusive, and so a derivative claim could be joined with a representative claim in the same proceedings. The Court of Appeal, however, took a different view: the alleged loss suffered by the minority shareholders was not distinct from that suffered by the company and as only one loss had occurred only one action could be brought.

Further, the Court of Appeal made it clear that no shareholder is ever entitled to 'double recovery', i.e. he cannot recover damages merely because the company in which he is interested has suffered damage. He can bring a personal action only where he has suffered personal loss which is not 'merely a reflection of the loss suffered by the company', e.g. the expenses of attending a meeting.

5. Statutory protection of the minority

Throughout this book many statutory provisions for the protection of specified minorities of shareholders are included in the context of the statutory subject-matter to which they relate, e.g. the right of a 15 per cent minority to object to an alteration of the company's objects is dealt with in 2:**27**, the right of a 15 per cent minority to object to variation of class rights is dealt with in 11:**15** and the right of holders of one-tenth of issued shares to have an inspector appointed by the Secretary of State for Trade and Industry to investigate ownership of the company's shares is dealt with in 22:**9**.

It remains to consider in this chapter a group of provisions which stand on their own and now comprise Part XVII (ss. 459–461) of the Act under the heading 'Protection of Company Members against Unfair Prejudice'.

6. Former legislation

The first statutory provision in this area was s. 210 Companies Act 1948 which authorised any shareholder who complained that the company's affairs were being conducted in an *oppressive* manner to petition the court for an order to deal with the position.

Although this provision received a considerable amount of academic attention, it was in practice of very little value. It had two major weaknesses. First, it had no application to isolated acts—the petitioner had to show that there had been an oppressive *course of conduct*. Secondly, the petitioner was required to convince the court that the facts of which he complained would *justify the making of a winding-up order* by the court on the ground that it was *just and equitable* to wind the company up (*see*

30:**1** and **3**). Often he could not establish this and accordingly orders under the section were a rarity.

7. Present legislation
The Companies Act 1980 repealed and replaced s. 210 and removed both of the weaknesses mentioned above. It is the provisions derived from the 1980 Act which are now applicable under ss. 459–461 Companies Act 1985, as amended by s. 145 and Schedule 19 Companies Act 1989.

8. The petition
Section 459 provides that any member may petition the court for an order on the ground that the company's affairs are being or have been conducted in a manner which is *unfairly prejudicial* to the interests of its members generally or of some part of its members, including himself, or that any actual or proposed act or omission of the company is or would be so prejudicial.

This provision clearly enlarged the scope of the remedy in several respects. The remedy now covers the past conduct of affairs as well as the present. It covers not only an isolated act but also an isolated omission or failure to act; and it extends to a proposed or contemplated act or omission.

Further, under s. 461 the court may make such order as it thinks fit if it is satisfied that the petition is *well founded*. No mention is made of a winding-up order being justified.

By s. 459 the remedy is available to a person who is not a member but to whom shares have been transferred (i.e. an unregistered transferee) or transmitted by operation of law (i.e. a personal representative or trustee in bankruptcy). The conduct complained of, however, must have been suffered by members as members and not as directors or employees: *Elder* v. *Elder & Watson Ltd* (1952) [B241].

Finally, s. 160 provides that in certain circumstances, mentioned in 22:**7**, the Secretary of State may petition under the section.

9. The court order
As stated in **8** above, the court may make such order as it thinks fit to give relief to the petitioner in respect of the matters complained of: s. 461.

However, it is further provided that, without prejudice to the generality of that provision, a court order may:

(a) regulate the conduct of the company's affairs in the future;
(b) require the company to refrain from doing an act complained of by the petitioner or to do an act which he has complained it has omitted to do;

(c) authorise civil proceedings to be brought in the name and on behalf of the company by such person as the court directs;

(d) provide for the purchase of the shares of any members of the company by other members or by the company itself, and in the latter case for the resulting reduction of capital (*see* 13:**19**).

It should be noted that **(c)** authorises a *derivative action*—the first time that such a course has been given a statutory basis in English or Scots law (*see* **4**). Nothing is said, however, about the costs of such an action. Presumably the plaintiff would be entitled to be indemnified by the company against all costs reasonably incurred in the proceedings: *Wallersteiner* v. *Moir (No. 2)* (1975) (*see* **3**).

Lastly, it is clear from the section that the court may alter the company's memorandum or articles if it so desires, and can prohibit the company from altering these documents without the court's consent (*see* 3:**9(e)**).

10. Judicial decisions
Most of the cases which have been decided under the provisions since their amendment in the 1980 Act have arisen in small quasi-partnership companies and been concerned with attempts to exclude a shareholder from participation in the company's affairs.

The chance of success is much greater under the present provisions than it was under s. 210 Companies Act 1948. The court has a wide discretion, e.g. in fixing the price for the sale of shares in a quasi-partnership company: *Re Bird Precision Bellows Ltd* (1986) [B246]. However, the procedure is not always available, e.g. in *Re a Company No. 006834 of 1988, ex parte Kremer* (1989) where it was plain that the appropriate solution to a breakdown in the relationship of members was for the petitioner to sell his shares to the respondent or to the company *and there was machinery in the articles for determining a fair price*, the petition under s. 459 was held to be an abuse of the process of the court and was struck out.

The cases fall into three main groups:

(a) those on the interpretation of the term 'unfair prejudice';

(b) those in which the remedy was sought as an alternative to a winding-up order on 'just and equitable' grounds;

(c) those involving valuation of shares.

> An instance of **(a)** is *Re Bovey Hotel Ventures* (1981). A company was owned in equal shares by husband and wife, with two nominee shareholders each holding one share. On the breakdown of the marriage the wife was excluded from the management. The company incurred a large VAT bill. The wife applied for an order under what is now s. 461 for the purchase of either her own or her husband's shares on the ground of unfair prejudice. HELD: A

shareholder could bring himself within the provision if he could show that the value of his shares had been seriously diminished or at least seriously jeopardised by a course of conduct by those in *de facto* control of the company. The test is objective: there is no need to show bad faith on the part of the controller and the question is whether a reasonable bystander would regard the conduct as unfairly prejudicial. In this case the exclusion from management and loss of profit by payment of the unpaid VAT diminished the value of the wife's shares and was unfairly prejudicial.

Re a Company No. 002612 of 1984 is an instance of a *proposed* act being held unfairly prejudicial. The petitioner wished to prevent a proposed rights issue from being placed before an extraordinary general meeting. HELD: Although the proposal was on the face of it fair, the petitioner was unfairly prejudiced because, owing to his financial position, he would be unable to take up his allocation in the issue. The judge issued orders restraining two members from voting in favour of the proposal.

An instance of **(b)** is *Re R A Noble & Son (Clothing) Ltd* (1983). A small private company was incorporated by two persons, as shareholders and directors, to expand the business started by one of them and to be continued by him. Disputes as to the number of shares held by each and as to other financial matters arose and the second shareholder, wishing to sever his connections, petitioned alternatively for relief on the ground of unfair prejudice or a winding-up order on just and equitable grounds. HELD: As the second shareholder had for the previous five years taken no real interest in the company and the first shareholder had done little to involve him, the company's affairs were being conducted in an unfairly prejudicial manner. Mutual trust had, however, been destroyed and a winding-up order on just and equitable grounds was justified.

An instance of **(c)** is *Re London School of Electronics* (1985) [B243]. In a two-shareholder company which ran degree courses the majority shareholder appropriated potential students to its own courses. The minority shareholder set up a rival organisation and took some students with him. He then petitioned the court on the grounds of unfair prejudice. HELD: Although *prima facie* an interest in a going concern ought to be valued at the date of the order, there were in some circumstances overriding considerations of fairness which required some other date to be chosen such as the date before the conduct complained of took place. In this case the valuation had to be on the basis that the students who had gone with the petitioner had remained with the company.

24

Insider dealing

1. General meaning of expression 'insider dealing'

The expression 'insider dealing' is used to mean the dealing in the securities of a company for the purpose of private gain by a person who has inside information about them which would affect their price if it were generally known.

The topic was not covered by the Companies Act 1948 at all. The earliest legislation on it was contained in the Companies Act 1967 which made it a criminal offence in certain circumstances for a director to deal in options (*see* 16:**59**).

After that Act was passed repeated attempts were made to draft comprehensive provisions on the topic which would trap the culpable without at the same time punishing the blameless. The result of these efforts finally took statutory form in provisions of the Companies Act 1980.

In the 1985 consolidation these provisions became, without any amendment, the Company Securities (Insider Dealing) Act 1985. That consolidating Act was amended by Part VII (i.e. ss. 173–178) of the Financial Services Act 1986.

Further legislation was required to implement a Directive of the EC Council and in addition decided cases had shown that further reform of the legislation was desirable.

The legislation applicable to insider dealing is now mainly to be found in the Criminal Justice Act 1993, which wholly repealed the 1985 Act and also repealed ss. 173–176 of the Financial Services Act 1986. The statutory provisions, as reformed, now consist of Part V (ss. 52–64) and Schedules 1 and 2 Criminal Justice Act 1993 and ss. 177–178 Financial Services Act 1986 as amended by the 1993 Act.

In this chapter references to sections are to sections of the Criminal Justice Act 1993 unless the contrary is indicated.

2. The offences

There are three types of the offence of insider dealing. In each case the person guilty of the offence is 'an individual who has information as an insider', and in each case the offence relates to 'price-affected securities'.

The three types of offence are:

(a) *dealing* in price-affected securities;
(b) *encouraging another person* to deal in price-affected securities; *and*
(c) *disclosing the information*, otherwise than in the proper performance of the functions of his employment, office or profession, to another person.

For an offence to be committed under (a) or (b) the acquisition or disposal must occur on a regulated market or the person dealing must be relying on a professional intermediary or be himself acting as a professional intermediary (s. 52). By s. 60 a 'regulated market' in this context means any market identified as a regulated market by an order made by the Treasury. By s. 59 a 'professional intermediary' means a person who carries on the business of acquiring or disposing of securities or of acting as an intermediary between persons taking part in any dealing in securities, but a person is not to be treated as carrying on such a business if his activity is merely incidental to some other activity or if he merely conducts such an activity occasionally.

For the full understanding of these provisions, a number of definitions must be studied.

3. Definition of 'securities'

By s. 54 the securities to which the Act applies are those which are listed in Schedule 2 to the Act *and* which satisfy any conditions applying to them under an order made by the Treasury for the purposes of s. 54.

The list in Schedule 2 includes shares and stock of a company and debentures and debenture stock of a company or public sector body.

4. Definition of 'dealing in securities'

Section 55 provides that a person 'deals in securities' if:

(a) he acquires or disposes of the securities (as principal or as agent); *or*
(b) he procures, directly or indirectly, an acquisition or disposal of the securities by any other person.

The word 'acquire' includes agreeing to acquire the security and also entering into a contract which creates the security. Similarly, the word 'dispose' includes agreeing to dispose of the security and also bringing to an end a contract which created the security.

For the purposes of (b), above, a person procures an acquisition or disposal of a security if it is acquired or disposed of by a person who is his agent or his nominee or acts at his direction in connection with the acquisition or disposal. There may also be other circumstances in which a person is to be regarded as procuring an acquisition or disposal.

5. Definition of 'insider'

As was seen in **2** above, the offences are committed by *a person who has* *information as an insider.* Section 57 provides that a person has information as an insider if and only if:

(a) it is, and he knows that it is, *inside information; and*
(b) he has it, and knows that he has it, from an *inside source.*

The definition of 'insider', therefore, cannot be fully understood without turning to the definition of 'inside information' and of 'inside source'. The latter is the more simple and will be taken first.

By s. 57 a person has information from an inside source if and only if:

(a) he has it through being a director, employee or shareholder of an *issuer* of securities or having access to the information because of his employment, office or profession; *or*
(b) the direct or indirect source of his information is a person within **(a)**, above.

The word 'issuer,' in **(a)**, above, means, by s. 60, any company, public sector body or individual by which or by whom the securities have been or are to be issued, and 'public sector body' means a government, a local authority, an international organisation, the Bank of England or the central bank of any sovereign State.

By s. 56 'inside information' means information which:

(a) relates to particular securities or to particular issuers of securities and not to securities generally or to issuers of securities generally;
(b) is specific or precise;
(c) has not been *made public; and*
(d) if it were *made public*, would be likely to have a significant effect on the price of any securities.

Section 58 gives guidance on how information may be 'made public', but the provisions are not exhaustive as to the meaning of that expression. The section provides that information is made public if:

(a) it is published in accordance with the rules of a regulated market to inform investors and their professional advisers;
(b) it is contained in records which by any Act are open to inspection by the public;
(c) it can be readily acquired by those likely to deal in any of the securities; *or*
(d) it is derived from information which has been made public.

It is also provided, however, that information may be treated as made public even though:

(a) it can be acquired only by persons exercising diligence or expertise;

(b) it is communicated to a section of the public and not to the public at large;
(c) it can be acquired only by observation;
(d) it is communicated only on payment of a fee; *or*
(e) it is published only outside the UK.

6. Definition of 'price-affected securities'

Section 56 provides that securities are 'price-affected securities' in relation to inside information, and inside information is 'price-sensitive information' in relation to securities, if and only if the information would, if made public, be likely to have a significant effect on the price of the securities.

7. Defences

Defences are set out separately in s. 53 for each of the three types of offence.

First, in relation to *dealing*, an individual is not guilty if he shows:

(a) that he did not at the time expect the dealing to result in a profit attributable to the fact that the information was price-sensitive; *or*
(b) that at the time he believed on reasonable grounds that the information had been disclosed widely enough to ensure that none of those taking part in the dealing would be prejudiced by not having the information; *or*
(c) that he would have done what he did even if he had not had the information.

Secondly, in relation to *encouraging another person* to deal in securities, the defences are the same except that in **(b)** the words 'had been disclosed' become 'had been or would be disclosed'.

Thirdly, in relation to *disclosure of information*, an individual is not guilty if he shows:

(a) that he did not at the time expect any person, because of the disclosure, to deal in the securities; *or*
(b) that, although he had such an expectation at the time, he did not expect the dealing to result in a profit attributable to the fact that the information was price-sensitive information.

In addition, Schedule 1 to the Act enables *market makers* to avail themselves of special defences. A 'market maker' is a person who:

(a) holds himself out at all normal times in compliance with the rules of a regulated market or an *approved organisation* as willing to acquire or dispose of securities; *and*
(b) is recognised as doing so under those rules.

The term 'approved organisation' means an international securities self-regulating organisation approved under para. 25B of Schedule 1 to the Financial Services Act 1986.

8. Penalties and prosecution
An individual guilty of insider dealing is liable:

(a) on summary conviction, to a fine not exceeding the statutory maximum or imprisonment for a term not exceeding six months or to both; *or*
(b) on conviction on indictment, to a fine or imprisonment for a term not exceeding seven years or to both.

Proceedings for offences cannot be instituted in England and Wales except by or with the consent of the Secretary of State or the Director of Public Prosecutions: s. 61.

9. Effect of offence of insider dealing on contract
Section 63 provides that no contract is void or unenforceable merely because an offence of insider dealing is being committed.

10. Investigations into insider dealing
Provisions for investigations into insider dealing were introduced by the Financial Services Act 1986 to enable the offences relating to insider dealing to be more effectively detected.

Section 177 of that Act, as amended by s. 74 Companies Act 1989 and Schedule 5 Criminal Justice Act 1993, provides that if it appears to the Secretary of State that there are circumstances suggesting that an offence under Part V of the Criminal Justice Act 1993 may have been committed, he may appoint an inspector to investigate and report to him.

The inspector has power to require any person whom he considers may be able to give information concerning the subject of his investigation:

(a) to produce documents;
(b) to attend before him; *and*
(c) in any other way to give him all reasonable assistance in connection with the investigation.

The inspector may make interim reports if he thinks fit, and must make such reports if so directed by the Secretary of State. At the end of the investigation he must make a final report to the Secretary of State unless the Secretary of State has given a direction at some earlier stage that the inspector should take no further steps in the investigation.

A statement made by a person in compliance with a requirement imposed by s. 177 may be used in evidence against him, but it is permissible to refuse disclosure of information or production of documents on the grounds of legal professional privilege, and bankers have a more limited exemption.

Section 178 deals with penalties which may be imposed on a person who refuses to comply with a request made under s. 177 above or refuses to answer a question on a relevant matter.

The inspector may certify the refusal to the court and, if the court is satisfied that the alleged offender had no reasonable excuse for his refusal, it may:

(a) punish him as if he had been guilty of contempt of the court; *or*

(b) direct that the Secretary of State may cancel his authority to carry on investment business or may restrict his authority to do so to a specified extent.

25

Private companies

1. Definition of a private company

The Companies Act 1985 in s. 1 defines a private company simply as a company which is not a public company (*see* 2:**2**).

Two restrictions on offers of shares in a private company were noted in 7:**1**: ss. 143 and 170 Financial Services Act 1986.

Apart from these two provisions, there are no further *restrictions* on a private company as such, and the differences between public companies and private companies arise from the *privileges* which the Acts have conferred on the latter.

These privileges have been substantially increased by the Companies Act 1989, in particular by a group of provisions (ss. 113–117) under the heading 'De-regulation of private companies'.

A further important piece of legislation took the form of a statutory instrument — the Companies (Single Member Private Limited Companies) Regulations 1992 (SI 1992, No. 1699) — to implement the Twelfth EC Company Law Directive. It provided that from 15 July 1992 a private limited company could be formed with only one member.

The differences between public and private companies have already been dealt with according to their subject-matter in earlier chapters but it may be convenient to have them also listed in this chapter (*see* **6**).

First, however, it is appropriate to deal with the statutory provisions governing the procedure by which a private company converts into a public company, and vice versa.

2. Capital requirements for conversion to public company

Section 45 imposes strict initial rules regarding the share capital of any private company seeking conversion. Before it can be re-registered as a public company, it must satisfy two of the same conditions required of a company registered as a public company on its original incorporation when such a company applies for a trading certificate, namely:

(a) the nominal value of its allotted share capital must be not less than the authorised minimum (*see* 2:**34**); *and*
(b) not less than one quarter of the nominal value of each allotted share, together with the whole of any premium on it, must have been paid up (*see* 5:**2** and 9:**15**).

There are, however, two further conditions to be satisfied under s. 45 owing to the fact that ss. 99 and 102 do not apply to private companies (*see* 10:**1** and 9:**16**). Thus safeguards are required when conversion is sought:

(c) where any share in the company, or any premium on it, has been paid up by *an undertaking to do work or perform services* for the company, that undertaking must have been performed; and
(d) where shares have been allotted as paid up as to their nominal value or any premium on them *otherwise than in cash*, and the consideration for the allotment includes an undertaking to the company which *does not fall within* **(c)** *above*, then *either*:
  (*i*) that undertaking must have been performed; *or*
  (*ii*) there must be a contract between the company and some person under which that undertaking is to be performed *within five years*.

Where **(b)** above has not been complied with as regards shares allotted under a share scheme for employees, those shares may be disregarded for the purpose of compliance with **(b)**–**(d)**, but must then be treated for the purpose of **(a)** as though they were not part of the allotted share capital.

In addition to the four requirements of s. 45, s. 44 imposes two more conditions which apply where, between the date of the balance sheet and the passing of the special resolution for re-registration, shares are allotted as paid up as to their nominal value or any premium on them *otherwise than in cash*. In these circumstances the company may not apply for re-registration as a public company unless:

(a) the consideration has been valued in accordance with s. 108; *and*
(b) a report has been made on its value during the six months immediately preceding the allotment (*see* 9:**18** and **19**).

3. Procedure for re-registration of private company as public company.
Section 43 governs the procedure to be followed for the re-registration of a private company with a share capital as a public company.

The first step is for the company to pass a special resolution for re-registration which:

(a) alters its memorandum so that it states that the company is to be a public company; *and*
(b) makes all other necessary alterations in both its memorandum and articles.

Next, an application for re-registration, signed by a director or secretary, must be delivered to the registrar along with the following documents:

(a) a printed copy of the *altered memorandum and articles*;

(b) a copy of a written *statement by the company's auditors* that in their opinion the relevant balance sheet shows that the amount of the company's net assets at the date of the balance sheet was not less than the aggregate of its called-up capital and undistributable reserves;

(c) a copy of the *relevant balance sheet*, i.e. one prepared as at a date not more than seven months before the company's application, together with a copy of an *unqualified report by the auditors*;

(d) a copy of any *report* prepared under s. 44 (*see* **2** above); *and*

(e) a *statutory declaration* by a director or secretary:

> (*i*) that the special resolution for re-registration has been passed and the conditions specified in ss. 44 and 45 have been satisfied (*see* **2** above); *and*
>
> (*ii*) that between the date of the balance sheet and the application for re-registration there has been no change in the company's financial position resulting in the amount of its net assets falling below the aggregate of its called-up capital and undistributable reserves.

Under s. 47 the registrar may accept this declaration as sufficient evidence that the special resolution has been passed and the conditions satisfied. He then retains the application and other documents and issues the company with a certificate of incorporation stating that it is a public company. On the issue of the certificate the company becomes a public company and any alteration in its memorandum and articles takes effect. The certificate is conclusive evidence that all the requirements of the Act regarding re-registration have been complied with, and that the company is a public company.

It should be noted that under s. 48 the same procedure, with slight and obvious modifications, is required for the re-registration of an *unlimited* (and therefore necessarily private) company as a public company. Furthermore, s. 77 Insolvency Act 1986 protects the interests of creditors where an unlimited company re-registers as a limited company and then goes into liquidation within the next three years (*see* 28:**4**).

Finally, s. 104, which brings into play the rules in s. 109 relating to the valuation of non-cash assets when acquired by the company from a subscriber to the memorandum, applies where a private company re-registers as a public company and non-cash assets equal to one-tenth or more of the nominal value of its issued share capital are acquired by the company from persons who were members at the date of re-registration within two years from that date (*see* 6:**5–7** and 9:**18–20**).

4. Procedure for re-registration of public company as private company

Section 53 prescribes the procedure for the converse operation, namely the re-registration of a public company as a private company. Although this is a far less common occurrence, it is sometimes seen where one company has taken over another and the holding company wishes to alter the status of its subsidiary (*see* 13:13).

The first step, once again, is the passing of a special resolution for re-registration by the company which:

(a) alters its memorandum so that it no longer states that the company is a public company; *and*
(b) makes all other necessary alterations in both its memorandum and articles.

Next, an application for re-registration, signed by a director or secretary, must be delivered to the registrar together with a printed copy of the altered memorandum and articles.

Furthermore, either the period for making an application to the court under s. 54 to cancel the resolution must have expired without such an application having been made or, if such an application has been made, it must have been withdrawn or a court order made confirming the resolution and a copy of that order delivered to the registrar.

Under s. 55 the registrar then retains the application and other documents and issues the company with an appropriate certificate of incorporation. On the issue of the certificate the company becomes a private company and the alterations in its memorandum and articles take effect. The certificate is conclusive evidence that all the requirements of s. 53 regarding re-registration have been complied with, and that the company is a private company.

5. Provision for dissentient members

It can be seen from **4** above that an application can be made to the court to cancel a resolution passed by a public company for re-registration as a private company. Section 54 governs such an application, dealing with the applicants, the period of time allowed and the powers of the court.

Such an application may be made:

(a) by the holders of not less than 5 per cent in nominal value of the company's issued share capital or any class thereof;
(b) if the company is not limited by shares, by not less than 5 per cent of its members; *or*
(c) by not less than 50 of the company's members.

No person who has voted in favour of the resolution can apply.

The application must be made within 28 days of the passing of the resolution. The court must then make an order either cancelling or confirming the resolution on such terms as it thinks fit, and may adjourn the proceedings in order that an arrangement may be made for the purchase of the interests of the dissentient members.

The court order may provide for the purchase by the company of the shares of any members and for the resulting reduction of capital (*see* 13:**20**). It can also make any alterations to the memorandum or articles which are thereby rendered necessary and prohibit the company from making subsequent alterations to these documents. The company may then make such alterations only with the leave of the court (*see* 3:**9(d)**).

Finally, the registrar must be kept informed. As soon as an application to the court is made, the company must notify him. Then, when the court order is made, the company must deliver to him within 15 days an office copy of it.

6. Differences between public and private company
A private company differs from a public company in the following ways:

(1) The statutory minimum of directors is one: s. 282.

(2) Two or more directors can be appointed by a single resolution of a general meeting: s. 292.

(3) A director holding office for life on 18 July 1945 (now almost extinct) cannot be removed by ordinary resolution under s. 303: s. 14 Companies Consolidation (Consequential Provisions) Act 1985.

(4) There is no statutory age-limit on the directors unless the company is a subsidiary of a public company: s. 293.

(5) There is no requirement that the secretary shall have qualifications: s. 286.

(6) A private company can convert from a limited company to an unlimited company: s. 49.

(7) A private company limited by guarantee is, on complying with certain conditions, exempt from the provisions of the Act regarding the use of the word 'limited' as part of its name: s. 30.

(8) A proxy may speak at general meetings: s. 372.

(9) The directors are not required to convene an extraordinary general meeting where the company's net assets fall to half or less of its called-up capital: s. 142.

(10) No minimum authorised capital is required on registration: s. 11.

(11) A private company can commence business immediately on registration and requires no trading certificates: s. 117.

(12) A private company must not apply for its shares to be listed on the Stock Exchange: s. 143 Financial Services Act 1986.

(13) A private company must not offer its shares by advertisement unless exempted by the Secretary of State for Trade and Industry: s. 170 Financial Services Act 1986.

(14) Shares issued by a private company to a subscriber to the memorandum are not required to be paid up in cash: s. 106.

(15) Where a subscriber to the memorandum of a private company sells non cash assets to the company, there is no requirement that those assets shall be valued by an expert: s. 104.

(16) It is unnecessary for 25 per cent of the nominal value of the shares in a private company to be paid up on allotment: s. 101.

(17) A private company is not prohibited from accepting payment for its shares in the form of an undertaking to do work or perform services for the company: s. 99.

(18) Non-cash consideration to be furnished to a private company in respect of an allotment of shares need not be so furnished within five years: s. 102.

(19) Non-cash consideration furnished to a private company in respect of an allotment of shares need not be valued by an expert: s. 103.

(20) The statutory pre-emption rights can be totally excluded by the memorandum or articles of a private company: s. 91.

(21) A private company may declare a dividend even though the amount of its net assets is less than the aggregate of its called-up share capital and its undistributable reserves: s. 264.

(22) A private company is not required to file interim accounts to support a proposed interim dividend: s. 272.

(23) The strict rules applicable to shares in which the company itself has a beneficial interest do not apply to private companies: s. 146.

(24) A private company is not subject to the statutory restrictions on the taking of a lien or charge on its own shares: s. 150.

(25) A private company which is not in the same group as a public company is not prohibited from making quasi-loans to its directors or entering into credit transactions with them: ss. 330 and 331.

(26) A private company which is not in the same group as a public company is not prohibited from making loans to persons connected with a director: ss. 330 and 331.

(27) The rules relating to the giving of financial assistance by a company for the purpose of the acquisition of its own shares are less stringent for a private company: ss. 151–158.

(28) Only a private company may be entitled to deliver modified accounts to the registrar: s. 246.

(29) A private company is subject to one less rule than a public company in the case of an off-market purchase by the company of its own shares: s. 164.

(30) A private company is subject to fewer rules regarding the disclosure of purchases of its own shares: s. 169.

(31) Only a private company is permitted to purchase its own shares out of capital: s. 171.

(32) A private company is not required to keep a register of interests in shares under s. 211.

(33) A private company, if limited by shares or by guarantee, need have only one member: Companies (Single Member Private Limited Companies) Regulations 1992 (SI 1992, No. 1699).

The following further differences were added by the Companies Act 1989, by provisions inserted in the 1985 Act by ss. 113–117 Companies Act 1989:

(34) A private company may operate by written resolutions instead of by resolutions (of any type) passed at meetings, with the exceptions of a resolution under s. 303 for the removal of a director and a resolution under s. 391 for the removal of an auditor: ss. 381A and Schedule 15A.

(35) By an elective resolution under s. 379A, a private company may extend the authority of the company required for allotment under s. 80 to an unrestricted period or to a fixed period exceeding five years: s. 80A.

(36) By an elective resolution under s. 379A, a private company may dispense with the laying of accounts and reports before the company in general meeting: s. 252.

(37) By an elective resolution under s. 379A, a private company may dispense with holding an annual general meeting: s. 366A.

(38) By an elective resolution under s. 379A, a private company may authorise shorter notice for a meeting where there is a 90 per cent (instead of 95 per cent) approval of persons entitled to attend and vote: ss. 369 and 378.

(39) By an elective resolution under s. 379A, a private company may dispense with annual appointment of auditors.: s. 386.

Finally, it should be noted that, by s. 117 Companies Act 1989, the Secretary of State may by regulations extend the right of private companies to elect, by elective resolution under s. 379A, to dispense with any further statutory requirements which are specified in the regulations, provided the Secretary of State considers that the requirements relate primarily to the internal administration and procedure of companies.

26

Dissolution and insolvency

1. Methods of dissolution

A company is like a contract in that, having been created by a legal process, it can only be destroyed by a legal process. It will not evaporate or disappear. A contract is created by agreement supported by consideration, and destroyed by one of the methods of discharge familiar to students of commercial law. [In Scots law consideration is not necessary for the creation of a contract.] A company is created by registration, and destroyed by one of the methods of dissolution which we are about to consider. They are as follows:

(a) A company which has been registered with *illegal* objects can be dissolved by the taking of proceedings by the Attorney General for *cancellation of the registration*.

> Thus *R. v. Registrar of Companies, ex parte Attorney General* (1991) [B34], Miss St Claire, who was engaged in the business of prostitution, was advised to register a limited company for the purposes of her business. The registrar rejected the names of Prostitutes Ltd, Hookers Ltd, and Lindi St. Claire French Lessons Ltd, but finally accepted the name of Lindi St. Claire (Personal Services) Ltd and the company was duly registered. The Attorney General successfully applied to have the registration cancelled on the ground that the purpose of the company was unlawful.

(b) A company which is transferring its undertaking to another company under a scheme for reconstruction or amalgamation may, according to s. 427, be *dissolved without winding up*, if the court so orders (*see* 32:**1–5**).
(c) A company which is *defunct* may be *struck off the register* by the registrar, under s. 652, and will then be *dissolved* (*see* 31:**26–27**).
    This is now a very common method of dissolution, as it is both cheap and easy.
(d) A company may be *wound up*, i.e. *liquidated*.

It is unnecessary to say more about **(a)**, and there is very little to be learnt about **(b)** and **(c)**, both of which will be discussed later. Liquidation, however, is a lengthy topic and it must be studied in more detail (*see* Chapters 28-31).

2. The Insolvency Act 1986

The provisions of the Companies Act 1985 relating to winding up were amended by the Insolvency Act 1985. The amended provisions together with the unamended provisions were then consolidated in the Insolvency Act 1986. Therefore *in the remainder of this chapter and in Chapters 28-31* which are devoted to winding-up *references to sections are to be taken as references to sections of the Insolvency Act 1986 unless the contrary is indicated.*

It should be kept clearly in mind throughout this and the succeeding chapters that, while most companies which go into liquidation are insolvent, i.e. cannot pay their debts in full, insolvency is not an essential ingredient of liquidation. Indeed, it will be seen that in one type of liquidation — a members' voluntary winding up — it is essential that the company *is able* to pay its debts in full. Fortunately, *all* the winding-up provisions, including those relating to companies which are not insolvent, have been consolidated in the Insolvency Act 1986. One should not be misled by the short title 'Insolvency Act 1986' into thinking otherwise.

A further preliminary point which must be mentioned is that the Insolvency Act 1986 also includes Parts which deal with the bankruptcy of individuals in England and Wales. These Parts can for present purposes be omitted. However, there are certain provisions in the Act which relate both to insolvent companies and to insolvent individuals, e.g. the categories of preferential debts and the qualification of being an insolvency practitioner. Such matters, so far as they affect companies, are treated within Chapter 31, which deals with the provisions of general application in winding up.

3. Methods of winding up and sections to be studied

There are two methods of winding up, according to s. 73:

(a) *voluntary* winding up, which may, by s. 90, be either:
   (*i*) a *members'* voluntary winding up; *or*
   (*ii*) a *creditors'* voluntary winding up; *and*
(b) winding up *by the court*, i.e. *compulsory* liquidation.

The main problem in studying liquidation is not its difficulty, but its length. Students find it an unmanageable topic, and do not know where to start. Here an attempt has been made to simplify it so that they will not feel too aware of the size of the subject, and it is hoped that they will then be able to read the many detailed books on it without losing their way.

The provisions to be studied comprise *principally Part IV* of the Insolvency Act 1986 and range from s. 73 to s. 219. This need cause no alarm, for there are many sections which can be omitted, and there are many to which a very short reference is enough. It is helpful if they are grouped so that the student knows where he is:

Sections 73–83	These are general sections applying to both methods of winding up and concerning *contributories*.
Sections 84–116	These sections deal with *voluntary* winding up, but are subdivided:
ss. 84–90	General sections.
ss. 91–96	*Members'* voluntary winding up.
ss. 97–106	*Creditors'* voluntary winding up.
ss. 107–116	Sections applying to both kinds of voluntary winding up.
Sections 117–162	These sections deal with winding up *by the court*.
Sections 163–219	These again are general sections applying to both methods of winding up.

In addition there are provisions in *Part VI* of the Act which must be looked at. Part VI covers miscellaneous provisions applying to *companies* which are *insolvent or in liquidation*, e.g. the liquidator's administration in getting in the company's property, his right to apply to court for inquiry to be made into the company's dealings, and what challenge can be made of transactions at an undervalue, preferences, extortionate credit transactions and floating charges [and the distinctive provisions for gratuitous alienations and unfair preferences in Scotland].

It should be noted that these provisions apply not only to a liquidator but also to the administrator, if an administration order is made under Part II of the Act (*see* Chapter 27).

Finally, as has been stated above, there are a few other provisions which are common to *company and individual insolvency*: of these, preferential debts are dealt with in Part XII of the Act and the qualifications of insolvency practitioners in Part XIII.

4. Company insolvency rules

Despite the numerous sections to be studied, there is also a substantial volume of subordinate legislation, since many of the detailed provisions relating to winding up are contained not in the Act itself but in company insolvency rules.

The rules at present in force are the Insolvency Rules 1986 (SI 1986, No. 1925), as amended, for England and Wales and the Insolvency (Scotland) Rules 1986 (SI 1986, No. 1915 (S. 139)), as amended, for Scotland.

Section 411 provides for the making of such rules by the Lord Chancellor with the concurrence of the Secretary of State for Trade and Industry [in Scotland by the Secretary of State alone], and Schedule 8 indicates the provisions which are capable of being included in the rules.

These provisions include provisions relating to:

(a) *court procedure* when a court is involved in the winding up;
(b) the form, contents and publication of *notices* and the persons to whom they are to be given;
(c) the way in which a *provisional liquidator* is to carry out his functions;

(d) the way in which the various *meetings* are to be summoned and conducted;

(e) the establishment and proceedings of the various *committees* of creditors and liquidation committees for which the Act provides;

(f) the *proving of debts*;

(g) the *distribution* of the company's property, including unclaimed funds and dividends;

(h) financial matters including the *liquidator's remuneration, investment* of receipts and winding-up *expenses*;

(i) *records* required to be kept *by officers of courts* in England and Wales and the inspection of these records by contributories and creditors;

(j) proceedings at *public examinations*;

(k) the *liquidator's books*, accounts and other records and their inspection and disposal;

(l) the *auditing* of the liquidator's accounts; *and*

(m) making non-compliance with any of the rules a *criminal offence*.

The matters for which provisions may be made under Schedule 8 include matters arising under voluntary arrangements (*see* **6–8**) or where there is an administration order (*see* Chapter 27).

The content of the rules is beyond the scope of this book, but the existence of the rules and the general nature of the matters for which they may provide must be constantly borne in mind in the study of the provisions of the Act itself as given in the remaining chapters of this book.

5. Alternatives to winding up

The winding-up procedure has been recognised as being in some situations an over-drastic means of dealing with a state of insolvency. The Insolvency Act 1985 introduced two new alternatives to liquidation, namely:

(a) company voluntary arrangements; *and*

(b) administration orders.

The provisions relating to **(a)** now comprise Part I of the Insolvency Act 1986 and are outlined in **6–8** below. The provisions relating to **(b)** now comprise Part II of that Act and are the subject-matter of Chapter 27.

6. Company voluntary arrangements

Sections 1–7 relate to a new procedure introduced by the Insolvency Act 1985 with a view to enabling a company which is nearly or actually insolvent to resolve its financial difficulties to the satisfaction of its creditors without the formality and expense necessarily involved in other procedures available under the Acts.

Safeguards are, however, necessary to prevent abuse of an informal procedure, and the principal safeguard in this case is the requirement that the person who acts in connection with the voluntary arrangement and sees to its implementation must be qualified as an 'insolvency practitioner'.

7. The proposal

Section 1 provides that the directors of a company may make a proposal to the company and to its creditors for a *composition in satisfaction of its debts* or a *scheme of arrangement of its affairs*. The term 'voluntary arrangement' is used to cover both of these.

The proposal is that some person (at this stage referred to as 'the nominee') should act in relation to the voluntary arrangement either as trustee or otherwise for the purpose of supervising its implementation, and the nominee must be a person who is qualified to act as an insolvency practitioner in relation to the company (*see* 31:**15**).

The proposal may be made even if an administration order (*see* Chapter 27) is in force and even if the company is being wound up, but in those circumstances it is not the directors who make the proposal but the administrator or the liquidator as the case may be.

Section 2 provides that where the nominee is not the administrator or liquidator, he must, within 28 days after he has been given notice of the proposal (or longer if the court allows), submit a report to the court, stating:

(a) whether, in his opinion, meetings of the company and of its creditors should be summoned to consider the proposal; *and*
(b) the date, time and place at which he proposes that any such meetings should be held.

For the purposes of enabling the nominee to prepare his report, the person intending to make the proposal must submit to the nominee:

(a) a document setting out the terms of the proposed voluntary arrangement; *and*
(b) a statement of the company's affairs containing prescribed information including particulars of its creditors, of its debts and other liabilities and of its assets.

If the nominee fails to submit the required report, the person intending to make the proposal may apply to the court for the nominee to be replaced by another qualified insolvency practitioner.

By s. 3 the nominee, if he is not the administrator or liquidator and has reported to the court under s. 2 that meetings of the company and its creditors should be summoned, must proceed to do so unless the court directs otherwise.

Section 3 provides that where the nominee is the liquidator or administrator he must summon meetings of the company and of its creditors to consider the proposal for such a time, date and place as he thinks fit. There is no need for a report to be made to court in this situation.

8. Consideration and implementation of proposal

Section 4 provides that the meetings summoned under s. 3 must decide whether to approve the proposed voluntary arrangement, with or without modifications, e.g. they may make a change of nominee. However, a modification must not be so radical as to take the arrangement outside the definition of 'voluntary arrangement' in s. 1, and the rights of secured and preferential creditors cannot be altered by the proposal (or by any modification of it) without the concurrence of the creditor concerned. At the end of either meeting the chairman reports the result of it to the court and to prescribed persons.

By s. 5 where each of the meetings summoned under s. 3 approves the proposed voluntary arrangement either with the same modifications or without modifications, then the arrangement takes effect as if made by the company at the creditors' meeting and binds every person who had notice of, and was entitled to vote at, that meeting (whether or not he was present or represented) as if he were a party to the arrangement.

Section 5 further provides that if an administration order is in force or the company is being wound up, the court may do one or both of the following:

(a) by order, discharge the administration order or stay the winding-up proceedings;

(b) give directions as to the conduct of the administration or winding up to facilitate the implementation of the voluntary arrangement.

An order under **(a)** must not be made until 28 days from the date of the chairman's reports or, where an application is made to court under s. 6, a final decision has been reached by the court.

Section 6 allows the decisions taken at the meetings to be challenged by an application to the court on one or both of the following grounds:

(a) that the arrangement unfairly prejudices the interests of a creditor, member or contributory of the company;

(b) that there has been some material irregularity at or in relation to either of the meetings.

The persons who may make such an application are:

(a) a person entitled to vote at either of the meetings;

(b) the nominee; *and*

(c) if an administration order is in force or the company is being wound up, the administrator or liquidator.

The application must be made within 28 days of the chairman's reports to the court under s. 4.

If the court is satisfied as to either of the grounds mentioned above, it may do one or both of the following:

(a) revoke or suspend the approval given by the meetings;
(b) give a direction to any person for the summoning of further meetings.

Section 7 provides that once a voluntary arrangement has taken effect, the nominee becomes known as the 'supervisor' of the arrangement.

The remainder of s. 7 concerns the role which the court may play in relation to the implementation of the proposal:

(a) If any of the company's creditors or any other person is dissatisfied by an act, omission or decision of the supervisor, he may apply to the court, and on such an application the court may:

(*i*) confirm, reverse or modify any act or decision of the supervisor;
(*ii*) give him directions; *or*
(*iii*) make such other order as it thinks fit.

(b) The supervisor may apply to the court for directions as to any particular matter arising under the arrangement, and he is included among the persons who may apply to the court for an administration order or for winding up.

(c) The court may make an order appointing a qualified insolvency practitioner in substitution for the existing supervisor, to fill a vacancy or to be an additional supervisor. These powers are to be exercised only where it is difficult for an appointment to be made without the court's assistance.

Administration orders

1. The object of administration orders

The Insolvency Act 1985 introduced administration orders as a new procedure for dealing with the affairs of a company which was likely to be or which actually was insolvent. The aim is to rescue and rehabilitate the company so that it will survive as a going concern, or, if that proves impossible, to ensure a more advantageous realisation of its assets than would result from a winding up.

The statutory provisions on administration orders now comprise Part II (i.e. ss. 8–27) of the Insolvency Act 1986.

2. Definition of 'administration order'

By s. 8 an administration order is an order of the court directing that, during the period for which the order is in force, the affairs, business and property of the company shall be managed by a person ('the administrator') appointed for the purpose by the court.

3. Circumstances in which an administration order may be made

Section 8 provides that the court may make an administration order in relation to a company if the court:

(a) is satisfied that the company is or is likely to become unable to pay its debts; *and*
(b) considers that the making of an order would be likely to achieve one or more of the following purposes:

  (*i*) the survival of the company, and the whole or any part of its undertaking, as a going concern;
  (*ii*) the approval of a voluntary arrangement under Part I of the Act (*see* 26: **6–8**);
  (*iii*) the sanctioning under s. 425 Companies Act 1985 of a compromise or arrangement between the company and its creditors or members (*see* 32:**1–5**); *and*
  (*iv*) a more advantageous realisation of the company's assets than would be obtained on a winding up.

An administration order must not be made in relation to a company after it has gone into liquidation.

The interpretation of the words 'likely to achieve one or more of the purposes' as used in s. 8 was considered in *Re Harris Simons Construction Ltd* (1989). The court has to be satisfied that there is a real prospect that one or more of the stated purposes may be achieved, but it is not necessary for the evidence to establish that the purpose will more probably than not be achieved. See also *Re Primlaks (UK) Ltd* (1989) [B231] for the same point and for the reasons why an administration order was granted in that case. The court retains a discretion to refuse to make an appointment. In this case an order was made.

4. Application for and making the order

Section 9 provides that an application for an administration order is by petition presented to the court by the company or its directors or by a creditor or creditors or by all or any of those parties.

Notice of the petition must immediately be given to any person who has appointed, or is entitled to appoint, an administrative receiver and to other prescribed persons.

Where there is an administrative receiver of the company and the person by whom he was appointed has not consented to the making of an administration order, the court must dismiss the petition unless the security which led to the appointment of the receiver is open to challenge under the provisions dealing with transactions at an undervalue and preferences (*see* 31:**20, 21**) or avoidance of floating charges (*see* 31:**23**).

Section 10 provides that during the period between the presentation of the petition and the making of the order (or the dismissal of the petition as the case may be):

(a) no resolution may be passed or order made for winding up the company;
(b) no steps may be taken to enforce any security over the company's property or to repossess goods in the company's possession under a hire-purchase agreement except with the leave of the court. *and*
(c) no other proceedings and no execution or other legal process may be begun or continued against the company or its property except with the leave of the court.

That provision, however, does not prevent a petition for winding up from being *presented*, or an administrative receiver from being appointed or a receiver (whenever appointed) from carrying out any of his functions.

5. Effect of order

Section 11 provides that the making of an administration order has the following consequences:

(a) Any petition for the winding up of the company must be dismissed.

(b) Any administrative receiver of the company must vacate office.

(c) Any receiver of part of the company's property must vacate office on being required to do so by the administrator.

Section 11 also provides that during the period for which an administration order is in force:

(a) no resolution may be passed or order made for the winding up of the company;

(b) no administrative receiver of the company may be appointed;

(c) no other steps may be taken to enforce any security over the company's property or to repossess goods in the company's possession under a hire-purchase agreement except with the consent of the administrator or the leave of the court: *and*

(d) no other proceedings and no execution or other legal process may be begun or continued against the company or its property except with the consent of the administrator or the leave of the court.

In an application to court for leave to enforce a security (*see* **(c)** above), the onus is on the secured creditor to show that it is a proper case for leave to be given but it is not essential to show some criticism of the administrator's conduct: *Royal Trust Bank* v. *Buchler* (1989).

The words 'other proceedings' in **(d)** above should be interpreted narrowly using the *ejusden generis* rule: *Air Ecosse Ltd* v. *Civil Aviation Authority* (1987) [B232].

Further, s. 12 provides that while the administration order is in force every document issued by the company or by the administrator on which the company's name appears must also contain the administrator's name and state that the affairs, business and property of the company are being managed by him. Failure to comply with this provision makes the company and any officer or the administrator who without reasonable excuse authorises or permits the default liable to a fine.

6. Appointment of administrator

Section 13 provides that the administrator is appointed by the administration order or, if a vacancy occurs by death, resignation or otherwise, by the court on an application being made to it:

(a) by any continuing administrator; *or*

(b) where there is none, by the creditors' committee (*see* **10**); *or*

(c) where there is neither a continuing administrator nor a creditors' committee, by the company or the directors or any creditor.

7. Powers of administrator

Section 14 confers on the administrator the general power to do all such things as may be necessary for the management of the affairs, business and property of the company, and provides that that general power covers all the 23 specific powers listed in Schedule 1. The 23 listed powers are the same as the powers which, by s. 42, are conferred on the administrative receiver (unless they are inconsistent with the provisions of the debentures under which the administrative receiver was appointed), (*see* 21: **18**).

By s. 14 the administrator also has power:

(a) to remove any director and appoint a director;
(b) to call any meeting of members or creditors; *and*
(c) to apply to the court for directions with regard to any particular matter arising in carrying out his functions.

Any power conferred on the company or its officers by the Companies Act 1985 or the Insolvency Act 1986 or by the memorandum or articles cannot be exercised without the administrator's consent if its exercise would interfere with the exercise by the administrator of his powers.

The administrator in exercising his powers is deemed to act as the company's agent, and a person dealing with him in good faith and for value is not concerned to inquire whether he is acting within his powers.

Section 15 makes special provision to enable the administrator to dispose of secured property as if it were not subject to the security.

If the security is a floating charge, the holder of it must be treated as having the same priority over company property representing the property disposed of as he would have had over the secured property itself.

In the case of a security other than a floating charge, the administrator must apply to court and satisfy the court that the disposal would be likely to promote one of the purposes specified in the administration order (*see* **3**). The net proceeds of the disposal and any sum necessary to make that amount up to the amount which would have been obtained if the property had been sold in the open market by a willing seller must be applied towards discharging the sum secured. An office copy of the court's order must be sent by the administrator to the registrar of companies within 14 days.

8. Duties of administrator

The Act imposes the following duties on the administrator:

(a) By s. 17 he must, on his appointment, *take into his custody* all the property to which the company is entitled.
(b) He must then *manage* the affairs, business and property of the company in accordance with any directions given by the court up to the time

when his proposals have been approved by a meeting of creditors (*see* 9). After that time he must act in accordance with the approved proposals.

(c) By s. 21 he must *immediately* after the administration order has been made send to the *company and publish in the prescribed manner a notice of the order*, and, *within 28 days* after the making of the order (unless the court otherwise directs), send the *same notice to all creditors* whose addresses he knows.

(d) He must also, *within 14 days* after the making of the order, send an office copy of the order to the *registrar of companies and other prescribed persons*.

(e) By s. 22 he must *immediately* after the order has been made require a *statement of the company's affairs* to be made out and submitted to him.

It must be in the prescribed form, verified by affidavit, and show:

(*i*) particulars of assets, debts and liabilities;

(*ii*) names and addresses of creditors;

(*iii*) securities held by them, and the dates when these were given; *and*

(*iv*) any further information which may be prescribed.

The persons who may be required to submit the statement are:

(*i*) past or present officers of the company;

(*ii*) persons who have taken part in its formation within one year before the date of the administration order;

(*iii*) persons who are, or have been within that year, in the company's 'employment' (widely defined as including employment under a contract for services) and who are capable of giving the required information;

(*iv*) persons who are, or have been within that year, officers or in the employment of another company which is or has been within that year, an officer of the company concerned.

The statement must be submitted *within 21 days* from the administrator's notice requiring it.

(f) By s. 23 the administrator must, *within three months* (or longer if the court allows) after the making of the order:

(*i*) send to the registrar of companies and to all creditors whose addresses he knows a *statement of his proposals* for achieving the purposes specified in the order; *and*

(*ii*) lay a copy of the statement before a meeting of creditors summoned for the purpose on not less than 14 days' notice.

(g) He must also, *within the same three months* (or longer if the court allows, *either*:

(*i*) send a copy of the statement to all members whose addresses he knows; *or*

(*ii*) publish in the prescribed manner a notice stating an address to which members should write for copies of the statement to be sent to them free of charge.

(h) After the creditors' meeting at which his proposals are considered, he must, by s. 24, report the result of the meeting to the court, and give notice of the result to the registrar of companies and to prescribed persons.

(i) When the administration order is discharged, he must, by ss. 18, 24 and 27, *within 14 days* after the order effecting the discharge, send an office copy of that order to the registrar of companies.

(j) If, after proposals have been approved, he proposes to make substantial revisions of them, he must, by s. 25, follow the same procedure as in **(f)**, **(g)** and **(h)** above except that the result of the meeting need not in this case be reported to the court.

9. Consideration of proposals

Section 24 provides that the meeting of creditors summoned under s. 23 must decide whether to approve the administrator's proposals. By s. 24 the meeting may approve the proposals *with modifications*, but only if the administrator consents to each modification.

If the meeting declines to approve the administrator's proposals, the court may by order discharge the administration order or adjourn the hearing or make an interim or any other order that it thinks fit.

10. Creditors' committee

Section 26 provides that where the creditors' meeting has approved the administrator's proposals (with or without modifications), the meeting may, if it thinks fit, establish a committee ('the creditors' committee') which may, on giving not less than seven days' notice, require the administrator to attend before it and furnish it with such information relating to the carrying out of his functions as it may reasonably require.

11. Protection of creditors and members

Section 27 is designed to protect the interests of creditors and members where an administration order is in force.

By this section a creditor or member may apply to the court by petition for an order on the ground that:

(a) the company's affairs, business and property are being managed by the administrator in a manner which is *unfairly prejudicial* to the interests of its creditors or members generally or of some of them (including at least himself); *or*

(b) any actual or proposed act or omission of the administrator is or would be of that nature.

The court may make such order as it thinks fit for giving relief or it may adjourn the hearing or make an interim or any other order that it thinks fit. In particular the order may:

(a) regulate the future management by the administrator of the company's affairs, business and property;
(b) require the administrator to refrain from doing or continuing an act complained of or to do an act which he has omitted to do;
(c) require the summoning of a meeting of creditors to consider such matter as the court may direct;
(d) discharge the administration order.

On the other hand, an order under s. 27 must not prevent either:

(a) the implementation of a voluntary arrangement under Part I of the Act (*see* 26:**6–8**) or any compromise or arrangement under s. 425 Companies Act 1985 (*see* 32:**1–5**); *or*
(b) the implementation of proposals or revised proposals if the application for the order has not been made within 28 days after the approval of the proposals or revised proposals as the case may be.

12. Discharge or variation of order.

Section 18 provides that the administrator may at any time apply to the court for the administration order to be discharged or to be varied so as to specify an additional purpose.

The administrator *must* make such an application if:

(a) it appears to him that the purposes specified in the order either have been achieved or are incapable of being achieved; *or*
(b) he is required to do so by a meeting of the company's creditors.

On hearing the application, the court may order the administration order to be discharged or varied, or may adjourn the hearing or make any interim or other order that it thinks fit.

13. Vacation of office

Section 19 provides that the administrator may at any time be removed from office by order of the court, and may, in prescribed circumstances, resign his office by giving notice to the court.

He *must* vacate office if:

(a) he ceases to be qualified to act as an insolvency practitioner in relation to the company; *or*
(b) the administration order is discharged.

Where a person ceases to be administrator, his remuneration, any expenses properly incurred and debts and liabilities arising out of contracts entered into or contracts of employment adopted by him in carrying out his functions are paid out of any property in his custody in priority to any floating charge over that property.

14. Release of administrator

Section 20 provides that a person who has ceased to be the administrator has his release from the following times:

(a) if he has died, the time at which notice is given to the court;
(b) in any other case, the time decided on by the court.

The effect of the release is to discharge him from all liability for acts or omissions in his conduct as administrator, but this does not prevent the exercise against him of the summary remedy under s. 212 (misapplication of property or breach of duty to the company).

15. Other provisions applicable to administration orders

The account given above is confined to the provisions of Part II of the Act. There are, however, provisions elsewhere in the Act which apply to administration orders. In particular, in Part VI of the Act ('Miscellaneous Provisions Applying to Companies which are Insolvent or in Liquidation'), s. 230 provides that the administrator must be a person who is qualified to act as an insolvency practitioner in relation to the company (*see* 31: **15**), and several later sections in that Part provide that the administrator is an 'office-holder' for the purposes of the section in question. These sections deal with supplies of the public utilities such as gas, electricity and water (s. 233), getting in the company's property (s. 234), the duty to co-operate with the office-holder (s. 235), application to court for inquiry (ss. 236–237), and the challenge of prior transactions which were at an undervalue (s. 238) or preferences (s. 239), or extortionate credit transactions (s. 244), or invalid floating charges (s. 245), or unenforceable liens (s. 246). These will be dealt with in Chapter 31 since they are provisions of general application in winding up as well as where an administration order has been made (*see* 31:**16–24**).

Contributories

1. Definition of a contributory

Section 79 defines a contributory as *every person liable to contribute to the assets of a company in the event of its being wound up.*

Section 81 provides that if a contributory dies, his personal representatives become liable to contribute to the assets and so become contributories. Moreover, if they default in paying any money due, the company may take administration proceedings in order to compel payment out of the estate (*see* 13:**10**)

Section 82 provides that if a contributory becomes bankrupt, his trustee in bankruptcy represents him and becomes a contributory, and that the estimated value of his liability to future calls, as well as calls already made, may be proved against (i.e. claimed from) the bankrupt's estate.

2. Liability of a contributory

Section 80 provides that the liability of a contributory creates a *debt* (in England and Wales in the nature of a *specialty*) accruing due from him at the time when his liability commenced (i.e. when he acquired the shares), but *payable when calls are made.*

Section 74 is a lengthy section, giving the details of the liability of the contributories. It does not refer to the terms 'A list' and 'B list' so that these require some explanation. The term 'A list' denotes the list of all those persons whose names were on the company's register of members at the commencement of the liquidation. The term 'B list' denotes the list of all those persons who were members *within the year preceding the commencement of the liquidation*, but who had transferred their shares before liquidation commenced. The two lists together form the contributories, i.e. persons who are liable to contribute to the assets in accordance with s. 74.

Section 74 provides first, in a general statement, that every present and past member is liable to contribute to the assets of the company on liquidation an amount sufficient to pay its debts. It then proceeds to qualify this statement in the following way:

(a) A *past* member (B list) is not liable to contribute if he ceased to be a member a year or more before the commencement of the winding up, i.e.

he is liable *only* if he ceased to be a member *within a year* preceding the winding up.

(b) A *past* member is not liable in respect of any debt contracted after he ceased to be a member.

(c) A *past* member is not liable unless the *existing* members (A list) are unable to satisfy the contributions required from them.

(d) In a company limited by shares, no contribution is required from *any member*, past or present, exceeding the amount, if any, *unpaid on the shares* in respect of which he is liable (limited liability).

(e) In a company limited by guarantee, no amount is required from any member exceeding the amount of the guarantee. If, however, such a company also has a share capital, then the member will be liable not only up to the amount of the guarantee, but also up to the amount unpaid on the shares, so that he has a double, if limited, liability.

(f) A sum due to a member *in his character of member,* by way of dividends, profits or otherwise, shall not be deemed a debt of the company payable to that member in the case of competition between himself and any other creditor not a member, though it may be taken into account in adjusting the rights of the contributories among themselves.

This curiously worded little paragraph is, of course, a reference to the order of distribution of assets. Students are often puzzled by it, asking what is the position if a trade creditor is also a member. Does the fact that he is a member deprive him of his priority, since the Act says 'creditor not a member'? Probably the correct view to take is that the Act means 'creditor regarding a debt which has *not arisen* in respect of his shares'.

3. Contribution and distribution

The rules given above, apart from **(f)**, relate to *contribution*. They do not affect *distribution* by the liquidator of the assets on which he can lay his hands. This can have some odd practical results.

Thus the liquidator must first call upon persons on the A list (*see* **(c)** above). Only if the individual A list member cannot pay the amount due on his shares may the liquidator resort to the person on the B list, if any, in respect of those shares. If the A list member has owned the shares for a year or more, there is then no one to whom the liquidator can resort in respect of those shares.

Having received such A list assets as he can collect, the liquidator applies those assets to *all the debts of the company, pari passu, in the order of distribution of assets, irrespective of the date when any particular debt was contracted.* Thus he will dispose of the creditors with fixed charges first, set aside a sum for costs, pay the preferential creditors next, and then the creditors with floating charges. Finally he will reach the unsecured creditors. Let us suppose that at this point he has not enough money to pay them all in full: he will then pay them, *pari passu*, as much as he can, e.g. 50p in £1.

Only then can he resort to the B list, and even when he does so he can only claim from a B list member when the corresponding A list member has been unable to pay. Moreover, he is now restricted by **(b)** above. If all the outstanding debts were contracted *after* the persons on the B list had transferred their shares, he cannot claim contribution from any of them. But let us suppose that there is one debt of £500 contracted *before* six B list members had transferred their shares. There are many other debts amounting to £10,000 in all contracted *after* all the B list members had transferred their shares. The total liability on the shares of the six B list members is £1000. In such a case the liquidator can demand from them *only* £500, **(b)**, and he must apply this £500 *pari passu* towards *all the debts*. It is clear that if he has £500 to apply towards debts of £10,500, each creditor will receive only one-twenty-first of the amount which he is owed. The single B list creditor will therefore receive one-twenty-first of £500; yet there is still a liability on the B list shares of £500.

4. Special rules where an unlimited private company re-registers as limited

Section 77 lays down special rules which apply where an unlimited private company has re-registered as limited (*see* 2:**32**) and then goes into liquidation. These rules also apply where an unlimited private company re-registers as a public (and therefore necessarily limited) company. They are as follows:

(a) Despite s. 74 (*see* **2 (a)**) (which imposes a time limit of one year on the liability of a past member), a past member who was a member of the company *at the time of re-registration* is liable to contribute to the assets in respect of debts contracted *before* that time if the winding up commences within *three years* from re-registration.

(b) Despite s. 74 (*see* **2 (c)**) (which exonerates past members entirely unless the existing members are unable to meet their obligations), where *all* the existing members have become members *since* the time of re-registration, a person who was a past or present member *at that time* is liable to contribute to the assets in respect of debts contracted *before* that time, even though the existing members have satisfied the contributions required from them.

This rule is subject to the time limits imposed on liability both by s. 74 (*see* **2 (a)**) and s. 77 (*see* **(a)**, above).

(c) Despite s. 74 (*see* **2 (e)**) (which imposes a limit on the liability of a member of a company limited by shares or guarantee), the liability of any person who was a *past or present member* of the company *at the time of re-registration* in respect of debts contracted *before* that time is *unlimited*.

The intention of the section is clearly to ensure that the members of an unlimited company do not escape their obligations by re-registering the company as limited. No provision, however, seems to have been made for *distribution*, and it seems a little hard on the creditors who dealt with an unlimited company that they should receive exactly the same proportion of the distributed assets as those creditors who dealt with the company after it re-registered as limited. This is especially the case where the distributed assets are greatly increased by the rules of *contribution* given above.

Voluntary winding up

1. Resolutions for voluntary winding up

Section 84 provides that a company may be wound up voluntarily:

(a) when the *period*, if any, fixed for its duration by the articles *expires*, or the *event*, if any, *occurs*, on the occurrence of which the articles provide that it is to be dissolved, and the company has passed an *ordinary resolution* to be wound up voluntarily;

(b) if the company passes a *special resolution* to be wound up voluntarily;

(c) if the company passes an *extraordinary resolution* to the effect that it cannot continue its business *by reason of its liabilities*, and that it is advisable to wind up.

Section 85 requires notice of any of the above resolutions to be given by the company within 14 days by advertisement in the *Gazette*.

2. The commencement of voluntary winding up

As in bankruptcy, the *moment of commencement* of the winding up is of great legal importance. Section 86 states that the moment of commencement of a voluntary winding up is the time of the *passing of the resolution.*

3. The consequences of a voluntary winding up

These are:

(a) Under s. 87, the company ceases to carry on business, except so far as is required for its beneficial winding up.

(b) Also under s. 87, the company's corporate state and powers continue until dissolution.

(c) Under s. 88, any transfer of shares without the sanction of the liquidator, and any alteration in the status of members, is void.

(d) Under s. 91 and s. 103, the powers of the directors cease on the appointment of a liquidator. But in a *members'* voluntary winding up the company in general meeting or the liquidator can sanction their continuance, while in a *creditors'* voluntary winding up the liquidation committee (*see* 11) or, if there is no such committee, the creditors may do so. If the company has passed the resolution for winding up but no liquidator has yet been appointed, the directors must not, by s. 114, exercise their powers without the sanction of the court except for the limited purposes of disposing of perishable goods and other goods the value of which is likely to diminish if they are not immediately disposed of and of doing all other things as may be necessary for the protection of the company's assets.

(e) If the liquidation occurs because of insolvency, the company's servants are dismissed. The liquidator may continue the employment of the servants, but this will be a new contract.

(f) By s. 112 the liquidator or any contributory or creditor may apply to the court to decide any question arising in the winding up and to exercise any of the powers which the court might exercise in a winding up by the court (*see* 30:**26–29**).

4. The declaration of solvency

Section 89 provides that where it is proposed to wind up a company voluntarily, the *directors* or, *if more than two, the majority of them,* may at a board meeting make a statutory declaration that they have inquired into the company's affairs and have formed the opinion that it will be able to pay its debts in full within a specified period not exceeding 12 months from the commencement of winding up.

This declaration is ineffective unless:

(a) it is made *within the five weeks preceding* the date of the passing of the resolution for winding up, or on that date but before the passing of the resolution; *and*

(b) it contains a *statement of assets and liabilities* as at the latest practicable date.

The declaration must be delivered to the registrar within 15 days after the passing of the resolution.

A director who makes this declaration without reasonable grounds for his opinion is liable to imprisonment or a fine or both. Further, if the company is duly wound up but its debts are not paid in full within the specified period, it is presumed (unless the contrary is shown) that the director did not have reasonable grounds for his opinion. This provision puts the burden of proof on the director concerned.

The declaration of solvency is extremely important, for it *determines the nature of the winding up.* Section 90 provides that when such a declaration *has been* made as above, the winding up is a *members'* voluntary winding up. When it *has not been* made, the winding up is a *creditors'* voluntary winding up.

Accordingly we must now see first what the Act provides regarding a members' voluntary winding up, and then what it provides regarding a creditors' voluntary winding up.

5. Appointment of liquidator in members' voluntary winding up

Section 91 empowers the *company* in general meeting to appoint a liquidator.

Section 92 empowers the *company* in general meeting also to fill any casual vacancy in the office of liquidator, subject to any arrangement with its creditors.

6. Liquidator's duty to call meetings in members' voluntary winding up

Section 93 requires the liquidator to summon a general meeting of the company at the end of the first year from the commencement of the winding up, and of each succeeding year, or at the first convenient date within three months from the end of the year or such longer period as the Secretary of State may allow, and to lay before the meeting an account of his acts and dealings and of the conduct of the winding up during the preceding year.

7 Final meeting and dissolution in members' voluntary winding up

Section 94 provides that, as soon as the winding up is completed, the liquidator must make up an account of the winding up, showing how it has been conducted and the property disposed of, and must call a general meeting by advertisement in the *Gazette*, stating the time, place and object of the meeting, and published at least one month before the meeting. He must lay the account before this meeting.

Within a week after the meeting, he must send a copy of the account to the registrar, and make a return to him of the holding and date of the meeting. If, however, a quorum is not present at the meeting, he must make a return that the meeting was duly called, and that no quorum was present.

The registrar, under s. 711 Companies Act 1985, must publish in the *Gazette* the receipt by him of the return.

By s. 201 the registrar, on receiving the account and return under s. 94, must immediately register them, and on the expiration of three months from the registration of the return the company is *deemed to be dissolved*. However, by s. 201, the court, if applied to by the liquidator or other interested person, may make an order deferring the date of dissolution.

8. Insolvency of company in members' voluntary winding up

If in a *members'* voluntary winding up the liquidator is at any time of the opinion that the company will not be able to pay its debts in full within the period stated in the declaration of solvency, s. 95 requires him:

(a) to summon a meeting of creditors for a day not later than the 28th day after the day on which he formed that opinion;

(b) to post notices of the meeting to the creditors not less than seven days before the date of the meeting;

(c) to cause notices of the meeting to be advertised in the *Gazette* and in two local newspapers;

(d) during the period before the meeting, to furnish creditors free of charge with such information concerning the company's affairs as they may reasonably require; *and*

(e) to make out a statement in the prescribed form as to the affairs of the company, lay that statement before the meeting and attend and preside at the meeting.

The statement under **(e)** must show:

    (*i*) particulars of the company's assets, debts and liabilities;

    (*ii*) the names and addresses of the creditors;

    (*iii*) the securities held by each of them;

    (*iv*) the dates when these securities were given; *and*

    (*v*) such other information as may be prescribed.

By s. 96 the winding up, as from the day of the creditors' meeting, is in effect converted into a creditors' voluntary winding up, as if no declaration of solvency had been made.

9. Creditors' meeting in a creditors' voluntary winding up

In a creditors' voluntary winding up s. 98 requires the company:

(a) to cause a meeting of its creditors to be summoned for a day not later than the 14th day after the day on which there is to be held the company meeting at which the resolution for voluntary winding up is to be proposed;

(b) to cause the notices of the creditors' meeting to be posted to the creditors not less than seven days before the date of the meeting; *and*

(c) to cause notice of the creditors meeting to be advertised in the *Gazette* and in two local newspapers.

The notice of the creditors' meeting must state *either*:

(a) the name and address of a person qualified to act as an insolvency practitioner (*see* 31:**15**) who, during the period before the meeting, will furnish creditors free of charge with such information concerning the company's affairs as they may reasonably require; *or*

(b) a place in the locality of the company's principal place of business where, on the two business days immediately before the date of the meeting, a list of the names and addresses of the company's creditors will be available for inspection free of charge.

Section 99 provides that the directors must:

(a) make out a statement in the prescribed form as to the company's affairs;

(b) cause that statement to be laid before the creditors' meeting; and

(c) appoint one of themselves to preside at the meeting;

and that it is the duty of that director to attend the meeting and preside over it. The statement of the company's affairs must show the same information as the statement of affairs required under s. 95 (*see* **8**).

10. Appointment of liquidator in creditors' voluntary winding up

Section 100 provides that both the creditors and the company at their respective meetings may nominate a liquidator. If they nominate different persons, the *creditors'* choice prevails. If the creditors do not make a nomination, then the *company's* nominee becomes the liquidator.

If two different persons are nominated so that the creditors' nominee becomes the liquidator, any director, member or creditor may apply to the court within seven days for an order either that the company's nominee shall be the liquidator instead of or together with him, or appointing some other person.

If a vacancy occurs in the office of liquidator, s. 104 provides that, unless the liquidator was appointed by the court, the creditors may fill the vacancy.

11. Liquidation committee in creditors' voluntary winding up

Section 101 provides that the creditors at their first or any subsequent meeting may appoint a committee (the 'liquidation committee') consisting of *not more than five* persons. If they do so, the company may also appoint *not more than five* persons to act as members of the committee.

If, however, the creditors resolve that all or any of the persons appointed by the company ought not to be members, then those persons are not qualified to act unless the court directs otherwise, and the court may appoint other persons to act as members instead of those mentioned in the resolution.

12. Liquidator's duty to call meetings in creditors' voluntary winding up

Section 105 makes the same provision for the holding of general meetings of the company as is made by s. 93 relating to a members' voluntary winding up (*see* **6**), but adds that *creditors' meetings* must also be held at the same times.

13. Final meeting and dissolution in creditors' voluntary winding up

Section 106 makes the same provision for the holding of a final general meeting of the company as is made by s. 94 (*see* 7), relating to a members' voluntary winding up, but adds that a final *creditors' meeting* must also be held.

Section 711 Companies Act 1985 and s. 201 Insolvency Act 1986 also apply in the same way (*see* 7).

14. Powers of liquidator in voluntary winding up

The remaining sections of the Act dealt with in this chapter apply to either voluntary winding up, whether it is a members' or a creditors' winding up.

The powers of the liquidator in a voluntary winding up are to be found in ss. 165 and 166 taken along with Schedule 4, which is in three Parts.

Part I of Schedule 4 sets out the powers which are exercisable *with sanction*. By s. 165 the sanction required by the liquidator for the exercise of these powers is in a *members'* voluntary winding up the sanction of an extraordinary resolution of the company, and in a *creditors'* voluntary winding up the sanction of the court or the liquidation committee (or, if there is no such committee, a meeting of the company's creditors).

The powers in Part I of Schedule 4 are:

(a) power to pay any class of creditors in full;
(b) power to make any compromise or arrangement with creditors; *and*
(c) power to compromise all calls, debts and liabilities and all claims between the company and a contributory or other debtor and all questions in any way relating to the assets or the winding up of the company.

By s. 165 the liquidator in either type of voluntary winding up may *without sanction* exercise either of the powers specified in Part II of Schedule 4, which are:

(a) the power to bring or defend any action or legal proceeding in the name and on behalf of the company; *and*
(b) the power to carry on the business of the company so far as may be necessary for its beneficial winding up.

He may also *without sanction* exercise any of the *general* powers specified in Part III of Schedule 4. It will be seen in the next chapter that these general powers can be exercised without sanction in a winding up by the court also.

The general powers set out in Part III of Schedule 4 are:

(a) power to sell any of the company's property by public auction or private contract;
(b) power to do all acts and execute, in the name and on behalf of the company, all deeds, receipts and other documents and for that purpose to use, when necessary, the company's seal if the company has a seal;

(c) power to prove, rank and claim in the bankruptcy or insolvency of any contributory;

(d) power to draw, accept, make and indorse any bill of exchange or promissory note in the name and on behalf of the company;

(e) power to raise on the security of the assets of the company any money which is necessary;

(f) power to take out in his official name letters of administration to any deceased contributory, and to do in his official name any other act necessary for obtaining payment of any money due from a contributory or his estate which cannot conveniently be done in the name of the company;

(g) power to appoint an agent to do any business which he is unable to do himself; *and*

(h) power to do all such other things as may be necessary for winding up the company's affairs and distributing its assets.

By s. 165 the liquidator in either type of voluntary winding up may:

(a) settle a list of contributories (which is *prima facie* evidence of the liability of the persons named in it to be contributories);

(b) make calls; *and*

(c) summon general meetings of the company for the purpose of obtaining its sanction by special or extraordinary resolution or for any other purpose he may think fit.

Section 165 further provides that where the liquidator in exercising his powers disposes of any of the company's property to a person who is 'connected' with the company, he must notify the liquidation committee, if there is one, of that fact. By s. 249 a person is 'connected' with a company if *either*:

(a) he is a director or shadow director of the company or an associate of such director or shadow director; *or*

(b) he is an associate of the company.

The term 'associate' for this purpose has a wide and detailed definition set out in s. 435 of the Act. It covers a great variety of family, partnership, employment, trust and corporate relationships.

15. Restriction on liquidator's powers in creditors' voluntary winding up

Section 166 imposes a restriction on the powers of a liquidator in a *creditors'* voluntary winding up during the period after the liquidator has been nominated by the company and before the holding of the creditors' meeting under s. 98, at which a different person may be nominated as liquidator (*see* **10**). The restriction is that the liquidator during that period requires the sanction of the court for the exercise of his powers, except that he may, without sanction:

(a) take into his custody or under his control all the property to which the company is or appears to be entitled;
(b) dispose of perishable goods and other goods the value of which is likely to diminish if they are not immediately disposed of; *and*
(c) do all such other things as may be necessary for the protection of the company's assets.

It is further provided that the liquidator must attend the creditors' meeting held under s. 98 and report to the meeting on any exercise by him of his powers.

16. Court's power to appoint and remove liquidator in voluntary winding up

Section 108 empowers the court to appoint a liquidator in a voluntary winding up if from any cause whatever there is no liquidator acting.

The same section empowers the court to remove a liquidator *on cause shown* and to appoint another.

The widely worded phrase 'on cause shown' is clearly intended to give the court an unfettered discretion in the matter, and the expression certainly includes insanity, bias, dishonesty, and undesirability on any grounds. It is not necessary to show personal misconduct or unfitness: failure to carry out his duties with sufficient vigour is enough: *Re Keypak Homecare* (1987).

17. Notice by liquidator of his appointment

Regardless of the manner in which he is appointed, the liquidator is required within 14 days by s. 109 to publish in the *Gazette* and deliver to the registrar a notice of his appointment.

If the appointment is not duly notified and is not shown by the company to have been known at the time to the person concerned then, under s. 42 Companies Act 1985, it cannot be relied on by the company against that person.

18. Removal of liquidator in voluntary winding up otherwise than by order of court

Section 171 provides that, as a general rule, the liquidator in a voluntary winding up may be removed from office only by an order of the court (*see* **16**) or:

(a) in a *members'* voluntary winding up, by a general meeting of the company summoned specially for that purpose; or

(b) in a *creditors'* voluntary winding up, by a general meeting of the company's creditors summoned specially for that purpose.

By s. 171, however, there is this exception. if the liquidator was appointed by the court under s. 108 (*see* **16**), a meeting for replacing him can only be summoned if he thinks fit *or* the court so directs *or* the meeting is requested:

(a) in a *members'* voluntary winding up, by members representing at least one-half of the total voting rights; *or*
(b) in a *creditors'* voluntary winding up, by at least one-half in value of the company's creditors.

19. Vacation of office by liquidator in voluntary winding up
By s. 171 a liquidator must vacate office if he ceases to be a person who is qualified to act as an insolvency practitioner in relation to the company.

He must also vacate office after the holding of the final meeting or, in the case of a creditors' voluntary winding up, meetings, as soon as he has complied with the requirement for giving notice to the registrar that the meeting or meetings have been held and of the decisions (if any) of the meeting or meetings.

Section 171 also provides that a liquidator may, in prescribed circumstances, resign his office by giving notice of his resignation to the registrar.

20. Release of liquidator in voluntary winding up
The release of the liquidator in a voluntary winding up is dealt with in s. 173.

A person who has ceased to be a liquidator has his release from the following times:

(a) if he has been removed from office by a general meeting of the company or of the company's creditors which has not resolved against his release, or if he has died, the time at which notice is given to the registrar that he has ceased to hold office;
(b) if he has been removed from office by a general meeting of creditors which has resolved against his release, or by the court, or if he has vacated office under s. 171 on the ground that he is no longer qualified to act as insolvency practitioner, the time fixed by the Secretary of State [in Scotland, by the Accountant of Court] on an application being made to him by that person;
(c) if he has resigned, the time prescribed;
(d) if he has vacated office under s. 171 after the holding of the final meeting of the company in a members' voluntary winding up, or the holding of the final meetings of the company and of creditors in a creditors' voluntary winding up, the time at which he vacated office,

unless the final meeting of creditors resolved against his release, in which case he must apply to the Secretary of State [in Scotland, to the Accountant of Court] for a time to be fixed.

The effect of a release is to discharge the liquidator from all liability for his conduct in the winding up, but this does not prevent the exercise of the summary remedy under s. 212 against a liquidator who has misapplied the company's property or been guilty of any misfeasance or breach of any duty in relation to the company: s. 173.

21. Power of liquidator to sell the company's property for shares

Usually the liquidator sells the undertaking and all the property of the company for *cash*, which is then distributed in the normal way to creditors and members. But sometimes he sells them for *shares* in another company, so that the members, instead of receiving their capital and any surplus assets in the form of money, become *shareholders in another company*.

In the final chapter we shall consider the various methods of company reconstruction and amalgamation, of which this is one. At this point, however, we must consider the provisions of s. 110 which enable the liquidator to make this arrangement.

The section provides that when a company is in a *members' voluntary liquidation*, and the whole or part of its business or property is to be transferred to *another company*, the liquidator may, with the sanction of a *special resolution*, accept in compensation *shares in the transferee company* for distribution among the members of the transferor company.

Such an arrangement is binding on the members of the transferor company, but s. 111 protects dissentients. It permits any member who did not vote in favour of the special resolution to dissent in writing to the liquidator at the registered office within seven days of the passing of the resolution, and to require the liquidator *either* to abstain from implementing the arrangement *or* to purchase his shares.

If, as is usually the case, the liquidator decides to purchase his shares, the purchase-money must be paid before the company is dissolved, and it must be raised by the liquidator in such a way as is determined by special resolution.

The provisions of ss. 110 and 111 apply in exactly the same way in a *creditors'* voluntary winding up, except that s. 110 prevents the liquidator from exercising his powers without the *sanction of the court or the liquidation committee*.

22. Expenses of voluntary winding up

By s. 115 all expenses properly incurred in the winding up, including the remuneration of the liquidator, are paid out of the company's assets in priority to all other claims.

23. Right of creditor or contributory to winding up by the court

Section 116 provides that the fact that a company is in voluntary liquidation does not bar the right of a creditor or contributory to have it wound up *by the court*, if there are proper grounds. If a contributory should apply, however, the court will not make an order for winding up by the court unless it is satisfied that the rights of the contributories will be prejudiced by a voluntary winding up.

Winding up by the court

1. Circumstances in which a company may be wound up by the court

Section 122 Insolvency Act 1986 provides that a company may be wound up by the court if:

(a) the company has passed a special resolution to that effect;

(b) a public company registered as such on its original incorporation has not been issued with a certificate under s. 117 Companies Act 1985 within a year from registration (*see* 5:3);

(c) the company does not commence business within one year from incorporation or suspends business for a whole year;

(d) (as amended by the Companies (Single Member Private Limited Companies) Regulations 1992) except in the case of a private limited company, the number of members is reduced below two;

(e) the company is unable to pay its debts;

(f) the court is of the opinion that it is just and equitable that the company should be wound up;

[(g) in Scotland, there is a floating charge and the court is satisfied that the security of the creditor entitled to the benefit of the charge is in jeopardy, as is deemed to be the case where events have occurred or are about to occur which make it unreasonable in the creditor's interests that the company should retain power to dispose of the property which is subject to the floating charge].

2. Definition of inability to pay debts

Section 123 explains what is meant by **(e)** above. It provides that a company is deemed unable to pay its debts if:

(a) a creditor for more than £750 has served on the company a demand for the sum due, and the company has for three weeks neglected to pay it or to secure or compound for it to his satisfaction; *or*

(b) in England and Wales execution is unsatisfied [in Scotland, the induciae of a charge for payment on an extract decree have expired without payment being made]; *or*

(c) it is proved to the court's satisfaction that the company is unable to pay its debts as they fall due; *or*

(d) it is proved to the court's satisfaction that the value of the company's assets is less than the amount of its liabilities, taking into account its contingent and prospective liabilities.

In *Taylor's Industrial Flooring Ltd* v. *M. & H. Plant Hire (Manchester) Ltd* (1990) the Court of Appeal held that if a debt is due from a company and it is not disputed, the failure of the company to pay it is evidence of an inability to pay debts and there is no need to serve a statutory demand.

3. The meaning of 'just and equitable'

The court's power under s. 122 to wind a company up on the ground that it is just and equitable to do so is purely discretionary. There is therefore no definite number of occasions on which the court will exercise its power, but it has done so in the following cases:

(a) Where the substratum or main object has failed: *Re German Date Coffee Co.* (1882) [B72].
(b) Where there was deadlock in the management: *Re Yenidje Tobacco Co. Ltd* (1916) [B272].
(c) Where the company was formed for a fraudulent purpose.
(d) Where the company was a 'bubble', i.e. it never in fact had any business or property.
(e) Where a director had voting control and refused to hold meetings, produce accounts or pay dividends: *Loch* v. *John Blackwood Ltd* (1924).
(f) Where, in a private company which distributed its profits as directors' remuneration and paid no dividends, all three of the members were directors, and one of them was removed from office as director under what is now s. 303 Companies Act 1985 by the other two: *Ebrahimi* v. *Westbourne Galleries Ltd* (1973) [B273].

Here the House of Lords held that the words 'just and equitable' are *general words* of wide application and must not be restricted:

(*i*) to particular instances; *nor*
(*ii*) by the previous clauses of the section; *nor*
(*iii*) to cases where *mala fides* can be provided; *nor*
(*iv*) to circumstances where the petitioner is wronged in his capacity of *shareholder*.

Further, while the concepts of probity, good faith and mutual confidence, and the remedies where these are absent, developed in the law of partnership, they apply in the same way to registered companies, and it is merely confusing to refer to small companies of this kind as 'quasi-partnerships'. Individuals in companies have rights and obligations *inter se* which are not submerged in the company structure, and the 'just and equitable' provision enables the court to subject the exercise of legal rights (such as the right to remove a director under what is now s. 303 Companies Act 1985) to equitable considerations.

The court will not, however, grant an injunction to *prevent* the exercise of legal rights, even though it may give a remedy for the inequitable use of them: *Bentley-Stevens* v. *Jones* (1974).

Where the entitlement to management participation is the basis of the relationship between the members, it appears that exclusion from management will be a ground for winding up whether it arises from the inequitable exercise of legal rights or a repudiation of the legal rights of others: *Re A. & B. C. Chewing Gum* (1975).

4. The presentation of the winding-up petition

While s. 122 (*see* **1**) gives the *grounds* on which a company may be wound up by the court, s. 124 gives the *persons* by whom the petition for winding up may be presented.

Under s. 124 there are *the following possible petitioners*:

(a) The *company*, after passing a special resolution (*see* **1**).
(b) The *directors*.

The petition must be presented by *all* the directors and not merely by two out of three of them: *Re Instrumentation Electrical Services* (1988).
(c) A *creditor*, including a contingent or prospective creditor.

A judgment creditor has a right to a winding-up order even though the company has a disputed claim for a larger sum against him: *Re Douglas Griggs Engineering Co.* (1963).
(d) A *contributory*, whether A list or B list. Despite the definition of a contributory in s. 79, the term includes for the purposes of s. 124 a holder of *fully-paid shares*: *Re National Savings Bank Association* (1866) [for Scotland, *Walker and Others, Petitioners* (1894)] (*see* 28:**1, 2**).

A contributory, however, may petition only if one of the following conditions is fulfilled:

(*i*) if the membership is reduced below two (*see* 2:**33**); *or*
(*ii*) if he is an original allottee; *or*
(*iii*) if he has held his shares for any six out of the previous 18 months; *or*
(*iv*) if the shares devolved on him through the death of a former holder.

The last three provisions are designed to prevent a person from buying shares in a company with the sole intention of qualifying himself to bring a winding-up petition. Section 124, however, permits a contributory to bring a winding-up petition under grounds **(e)** or **(f)** in **1** above where he is liable under s. 76 (*see* 11:**36**).

A *personal representative* of a *deceased* contributory, even though he is not registered as a member in respect of the shares, is a contributory for the purposes of s. 124: *Re Bayswater Trading Co. Ltd* (1970) [for Scotland, *Howling's Trustees* v. *Smith* (1905)]. An *unregistered* allottee of shares is likewise a contributory for the purposes of s. 124 since there is nothing in that section which expressly requires registration: *Re J.N.2 Ltd* (1978). An unregistered *trustee in bankruptcy* of a *bankrupt* contributory, however, is not: *Re Bolton Engineering Co. Ltd* (1956).

(e) The *Secretary of State*, if the ground of the petition is that specified in **(b)** in 1 above or in a case falling within s. 124A inserted in the Insolvency Act 1986 by s. 60 Companies Act 1989 (expedient in the public interest, following report of inspectors, etc.) (*see* 22:7).

(f) In England and Wales, the *official receiver*, where the company is already in voluntary liquidation, and the interests of the creditors or contributories are not adequately protected.

An example of this occurred in *Re Ryder Installations Ltd* (1966), where the voluntary liquidator's conduct was irregular and his accounts unsatisfactory.

The statutory right to present a winding-up petition in accordance with the section cannot in any way be restricted or excluded by provisions to that effect in the articles.

5. Non-statutory rules concerning petitioners
Apart from the possible petitioners under s. 124, there are decisions establishing that the following persons may present a winding-up petition:

(a) a secured creditor (who will not lose his security by doing so);

(b) a creditor's executor;

(c) an assignee of a debt or part of a debt, including in England and Wales an equitable assignee;

(d) a holder of bearer debentures;

(e) a mortgagee who intends to exercise his power of sale (but he will be restrained from so doing until his petition is heard);

(f) a shareholder whose calls are in arrear (but he must first pay the amount of the call into court).

Conversely, the holder of a share warrant cannot present a petition.

6. Powers of court on hearing petition
Section 125 empowers the court to dismiss the petition, or adjourn the hearing, or make any order that it thinks fit, but provides that it *must not refuse* to make a winding-up order merely because the assets have been fully mortgaged or because there are no assets at all. Despite this provision, however, a fully-paid shareholder is not entitled to a winding-up

order unless he can show that he, as a member of the company, will achieve some advantage or avoid or minimise some disadvantage which would accrue to him by virtue of his membership: *Re Chesterfield Catering Co. Ltd* (1977).

Section 125 further provides that where the petition is presented by members on the ground that it is just and equitable that the company should be wound up, the court must make a winding-up order unless it is of the opinion that the petitioners have some other remedy available to them, and that they are acting unreasonably in failing to pursue it. A good example of this situation occurred in *Charles Forte Investments* v. *Amanda* (1964) (*see* 12:7).

7. Power of court to stay proceedings against the company

Section 126 is a section applying only to the period of time *after* the presentation of the petition and *before* a winding-up order has been made.

It states that during this period the company, or any creditor or contributory, may apply to the appropriate court to stay any proceedings which are pending against the company, and the court may do so.

8. The commencement of winding up by the court

Section 129 provides that where *before the presentation of a petition* for winding up by the court, the company has passed a resolution for *voluntary* winding up, the winding up is deemed to have commenced *at the time of the passing of the resolution*.

In all other cases (i.e. where the company has *not* previously resolved to wind up voluntarily) a winding up by the court commences *at the time of the presentation of the petition*.

It is helpful at this point to compare s. 86 which deals with the moment of commencement of a voluntary winding up, providing that it is the time of the passing of the resolution to wind up. This explains the provisions of s. 129 and the two sections should always be studied together.

9. The consequences of a winding-up order

Once the winding-up order is made, its consequences *date back* to the commencement of the winding up. This is the reason why it is essential to know exactly when the moment of commencement is. Section 129, as we have just seen, provides that as a rule it is *the time of the presentation of the petition*, so that in the normal case the consequences of the winding-up order will date back to that time.

These consequences are:

(a) Under s. 127, any disposition of the company's property, any transfer of shares, and any alteration in the status of members is void, unless the court orders otherwise.

(b) Under s. 128, any execution against the company's property in England and Wales is void. [In Scotland, by s. 185 the provisions of the Bankruptcy (Scotland) Act 1985 as to the effect of sequestration on diligence are made to apply also to winding up.]

(c) Under s 130, a copy of the winding-up order must be sent at once by the company to the registrar who, under s. 711 Companies Act 1985, must publish notice of its receipt by him in the *Gazette*.

If its receipt has not been officially notified by the registrar at the material time and if the company cannot show that it was known at that time to the person concerned, then, under s. 42 Companies Act 1985, the company cannot rely on the making of the order against that person.

(d) Also under s. 130, actions against the company are stayed. (This section does not come into operation until the winding-up order is made, and s. 126 no longer applies (*see* 7 above).)

(e) Under s. 136 in England and Wales the official receiver automatically becomes the liquidator, unless, under s. 140, the court appoints as liquidator the person who has just ceased to be the administrator of the company under an administration order or the person who has been the supervisor under an approved voluntary arrangement.

(f) The powers of the directors cease.

(g) The servants of the company are dismissed.

10. The official receiver in England and Wales

The appointment and functions of official receivers are provided for in ss. 399–401. [These provisions do not apply to Scotland.] Official receivers are appointed by the Secretary of State for Trade and Industry and are attached to the courts. Their functions extend to individual bankruptcy in England and Wales as well as to the winding up of companies. The Secretary of State may, in order to facilitate the disposal of the business of official receivers, give directions such as authorising an official receiver attached to one court to act as the official receiver in relation to cases before another court.

11. The provisional liquidator

Section 135 empowers the court in England and Wales to appoint a provisional liquidator at any time *after* the presentation of the petition and *before* the making of the winding-up order. Either the official receiver or any other fit person may be appointed. [In Scotland a provisional liquidator may be appointed at any time before the first appointment of liquidators.]

This is a purely *temporary* appointment, for as soon as the winding-up order is made the official receiver in England and Wales automatically becomes the liquidator (*see* 9(e)). It is not made in every case, but only where proof by affidavit is given that there are sufficient grounds for the appointment, usually that the assets are in jeopardy.

To secure the appointment, application must be made to the court by a creditor, a contributory, or the company. If the court grants the application, it must notify the official receiver who is usually, though not necessarily, the person appointed.

Section 135 makes it clear that the powers of the provisional liquidator depend on the order appointing him. He is merely a receiver, his function being to protect the assets of the company; thus he would not be given power to sell the assets unless they are perishable.

12. The appointment of the liquidator

Section 136 [which is not applicable to Scotland] deals with the functions of the official receiver in relation to the office of liquidator, but it must be remembered that these provisions are subject to s. 140 by which in certain circumstances the court may appoint the administrator or supervisor as the case may be (*see* **9**).

Section 136, as we have already seen in **9(e)**, provides that as soon as the winding-up order is made, the *official receiver* automatically becomes *liquidator* and acts as such until another person is appointed. This occurs in *every* compulsory liquidation and is in no way connected with the appointment of a *provisional* liquidator under s. 135 between the time of the presentation of the petition and the making of the winding-up order.

Section 136 provides that the official receiver is, by virtue of his office, the liquidator during any vacancy.

The section entitles the official receiver, at any time when he is the liquidator, to summon separate meetings of the creditors and contributories for the purpose of choosing a person to be liquidator in his place. He *must* summon such meetings if he is at any time requested to do so by one-quarter in value of the company's creditors.

By s. 137 [which also does not apply to Scotland] the official receiver may, at any time when he is the liquidator, apply to the Secretary of State for the appointment of a person as liquidator in his place.

If the official receiver has exercised his power of summoning meetings under s. 136, but no person has been chosen to be liquidator as a result of those meetings, then it is the duty of the official receiver to decide whether to refer the need for an appointment to the Secretary of State: s. 137.

On an application or a reference under s. 137 the Secretary of State may either make or decline to make an appointment. If he makes an appointment, then the liquidator must notify his appointment to the company's creditors.

[Section 138 deals with the appointment of a liquidator in Scotland. The liquidator is appointed by the court at the time when the winding-up order is made, he is referred to as 'the interim liquidator' and he continues in office until another person becomes liquidator in his place.

The interim liquidator must as soon as practicable summon meetings of the creditors and contributories for the purpose of choosing a person to be liquidator in his place. He may himself be chosen. If it appears to the interim liquidator, in a case where the company is being wound up on grounds including its inability to pay its debts, that it would be inappropriate to summon a meeting of the contributories, he may summon only a meeting of the creditors.

If one or more meetings are held but no person is appointed or nominated by the meeting or meetings, the interim liquidator must make a report to the court, and the court must then appoint either the interim liquidator or some other person to be liquidator.

A person who becomes liquidator in place of the interim liquidator must, unless he is appointed by the court, immediately notify the court of that fact.]

Section 139 deals with the choice of a liquidator at the meetings of creditors and contributories summoned for that purpose. Each meeting may nominate a person to be liquidator and the creditors' nomination prevails if different persons are nominated, except that a creditor or contributory may, within seven days of the creditors' nomination, apply to the court for an order appointing the contributories' nominee or some other person as liquidator instead of the creditors' nominee.

13. The statement of affairs

Section 131 provides that where the court has made a winding-up order, a statement of the company's affairs must, unless the court orders otherwise, be made out and *submitted to the official receiver* in England and Wales.

It must be in the prescribed form, verified by affidavit, and show:

(a) particulars of assets, debts and liabilities;
(b) names and addresses of creditors;
(c) securities held by them, and the dates when these were given; *and*
(d) any further information which may be prescribed or which the official receiver may require.

The statement must be submitted and verified by some or all of the following persons, as the official receiver may require:

(a) past or present officers of the company;
(b) persons who have taken part in its formation within one year before the winding-up order;
(c) persons who are, or have been within that year, in the company's

'employment' (widely defined as including employment under a contract for services) and who are capable of giving the required information;
(d) persons who are, or have been within that year, officers or in the employment of another company which is, or has been within that year, an officer of the company now in liquidation.

The statement must be submitted *within 21 days* from the official receiver's notice requiring it.

[In the application of s. 131 to Scotland, references to the official receiver are to the liquidator or, in a case where a provisional liquidator has been appointed, to the provisional liquidator.]

14. Investigation by official receiver
In England and Wales section 132 requires the official receiver to investigate:

(a) if the company has failed, the causes of its failure; *and*
(b) generally, the promotion, formation, business dealings and affairs of the company;

and to make such report (if any) to the court as he thinks fit.

The official receiver [in Scotland the liquidator] may also, at any time during the winding up, apply to the court for the public examination of officers and others under s. 133 (*see* **28**).

15. Summary of the duties of the official receiver

(a) He may be appointed *provisional liquidator after* the presentation of the petition and *before* the winding-up order is made, under s. 135. He is then merely a receiver and his function is to protect the assets during this intervening period.
(b) He becomes the *liquidator* automatically in all cases as soon as the winding-up order is made, under s. 136 (unless the court makes an appointment under s. 140). He acts as liquidator until another person is appointed.
(c) He may summon separate *meetings* of creditors and contributories, under s. 136 for the purpose of choosing a person to be liquidator in his place.
(d) He may apply to the *Secretary of State* for the appointment of a liquidator, under s. 137.
(e) He is, by virtue of his office, the *liquidator* during any *vacancy*, under s. 136.
(f) He receives and considers the *statement of affairs*, under s. 131.
(g) He makes an *investigation* and may *report* to the court, under s. 132.
(h) He may apply to the court for the *public examination* of officers and others under s. 133 and take part in that examination.

[In Scotland, there is no official receiver and the procedure is somewhat different:

(a) There may be a provisional liquidator, appointed by the court at any time *before the first appointment of liquidators,* under s. 135.

(b) After a winding-up order has been made a liquidator (referred to as 'the interim liquidator') *must* be appointed by the court at the time when the order is made, under s. 138.

(c) The interim liquidator may summon separate *meetings* of creditors and contributories for the purpose of choosing a person to be liquidator in his place.

(d) If no person is appointed or nominated at the meetings, the interim liquidator must make a report to the *court* for the court to appoint a liquidator, under s. 138.

(e) The interim liquidator continues in office until another person becomes liquidator in his place, under s. 138.

(f) He may apply to the court for the *public examination* of officers and others under s. 133 and take part in that examination.]

16. Resignation and vacation of office of liquidator

Section 172 provides that a liquidator may, in prescribed circumstances, *resign* his office by giving notice of his resignation to the court.

By the same section a liquidator or provisional liquidator (other than the official receiver) must *vacate office* if he ceases to be a person who is qualified to act as an insolvency practitioner in relation to the company.

The other case in which a liquidator must *vacate office* comes at the end of the winding up. If it appears to the liquidator that the winding up is for practical purposes complete and if the liquidator is not the official receiver, the liquidator must, by s. 146, summon a final general meeting of the creditors to receive his report on the winding up. The liquidator must then, by s. 172, vacate office as soon as he has given notice to the court and the registrar of companies that the meeting has been held and of its decisions (if any). [In Scotland a liquidator must also vacate office where the court has ordered an early dissolution under s. 204 (*see* **31**.)]

17. Removal of liquidator

Two provisions in s. 172 deal with removal of a liquidator:

If the liquidator was appointed by the Secretary of State in England and Wales, he may be removed from office by a direction of the Secretary of State.

In all other cases, the liquidator may be removed from office only by an order of the court or by a general meeting of the creditors summoned specially for that purpose, and a provisional liquidator may be removed from office only by an order of the court.

18. Release of liquidator

The release of the liquidator is dealt with in s. 174:

Where the official receiver in England and Wales has ceased to be liquidator and a person becomes liquidator in his stead, the official receiver has his release:

(a) if the person was nominated by a general meeting of creditors or contributories, or was appointed by the Secretary of State, from the time at which the official receiver gives notice to the court that he has been replaced;

(b) if the person is appointed by the court, from the time fixed by the court.

If the official receiver while he is a liquidator gives notice to the Secretary of State that the winding up is for practical purposes complete, he has his release from the time fixed by the Secretary of State.

A person other than the official receiver who has ceased to be a liquidator has his release from the following times:

(a) if he has been removed from office by a general meeting of creditors which has not resolved against his release, or if he has died, the time at which notice is given to the court that he has ceased to hold office;

(b) if he has been removed from office by a general meeting of creditors which has resolved against his release, or by the court or the Secretary of State, or if he has vacated office under s. 172 on the ground that he is no longer qualified to act as an insolvency practitioner, [or, in Scotland, he has vacated office when the court has made an order for an early dissolution under s. 204], the time fixed by the Secretary of State [in Scotland, the Accountant of Court] on an application being made to him by that person;

(c) if he has resigned, the time prescribed;

(d) if he has vacated office under s. 172 on the completion of winding up, the time at which he vacated office unless the final meeting resolved against his release, in which case he must apply to the Secretary of State [in Scotland, the Accountant of Court] for a time to be fixed.

A person who has ceased to hold office as a provisional liquidator has his release from the time fixed by the court on an application being made by him.

The effect of a release is to discharge the official receiver or a liquidator or provisional liquidator from all liability for his conduct in the winding up, but this does not prevent the exercise of the summary remedy under s. 212 against a liquidator who has misapplied the company's property or been guilty of any misfeasance or breach of any duty in relation to the company.

19. General functions of liquidator

By s. 143 the functions of the liquidator are to secure that the assets of the company are got in, realised and distributed to the creditors and, if there is a surplus, to the persons entitled to it.

If in England and Wales the liquidator is not the official receiver, it is his duty:

(a) to furnish the official receiver with such information;
(b) to produce to the official receiver, and allow him to inspect, such books, papers and other records; *and*
(c) to give him such other assistance,

as the official receiver may reasonably require for the purpose of carrying out his functions in relation to the winding up.

20. The position of the liquidator regarding the company's property

Section 144 provides that the liquidator obtains *custody and control* of the company's property. [In Scotland, if and so long as there is no liquidator the company's property is deemed to be in the *custody* of the court.] It is important to notice that he does not obtain *title* to it, i.e. *ownership*, unless he applies to the court under s. 145 for a *vesting order* to be made and the court makes an order to that effect.

This is one of the ways in which a liquidation differs from a bankruptcy, for in a bankruptcy the property of the debtor (with minor exceptions) vests in the trustee in bankruptcy.

21. Duty to summon final meeting

If it appears to the liquidator that the winding up is for practical purposes complete and if the liquidator is not the official receiver, the liquidator must, by s. 146, summon a final general meeting of the creditors to receive his report of the winding up and to decide whether he should have his release under s. 174.

It is the duty of the liquidator to retain sufficient sums from the company's property to cover the expenses of summoning and holding this final meeting.

22. Liquidation committees

Sections 141 and 142 deal with the liquidation committees which may be set up in a winding up by the court in England and Wales and in Scotland, respectively.

Where separate meetings of creditors and contributories have been summoned for the purpose of choosing a person to be liquidator, those meetings may establish the liquidation committee.

Alternatively, the liquidator, provided he is not the official receiver, may at any time, if he thinks fit, summon separate general meetings of the creditors and contributories to decide whether such a committee should be established. Further, he *must* summon such a meeting if he is requested to do so by one-tenth in value of the creditors.

If the meetings of creditors and contributories are in disagreement as to whether a committee should be established, a committee must be established unless the court orders otherwise.

The liquidation committee is not able or required to carry out its functions at any time when the official receiver is liquidator; at such a time its functions are vested in the Secretary of State except to the extent that rules made under s. 411 provide otherwise.

Where there is for the time being no liquidation committee, and the liquidator is a person other than the official receiver, the functions of such a committee are vested in the Secretary of State [in Scotland, in the court] except to the extent that the rules provide otherwise.

[In Scotland, a liquidation committee has in addition such of the powers and duties of commissioners in a sequestration as may be conferred and imposed on such committees by the rules.]

23. The powers of the liquidator
The powers of the liquidator in a winding up by the court are to be found in s. 167 taken along with Schedule 4. The form and contents of that Schedule have already been detailed in relation to voluntary winding up (*see* 29:**14**) and may therefore be more briefly treated here.

Section 167 provides that in a winding up by the court any of the powers specified in Parts I and II of Schedule 4 may be exercised by the liquidator with the sanction of the court or the liquidation committee, and that any of the general powers in Part III of that Schedule may be exercised by him with or without sanction.

Where the liquidator (provided he is not the official receiver) in the exercise of his powers disposes of any of the company's property to a person who is 'connected' with the company or employs a solicitor to assist him in the carrying out of his functions, he must, if there is for the time being a liquidation committee, give notice to the committee of that exercise of his powers. The term 'connected' is defined in s. 249 (*see* 29:**14**).

The liquidator, in exercising any of the powers conferred by s. 167 and Schedule 4, is subject to the control of the court, and any creditor or contributory may apply to the court regarding them.

24. Supplementary powers of liquidator
Section 168 which applies to England and Wales empowers the liquidator

to call meetings of creditors or contributories in order to ascertain their wishes, and requires him to do so whenever the creditors or contributories *by resolution so direct,* or whenever *requested in writing* to do so by *one-tenth in value* of the creditors or contributories.

The section also empowers the liquidator to apply to the court for directions in any matter which arises in the winding up, and enables any person who is aggrieved by an act of the liquidator to apply to the court, which may then make such order as it thinks just.

[Section 169 applies to Scotland only. Where there is no liquidation committee, the court may provide by order that the liquidator may bring or defend any legal proceeding in the name and on behalf of the company or that he may carry on the business of the company so far as may be necessary for its beneficial winding up, *without the sanction or intervention of the court.* A liquidator in Scotland also has (subject to the rules) the same powers as a trustee on a bankrupt estate.]

25. Liability of the liquidator

We have already seen that the ownership of the company's property remains in the company and does not pass to the liquidator on the making of the winding-up order **(20)**. He is not, therefore, a *trustee* either for the company or for the creditors or contributories, any more than a director is (*see* 16:**56**).

He is, however, in a *fiduciary relation* towards the company and the creditors, and for *breach of the many statutory duties* imposed on him he will be liable to pay damages to any creditor or contributory who has been injured by the breach. Moreover, if he is *negligent* in his application of the company's assets, he will likewise incur liability to any person who suffers as a result, and proceedings can be taken against him, as against a promoter, director, or any officer of the company under s. 212 for *misfeasance* (*see* 31:**13**).

In *Pulsford* v. *Devenish* (1903), the liquidator advertised in the usual way for creditors to make their claims against the company, but took no further steps to notify a creditor whose debt appeared in the company's books, but who did not know of the liquidation. HELD: The liquidator was liable to compensate him.

26. General powers of the court

The remainder of the sections on compulsory winding up deal with the powers of the court. Some of these powers must be considered in detail, and the rest of this chapter is concerned with them, but others require no explanation, and a short list of them will suffice:

(a) Section 147 empowers the court to *stay the winding up proceedings* at any time in a proper case, on the application of the liquidator, the official receiver, any creditor or contributory.

(b) Section 148 requires the court to *settle a list of contributories*, and empowers it to *rectify the register of members*. It also requires it to *collect the company's assets and apply them towards its liabilities*. A list of contributories is not necessary where calls need not be made on them.

(c) Section 150 empowers the court to *make calls* on the contributories on the list.

(d) Section 153 empowers the court to *fix a time within which creditors must prove their debts*, or be excluded from the benefit of any distribution made before proof.

(e) Section 155 empowers the court to specify the rights of inspection of the company's books and papers by creditors and contributories.

(f) [In a winding up in Scotland, s. 157 empowers the court to require the attendance of any officer of the company at any meeting of creditors or of contributories, or of a liquidation committee, for the purpose of giving information as to the trade, dealings, affairs or property of the company.]

Under s. 160, the powers of the court conferred by ss. 148, 150 and 153 may be *delegated to the liquidator* as an officer of the court and subject to the control of the court, though he may not, without the special leave of the court, *rectify the register of members*. Nor can he *make a call* without either the special leave of the court or the sanction of the liquidation committee.

27. Extent to which set-off allowed

Section 149 empowers the court to order any contributory to pay any money which he owes to the company, exclusive of calls. If, however, the company at the same time owes money to the contributory, the debts may be set off against each other *when all the creditors have been paid in full*.

Further, it has been held that set-off must be allowed when the contributory *becomes bankrupt* after the commencement of the winding up.

28. Court's power of public examination

Section 133 provides that the official receiver [or, in Scotland, the liquidator] *may* at any time during the winding up apply to the court for the public examination of any person who is or has been an officer of the company, or has acted as liquidator or administrator or as receiver or manager or has in some other way taken part in the company's promotion, formation or management.

The official receiver [or, in Scotland, the liquidator] *must* make such an application, unless the court orders otherwise, if he is requested to do so by:

(a) one-half in value of the creditors; *or*

(b) three-quarters in value of the contributories.

If the court directs that a public examination be held, the person concerned must attend on a day appointed by the court and be publicly examined as to the promotion, formation or management of the company or as to the conduct of its business and affairs, or his conduct or dealings in relation to the company.

Questions concerning these matters may be put by any of the following persons:

(a) the official receiver;
(b) the liquidator;
(c) any person who has been appointed as special manager of the company's property or business (*see* 31:3);
(d) any creditor who has tendered a proof [or in Scotland, submitted a claim] in the winding up; *and*
(e) any contributory.

29. Court's power to arrest absconding contributory

It has been said that by far the most delightful section in the Companies Act 1948 was s. 271, giving the court power to arrest a contributory. The section, now s. 158 Insolvency Act 1986, provides that on proof that a contributory is about to quit the United Kingdom or to abscond or to remove or conceal his property in order to evade payment of calls, the court may have him arrested, and his books, papers and movable personal property seized, and him and them safely kept for such time as the court may order.

> NOTE: The meaning is clear, but the language picturesque, conjuring up an image of a disconsolate contributory incarcerated along with and entirely surrounded by his books, papers, and movable personal property, while acres of good arable land (unaffected by the section) lie abandoned.

30. Dissolution

Where a winding up follows its full course, the procedure for the dissolution of the company is governed by s. 205.

The registrar of companies will have received *either*:

(a) a notice under s. 172 from the liquidator (other than the official receiver) that a final meeting of creditors has been held to consider the liquidator's report; *or*
(b) in England or Wales a notice from the official receiver that the winding up is complete.

On receiving either notice, the registrar must immediately register it, and at the end of three months after that registration, the company is dissolved.

This is, however, subject to the exception in England and Wales that the Secretary of State, if applied to by the official receiver or by any other person appearing to be interested, may defer the date of the dissolution for such period as he thinks fit.

An appeal may be made to the court against the Secretary of State's decision, and it is the duty of the person who has applied for such a deferment to deliver to the registrar a copy of the Secretary of State's direction within seven days after it has been given.

[In Scotland, the exception is that the court, if applied to by any person appearing to have an interest, may order the date of the dissolution to be deferred for such period as the court thinks fit. It is the duty of the person who applied to the court to deliver to the registrar a copy of the court order within seven days after it has been made.]

31. Early dissolution

An alternative to dissolution under s. 205 is the early dissolution procedure provided for by ss. 202-204. Up to a third of the companies which go into compulsory liquidation have few or no assets, and the aim of this alternative procedure is to save the time of the official receiver or liquidator and the expense of following through the full procedure.

Section 202 provides that the early dissolution procedure is available only if the official receiver is the liquidator and if it appears to him:

(a) that the realisable assets are insufficient to cover the expenses of the winding up; *and*
(b) that the affairs of the company do not require any further investigation.

The application is made by the official receiver to the registrar of companies and the official receiver must give at least 28 days' notice of his intention to make such application to the creditors and contributories and to the administrative receiver (if any). With the giving of that notice the official receiver ceases to be required to perform any duties in relation to the company.

The official receiver's application is registered by the registrar and at the end of three months from registration the company is dissolved.

Section 203 permits an application to be made by the official receiver or any creditor or contributory or the administrative receiver (if any) to the Secretary of State for a direction that the winding up should proceed as if no notice under s. 202 had been given, on the ground that:

(a) the realisable assets are sufficient to cover the expenses of the winding up; *or*

(b) the affairs of the company do require further investigation; *or*

(c) the early dissolution is for any other reason inappropriate.

The Secretary of State may also defer the date of the dissolution beyond the three months' period.

In s. 203 there are the same provisions as in s. 205 regarding appeal to court against a Secretary of State's direction and regarding delivery of a copy of his direction to the registrar within seven days.

Section 204 applies to early dissolution in Scotland.

If it appears to the liquidator that the realisable assets are insufficient to cover the expenses of the winding up, he may apply to the court for an order that the company be dissolved, and the court must make such an order if:

(a) the court is satisfied that the realisable assets are insufficient to cover the expenses of the winding up; *and*

(b) it appears to the court appropriate to do so.

A copy of the order must within 14 days of its date be forwarded by the liquidator to the registrar, and at the end of three months from its registration the company is dissolved.

The court may, if applied to by a person who appears to have an interest, order the date of dissolution to be deferred for such period as the court thinks fit. It is the duty of the person who applied for such an order to deliver a copy of the order to the registrar within seven days after the making of the order.

Provisions of general application in winding up

1. Proof of debts

Provisions as to the debts which may be proved [in Scots law, claimed] in a winding up, as to the manner and conditions of proving a debt and as to the manner and expenses of establishing the value of any debt or security are amongst the matters capable of inclusion in rules made by statutory instrument under s. 411 and Schedule 8.

2. Preferential debts

Section 175 provides that the company's preferential debts, listed in Schedule 6, must be paid in priority to all other debts. They rank equally among themselves after the expenses of the winding up and must be paid in full, unless the assets are insufficient to meet them, in which case they abate in equal proportions.

Further, they have priority over the claims of holders of a floating charge created by the company.

There are five categories of preferential debts listed in Schedule 6:

(a) debts due to the Inland Revenue, i.e. principally sums deducted by the company as PAYE from remuneration paid during the preceding year;

(b) debts due to Customs and Excise, i.e. principally VAT referable to the preceding six months, any car tax which has become due within the preceding year, and various duties under the Betting and Gaming Duties Act 1981 which have become due within the preceding year;

(c) social security contributions which have become due within the preceding year;

(d) sums owed by the company as contributions to occupational pension schemes and state scheme premiums;

(e) remuneration, including holiday remuneration, owed by the company to employees for the preceding four months, not exceeding a prescribed amount for each employee, with the same preference extended to sums owed by the company to any person (e.g. a bank) who has advanced money to the company to enable it to pay the remuneration.

The relevant date which fixes the period of the preceding year, six months, etc., for the purposes of these debts is, by s. 387:

(a) in the case of a voluntary winding up, the date of the passing of the resolution for winding up; *and*

(b) in the case of a winding up by the court, the date of the appointment of a provisional liquidator or, if no such appointment was made, the date of the winding-up order, except that if the winding up by the court has followed immediately upon the discharge of an administration order, the relevant date is the date of the making of the administration order.

Section 176, which applies to England and Wales only, provides that when a landlord or other person has distrained on the company's property *within three months* before the winding-up order, the preferential debts are a *first charge* on the goods distrained on, or the proceeds of sale, but the landlord or other person will have the *same priority* as the person to whom the payment is made. Thus a landlord must return the goods distrained on, or the proceeds of sale, if he exercised his rights within the previous three months, but he then ranks equally with the other preferential creditors, over whom he would otherwise have an advantage.

3. Appointment of special manager

Section 177 provides that, where a company has gone into liquidation or a provisional liquidator has been appointed, the court may appoint any person to be the special manager of the business or property of the company.

The application may be made by the liquidator or provisional liquidator in any case where it appears to him that the nature of the business or property or the interests of the creditors or contributories or members require the appointment.

It is for the court to decide what powers the special manager has.

His remuneration may be provided for in rules under s. 411 and Schedule 8.

4. Disclaimer of onerous property

Sections 178 to 182, which apply to England and Wales only, deal with a liquidator's power to disclaim onerous property. The law on this subject was substantially amended by the Insolvency Act 1985.

The leading provision is in s. 178: the liquidator may, by giving the prescribed notice, disclaim any 'onerous property', even though he has taken possession of it, tried to sell it or in some other way exercised rights of ownership in relation to it.

The following is 'onerous property':

(a) any unprofitable contract; *and*

(b) any other property of the company which is unsaleable or not readily saleable or is such that it may give rise to a liability to pay money or perform any other onerous act.

The effect of the disclaimer is to terminate the company's rights and liabilities in respect of the property, but not the rights and liabilities of other persons.

The section prevents a liquidator from giving a notice of disclaimer if a person interested in the property has first applied in writing to him requiring him to decide within 28 days whether he will disclaim or not and the liquidator has not given notice of disclaimer within that period.

Any person who sustains loss or damage as a result of a disclaimer is deemed a creditor of the company to the extent of the loss or damage and so may prove for the loss or damage in the winding up.

Section 181 provides that an application may be made to the court by any person who claims an interest in the disclaimed property or by any person who is under any liability in respect of it (other than a liability discharged by the disclaimer) for the court to make an order for the vesting of the disclaimed property in, or for its delivery to, the applicant or a trustee for him. The effect of any such court order must be taken into account in assessing the loss or damage sustained by any person for the purposes of s. 178.

Section 179 provides that a disclaimer of *leasehold* property does not take effect unless a copy of the disclaimer has been served on every underlessee or mortgagee whose address is known to the liquidator, and *either:*

(a) no application to the court under s. 181 is made within the next 14 days after the notice; *or*
(b) where such an application has been made, the court directs that the disclaimer shall take effect.

By s. 182 the court must not make an order under s. 181 vesting leasehold property in any underlessee or mortgagee except on terms making that person:

(a) subject to the same liabilities as the company was subject to under the lease at the commencement of the winding up; *or*
(b) if the court thinks fit, subject to the same liabilities as that person would be subject to if the lease had been assigned to him at the commencement of the winding up.

Where no underlessee or mortgagee is willing to accept such terms the court may vest the company's interest in the property in any person who is liable to perform the lessee's covenants in the lease, and the court may vest the interest in such a person freed from all incumbrances created by the company.

5. Rights of creditors as to execution or attachment

Section 183, which applies only to England and Wales, provides that where a creditor has issued execution against the company's goods or land, or has attached any debt due to the company, he may not keep the benefit of the execution or attachment against the liquidator unless he completed it before *the commencement of the winding up.*

However, where a creditor has had notice of a meeting at which a resolution for voluntary winding up is to be proposed, he must complete the execution or attachment *before the date on which he had the notice.*

A person who buys under a sale by the sheriff any of the company's goods on which execution has been levied acquires a good title against the liquidator provided he buys in good faith. Further, the court may set aside the liquidator's rights in favour of the creditor if it thinks fit.

The section explains what is meant by 'completion'. It provides that execution against goods is completed by seizure and sale, or by the making of a charging order under s. 1 of the Charging Orders Act 1979, attachment by receipt of the debt, and execution against land by seizure, by the appointment of a receiver, or by the making of a charging order as above.

[For Scotland, s. 185 applies to winding up provisions derived from the Bankruptcy (Scotland) Act 1985. The 1985 Act relates to the sequestration of a debtor's estate, and the sections which are made to apply to a company being wound up are in s. 37 (effect of sequestration on diligence) and s. 39 (realisation of estate). Some substitutions are provided for in s. 185:

(a) for debtor, substitute company;
(b) for sequestration, substitute winding up;
(c) for date of sequestration, substitute commencement of the winding up;
(d) for permanent trustee, substitute liquidator.

It should be noted that, whereas the commencement of a winding up by the court normally dates back to the presentation of the petition (*see* 30.8), for the purposes of **(c)**, above, it is the day on which the winding-up order *is made.*

The rules which apply are:

(a) The winding up is, at the date of its commencement, equivalent to an arrestment in execution and decree of furthcoming, and to a completed poinding, and no arrestment or poinding executed on or after the sixtieth day before that date is effectual against the liquidator except to the limited extent that an arrester or poinder who is thus deprived of the benefit of his diligence is entitled to a preference for the expense *bona fide* incurred by him in his diligence.

(b) The winding up is, at its commencement, equivalent to a decree of adjudication of the heritable estate of the company for payment of the whole debts of the company, subject to any preferable heritable rights and securities which are valid and unchallengeable and subject to (c), below.

(c) A poinding of the ground which has not been carried into execution by a sale 60 days before the commencement of the winding up is of no effect in a question with the liquidator unless the poinder holds a heritable security which is preferable to the right of the liquidator, in which case the poinding is available for the interest for the current half-year and for the arrears of interest for the preceding year, but for no more.

The provisions in s. 39 Bankruptcy (Scotland) Act 1985, as adapted for winding up by s. 185 Insolvency Act 1986, are intended to ensure that, while either the liquidator or the creditor may sell the estate, the interests of the liquidator (for the benefit of the other creditors) are protected as well as the interests of the creditor who has security over the estate.]

6. Duties of sheriff as to goods taken in execution

Section 184, which does not apply to Scotland, provides that where a company's goods are taken in execution, and *before their sale* notice is served on the sheriff that a provisional liquidator has been appointed, a winding-up order made, or a resolution for voluntary winding up passed, he must if required deliver the goods and any money seized or received in part satisfaction of the execution to the liquidator.

The costs of the execution are a first charge on the goods or money, and the liquidator may sell those goods to satisfy that charge.

Section 184 further provides that where under an execution for a sum of more than £500 goods are sold or money paid to avoid sale, the sheriff must deduct the costs of the execution from the proceeds of sale or the money paid, and *hold the balance for 14 days*. If within that time notice is served on him of the presentation of a petition for winding up, or of a meeting being called at which a resolution for voluntary winding up is to be proposed, and then a winding-up order is in fact made, or the resolution for voluntary winding up passed, he *must pay the balance to the liquidator*, who may retain it as against the execution creditor. Notice of a meeting of *creditors*, however, will not defeat the execution creditor. The words of the provision must be strictly construed, and the execution creditor will only be defeated by notice of a meeting of the *company* to pass a winding-up resolution: *Re T.D. Walton* (1966).

Section 184 provides again that the court may set aside the liquidator's rights in favour of the creditor if it thinks fit.

7. Rescission of contracts by the court

Section 186 permits a person who is, as against the liquidator, entitled to the benefit or subject to the burden of a contract made with the company to apply to the court for the court to make an order rescinding the contract on such terms as to payment by or to either party of damages for non-performance or otherwise as the court thinks just.

Any damages payable under the order to such a person may be proved [in Scots law, may be claimed], by him as a debt in the winding up.

8. Notification of liquidation

Section 188 provides that where a company is in liquidation, every business document on which the company's name appears must contain a statement that the company is being wound up.

9. Interest on debts

Interest up to the date of winding up is included in the debt proved by [in Scots law, claimed by] a creditor.

Section 189, which originated in the Insolvency Act 1985, provides for interest in respect of the period for which the debt has been outstanding *since the company went into liquidation.*

Any surplus remaining after full payment of the debts proved in the winding up, must be applied in paying interest on those debts.

The rate of interest is whichever is the greater of:

(a) the rate in s. 17 of the Judgments Act 1838, which is varied from time to time by statutory instrument; [for Scotland, substitute the Insolvency (Scotland) Rules 1986 (SI 1986, No. 1915 (S. 139)) for s. 17 of the Judgments Act 1838;] *and*

(b) the rate applicable to the debt apart from the winding up.

All interest payable under s. 189 ranks equally, whether or not the debts on which it is payable rank equally.

10. Information as to pending liquidations

If any winding up is not concluded within one year after its commencement, the liquidator must, by s. 192, at prescribed intervals until the winding up is complete, send to the registrar of companies statements containing prescribed particulars concerning the proceedings in, and position of, the liquidation.

11. Meetings to ascertain wishes of creditors or contributories

Section 195 provides that the court may have regard to the wishes of creditors or contributories as regards all matters relating to the winding up, and, if it thinks fit, for the purpose of ascertaining those wishes, may direct meetings of creditors or contributories to be held, and may appoint a person to act as chairman and report the result to the court.

In the case of creditors regard must be had to the value of each creditor's debt, and in the case of contributories regard must be had to the number of votes conferred on each contributory by the Companies Act 1985 or the articles.

12. Offences of fraud, deception, etc., before and during winding up

Sections 206 to 211 specify numerous offences of which a past or present officer of a company in liquidation can be found guilty.

The offences include the following:

(a) concealing any part of the company's property to the value of £500 or more: s. 206;

(b) concealing or falsifying books or papers relating to the company's affairs: ss. 206 and 209;

(c) pawning, pledging or disposing of any property of the company which has been obtained on credit and has not been paid for (unless such disposal was in the ordinary way of the company's business): s. 206;

(d) having made a gift of the company's property within five years before the commencement of winding up: s. 207;

(e) failing to hand over to the liquidator company property, books and papers: s. 208;

(f) making any material omission from any statement relating to the company's affairs: s. 210; *and*

(g) making a false representation to creditors for the purpose of obtaining their consent to some agreement: s. 211.

With regard to most of these offences the Act provides that it is a defence for the person charged to prove that he had no intent to defraud or no intent to conceal the company's state of affairs or to defeat the law. It is important to note that the onus of proving innocence thus lies on the person charged.

13. Misfeasance

Section 212 is an important section. It provides that if it appears in liquidation that any past or present officer, promoter, liquidator, administrator or administrative receiver or person who has otherwise taken part in the management of the company has misapplied or retained any of the company's money or property, or been guilty of any misfeasance, or breach of any fiduciary or other duty towards the company, the court may examine into his conduct on the application of:

(a) the official receiver in England or Wales; *or*

(b) the liquidator; *or*
(c) any creditor; *or*
(d) any contributory, with leave of the court.

The court may then compel him to *restore the money or property*, or to *contribute such sum as the court thinks just* to the company's assets *by way of compensation*.

For the purposes of this section, an auditor is an officer of the company (*see* 19:**18**).

For an example of the application of s. 212 see *Re Purpoint Ltd* (1991) [B291].

14. Fraudulent and wrongful trading and use of prohibited company names
The court may impose *personal liability* for a company's debts on:

(a) persons who have been knowingly parties to the carrying on of the company's business to defraud creditors ('fraudulent trading'): s. 213;
(b) directors who ought to have realised that insolvent liquidation was inevitable but failed to take every step to minimise the potential loss to creditors ('wrongful trading'): s. 214; *and*
(c) persons involved in the management of a company which went into insolvent liquidation within the previous five years: ss. 216 and 217.

These provisions have already been considered in relation to the limited liability clause of the memorandum (*see* 2:**33**).

15. Qualification of liquidator
Section 230 requires a liquidator and a provisional liquidator to be qualified to act as an insolvency practitioner in relation to the company.

Part XIII (i.e. ss. 388–398) deals with insolvency practitioners and their qualification. By s. 388 these provisions cover not only liquidators, provisional liquidators, administrators, administrative receivers and supervisors of voluntary arrangements in relation to companies but also trustees and other persons in relation to individual bankruptcy. They do not, however, apply to the official receiver.

By s. 390 only an individual may become qualified to act as an insolvency practitioner. Normally, he must be a member of a professional body recognised by the Secretary of State under s. 391. Otherwise he must obtain a special authorisation from a competent authority under ss. 392–393, by applying to the Secretary of State or other authority specified by him and furnishing such information (including information as to his education and practical training and experience) as may be required. If the competent authority proposes to refuse authorisation or proposes to withdraw it, the person concerned has a right to make representations to the competent authority under s. 395, and if necessary to have his case referred to and decided by the Insolvency Practitioners Tribunal under ss. 396–397. The constitution and procedure of the Tribunal are governed by Schedule 7.

There must be security [or, in Scotland, caution] for the proper performance of the liquidator's functions: s. 390.

Section 390 further provides that a person is disqualified from acting as an insolvency practitioner if:

(a) he has been adjudged bankrupt [or, in Scotland, sequestration of his estate has been awarded] and he has not yet been discharged;
(b) he is subject to a disqualification order under the Company Directors Disqualification Act 1986; *or*
(c) he is a patient under the Mental Health Act 1983 or the Mental Health (Scotland) Act 1984.

While, by s. 389, it is an offence for a person to act as an insolvency practitioner when he is not qualified to do so, s. 232 provides that the acts of the liquidator are valid notwithstanding any defect in his appointment, nomination or qualifications.

16. Supplies of gas, electricity, water and telephone

Formerly the suppliers of public utilities, though they were not preferential creditors, were, because of their monopoly position, able to compel the liquidator to pay outstanding accounts in full under the threat that otherwise the supplies would be discontinued. The Insolvency Act 1985 altered the law on this matter.

The rights of the suppliers of the public utilities of gas, electricity, water and telephone in a liquidation are now stated in s. 233 Insolvency Act 1986. The supplier *may* impose on the liquidator the condition that he will personally guarantee the payment of the charges for the *continuing* supply, but *must not* impose the condition that any outstanding charges for the *pre-liquidation* supply are paid.

17. Getting in the company's property

Section 234 provides that, where *any person* has in his possession or control any property, books, papers or records to which the company appears to be entitled, the court may require that person to hand over the items to the liquidator.

If the liquidator seizes or disposes of property which is not property of the company at a time when he has reasonable grounds for believing that it is company property, he has:

(a) no liability for any loss or damage resulting from the seizure or disposal unless it was caused by his own negligence; *and*

(b) a lien on the property (or proceeds of sale) for expenses incurred in the seizure or disposal.

18. Duty to co-operate with liquidator

Section 235 makes it the duty of past and present officers of the company and other persons (including employees) who have had connections with the company during the previous year to give to the liquidator (defined here as including, in a compulsory winding up, the official receiver in England and Wales) such information concerning the company and its affairs as the liquidator may reasonably require and also to attend on him at such times as he may reasonably require.

19 Inquiry by court into company's dealings

Under s. 236 the court may, if applied to by the liquidator (including again the official receiver in a compulsory winding up in England and Wales), summon to appear before it:

(a) any officer of the company;
(b) any person known or suspected to have in his possession any property of the company or supposed to be indebted to the company; *or*
(c) any person whom the court thinks capable of giving information concerning the company's affairs.

The court has, in this connection, powers to arrest persons and keep them in custody and to seize and hold books, papers, records, money or goods in their possession.

- By s. 237 the court has further enforcement powers which may be exercised in the light of evidence obtained from the inquiry under s. 236.

20 Transactions at an undervalue

Section 238, which applies to England and Wales only, provides that where a company has entered into a transaction with any person *at an undervalue*, the liquidator may, if the transaction falls within a *specified period* before the winding up, apply to the court for an order to restore the position to what it would have been if the company had not entered into the transaction.

A company enters into a transaction at an undervalue for the purposes of this provision if:

(a) the company makes a *gift* to the person or receives *no consideration; or*
(b) the value of the consideration is *significantly less* than the value of the consideration provided by the company.

However, the court must not make an order under s. 238 if it is satisfied:

(a) that the company entered into the transaction in good faith and for the purpose of carrying on its business; *and*
(b) that at the time when it did so there were reasonable grounds for believing that the transaction would benefit the company.

By s. 240 the transaction must have been entered into *within two years* before the commencement of the winding up, and, in addition, the company must *either* have been unable to pay its debts at the time of the transaction *or* have become unable to pay its debts as a result of the transaction. However, these requirements are presumed to be satisfied unless the contrary is shown, if the transaction is entered into by the company with a person who is 'connected' with the company, as defined in ss. 249 and 435.

Section 241, without restricting the court's general power to make under s. 238 such order as it thinks fit, specifies some particular orders which it may make. For example, the court may:

(a) require any property transferred as part of the transaction to be vested in the company;
(b) require any property to be vested in the company if it represents the application of the proceeds of sale of the property transferred;
(c) release or discharge any security given by the company;
(d) require any person to pay money to the liquidator for benefits received from the company; *and*
(e) provide for any surety or guarantor whose obligations were released or discharged under the transaction to be under a new or revived obligation.

Although the court order may affect property of a person other than the person with whom the company entered into the transaction, it must not prejudice any interest in property which was acquired from a person other than the company *and* which was acquired in good faith, for value and without notice of the relevant circumstances, i.e. the circumstances which make an order under s. 238 appropriate.

[Corresponding provisions applicable to Scotland only comprise s. 242 and come under the heading 'gratuitous alienations'.

The challenge of an alienation can be made by:

(a) any creditor the debt to whom was incurred on or before the commencement of the winding up; *or*
(b) the liquidator; *or*
(c) if an administration order is in force in relation to the company, the administrator.

The alienation which can be challenged is any transfer of any part of the company's property or any discharge or renunciation of any claim or right of the company, provided it takes place:

(a) if the person is an *associate*, on a day not earlier than five years before the date of the commencement of the winding up or the date of the making of the administration order;

(b) if the person is not an *associate*, on a day not earlier than two years before that date.

The term 'associate' in that context is incorporated from s. 74 Bankruptcy (Scotland) Act 1985, where it is defined as including a wide range of relatives as well as employers, employees and directors.

If the challenge is successful, the court grants a decree of reduction or for restoration of property to the company's assets or other redress as may be appropriate. The court must not grant such a decree if the person seeking to uphold the alienation establishes:

(a) that at any time after the alienation, the company's assets were greater than its liabilities; *or*

(b) that the alienation was made for adequate consideration; *or*

(c) that the alienation was a reasonable birthday, Christmas or other conventional gift; *or*

(d) that the alienation was the gift for a charitable, benevolent or philanthropic purpose to a person who is not an associate of the company.

The court's decree does not prejudice any right or interest acquired in good faith and for value from or through the transferee in the alienation, i.e. third parties are protected.

At common law, a creditor has a right to challenge an alienation made for no consideration or no adequate consideration. By s. 242 a liquidator or an administrator is given the same common law right. The requirements for a common law challenge are, however, difficult to prove.]

21 Preferences

The provisions relating to preferences are similar to those relating to transactions at an undervalue. Section 239, which applies to England and Wales only, provides that where a company has *given a preference* to any person within a *specified period* before the winding up, the liquidator may apply to the court for an order to restore the position to what it would have been if the company had not given the preference.

A company gives a preference for the purposes of this provision if:

(a) the person is one of the company's creditors or a surety or guarantor for any of the company's debts or liabilities; *and*

(b) the company does anything which has the effect of putting that person into a better position, in the event of the company going into insolvent liquidation, than he would have been in if the thing had not been done.

The court must not make an order unless the company was influenced by a desire to produce the effect stated in (b) above, but if the preference is given to a person 'connected' with the company (otherwise than by mere employment), the company is presumed, unless the contrary is shown, to have been influenced by such a desire.

By s. 240 the specified period relating to preferences is:

(a) *two years* before the commencement of winding up if the preference has been given to a person who is 'connected' with the company; *and*
(b) *six months* before the commencement of winding up in any other case.

The company must *either* have been unable to pay its debts at the time of the preference *or* have become unable to pay its debts as a result of the preference. The presumption in s. 240 relating to transactions at an undervalue with a 'connected' person does not apply to preferences.

In other respects the provisions relating to preferences are the same as those relating to transactions at an undervalue (*see* **20**).

[Corresponding provisions applicable to Scotland only comprise s. 243 and come under the heading 'unfair preferences'.

An 'unfair preference' is a transaction which creates a preference in favour of a creditor to the prejudice of the general body of creditors and taking place not earlier than the commencement of the winding up or the making of an administration order in relation to the company.

The challenge can be made by:

(a) any creditor the debt to whom was incurred on or before the commencement of the winding up; *or*
(b) the liquidator; *or*
(c) in the case of an administration order, the administrator.

If the challenge is successful, the court grants a decree of reduction or for restoration of property to the company's assets or other redress as may be appropriate, but, as for gratuitous alienations, the court's decree does not prejudice any right or interest acquired in good faith and for value from or through the creditor in whose favour the preference was created.

The following transactions cannot be challenged:

(a) a transaction in the ordinary course of trade or business;
(b) a payment in cash for a debt which had become payable, unless the transaction was collusive with the purpose of prejudicing the general body of creditors;
(c) a transaction by which the parties undertake reciprocal obligations,

i.e. a new transaction, unless the transaction was collusive as in **(b)**, above; *and*

(d) the granting of a mandate by a company authorising an arrester to pay over the arrested funds to the arrester where:

(*i*) there has been a decree for payment or a warrant for summary diligence; and

(*ii*) the decree or warrant has been preceded by an arrestment on the dependence of the action or followed by an arrestment in execution.

At common law, a creditor has a right to challenge a preference created by a debtor, and by s. 243 a liquidator or an administrator is given the same common law right.]

22. Extortionate credit transactions

Section 244 provides that the court may, if applied to by the liquidator, make an order with regard to a transaction for providing credit to the company if the transaction:

(a) is or was *extortionate; and*

(b) was entered into in the period of *three years* before the company went into liquidation.

A transaction is extortionate for the purposes of this provision if, considering the risk accepted by the person providing the credit:

(a) the terms of it are or were such as to require grossly exorbitant payments to be made in return for the provision of the credit; *or*

(b) it grossly contravened ordinary principles of fair dealing in some other way.

It is presumed, unless the contrary is proved, that a transaction is or (as the case may be) was extortionate.

An order may contain one or more of the following as the court thinks fit:

(a) provision setting aside any obligation created by the transaction;

(b) provision varying the terms of the transaction in some other way;

(c) provision requiring a party to the transaction to pay to the liquidator any sums paid to that person by the company;

(d) provision requiring any person to surrender to the liquidator any property held by him as security for the transaction; *and*

(e) provision directing accounts to be taken between any persons.

23. Avoidance of certain floating charges

The aim of the statutory provisions for the avoidance of certain floating charges, now in s. 245 Insolvency Act 1986, is to prevent a company from selecting one of its existing unsecured creditors and, by giving him a floating charge on its assets, enabling him to claim a priority over the others. It is similar in principle to the rules regarding preferences (*see* **21**).

The provisions were strengthened by the Insolvency Act 1985.

Section 245 provides that a floating charge on a company's undertaking or property created at a *specified time* is invalid except to the extent of the total of:

(a) the money paid or the value of the goods or services supplied to the company at the same time as, or after, the creation of the charge;
(b) the value of the discharge or reduction, at the same time as, or after, the creation of the charge, of any debt of the company; *and*
(c) the amount of interest (if any) payable on **(a)** or **(b)** in accordance with the agreement under which the money was paid, the goods or services supplied or the debt discharged or reduced.

The relevant period of time for this provision is the period of *two years* before the commencement of winding up if the charge is created in favour of a person who is 'connected' with the company, and the period of 12 *months* before the commencement of winding up in other cases.

However, where a company creates a floating charge within the 12 months before the commencement of winding up *and* the person in favour of whom the charge is created is not 'connected' with the company, then the floating charge will not be invalid unless:

(a) the company is at the date of the creation of the charge unable to pay its debts; *or*
(b) the company becomes unable to pay its debts as a result of the transaction under which the charge was created.

24 Unenforceability of liens on books, etc.
Section 246 provides that a lien or other right to retain possession of any of the books, papers or other records of the company is unenforceable in so far as its enforcement would deny possession of these items to the liquidator.

This provision does not apply to a lien on documents which give a title to property.

25 Court's power to declare dissolution void
Section 651 Companies Act 1985, as amended by the Insolvency Act 1985 and by s. 141 Companies Act 1989, provides that a dissolved company can be revived for certain purposes. This process of resurrection is some-times advisable if the company is subsequently found to have had either unpaid debts or undistributed property.

The section, as amended, provides that, on an application by the liquidator or any other interested person, the court may make an order, on such terms as the court thinks fit, declaring the dissolution to have been *void*.

Such proceedings may then be taken as might have been taken if the company had not been dissolved.

An application must be made *within two years from the date of dissolution except that* if the application is for the purpose of bringing proceedings against the company:

(a) for damages in respect of personal injuries, *or*
(b) for damages under the Fatal Accidents Act 1976 or the Damages (Scotland) Act 1976,

the application may be made at any time.

For an example see *Re Workvale Ltd (in Dissolution)* (1991) [B295].

It is the duty of the applicant to deliver to the registrar within seven days an office copy of the order.

26 Defunct companies

A company can also be restored to life under ss. 652–653 Companies Act 1985, the main purpose of which is to enable a company which is no longer carrying on business, but which has not been wound up, to be dissolved by removal from the register (*see* 26: **1**).

Section 652 provides that where the registrar has reasonable cause to believe that a company is not carrying on business, he may send a letter inquiring whether it is doing so.

If *within one month* he does not receive an answer, he must *within the next 14 days* send a registered letter, referring to the first letter, and stating that if an answer is not received within one month a notice will be published in the *Gazette* with a view to striking the company off the register.

If he receives an answer saying that the company is not carrying on business, or does not receive any answer within one month after sending the second letter, he may publish in the *Gazette* and send to the company a notice that *after three months* the name of the company will, unless cause is shown to the contrary, be struck off the register and the company dissolved.

Further, s. 652 requires the registrar to publish and send to the company or the liquidator (if any) a notice similar to that specified above where a company is in *liquidation*, but he has reasonable cause to believe either that no liquidator is acting, or that the affairs of the company have been fully wound up, and the returns required to be made by the liquidator have not been made *for six consecutive months*.

After the specified time the registrar may strike the company's name off the register, and must publish notice of the fact in the *Gazette*, whereupon the company is *dissolved*. This does not affect, however, either the liability, if any, of the directors, officers, or members, or the power of the court to wind up the company.

Finally, s. 653 provides that if the company, or any member or creditor, feels aggrieved by the company having been struck off, it or he may apply to the court *within 20 years*. If the court is satisfied that the company was carrying on business when it was struck off, or that it is just to restore it to the register, it may order the company's name to be restored. In order to qualify as an applicant the petitioner must show that he was a member or creditor *at the date of dissolution*. The words 'any member', however, extend to the personal representative of a deceased member, even though he was never on the register of members, since it is not unlikely that in the course of the 20 years a registered member might die: *Re Bayswater Trading Co. Ltd* (1970).

A copy of the court order must be delivered to the registrar, and the company is then *deemed to have continued to exist as if its name had not been struck off*. The court may place it and other persons in their original position. The effect of this provision is that all acts done by the company during the period between dissolution and restoration are validated, and this period is ignored for the purposes of the Limitation Act.

27 The property of a dissolved company

Section 654 provides that where a company is dissolved, all its property, except that which it holds on trust for another person, is deemed to be *bona vacantia*, and accordingly belongs to the Crown. Section 655 authorises the Crown to dispose of such property despite the possibility that an order may be made under s. 651 or 653 reviving the dissolved company. By s. 654 if such an order is made, the disposition is not affected but the Crown must pay to the company the amount received for the property or, if none, an amount equal to its value.

Alternatively, s. 656 empowers the Crown to *disclaim* the property by a notice signed by the Treasury Solicitor [or, in relation to property in Scotland, by the Queen's and Lord Treasurer's Remembrancer].

32

Arrangements and reconstructions

1. The scope of s. 425

We have already seen in 29:**21** that a company in voluntary liquidation may make an arrangement with its creditors under s. 110 Insolvency Act 1986. A company which is *not* in liquidation, however, cannot proceed under that section. It must instead enter into either a voluntary arrangement under Part I of the Insolvency Act 1986 (*see* 26:**6–8**) or a scheme of arrangement under s. 425 Companies Act 1985, under which almost any type of compromise, arrangement or reorganisation of the company's capital can be effected.

Section 425 has been mentioned before in connection with the alteration of rights attached to shares (*see* 11:**13**). But it has a far wider scope than this. Since, as we shall see below, the consent of the court has to be obtained, the section permits the company to enter into any type of scheme regarding either its creditors or its members which does not conflict with the general law or with any particular statutory provision. Thus the company could not under this section be empowered to do an unlawful act, or to convert its issued share capital into redeemable shares (*see* 11:**24**) but only to do acts which are lawful in themselves.

Moreover, the section does not enable the company to avoid a prescribed statutory procedure where there is one, e.g. for the reduction of capital.

2. Power to compromise with creditors and members

Section 425 (as amended by the Insolvency Act 1985) provides that where a compromise or arrangement is proposed between a company and its creditors or any class of them, or its members or any class of them, the court may, on the application of the company, or any creditor, or member, or liquidator or administrator, *order a meeting* of the creditors or members, or any class of them, as the case may be.

If a *majority in number* representing *three-quarters in value* of the creditors or members or any class of them, present and voting either in person or by proxy, agree to any compromise or arrangement, it is *binding if sanctioned by the court*.

The court will refuse to sanction the arrangement unless the class meetings are properly constituted. Thus where one of the members was the wholly-owned subsidiary of a company which was to purchase all the shares under the arrangement, Templeman J. held that that member formed a class on its own, separate from the other members, since it had different interests, and accordingly he refused to sanction the arrangement: *Re Hellenic & General Trust Ltd* (1976).

The court order has no effect until a copy has been delivered to the registrar for registration. Further, a copy of the order must be annexed to every copy of the memorandum subsequently issued.

3. Information to be sent with notice of the meeting

Section 426 requires the company to send with the notice of the meeting called under s. 425 a *statement* explaining the *effect of the scheme*, and stating in particular the *material interest of the directors* and the effect of the scheme on them.

If the notice is given by advertisement, such a statement must be included, or a place notified where creditors or members may obtain copies of one.

Where the scheme affects the rights of debenture holders, the statement must give a similar explanation with regard to the trustees of any deed for securing the issue as is required with regard to the directors.

4. Matters for which the court may provide

Section 427 provides that where an application is made to the court under s. 425 for the sanction of a scheme, and that scheme is one under which the whole or part of the company's undertaking or property is to be *transferred to another company*, the court may provide for the following matters:

(a) the transfer of the whole or part of the undertaking and property or liabilities of the transferor company to the transferee company;

(b) the allotting or appropriation by the transferee company of shares or debentures in that company;

(c) the continuation by or against the transferee company of legal proceedings which are pending by or against the transferor company;

(d) the dissolution, without winding up, of the transferor company (*see* 26:1);

(e) dissenting persons;

(f) any other incidental matters.

A copy of the court order must be delivered by the company to the registrar within seven days.

5. Comparison with a reconstruction under s. 110 Insolvency Act 1986

It is clear from s. 427 that it is possible under ss. 425–427 for companies to amalgamate, so that the undertaking and property of one is transferred to another. This may, as is obvious from **(d)** above, involve the dissolution of the transferor company without a winding up (i.e. a 'merger').

In **29:21** we saw that much the same sort of result can be achieved under s. 110 Insolvency Act 1986, and it is therefore interesting to compare and contrast the two types of reconstruction:

(a) Section 110 Insolvency Act 1986 is a much *narrower* section than s. 425. It permits only one type of reconstruction, by which a company in voluntary liquidation sells its undertaking for shares in another company. Section 425 covers a wide variety of activities, as was mentioned in 1.

(b) Section 110 Insolvency Act 1986 can be used only by a company in *voluntary liquidation*. Section 425 is frequently used by a company which is a going concern, even though the court may provide, under s. 427, for the dissolution of the transferor company in appropriate circumstances.

(c) Section 110 Insolvency Act 1986 can be used without obtaining the *sanction of the court*, unless the winding up is a *creditors'* voluntary winding up, when the sanction either of the court or of the liquidation committee must be obtained. Section 425 invariably requires the sanction of the court.

(d) A dissentient under s. 110 Insolvency Act 1986 can require the liquidator either to purchase his interest or to abandon the whole scheme. Under s. 425 the scheme will bind all the members once it is sanctioned by the court, though the court may make provision for dissentients (*see* **(e)** above).

6. Take-over offers

The statutory provisions relating to 'take-over offers' are contained in Part XIIIA of the Companies Act 1985.

Part XIIIA, consisting of ss. 428–430F of the Act, was added by s. 172 and Schedule 12 Financial Services Act 1986. Section 172 of that Act provides that the new ss. 428–430F Companies Act 1985 are to be substituted for the original ss. 428–430 Companies Act. 1985, which were within Part XIII of the Act. The provisions have now been allocated a Part for themselves and the term 'take-over offer', formerly merely a popular term, has now a statutory definition. The major principles have remained unchanged, but the provisions have been amended and their terminology modernised.

By s. 428 'a take-over offer' means an offer to acquire all the shares, or all the shares of any class, in a company (other than shares which at the date of the offer are already held by the offeror), and which is on terms which are the same for all the shares to which the offer relates or for all the shares of each class.

By s. 430E the provision that the take-over offer must extend to 'all the shares' is to be regarded as satisfied where the offer extends to all shares other than those of the offeror's associates (e.g. a company in the same group as the offeror).

It can often happen that the person making a take-over offer wishes to enhance his offer in order to attract further acceptances, and the question of the date when an offer is made must be provided for because of the time factors involved in the statutory provisions. Section 428 answers the question by stating that where the terms of an offer make provision for their revision and for acceptances on the previous terms to be treated as acceptances on the revised terms, the revision is not to be regarded as the making of a fresh offer, and so the date of the revised offer is to be taken to be the same as the date of the original offer.

The earlier versions of the take-over provisions referred to the offer as being made by the 'transferee company', while the term 'transferor company' was used of the company which was being taken over. These somewhat clumsy terms have been replaced by the terms 'offeror' and 'the company', respectively. Section 428, therefore, defines, 'the offeror' as meaning the person making a take-over offer and 'the company' as meaning the company whose shares are the subject of the offer.

With regard to the term 'offeror', it should be noted that it is possible for a take-over offer to be made by two or more persons jointly, and, by s. 430D, there are modifications to the statutory provisions in such a case.

It should also be appreciated that, although the term 'transferee company' has been dropped in favour of the term 'offeror', the person making the offer will in fact usually be another company (an artificial legal person) and not an individual (a natural person).

7. Right of offeror to buy out minority shareholders

Section 429 provides that, if the offeror has received acceptances for at least *nine-tenths* of the shares (or nine-tenths of the class) to which the offer relates, he may give notice to the holder of any shares (or shares of the class) not acquired that *he desires to acquire* those shares.

In order to be able to exercise this right the offeror must have acquired the minimum nine-tenths of shares *before the end of four months from the date of the offer,* and the notice which he gives to the holder of his desire to acquire the holder's shares must be given *within two months after he has acquired the necessary minimum nine-tenths.*

The offeror must send a copy of the notice to the company along with a statutory declaration stating that the conditions for the giving of the notice are satisfied. If the offeror is a company, this statutory declaration must be signed by a director.

If, while the take-over offer is open, the offeror acquires shares to which the offer relates but does so in some other way than by acceptances of the offer (e.g. he may purchase them in the market), then, provided that the price which he has paid for them does not exceed the price offered in the take-over offer, these shares can be counted towards the nine-tenths necessary for the exercise of the right to buy under s. 429.

The effect of a notice under s. 429 is that the offeror is *entitled and bound to acquire the shares on the terms of the offer: s. 430.*

At the end of *six weeks from the date of the notice,* the offeror must, by s. 430, pay or transfer *to the company* the consideration for the shares to which the notice relates, and must accompany it by a transfer executed on behalf of the shareholder by a person appointed by the offeror so that the company may register the offeror as the holder of the shares.

The consideration received by the company must be held on trust by it for the shareholder concerned.

8. Right of minority shareholder to be bought out by offeror

Section 430A provides that, if a take-over offer results in the offeror obtaining nine-tenths of the shares (or class of shares), counting in shares which he has acquired in some other way than by acceptances, the holder of any shares who has not accepted the offer may write to the offeror *requiring him to acquire his shares.* This enables a shareholder who refused to accept the offer to change his mind, as he may very well wish to do when he finds himself in a helpless minority.

The offeror must give any shareholder who has not accepted the offer notice of the rights which he may exercise under the section. He must do this *within one month* after the time when he acquires the necessary nine-tenths, and if at that point of time the offer is still open for acceptance, the offeror must mention that fact in the notice.

However, the shareholder is legally entitled to a longer period for the exercise of his right to be bought out. The notice given to him may specify a period for the exercise of the right, but this period must be *not less than three months after the end of the period within which the offer can be accepted.*

The provisions for notice under s. 430A do not apply if the offeror has given the shareholder a notice under s 429 that he desires to acquire the shares.

The effect of the exercise by a shareholder of his right to be bought out under s. 430A is that the offeror is *entitled and bound to acquire the shares on the terms of the offer or on such other terms as may be agreed: s. 430B.*

9. Applications to court

Under s. 430C there are three possible situations in which an application to court may be made in connection with a take-over offer:

(a) Where a shareholder has received a notice under s. 429 stating that the offeror, having obtained the necessary nine-tenths, desires to acquire his shares also, the court may, if the shareholder applies to it *within six weeks after the giving of the notice, either*:

(*i*) order that the offeror shall not be entitled and bound to acquire the shares; *or*

(*ii*) specify terms of acquisition different from those of the offer.

(b) Where the shareholder exercises his rights under s. 430A to be bought out, the court may, if an application is made to it by him or by the offeror, order that the terms on which the offeror is entitled and bound to acquire the shares shall be such *as the court thinks fit*.

(c) Where a take-over offer has not been accepted by the necessary nine-tenths, with the result that the offeror is not entitled to give notices under s. 429, the offeror may apply to the court for an order authorising him to give such notices. The purpose of this provision is to cover the situation where the offeror has not reached his target of nine-tenths because he has been unable to trace all the shareholders. The court must be satisfied:

(*i*) that the offeror has after reasonable inquiry been unable to trace one or more of the shareholders concerned;

(*ii*) that the shares of these shareholders, if added to the shares for which acceptances have been given, would amount to nine-tenths; *and*

(*iii*) that the consideration offered is fair and reasonable.

Further, the court must have regard to the number of shareholders who *have been traced but who have not accepted the offer*, and must not make an order unless it considers that it is just and equitable to do so.

10. View taken by court on application of dissenting shareholder

Under the former provisions also, an application to court within category **(a)** in **9** above could be made by a dissenting shareholder, and decided cases have established a number of points regarding the view taken by the court on such applications.

The court will normally take the view that since the required majority have approved the scheme, it is up to the dissenting shareholder to show grounds for his disapproval of it. Thus the offer will be treated as *prima facie* a fair one, and the burden of showing otherwise is on the dissentient who seeks relief. In discharging it he must show unfairness to the shareholders *as a body*, so that while the market price of the share is a relevant factor, the personal circumstances of the dissentient are not: *Re Grierson, Oldham and Adams* (1968).

Where, however, the offer is in reality being made by the same majority shareholders who have accepted it, the burden of proof is *reversed* and it is up to the offeror to *show that the scheme is fair*. This is a perfect example of what is meant by 'lifting the veil' of incorporation, and the facts of *Re Bugle Press Ltd* (1961) are interesting in this connection.

B.P. Ltd had an issued capital of 10,000 £1 shares, of which Jackson held 4500, Shaw held 4500, and Treby held 1000. Jackson and Shaw then incorporated a new company, called Jackson and Shaw (Holdings) Ltd, with an issued capital of 100 shares, of which each of them held 50. This company then made an offer under what is now s. 428 Companies Act 1985 to the shareholders of B.P. Ltd. Jackson and Shaw naturally accepted the offer, but Treby refused it on the ground that the price was too low. HELD: He was not bound to sell at that price. Where 'as a matter of substance the persons who are putting forward the offer are the majority shareholders', it is up to them to show that the scheme is fair and not to the dissenting shareholder to show that it is unfair.

NOTE: Here the corporate personality of Jackson and Shaw (Holdings) Ltd has been disregarded. The 'veil' has been lifted to reveal, behind the corporate person, the natural persons of Jackson and Shaw—those same natural persons who are accepting the offer made, in substance, by themselves.

11. The meaning of 'reconstruction' and 'amalgamation'

In his celebrated speech in *Liversidge* v. *Anderson* (1942), Lord Atkin quoted a passage from Lewis Carroll's *Through the Looking-Glass*: ' "When I use a word," Humpty Dumpty said, "it means just what I choose it to mean, neither more nor less." "The question is," said Alice, "whether you can make words mean so many different things." '

Unfortunately, you can. And the longer the word, the safer you are, for while people sometimes ask you what you mean by a *short* word, they rarely have the courage to inquire what a *long* word means.

Words such as 'reconstruction' and 'amalgamation' have *no fixed technical legal significance*, but are used loosely to indicate some sort of rearrangement or reorganisation entered into by companies. Examiners who ask students to explain what these words mean, therefore, are in effect asking for an account of procedures which can be adopted under ss. 425–427 and 428 Companies Act 1985 and 110 Insolvency Act 1986. All that can be said about the *meaning* of the words is that a 'reconstruction' can cover, for instance, a reorganisation of share or loan capital which is purely *internal* affecting *one company only* (s. 425), or the formation of a *new* company to carry on the business of the old one, with the same shareholders (s. 110 Insolvency Act 1986). The word 'amalgamation' necessarily involves *two companies*, but can cover the transfer of the whole undertaking from one company to another under ss. 425–427, or the absorption of one company by another under s. 110 Insolvency Act 1986, or even extend to the *economic*, though not the legal, unity obtainable under s. 428.

Humpty Dumpty clearly had the right idea, but it is very important for examination purposes not to be drawn into prolonged and inconclusive discussion, and instead to show a detailed knowledge of the procedures which can be adopted under the various sections. Too many students take refuge in complexity, no doubt believing with Oscar Wilde that 'to be intelligible is to be found out'. Examiners are not unaware of this, and the best marks will always go to a student who understands what he knows, knows what he means, and means what he says.

Index